WA 1371459 7

D1759176

STANDARD LOAN
UNIVERSITY OF GLAMORGAN
TREFOREST LEARNING RESOURCES CENTRE

Renew Items on PHONE-it: 01443 654456
Help Desk: 01443 482625 Media Services Reception: 01443 482610
Items are to be returned on or before the last date below

THE NEW MIDDLE AGES

BONNIE WHEELER, *Series Editor*

The New Middle Ages is a series dedicated to pluridisciplinary studies of medieval cultures, with particular emphasis on recuperating women's history and on feminist and gender analyses. This peer-reviewed series includes both scholarly monographs and essay collections.

PUBLISHED BY PALGRAVE:

The Vernacular Spirit: Essays on Medieval Religious Literature
edited by Renate Blumenfeld-Kosinski, Duncan Robertson, and Nancy Warren

Popular Piety and Art in the Late Middle Ages: Image Worship and Idolatry in England 1350–1500
by Kathleen Kamerick

Absent Narratives, Manuscript Textuality, and Literary Structure in Late Medieval England
by Elizabeth Scala

Creating Community with Food and Drink in Merovingian Gaul
by Bonnie Effros

Representations of Early Byzantine Empresses: Image and Empire
by Anne McClanan

Encountering Medieval Textiles and Dress: Objects, Texts, Images
edited by Désirée G. Koslin and Janet Snyder

Eleanor of Aquitaine: Lord and Lady
edited by Bonnie Wheeler and John Carmi Parsons

Isabel La Católica, Queen of Castile: Critical Essays
edited by David A. Boruchoff

Homoeroticism and Chivalry: Discourses of Male Same-Sex Desire in the Fourteenth Century
by Richard E. Zeikowitz

Portraits of Medieval Women: Family, Marriage, and Politics in England 1225–1350
by Linda E. Mitchell

Eloquent Virgins: From Thecla to Joan of Arc
by Maud Burnett McInerney

The Persistence of Medievalism: Narrative Adventures in Contemporary Culture
by Angela Jane Weisl

Capetian Women
edited by Kathleen D. Nolan

Joan of Arc and Spirituality
edited by Ann W. Astell and Bonnie Wheeler

The Texture of Society: Medieval Women in the Southern Low Countries
edited by Ellen E. Kittell and Mary A. Suydam

Charlemagne's Mustache: And Other Cultural Clusters of a Dark Age
by Paul Edward Dutton

Troubled Vision: Gender, Sexuality, and Sight in Medieval Text and Image
edited by Emma Campbell and Robert Mills

Queering Medieval Genres
by Tison Pugh

Sacred Place in Early Medieval Neoplatonism
by L. Michael Harrington

The Middle Ages at Work
edited by Kellie Robertson and Michael Uebel

Chaucer's Jobs
by David R. Carlson

Medievalism and Orientalism: Three Essays on Literature, Architecture and Cultural Identity
by John M. Ganim

Queer Love in the Middle Ages
by Anna Klosowska

Performing Women in the Middle Ages: Sex, Gender, and the Iberian Lyric
by Denise K. Filios

Necessary Conjunctions: The Social Self in Medieval England
by David Gary Shaw

Visual Culture and the German Middle Ages
edited by Kathryn Starkey and Horst Wenzel

Medieval Paradigms: Essays in Honor of Jeremy duQuesnay Adams, Volumes 1 and 2
edited by Stephanie Hayes-Healy

AUTHORITY AND SUBJUGATION IN WRITING OF MEDIEVAL WALES

Edited by
Ruth Kennedy and Simon Meecham-Jones

AUTHORITY AND SUBJUGATION IN WRITING OF MEDIEVAL WALES

First published in 2008 by
PALGRAVE MACMILLAN®
in the US—a division of St. Martin's Press LLC,
175 Fifth Avenue, New York, NY 10010.

Where this book is distributed in the UK, Europe and the rest of the world,
this is by Palgrave Macmillan, a division of Macmillan Publishers Limited,
registered in England, company number 785998, of Houndmills,
Basingstoke, Hampshire RG21 6XS.

Palgrave Macmillan is the global academic imprint of the above companies
and has companies and representatives throughout the world.

Palgrave® and Macmillan® are registered trademarks in the United States,
the United Kingdom, Europe and other countries.

ISBN-13: 978–0–230–60295–3
ISBN-10: 0–230–60295–9

Library of Congress Cataloging-in-Publication Data

Authority and subjugation in writing of medieval Wales / edited by
Ruth Kennedy and Simon Meecham-Jones.
    p. cm.—(The new Middle Ages)
Includes bibliographical references and index.
ISBN 0–230–60295–9 (alk. paper)
    1. Wales—In literature. 2. English literature—Middle English,
1100–1500—History and criticism. 3. Imperialism in literature.
4. Authority in literature. 5. Colonies in literature. 6. Welsh
literature—1100–1400—History and criticism. 7. Welsh literature—
1400–1550—History and criticism. 8. England—Relations—Wales.
9. Wales—Relations—England. 10. Politics and literature—England—
History—To 1500. I. Kennedy, Ruth, Dr. II. Meecham-Jones, Simon.

PR275.W36A87 2008
820.9′358429—dc22   2008007184

A catalogue record of the book is available from the British Library.

Design by Newgen Imaging Systems (P) Ltd., Chennai, India.

First edition: September 2008

10 9 8 7 6 5 4 3 2 1

Printed in the United States of America.

CONTENTS

ILLUSTRATIONS

ACKNOWLEDGMENTS

L omers is the London Old and Middle English Research Seminar, a convivial forum that brings together medievalists from the separate colleges of the Federal University of London but also reaches out to other parishes. The inspiration for a series of symposia studying the variety of cultural and national forms of expression in medieval Britain was initiated by an earlier stimulating Lomers seminar by John J. Thompson: "Irishness(es) and Middle English Literary Culture." This led to four summer symposia on Welshness(es) and Scottishness(es) and Medieval English literary culture, so thank you, John. This volume brings together revised papers from the Lomers summer symposia of 2004 and 2005, together with the Trevisa edition, discussed in 2005 but completed subsequently, and a series of commissioned chapters designed to present as comprehensive and balanced depiction of the complex meeting, interaction, evasion, and resistance of cultures in medieval Wales. Lomers could not run without the wonderful financial and general support of the Institute of English Studies in the School of Advanced Studies at Senate House, London; particular thanks here are due to Warwick Gould, Michael Baron, Joanne Grubb, Francesca Bettocchi, and Jon Millington, and to Julia Boffey, past chair of Lomers, for her continued unstinting advice and encouragement. We would also like to thank our editor, Bonnie Wheeler, and our extremely sympathetic anonymous reader—now revealed as Jeffrey Jerome Cohen—together with all who have worked on this book at Palgrave Macmillan; they have been especially patient this time round. Working on this second book with Newgen Imaging Systems, particularly our contact editor, Maran Elancheran, has been a consistent delight. The image reproduced on the front cover represents the conflict of Beli and Brân, and is from MS NLW Peniarth 23, one of the few surviving illustrated manuscripts from medieval Wales and the only illustrated Arthurian one. We are most grateful to Ceridwen Lloyd-Morgan for drawing our attention to the manuscript, to Llyfrgell Genedlaethol Cymru/The National Library of Wales for granting us permission to use this image, and to Camwy Macdonald for organizing the reproduction and permission. Our warmest thanks also go to Ceridwen for her help in confirming the details of Welsh manuscripts, some of which have been renamed and reclassified many times, and for her invaluable help in proofreading the orthography of Modern and Medieval Welsh throughout the entire volume. We are particularly grateful to Helen Fulton for suggesting Anna Ratcliffe to draw the maps. We are also grateful to the Dean and Chapter of Lichfield Cathedral who have granted permission to reproduce images from Lichfield Cathedral Library, MS 1, and to the British Library and Oxford New College for permission to edit the texts in chapter 6.

Many thanks and tributes are due to Rosamund Allen, Sioned Davies, Rosalind Field, Robert Hampson, Patricia Harris-Gillies, Jonathan Goodall, John Hines, Dianne Myers, Jennifer Neville, Nan Robertson, David and Gail Saville, Mark Smith, Michelle Warren, and Laura Wright for their invaluable input and support, and I would like to dedicate my own labors here to the memory of an extraordinary and revered teacher of English at Dame Allan's School, the redoubtable Welshwoman Elspeth [Blodwen] Williams. I believe she would have liked this book.

Ruth Kennedy

The work for this book was done half in Wales (in Swansea and at Llyfrgell Genedlaethol Cymru/The National Library of Wales in Aberystwyth) and half in England (at the University Library and Trinity Hall in Cambridge, the British Library and the Bodleian). A chance meeting with Daniel Huws at the British Library provided a valuable opportunity to discuss the project at an early stage. Particular thanks are also due to Farideh Koohi-Kamali at Palgrave for her commitment to this volume, to Huw Pryce, Helen Cooper, Neil Reeve, and Robin Chapman Stacey for helpful advice, and to Patrick Geary for his generous encouragement. As always, I owe a particular debt to my mother, to Laura Wright, to Maldwyn Mills, and to Colin and Betty Davies, for their unfailing support and encouragement at every stage. In addition, the work has benefited from the interest of Marian [Davies], Marilyn Roberts, Esta and the late Ieuan Jones, Jennifer Davies and the late Islwyn Evans, and from the always supportive curiosity of a number of fine undergraduates, most of whom were surprised to hear that a volume was planned to address this little-explored subject.

Simon Meecham-Jones

CONTRIBUTORS

Michelle P. Brown is Professor of Medieval Manuscript Studies at the Institute of English Studies in the School of Advanced Study, University of London. She was formerly the Curator of Illuminated Manuscripts at the British Library and has published, lectured and broadcast widely on medieval manuscripts and curated several major exhibitions. Publications include *The Holkham Bible, The Luttrell Psalter, The Lindisfarne Gospels* (facsimiles), and *The Lindisfarne Gospels: Society, Spirituality and the Scribe; The Book of Cerne: Prayer, Patronage and Power in Ninth-Century England, In the Beginning: Bibles before the Year 1000; How Christianity Came to Britain and Ireland; Manuscripts from the Anglo-Saxon Age; The Lion Companion to Christian Art.*

Tony Davenport is Emeritus Professor of Medieval Literature in the University of London and Fellow of the English Association. He is the author of *The Art of the Gawain Poet, Fifteenth-century English Drama, Chaucer: Narrative and Complaint, Chaucer and His English Contemporaries,* and *Medieval Narrative.*

Geraint Evans is a teaching fellow in the Department of Media and Communication at Swansea University. His research interests include publishing history since the sixteenth century, multilingual broadcasting and modernism, often with a focus on the language and culture of Wales and its interaction with England and international English culture. He has published widely on Celtic literature and culture and the early history of printing.

Helen Fulton is Professor of English and Acting Head of the School of Arts at Swansea University. She is currently working on editions of Welsh prophecies and is coinvestigator on the project "Mapping Medieval Chester," researching the links between the Welsh community and the medieval city of Chester. She is currently editing the *Blackwell Companion to Arthurian Literature*, forthcoming, 2008. Her most recent books include an edited collection *Medieval Celtic Literature and Society* and, with Ruth Evans and David Matthews, *Medieval Cultural Studies.*

Sally Harper is a Senior Lecturer in the School of Music at the University of Wales, Bangor and is Director of the Centre of Advanced Welsh Music Studies. She edits the bilingual journal *Welsh Music History/Hanes Cerddoriaeth Cymru.* She is author of *Music in Welsh Culture before 1650* and *Medieval English Benedictine*

Liturgy and has edited *Music in the Scottish Church up to 1603, Robert ap Huw Studies/Astudiaethau Robert ap Huw,* and with Wyn Thomas, *Welsh Music Studies: Bearers of Song.*

Sara Elin Roberts is Lecturer in the School of Welsh, University of Wales, Bangor. She researches and publishes on medieval Welsh literature and law, including fifteenth-century aspects and the law of the March; education of the lawyers and mnemonic techniques; legal triads; the poetry of the nobility, in particular the work of Dafydd ap Gwilym and bardic debates. She is author of *The Legal Triads of Medieval Wales.*

Ceridwen Lloyd-Morgan retired in 2006 as Head of Manuscripts and Visual Images at the National Library of Wales. She is Honorary Research Fellow in the School of Welsh, Cardiff University, and a Member of the Centre for Medieval Studies, Bangor University. She has published widely on external influences on the development of the Welsh prose tradition.

William Marx is Reader in Medieval Literature at the University of Wales, Lampeter and is one of the general editors of the international series *Middle English Texts.* He is the author of *The Devil's Rights and the Redemption in the Literature of Medieval England,* and has published a major study of the medieval English *Gospel of Nicodemus.* He is author of *An English Chronicle 1377–1461: A New Edition,* and, *most recently, w*ith Janet Burton, *Readers, Printers, Churchmen, and Travellers, and, with* Raluca Radulescu, *Readers and Writers of the Prose "Brut."*

Ruth Kennedy is a Senior Lecturer at Royal Holloway, University of London and is organizer and chair of the Lomers Seminars. She is editor of *Medieval English Measures, Three Alliterative Saints' Hymns* and coeditor, with Simon Meecham-Jones of *Writers of the Reign of Henry II.*

David N. Klausner is Professor of English and Medieval Studies and Vice Dean for Interdisciplinary Affairs in the University of Toronto. He has edited the volumes for Herefordshire, Worcestershire, and Wales in the series *Records of Early English Drama,* and has published on early drama in both England and Wales, as well as on the relationships between Old English and early Welsh poetry.

Simon Meecham-Jones is an affiliated lecturer for the English Faculty at Cambridge University and an associate research fellow of the Medieval and Early Modern Research Centre at the University of Swansea. He has written many articles on Chaucer, Gower, twelfth-century Latin lyrics, and coauthor, with Ruth Kennedy of *Writers of the Reign of Henry II.*

Peter Robson is a research scholar at Corpus Christi College, Oxford. His research interests are in Old English, particularly Alcuin and Alfredian literature.

Cory James Rushton is Assistant Professor in the Department of English at St. Francis Xavier University, Nova Scotia. He has published widely on Arthurian romance, and is coeditor, with Amanda Hopkins, of *The Erotic in*

Medieval British Literature, is coauthor, with Robert Rouse, of *The Medieval Quest for Arthur* and coeditor, with Raluca Radulescu, of *The Companion to Medieval Popular Romance*.

Ronald Waldron is Emeritus Reader in Medieval English Language and Literature from King's College, University of London. He has published a number of books and articles on medieval literature such as, with Malcolm Andrew, *The Poems of the "Pearl" Manuscript*. Most relevant to the present volume is his edition of *John Trevisa's Translation of the "Polychronicon" of Ranulph Higden, Book VI*.

The main divisions of Wales before 1100 and the main Market Towns and Abbeys in medieval Wales

Map of MEDIEVAL Wales

Wales and England after 1284

Map of MEDIEVAL Wales and England

INTRODUCTION

Simon Meecham-Jones

For more than a thousand years, Wales has been contested territory, and that contestation has been furthered and promoted as much by writers and scholars as by sovereigns and warlords. Throughout the medieval period, Wales suffered as the physical battleground for armies of opposing interests; but the textual battles to establish claims of justification and entitlement were no less important and scarcely less fierce. It is almost certainly the case that the importance in the subjugation of Wales of the role played by the colonizing history constructed by Bede exceeds even that of Edward I. The purpose of this volume is to draw back to prominence the role of English textual culture in inspiring and rationalizing these early campaigns in English Imperialism, and to set it alongside the complex and conflicted responses to that onslaught formulated in the Welsh literature of medieval Wales.

The Welsh nation is a child of the medieval world that, against most predictions, and despite lacking the sustenance of political expression, has survived into the modern world. Paradoxically, the lack of any defining political apparatus has allowed the signifiers of Welsh identity to develop, sometimes absorbing and sometimes resisting change across fifteen hundred years, allowing the people of Wales to continue "making and remaking themselves in generation after generation, usually against the odds, usually within a British context."[1] That remaking has never been practiced free from the coercion of external cultural pressures, as the Welsh have been forced to react to, and to live with the consequences of, the efforts of writers, lawyers, and soldiers to define the past, present, and future meaning of "Wales," its culture and its people in ways favorable to English, or, sometimes, British interests.

From the Norman invasion to the Tudor accession, English political and military engagement in medieval Wales was intense, as military intervention was followed by colonial appropriation of land, fortification and settlement, and then economic exploitation on a grand scale. The wealth to be made in Wales, and the relatively unsupervised exercise of military force by the Marcher Lords, made Wales a significant (if reluctant) influence on the development of English aristocratic culture, while the Border Country became the central playing field of recurring outbreaks of civil war between English royal and aristocratic factions. The subjugation and economic settlement of Wales provided a diversionary raison d'être for English aristocratic militarism that ironically also periodically provided the financial means and military organization to support attempts to overthrow the authority of the English Crown.

The cultural justification for the seizure of Wales was swiftly refined into four key concepts: the discourse of peripherality, the discourse of Britishness, the discourse of authority and discourse of racial inferiority. The discourse of peripherality drew attention to Wales's perceived status at the geographical margins of European civilization. The discourse of Britishness proclaimed the "natural" unity of the island(s) of Britain, inferring from physical continuity an inevitable political unity. The discourse of authority asserted the right of England to rule Wales, by virtue of tradition, God's favor, and England's greater civilization.[2] Allied to this was the myth of the racial inferiority of the Welsh (and Irish), a myth that Gillingham credits to William of Malmesbury (though his work certainly reflects assumptions that are scarcely concealed in the work of Bede):

> One of William of Malmesbury's most creative and influential achievements was to introduce this imperialist perception of Celtic peoples into history.[3]

In the most celebrated medieval commentaries on the Welsh, Walter Map's *De Nugis Curialium*[4] and Giraldus Cambrensis' *Descriptio Kambriae*,[5] can be seen the complex, often self-contradictory, nature of what resulted from the attempt to reconcile the contrary pressures released by the rehearsal of these traditional ideas. But Giraldus and Walter Map were sophisticated and self-aware artists, attempting to salvage their compromised integrity with the literary weapons of wit, irony, and eloquence. In the hands of a more blatant and less contemplative writer like William of Newburgh, the tropes are piled together in an offensive assault on the self-image of the Welsh:

> Quibus paulatim profligatis, miseras eorum reliquias, quae nunc Walenses vocantur, inviis montibus et saltibus coarctarunt.
>
> [The Britons were gradually crushed by them, and the invaders penned the wretched remnants, now called the Welsh, in trackless mountains and forests.][6]

Such repeated onslaughts could not be without some effect, both in undermining the Welsh will to resistance, and in persuading later historians and critics of the justice of what had been done. It was in the medieval period, through the exercise of military force and through the construction of a narrative of justification to vindicate that use of force, that the terms for both the constitutional and the cultural relationship of England and Wales were set—in an uneasy and enforced union of unequal respect. If the cultural relationship of England and Wales in the twenty-first century remains grudging and distrustful, it is to the medieval period that we must look for answers as to the reasons why.

From the first Norman incursions, the ethical and legal legitimacy of English intervention in Wales was, at best, obscure—a right assumed rather than asserted, and apparently requiring no explication. This failure to develop an overt and coherent ideology of conquest resulted in the relationship of Wales and the English throne being characterized by a fatal lack of clarity compared, for example, with the assertion of the English Crown's rights in France. This strategy of obscuration was made workable only by denying the legitimacy and distinctness of Welsh territorial markers, Welsh legal codes, the disputed independence of Welsh ecclesiastical structures from the control of Canterbury, and the separate development (after the decay of whatever Romano-British centralized power structures had survived) of Welsh linguistic and cultural traditions.

Certainly the most remarkable element of the relationship of the neighboring if economically and politically unequal cultures of medieval England and Wales is the sustained denial in Middle English culture of the existence of distinctive Welsh political and cultural concerns. The success and longstanding duration of this process of determined (if, at times, unconscious) denial could help to explain the paucity of references to Wales, the Welsh people, and the military campaigns in Wales to be found in popular and learned Middle English culture. Medieval English tradition developed no tradition of "Edward Longshank" romances or chronicles to rival the popularity of the Charlemagne romances. No less remarkable is the failure of three hundred years of scholarship and medievalist antiquarianism to notice, or consider worthy of comment, this absence of images of Wales and Welsh culture in the development of a discourse of British medieval history. If English medieval culture sought to render the Welsh invisible, subsequent study of these texts has done little to overturn this erasure. Nearly thirty years ago Rees Davies berated the reluctance of the British academic establishment to acknowledge how crucial a consideration of events in Wales (and Scotland and Ireland) must be to an understanding of the nature and development of medieval British history:

> It is one of the oddities, even absurdities, of academic history courses in Britain that they have generally chosen to ignore the peoples of Scotland, Ireland and Wales except at those moments when they have impinged, often unpleasantly and obstreperously, on the history of England.[7]

But it might be argued that the historians Davies criticizes were merely carrying on the practice of their medieval predecessors because for William of Malmesbury or William of Newburgh affairs in Wales are similarly worthy of commemoration only when they immediately concern English interests. Simultaneously in the medieval chronicles we see both an absence of curiosity about Wales and a (probably unconscious) determination to control, by limiting, the dissemination of information about Wales. In the writing of medieval England, later historians have too often averted their eyes, feigning an intellectual aloofness that the works of Davies, Bartlett, and others have scratched but scarcely fractured.[8] Even in Wales, despite R. S. Thomas's warning that Welsh cultural self-reflection had become so fixated on past defeat that it had become no more than "worrying the carcase of an old song,"[9] there has been remarkably little study of the representation of Wales and the Welsh people in medieval English literature.

The failure to accord due notice to the experience of medieval Wales is regrettable, since the records of that experience offer remarkable insights into the stumbling and inchoate development of the physical and intellectual structures of medieval military and cultural imperialism in the British Isles. Wales occupies a special place in the history of British imperialism as the first colony—in Rees Davies's phrase "England's first Empire."[10] It was in Wales that what Davies has described as a series of ad hoc and opportunistic interventions revealed the possibility of a more ambitious strategy of seizure and control:

> The Anglo-Normans did not set out self-consciously on a conquest of "Wales" or "Ireland" as such, or plot the take-over of the kingdom of Scotland; they were not informed by national ambitions or national animus; few of them could have guessed at, or cared about, what they might—or might not—achieve; [...] In short their enterprises were not national conquests in intention, scale or character.[11]

If the interventions in Wales did not begin as "national conquests in intention, scale or character," it was the contribution of textual culture to point the conclusion that such a policy of conquest was both possible and just. In tracing the strategies of justification, developed from the writings of Bede and William of Malmesbury, the preamble to the Statute of Wales,[12] and the punitive laws and levies imposed on Wales by English monarchs from Edward I to Henry IV, it is easy to trace the development of an ideology that distinguished the moral value of the conquerors from that of the conquered. In using the ideas of the discourse of authority and the discourse of racial inferiority to develop a justification for the unequal legal status of the Welsh and the English in medieval Wales, the English Crown developed a model that, it was to find, could be applied, first to Ireland and later to lands conquered in America, Africa, India, and elsewhere.

Another consequence of the processes of colonial seizure and plantation was the setting in motion of intense, and ideologically contested, processes of linguistic contact and conflict, introducing new strains into the already complex operation of models of multilingualism in Wales. But that linguistic contact helps also to explain the distinctive qualities of the Welsh experience. Though the Norman chroniclers might deride the Welsh as *barbari* [barbarians][13] it was far from the truth to imagine that Wales was a land without textual resources of its own. England's first colonial wars were aimed at subduing a people who, however fractious and fissiparous their political culture, nonetheless enjoyed both a highly developed and long-established legal code (albeit one based on a principle of design quite distinct from that of the developing English Common Law)[14] and a prolific and sophisticated literary culture that invested great prestige in the disciplines of *barddoniaeth* [poetry]. The literary witnesses of the conquest of Wales provide a variety of perspectives, perhaps without equal, in evidencing the creation of a colonial system and the ideology that would enable the system to become embedded, until its existence seemed inevitable. There are grave difficulties in reconciling the evidence of these partial witnesses—texts in Latin, Anglo-Norman and French, English, and Welsh (though these last have often been an underused source); texts written in Wales, in the Marches and in England about Wales and the Welsh, as well as a great body of English texts (in Latin, Anglo-Norman, and English) that, in their refusal to acknowledge the existence of Wales and the consequences of the wars in Wales, paradoxically speak eloquently about the fears and resentments that military victory and political annexation did not dispel.

The purpose of this volume is to draw together the evidence from this wealth of sources, written in or concerning medieval Wales, to examine the role played by medieval textual culture in constructing, fostering, embedding (and, sometimes, resisting) this medieval construction of an imposed union of unequal respect. In the first chapter, William Marx considers the uneven survival of manuscript sources that can be certainly identified with Welsh sites of patronage or production. He also considers the failure of large-scale studies of the development of Middle English, particularly the *Linguistic Atlas of Late Medieval English*, to attempt to distinguish identifiable dialectal characteristics of English spoken and written within Medieval Wales. In consequence the voice of a whole community—of English and Welsh men and women living in medieval Wales, but writing in English—has been obscured.

In chapter 2, Simon Meecham-Jones considers the baffling absence of references to Wales, the Welsh people, and the wars in Wales throughout the major Middle English literary texts—in the court poetry of Chaucer and Gower, in *Piers Plowman*, and in the limited use made of Welsh tradition and Welsh locations in the corpus of medieval romance. He identifies this absence as evidence of a semiconscious policy of cultural erasure, through which challenging questions about the legality and legitimacy of English intervention in Wales were evaded by the inability of English writers to acknowledge the cultural separateness and independence of Welsh cultural and political structures without seeming to challenge the political discourses of authority and racial inferiority.

One of the greatest difficulties in challenging the view of Anglo-Welsh history presented by Bede and the Norman historians lies in the apparent destruction of the great body of early Welsh manuscripts. The losses in Welsh literature are grievous, and many texts judged to be early survive only in manuscripts compiled two or three centuries later than the probable date of composition. The survival of Latin texts written in Wales seem to have been more precarious—Daniel Huws estimates that while

> There are good grounds for maintaining that in Wales fewer than one in a hundred medieval manuscripts have survived; certainly a lower percentage than in England. On the other hand, an informed guess might be that one in five medieval manuscripts in Welsh have survived, perhaps more.[15]

In the third chapter Michelle P. Brown considers the evidence provided by the Lichfield Gospels concerning the relationship of the English and Welsh church hierarchy in the pre-Conquest period. The gospel is an eighth century text that has been in the possession of Lichfield Cathedral for a thousand years but that contains some of the earliest surviving written Welsh sources in a series of marginalia. Although it is generally accepted that the manuscript was in Wales at the monastery of Saint Teilo (Llandeilo) in the ninth century, the question of the gospel's place of production has become a focus for "textual nationalism" in both Wales and England, and an important test of whether, in the absence of surviving other gospels,[16] it is likely that the Lichfield Gospels could have been produced in Wales, in imitation of English models, or whether they must be considered to be an English production, perhaps brought to Wales as the plunder of a raiding party (and maybe even "returned" to England through parallel means).

In chapter 4, Peter Robson considers an alternative source of evidence for Anglo-Saxon attitudes to the British population, offering a reading of the puzzling and disturbing references to captive Welsh women in one of the Exeter Book Riddles. An understanding of the riddle depends in part on whether the key term *Wealas* refers to the Welsh, to slaves, or puns on the connection between the Welsh and slavery. Robson sets this debate in context by using postcolonial theory to explore the politics of the double-entendre.

One of the greatest causes of the incompatibility of English and Welsh society was the fundamental difference in design and procedure between Welsh legal practice, which had become codified under the name of the tenth-century king Hywel Dda (Hywel the Good), and English systems. In the fifth chapter, Sara Elin Roberts considers the complex operation of systems of English and Welsh law within medieval Wales. The pattern of English incursion in Wales led to the simultaneous existence of Wales (until the Act of Union in 1536) of three distinct jurisdictions: English law in the English planted settlements in Wales, Welsh law in *pura Wallia*, and the law of the March (which was a "restricted" and distinctive brand of English law) in the Marcher lordships. "Permitting" the survival of Welsh legal remedies often served English interests, not least in establishing the paradox that while English law defined the Welsh as subjects of the English Crown, it also denied them access to the remedies and protection available to English-born subjects.

In modern times, historians and critics have been fascinated by the idiosyncratic, insightful, and maddeningly conflicted *Itinerarium Kambriae* and *Descriptio Kambriae* of Giraldus Cambrensis, but it seems certain that medieval English readers would more often have encountered Gerald's work at second hand, in the very popular adaptations by Ranulph Higden, a monk of Chester in his *Polychronicon*, and in the English translation of that work by Trevisa. In the sixth chapter Ronald Waldron presents a new edition of Trevisa's translation of Book 38 of Higden's *Polychronicon*, which provides an amusing and revealing account of the shape into which the image of Wales was being refigured by the English imagination. Higden and Trevisa draw selectively on the detailed accounts of wonders in Giraldus' *Descriptio*, ironing out the contradictions of Gerald's text, primarily by shortening or omitting anything that shows the Welsh in a positive light, to construct a vision of Wales as a space removed from contemporary reality and describable only as an expression of imaginative fantasy.

The seventh, eighth, and ninth chapters consider the evidence from medieval romance for the evolution of notions of the Welsh nation. First Tony Davenport, after noting the infrequency of Welsh scenes and locales in Middle English romance, offers a reading of the few notable examples of such scenes, in *Sir Cleges* and *Horne Childe*. Again images of Wales are associated with fantasy and the "wildness" of the forest—an earlier and preurbanized contrast to the development of English social values.

In his account of the "myth of nations," Geary reminds us that however compelling the similarities and continuities may appear "congruence between early medieval and contemporary 'peoples' is a myth."[17] One major cause for this noncongruence results from the developments and changes that result from cultural contact with the linguistic and narrative traditions of other societies. Even before the start of the Norman incursions, Welsh culture was already significantly influenced by a variety of other languages—not merely English and the Latin culture of the church, but also Norse, Danish, and Irish influences (the last preserved in the Ogham inscriptions of southwest Wales). In the eighth chapter Ceridwen Lloyd-Morgan draws attention to the most influential of these cultural contacts, considering the extensive and fruitful contact between Welsh and the French and Anglo-Norman traditions, as evidenced in romance texts. One consequence of the insistence of writers like William of Malmesbury on the "barbarity" of the Welsh has been to foster a belief that Welsh culture was not in regular and mutual communion with the mainstream of European literary culture. In demonstrating the level of familiarity with French literary culture in medieval Wales, and the extensive (and early) evidence for linguistic and thematic borrowing, Lloyd-Morgan proves the falsity of this assumption, while also highlighting the primacy of French and Anglo-Norman, rather than English, culture as the medium for the contact of Welsh and European culture almost to the very end of the medieval period.

In the ninth chapter Cory James Rushton analyzes Malory's representation of the Welsh. Though Malory wrote in a period of widespread anti-Welsh sentiment, in the generations following the Glyn Dŵr challenge, Rushton finds that Malory presents a subtle and balanced portrayal, in which south Wales is reinscribed at the heart of the Arthurian story, and distinguished from the more wayward and unpredictable north.

The tenth chapter views the social estrangement between English and Welsh speaking medieval cultures from a different perspective, as Helen Fulton examines the complex construction of ideas of English identity, and the relationship of race to social class, in the fourteenth-century Welsh lyrics of Dafydd ap Gwilym. Fulton demonstrates the covert tensions explored in Dafydd's work between Welsh discourses of accommodation with, and reserving separation from, dominant English cultural imperatives. The chapter draws on the postcolonial theory of Homi Bhabha, particularly his concepts of mimicry and doubling, to interrogate the complexities of Welsh-English relations in the late Middle Ages.

The eleventh and twelfth chapters investigate the climate of patronage in late medieval Wales, and the extent to which Welsh noble and gentry families were involved in maintaining and encouraging artistic forms that expressed a distinctive Welsh character. David N. Klausner offers an overview of the generally (and, perhaps, unjustly) neglected topic of late medieval drama in Wales. He notes that evidence survives for a considerable variety of dramatic performance in every part of Wales. Although many of the surviving works (such as the Passion play and the Nativity play) have analogues in medieval English drama, they also display many distinctive features that cannot be traced to English sources. No text exemplifies more clearly the simultaneous (though apparently not contradictory) processes of informed contact with English culture and the will to recast that culture into a distinctively Welsh form than the remarkable drama *Troelus a Chresyd,* which survives in Aberystwyth, National Library of Wales MS Peniarth 106. The play reimagines Chaucer's *Troilus and Criseyde* (supplemented by Henryson's *Testament of Cresseid*) in a dramatic form, perhaps influenced by the conventions of the court masque, providing unexpected evidence of a continuing critical response in Welsh to the achievements of Middle English (and Middle Scots) literature.

Giraldus had noted and praised both the skill of Welsh musicians and the high honor in which music was held in Wales (though he used the same terms in his description of the Irish). Sally Harper considers the survival of an extensive and distinctive secular musical tradition in Wales after the Edwardian conquest. In Harper's account, the paramount role of music in asserting a Welsh cultural identity is explored. Although the lack of accepted norms of musical notation have made the recovery of medieval music, and of medieval performance practice, a complex and frustrating search, there is considerable evidence from the surviving literary texts in Welsh to help reconstruct the respect in which music and musicians were held.

One of the most curious characteristics of the surviving corpus of Middle English literature is the meager harvest of lyrics, but in medieval Welsh, the opposite is true: much surviving Welsh medieval poetry is lyric in form, and has been presumed to have been designed to be sung. Harper explains the divergent paths of music in medieval Wales and England as a result of the nature of the Welsh lyric as a public event, designed for performance to a patron and his entourage, with the purpose of furthering the reputation of both poet and patron. She also shows that the distinctive development of Welsh music reflects the more formal links between professional poets and musicians in medieval Wales, working together, by comparison with contemporary English practices, where musicians were often described as being of a different class and level of education from those who wrote texts.

One serious consequence of repeated foreign incursions into Wales was the distortion of the "natural" development of urban culture in Wales. In the later Middle Ages, the differences in social organization between Wales and England became more, rather than less, marked, in particular as a result of the failure of Wales to develop important urban centers to rival those in the March: Shrewsbury, Oswestry, Hereford, and the rest. Furthermore, the developing urban centers in Wales were themselves scarcely Welsh. Each group of invaders established fortified settlements: first the Romans (Segontium/Caernarfon; Maridunum/Carmarthen; Nidum/Neath), then probably the Irish and the Danes (in legend, Swansea is believed to bear the name of Sweyn Forkbeard), and finally the Normans began the policy of encouraging English and Flemish migrants to establish towns under the protection of the Norman castles.[18] One strange consequence of this was that London, more than one hundred and fifty miles from the Welsh border, but allegedly founded by the Brythons, was scarcely more of a foreign city to the Welsh than Pembroke or Swansea—a city that, like Cardiff, has almost certainly never had a majority of Welsh-speaking inhabitants. By the 1530s, London could claim to be, by head of population, the largest "Welsh" city in the world, supporting the development of an expatriate community that sought to maintain its Welsh identity. The final chapter explores the role played by the Welsh in London in preserving and developing a Welsh literature outside Wales. Geraint Evans considers how this "London Welsh" community was quick to exploit the new technology of printing, and the cultural possibilities made available through protestant ideologies of the priesthood of all believers to maintain and promote the potentially threatened Welsh language tradition, creating an important corpus of early printed books in Welsh. In doing so, they initiated the significant, if surprising, role that London has played in helping to prevent the extinction of the Welsh nation. When Iolo Morganwg sought to revive the tradition of the National Eisteddfod in 1792, he summoned the *gorsedd* [assembly of bards] not in his native Glamorgan but in the more exotic setting of Primrose Hill. The same identification is made in the poetry of the contemporary (and London-born and raised) poet Ifor ap Glyn who reimagines the map of the London Underground in terms of the Welsh mythic and literary past, punning on the interchangeability of the branch lines of the underground and the *pedair cainc* [four branches of the Mabiniogion]:

Dyma Songlines Llundain:
pedair cainc ar ddeg chwedloniaeth y ddinas
a'u cledrau'n canu am yr hen amser
pan dynnwyd yr enfys dan y ddaear;

mae atsain sodlau lawr twneli'r nos
yn adrodd Mabinogi'r Northern Line
yn disgyn yn ddu i Annwn De Llundain

mae pob chwa o wynt o flaen trên
ar rimyn melynwy'r Circle Line
fel angerdd gwyrthiol y Pair Dadeni,

ond marŵn y Met Line oedd yn llywio
eneidiau blin ein llwyth Llundeinig ni,
ar ein teithiau Arthuriaidd dyddiol,
tua Greal Sanctaidd ymddeol.

Dyma Songlines Llundain.[19]

[Here are the London Songlines: / Fourteen branches of the city's mythology / And their tracks singing about the old time / When the rainbow was pulled under the ground; / There's the echo of heels down the tunnels of the night / Reciting the Mabinogi of the Northern Line / Descending darkly to the Hades of South London / Each gust of wind before a train. On the egg-yolk rim of the Circle Line / Is like the miraculous force of the cauldron of Rebirth, / But the maroon of the Met Line was directing / The weary souls of our London tribe, / On our daily Arthurian quests, / Towards the Holy Grail of retirement. / Here are the London Songlines.]

Ifor ap Glyn's willingness to interpret his experience in present-day London in terms derived from his Welsh (and "traditional," or inherited) identity sounds an optimistic note, but it is an optimism that was rarely signaled or deserved in the responses of medieval English culture to the Welsh nation. Ifor ap Glyn's playfulness in delighting in his command of two (or more) discrete visions of the world reveals an engaging confidence; the enduring failure of the English cultural tradition to accommodate, assimilate, or respect the distinct cultural traditions of England's closest neighbor and first imperial conquest must be considered tragic—not in its consequences that are (at best) inconclusive, but in its revealed fear of difference. Writing in 1983, Gellner propounded a doctrine of progressive uniformity that subsequent events have left sounding mandarin, if not quaint:

> It [late industrial society] will have to respect cultural differences where they survive, provided that they are superficial and do not engender genuine barriers between people, in which case the barriers, not their cultures, constitute a grave problem. Though the old plethora of folk cultures is unlikely to survive, except in a token and cellophane-packaged form, an international plurality of sometimes fairly diverse high cultures will no doubt (happily) remain with us.[20]

For Bede, for William of Malmesbury and William of Newburgh, for King Edward I and King Henry IV, for Higden and Trevisa, the existence of Welsh culture (and, maybe the existence of the Welsh people) constituted a "grave problem"—but a grave problem for which they saw a solution. They were wrong in believing that the extinction of the Welsh nation was likely, but the work of making visible their efforts at erasure is still at an early stage.

Notes

1. Gwyn A. Williams, *When Was Wales?* (London: Penguin, 1991), 304.
2. Gillingham quotes with approval the judgment of Corrigan and Sayer: "Corrigan and Sayer suggest, surely rightly, that for the English to construe the brutality of conquest and/or the rapacity of commerce as a 'civiliz- ing mission,' 'took a national culture of extraordinary self-confidence and moral rectitude'"; P. Corrigan and D. Sayer, *The Great Arch: English State Formation as Cultural Revolution* (Oxford: Blackwell, 1985), quoted in John Gillingham, *The English in the Twelfth Century* (Woodbridge, Suffolk: Boydell and Brewer, 2000), 3.
3. Gillingham, *English in Twelfth Century*, 9.

4. Walter Map, *De Nugis Curialium (Courtiers' Trifles)*, ed. M. R. James, rev. C. N. L. Brooke and R. A. B. Mynors (Oxford: Clarendon Press, 1983).

5. Giraldi Cambrensis, *Itinerarium Kambriae* and *Descriptio Kambriae*, ed. James F. Dimock, in *Giraldi Cambrensis: Opera*, ed. J. S. Brewer, J. F. Dimock, and G. F. Warner, 8 vols., RS 21 (London, 1861–91), 6: 3–227.

6. William of Newburgh, *Historia rerum Anglicarum, the History of English Affairs*, Book 1, ed. with trans. and commentary by P. G. Walsh and M. J. Kennedy (Warminster: Aris & Phillips, 1988), 30–31.

7. R. R. Davies, *Historical Perception: Celts and Saxons* (Cardiff: University of Wales Press, 1979), 24.

8. Norman Davies has attempted to formulate a style of writing British history in which the experiences of all the inhabitants of the "British" Isles are accorded equal status; Norman Davies, *The Isles: A History* (London: Macmillan, 1999).

9. R. S. Thomas, "Welsh Landscape," in R. S. Thomas, *Collected Poems, 1945–1990* (London: Weidenfeld & Nicholson, 1993), 37.

10. R. R. Davies, *England's First Empire: Power and Identity in the British Isles, 1093–1348* (Oxford: Clarendon Press, 2000).

11. R. R. Davies, *Domination and Conquest: The Experience of Ireland, Scotland and Wales 1100–1300*, Wiles Lectures 1988 (Cambridge: Cambridge University Press, 1990), 3.

12. *English Historical Documents Volume III*, ed. Harry Rothwell (London: Routledge, 1996), 422.

13. See further in chapter 2.

14. S. F. C. Milsom, *Historical Foundations of the Common Law* (London: Butterworths, 1981).

15. Daniel Huws, *Medieval Welsh Manuscripts* (Cardiff: National Library of Wales and University of Wales Press, 2000), 3.

16. The one other possible surviving Welsh book of this kind is the manuscript known as the Hereford Gospels: Hereford Cathedral MS P. i. 2—though Mercia has been offered as an alternative place of composition. The Lichfield Gospels offer a biblical text that has a very high number of divergences from the Vulgate, and a significant proportion of these divergences are found also in the Hereford Gospels, whereas the number of these divergences found in the Lindisfarne Gospels is very low.

17. Patrick J. Geary, *The Myth of Nations* (Princeton, NJ: Princeton University Press, 2002), 37.

18. This topic is dealt with in greater length in chapter 2.

19. Ifor ap Glyn, from "Map yr Underground," in *Cerddi Map yr Underground* [The Underground Map Poems] (Llanrwst: Carreg Gwallt Press, 2001), 8–9, reproduced by kind permission of the author and Carreg Gwallt Press.

20. Ernest Gellner, *Nations and Nationalism* (Oxford: Blackwell, 1983), 121.

CHAPTER 1

MIDDLE ENGLISH TEXTS
AND WELSH CONTEXTS

William Marx

A berystwyth, National Library of Wales MS Peniarth 39, is a fifteenth-century manuscript of the Welsh language *Law of Hywel Dda* [The Law of Hywel the Good]. Texts of the medieval Welsh laws are central to Welsh history; recognizing Welsh law was one of the definitions of being Welsh in a politically fragmented country.[1] This manuscript is not, however, entirely in Welsh; one folio, fol. 74r, contains a Middle English text "The Letter of Pope Leo to King Charles," that is, to Charlemagne:[2]

> Seynt Leon, þe Pope, wret þis letter and send hit to Kyng Charlis and seid, "He þat berith þis letter on hym ne dare he noȝt drede of hys enemys to be overcom neyþer felle to be ydamnyd ne with þe fend to ben overcome..."

This is a charm: whoever bears this letter will be free of dangers and evils. This is the only piece of Middle English writing in the manuscript. It was added in a later hand and has no explicit or implicit connection to the *Law of Hywel Dda*. This kind of later, seemingly random, addition is a familiar feature of medieval manuscripts. In this instance, it is linguistically different from the main text, and it is probable that the copyist did not consider the context as anything more than a convenient place to record this English language text. There was a blank space in the manuscript that could be used for this purpose. Here English is a minority language and the text is added without specific reference to the significance of the context. In that sense it is intrusive. At the same time, the scribe, who was probably Welsh, was willing and able to accommodate a brief English language text in a Welsh language manuscript and did not feel the need to translate it into Welsh. The picture suggests a culture at ease with its native language and prepared to incorporate material in a different language where it might be useful. Significantly, this brief Middle English text was incorporated into the cherished space of a culturally important text, the *Law of Hywel Dda*.

This example provides one model for the place of Middle English in Welsh manuscripts and, indeed, in medieval Welsh language culture, and what follows uses evidence from manuscripts of Welsh origin and provenance to consider what they can suggest about how Welsh culture in the fifteenth century and later responded to, interacted with, and used Middle English language materials.[3] This chapter has grown out of my volume for the *Index of Middle English Prose* for the National Library of Wales.[4] The series, which to date has published eighteen volumes, is an ambitious project that has been underway for over thirty years and may take the same number of years to complete. Each volume editor is responsible for examining manuscripts in a specific collection in a search for occurrences of Middle English prose texts, be they well known, substantial, and complete texts such as the Parson's Tale of the *Canterbury Tales,* fragments of texts, or recipes. The original aim of the project was to provide a census and inventory of the surviving Middle English prose texts and to classify these along the lines of the *Index of Middle English Verse.*[5] The *Index of Middle English Prose* is far from completion, but the volumes concerned with individual collections are valuable in themselves. A by-product of exploring collections in this way is that it provides an insight into the nature of the materials that were being brought together in manuscripts and the range of functions of Middle English prose, from the scientific to the historical, to the devotional, to what we would traditionally think of as the literary.

The National Library of Wales is of special interest because it is in the real sense of the term a national library, the library of a nation, and it was conceived as such in the late nineteenth century.[6] It was in 1873 at the National Eisteddfod held in Mold (Flintshire) that plans took shape and a committee was formed to campaign for a national library for Wales. Aberystwyth in Ceredigion became the chosen site, and Llyfrgell Genedlaethol Cymru/the National Library of Wales, opened its doors for readers in 1909. In the year 2007 Llyfrgell Genedlaethol Cymru celebrated the hundredth anniversary of the granting of its charter.

The library's main purpose was to gather together the historic libraries of manuscripts and books held in private collections in Wales, and to return to Wales collections of historic manuscripts and books that had found their way into England. A significant collection of medieval material had been assembled in the early eighteenth century by the Reverend Moses Williams, vicar of Llandyfrïog, Ceredigion, but by the middle of that century this had become the property of the earls of Macclesfield and was housed in Shirburn Castle in Oxfordshire. The individual who did most to establish the National Library of Wales and to bring together its manuscript collections was Sir John Williams (1840–1926), a medical doctor from Swansea who for most of his career was a senior member of the staff of University College Hospital, London. Sir John Williams arranged for the purchase of the Welsh collection from the earl of Macclesfield and its repatriation to Wales. He also negotiated for the sale to the National Library of a number of collections of Welsh material in Wales, most notably the Peniarth-Hengwrt collection, held in Peniarth house in Tywyn in Merionethshire. The Hengwrt part of the collection was begun by the distinguished antiquarian Robert Vaughan (1592–1667) of Hengwrt, near Dolgellau in Merionethshire. This was in time merged with another at Peniarth, and when the combined collection came to the National Library of Wales in 1909 it contained over five hundred manuscripts of Welsh, Cornish, English, Latin, and French material. Robert Vaughan was responsible for acquiring what is known as the "Hengwrt manuscript of Chaucer's *Canterbury Tales*," MS Peniarth 392.[7] This manuscript has been in Wales since before the middle of the seventeenth century, and along with other manuscripts points to the high standard of Vaughan's collecting activities. It was, however, Welsh material and material relating to Wales that interested Vaughan and other antiquarian collectors in Wales from the seventeenth century onward. Sir John Williams and others behind the project to establish the National Library of Wales carried on this interest and formed a public institution to preserve the historical identity of Wales and the Welsh language. One needs to keep in mind that very many of the historic manuscripts and books of the collections of the National Library of Wales have direct association with Welsh history and the history of Wales as a nation. One could say this about almost any collection, that it bears a relationship to the history of the country in which it is found, but for the National Library of Wales this aspect of its history and development is more pronounced and more significant.

Apart from a few famous manuscripts such as the "Hengwrt Manuscript of Chaucer's *Canterbury Tales*" and what is usually referred to as "Porkington 10"— actually Brogyntyn MS II.1[8]—the English language manuscripts in the National Library of Wales have remained unexplored. The Welsh manuscripts have been subject to intense scrutiny, but the English language texts found in these manuscripts are relatively little known outside Wales.[9] Over half of the manuscripts catalogued for the volume of the *Index of Middle English Prose* for the National Library of Wales were not listed in the *Index of Printed Middle English Prose*, and the treatment of National Library of Wales manuscripts in the volumes of the *Manual of the Writings in Middle English* is sketchy to say the least.

For the purposes of this collection of essays what is particularly fascinating about the manuscripts indexed from the National Library of Wales is the treatment of Middle English texts in manuscripts that also contain Welsh, French, and Latin texts. Researchers in Middle English writing are accustomed to find English as the dominant language, most often the only language, in manuscripts containing Middle English from the middle to late fourteenth century onward. But among manuscripts that originated in Wales and contain Middle English, English is frequently a minority language. This should not be surprising—Welsh is the vernacular language of Wales—but it is salutary to be reminded that in Wales, in the later Middle Ages, Middle English was a minority language and shared the linguistic stage with Welsh, French, and Latin. Wales's linguistic culture encompasses four languages, and some manuscripts contain material in all of them. What do Middle English texts in Welsh manuscripts suggest about Welsh identities? There follow four case studies based on manuscripts in the National Library of Wales that are designed to look at this question tentatively.

The first case study reflects something of what emerges from Peniarth 39 but in a more dynamic way. Aberystwyth, National Library of Wales (hereafter NLW) MS Peniarth 12 is a composite manuscript and its precise codicological history, not to mention its textual history, is difficult to untangle.[10] It is known primarily to Welsh scholars because it contains one of the more than twenty Welsh language witnesses to a text known as the *Elucidarius*.[11] This is a highly practical work of religious instruction in the form of a dialogue; it deals with doctrinal issues, for example, the nature of the Trinity, and with problems such as corrupt priests. The text was composed in Latin and was immensely popular in medieval Europe, and was translated into most European languages. Copies survive in their hundreds in French, German, and Spanish.

The basis of Peniarth 12 is a late sixteenth-century Welsh language manuscript with an inscription in Welsh in the hand of the main scribe, which reads (fol. 79v): "Llyfr Hugh Evans yw hwn Anno 1583" [This is Hugh Evans's book, in the year 1583]. The manuscript is mainly paper. Fols. 12r–73r contain the Welsh language text of the *Elucidarius*; of these, fols. 39r–58r are a fifteenth-century vellum fragment of the text, and Hugh Evans has constructed a complete Welsh language text of the *Elucidarius* around this earlier fragment. The remainder of the folios (fols. 73v–81v) contain, in Hugh Evans's hand, religious texts in Welsh, with the exception of a Latin text of the Creed. What had escaped the notice of English scholars, but not Welsh scholars, is that the first eleven folios contain a significant portion of a distinct Middle English translation also of the *Elucidarius*. The hand is not that of Hugh Evans, but is late fifteenth century. The *Elucidarius* is a problematic text for Middle English writing, for although it appears in such a large number of witnesses in most European languages, it survives in very small numbers in English: one twelfth-century manuscript of fragments, a late fourteenth- or early fifteenth-century translation found in two manuscripts, and two printings by Wynkyn de Worde translated from French. Peniarth 12 therefore provides a significant addition to the census of Middle English versions of the *Elucidarius*. I have edited this text with an introduction that includes a profile of the language using the *Linguistic Atlas of Late Medieval English*.[12] The linguistic profile (LP) locates this Middle English text to west Herefordshire where the Welsh language was widespread in the Middle Ages. The region in west Herefordshire known as "Archenfield" or, in Welsh, "Ergyng" was Welsh speaking until the eighteenth century and was effectively a part of Wales before the Act of Union in 1536 when it became absorbed into Herefordshire.[13]

Ergyng, or possibly west Herefordshire generally, provides a likely context for the origin of this Middle English version of the *Elucidarius*, and increases the possibility that it might have been translated from Welsh. No persuasive linguistic evidence, however, emerges for a Welsh language origin for this Middle English *Elucidarius* and the conclusion must be that it was translated from Latin. The codicological history of Peniarth 12 is complex and it is too tightly bound to discover whether the first eleven folios were copied separately from the main part of the manuscript. Circumstantial evidence, however, suggests that it was an independent fragment that Hugh Evans bound into his sixteenth-century book. Hugh Evans constructed his Welsh language text of the *Elucidarius* around an earlier fragment of a Welsh language *Elucidarius* and on fol. 55v notes in the margin *finis angli*, that is, at this point the English text finishes. This gives rise to the possibility that the English language text contributed something to the process of compilation that Hugh Evans initiated.

This example of a Middle English text in a Welsh context has some interesting suggestions to make about the interplay between English language and Welsh language texts in a Welsh linguistic and cultural environment. First, the Middle English text was produced in what can be assumed was a Welsh speaking region, which is known for other Middle English texts. The picture suggests a culture in which English, Welsh, Latin, and French were used side by side, a multilingual cultural environment. Whether Hugh Evans later, in 1583, compiled his manuscript in Welsh-speaking west Herefordshire, Archenfield, or Ergyng is not clear, but it is evident that when he came to assemble his collection, there was every reason for him to prefer Welsh to English. The codicological evidence shows that he actively sought to reconstruct a Welsh language *Elucidarius* around the fifteenth-century Welsh fragment of the text that he had in hand. He had, it would seem, an English language fragment around which he could have compiled a complete English language text, but his choice was for Welsh. What does this suggest about the status and function of English for Hugh Evans? In this instance, English is a relic of the past; English appears in a fifteenth-century fragment that the compiler chose to preserve, and another English language text also survives in the binding, "Instructions on Preparing for Death."[14] But the dominant language of this manuscript is Welsh. Here we can see how the Welsh language was regarded in relation to English within Wales. The Welsh language is functional and it has a purpose for a didactic compilation such as this. English is regarded as possibly a curiosity, or a point of reference that provides support for, but is by no means central to, the compilation.

The second case study is based on another Peniarth manuscript, MS Peniarth 50.[15] This is a predominantly Welsh language manuscript with some Middle English, and is an important manuscript for Welsh scholars. It is in one hand and dated to the first half of the fifteenth century. The manuscript has been associated with Neath Abbey, and it is highly probable that the compiler was a monk at this Cistercian abbey in Glamorgan.[16] This context for the manuscript is plausible given that the Cistercians are known to have been strong supporters of Wales and its politics as well as Welsh culture including Welsh literature, both oral and written. This was especially true of the Cistercian houses in central and north Wales, for example, Strata Florida. Neath Abbey was not located in this geographical region, but the Cistercians were a closely knit order both nationally and internationally, and Welsh bards such as Gutun Owain and Dafydd ap Gwilym frequently visited Cistercian houses and moved from one to the other.[17]

Peniarth 50 is known as *Y Cwtta Cyfarwydd* [The Short Guide] and although it is not the only manuscript to have this title, it is the most well known. Its main contents, in Welsh, are prophecies in prose and verse. A significant feature of the manuscripts held by the National Library of Wales is the sheer volume of prophecies, in prose and verse, in Welsh and English. Prophecies form one of the chief genres of writing in Welsh and English in Wales, and none of the other collections for the *Index of Middle English Prose* contains anything like the number of prophecies that are found in the manuscripts in the National Library of Wales. Welsh scholars have detected an important difference in the nature of the origins of prophecies in verse and in prose; Welsh verse prophecies tend to be native Welsh composition, whereas in the fifteenth century, prophecies in Welsh prose tend to be reworkings of English language texts. The last point needs qualification: the translation or adaptation of English material of this kind to Welsh does not mean that it was not of central concern to the compiler and the audience. Middle English prophecies were being given a new audience in Welsh.[18]

A second feature of Peniarth 50 is that despite the dominance of Welsh language texts, it also contains sixteen items of Middle English prose and seven of Middle English verse. These Middle English texts, both verse and prose, are mainly in the genre of prophecies, along with some charms. A brief extract from one of the Middle English prophecies illustrates the nature of these texts:

> A remembrance of termys of diuerse prophecyes that Wallyshmen fyn-
> dyth in her bokys. On of hem is that ther is a tyme of foxyes the whiche
> Merlyn spekyth of, how a foxe schall aryse and schall be take for a kyng,
> but nought by law, and schall gendyr whelpys that schall do moche steryng
> & moche woo make...[19]

The material here is conventional in terms of prophetic writing, but the first sentence is provocative. Is the sentence inclusive or exclusive? That is, does it mean that this text is a "record or list" (remembrance) of the prophecies that Welshmen—as the "Other"—"compose" or "produce" in their books, or does it mean that this text is a record of the prophecies that *we* Welshmen compose in *our* books? In other words, is the scribe compiling this *about* the culture or *for* the culture? Is English a foreign language? The evidence is ambiguous, but the manuscript gives space to a significant amount of English language material in a manuscript in which Welsh is the main language. It is probable that the compiler is not being hostile to or being threatened by English language culture, and that this English material is considered to be native writing, not foreign, imported writing. In Wales, English is one of the secondary languages, and as such has a place in Welsh culture.

One of the most interesting features of this manuscript comes with what the compiler has to say about Welsh identity. This appears in the Welsh language preface to the account in Welsh of the legend of the history and significance of the oil that was miraculously given to Thomas Becket. Ceridwen Lloyd-Morgan has written perceptively about this text and the preface, and what follows draws very much on her work.[20] The Welsh text is known as *Darogan yr Olew Bendigaid* [The Prophecy of the Sacred or Blessed Oil], and is found in a number of manuscripts; the preface, however, is found in no manuscript earlier than Peniarth 50. The compiler begins by lamenting the servitude of the Welsh under English domination and says that he suffered great despair because of this. He then remembers that Giraldus Cambrensis had attributed prophecy to divine inspiration. This realization leads him to search through prophecies, and these have the effect of assuring him that the Welsh could one day reestablish their nation. The compiler closes the preface by giving a brief account of how he compiled the *Darogan yr Olew Bendigaid*: "ryw dirgeledic gydymddaith ydolygawdd ym drossi man betheu droganawl o ladin franghec a saesnec ynghymraec" [some mysterious companion made me translate odds and ends of prophecy from Latin, French and English into Welsh].

The Welsh preface, which is probably the work of the compiler of the manuscript, seems personal, but its perspective is more broadly political, and in this respect it articulates a clear political stance of the Welsh nation in respect to the English. There is much that is compelling about this text and its context, but for this chapter one of the main points of interest is the attitude to language and the linguistic origin of texts: the compiler searched for and translated into Welsh material from Latin, French, and English. Is the compiler translating texts into Welsh for practical reasons—the audience is mainly Welsh speaking—or for political reasons, to assert Welsh identity and to appropriate to the Welsh language prophecies concerning the restoration of the Welsh nation? It is probable that both interpretations apply and are in some sense linked.

There is, however, yet another aspect of Peniarth 50 that should be considered when we try to assess the purpose and function of the manuscript, namely the sixteen items of Middle English prose and seven items of Middle English verse. Almost all of the Middle English texts are prophecies and so overlap with the main type of Welsh material, and in some instances they refer to places in Wales, for example, "Landaff," "Glamorgan," "Myllford," "Brechnoc" (Brecon), "Wenllouke" (Wenlock), and "Castell Morleys" (Morlais Castle, Glamorgan).[21] It would seem that in this manuscript and others like it, Middle English functions as one of the minority languages of Wales; that is, it is not regarded as a foreign language. The English may be seen as the oppressors, but the English language is not regarded as a symbol of the foreigners. I would argue that here, in this manuscript context, the Middle English language is functional and its use does not in itself carry political connotations.

Ceridwen Lloyd-Morgan describes the compiler of Peniarth 50 as a "magpie character searching hither and yon in old manuscripts for tidbits of interesting tradition or prophecy."[22] The same can be said of Wales's greatest copyist of the seventeenth century, John Jones of Gellilyfdy, who was born in the late 1570s or early 1580s and died around 1658.[23] He lived in Gellilyfdy in Flintshire and was a tireless transcriber of historic Welsh language texts, mostly prophetic writing; like the compiler of Peniarth 50, he was a magpie of a copyist. In the midst of his copying of Welsh language material—and this is his main interest—there are occasional patches of Middle English, mostly historical and prophetic writing, similar to what he is transcribing in Welsh. John Jones compiled NLW MS Peniarth 215 between 1604 and 1612, and the contents are mainly Welsh language historical chronicles, with some Latin, concerning the history of Wales.[24] Nevertheless, in the midst of this Welsh language chronicle narrative is a long passage of Middle English covering pages 164–76. This is made up of three separate passages that have been derived from John Trevisa's translation of the *Polychronicon*: Book V, Chap. 6 concerning King Arthur, Book VII, Chap. 23, the discovery of the graves of Arthur and Guinevere, and Book IV, Chap. 31, and Book V, Chap. 10, concerning the association of Pelagius with the abbey of Bangor and the slaughter of the monks of Bangor by King Ethelfrith.[25] This is a hotchpotch of English language material in the midst of Welsh language historical narrative. John Jones prefaces the English passage with this note, in Welsh:

> Sef a gefai i hyn o storia am gafadedigaeth angladd yr ardderchawg frenin arthvr yn y chweched gabidwl or pvmed llyfr o lyfr kronikl saesonaeg or eiddo harri Jones o lwyn y kosyn yn ysgeifiog fal hynn.[26]

> [I discovered this story concerning the finding of the burial place of the honorable king Arthur in the sixth chapter of the fifth book of an English chronicle book owned by Harri Jones of Llwyn-y-cosyn in Ysgeifiog, thus.]

Another of John Jones's manuscripts, NLW MS 3041, contains a similar prefatory note to a prophetic text:

> Sef a gefais y broffydoliaeth hon sydd yn dyfod yn saesneg mewn hen gronigl Saesneg (or eiddo Harri Jones o lwyn y kosyn).[27]

> [I found this prophecy which follows in English in an old English chronicle owned by Harri Jones of Llwyn-y-cosyn.]

Here again the English text is taken from Trevisa's translation of the *Polychronicon*.[28] Elsewhere in the same manuscript John Jones prefaces the text of a Latin prophecy with this note:

> llyma proffwydoliaeth lladin yr hom [*sic*] a gefais i yn ysgrifenedig mewn hen gronikl saesneg oedd breintiedig (or eiddo fy ewythr Sion Grvffydd or Brithdir).[29]

> [Here is a Latin prophecy which I found written in an old English chronicle which was highly esteemed, owned by my uncle Sion Gruffudd of Brithdir.]

The "hen gronikl saesneg" referred to here was probably a copy of Trevisa's Middle English translation of the *Polychronicon*. These instances are evidence of the circulation and use of a Middle English text that was well respected in Flintshire in north Wales, and was regarded as authoritative enough to use to interrupt a Welsh language narrative in order to provide some additional information. The way in which John Jones, here and elsewhere in his compilations, incorporates Middle English texts, which are available to him in Flintshire, argues again that the English language was functional and was part of Welsh culture. As far as it is possible to be, John Jones's purpose as a copyist was to preserve Welsh language texts concerned with Wales and its history, and in this respect his work can be said to have both cultural and political dimensions. At the same time he did not ignore material in English where it could contribute to his purpose. As with Peniarth 50 and other bilingual manuscripts, and those with French, English, and Latin, Welsh is the main language and the other written languages do not appear to pose a threat to Welsh, and their use does not seem to carry political connotations. The English people may be seen as the "Other," but the English language is a different matter.

The discussion so far has focused on bilingual and multilingual manuscripts from Wales where Middle English has a place as a minority language, and there are a number of examples of this type of manuscript. The next example is an exclusively Middle English manuscript which is known to have been in Wales from at least the sixteenth century. NLW MS 21608 is from the last quarter of the fifteenth century and is a text of the Middle English prose *Brut*, which is a large prose narrative beginning with the foundation of Britain by Brutus, and following the history of Britain in different forms to any number of points in the thirteenth, fourteenth, and fifteenth centuries.[30] It was originally compiled in Anglo-Norman, and was translated into Middle English in the fourteenth century.[31] The Middle English *Brut* was constantly being added to and revised, and is witnessed in many versions. Taking all the known Middle English manuscripts of the different versions together, there are approximately 180 manuscripts, making the *Brut* the text with the largest number of surviving Middle English manuscripts apart from the Wycliffite translation of the Bible. NLW MS 21608 contains one of the variant texts of the *Brut*, and is characterized by additions to and revisions of the "Common Version." Some of the revisions and additions are extensive, and these produce what is a highly sophisticated and subtly nuanced version of the narrative of British history up to 1461 and the accession of Edward IV.[32] They include the addition to chapter 163 of the "Common Version" two epitaphs on the death of Llywelyn ap Gruffydd (1282), the last native prince of Wales:

Off this Lewelyn .ii. clerkes, a Walshemon and an Englesshmon, wrote verse in ryme. The Walshemon wroote in commendacioun of hym in this wise:

Off Englisshemen here lieth the tormentour
Prince off Wales and protectour
Lewelyn reuler and gouernour
Off vertue and off kynges the floure
Fourme and ensample off quiete balaunce
Leder off his peple be vertues gouernaunce

And the Englishemon wrote in discommendacion off hym in this wise:

Heere lieth the prince off all errour
Off true men robbour and oppressour
Off Englishmen false traytour
A dede bronde off falshede mayntenour
God off Walshmen and honour
Pitousles prince off true men murdroure

Filth of Troianes stokke off decepcion
And of all evell cause and occasion.

The origin of these verses is the *Polychronicon* where they appear in Latin, but they have been purposefully and uniquely translated for and added to NLW MS 21608 of the *Brut*.[33] The two epitaphs acknowledge two points of view concerning Llywelyn ap Gruffydd. This balancing act is provocative and suggests that the compiler had loyalties in both England and Wales.

Another kind of intriguing evidence from the manuscript comes from its inscriptions, the most telling of which is the following, in a sixteenth-century hand:

> Lewis Dollgelley of Ruthyn ys the possessor of thys booke, God send hym loke. And he ys mercer of Ruthyn and ys an honeste and a veyrey rych mercer and disceaueth not the pore simple people but leadeth hys lyfe in equitye and iustyce and lyueth onlye wythout the preiudyce.[34]

This is the most extensive and revealing of the manuscript's inscriptions, but the manuscript contains also a number of names that Daniel Huws has located to Ruthin in Denbighshire.[35] This evidence shows that in the sixteenth century NLW MS 21608, a thoroughly English language text, was in Ruthin in the possession of a merchant. Could the text have been originally revised and the manuscript copied in Wales for a Welsh patron? Linguistic evidence from the LALME would be helpful to answer this question. I compiled the data from NLW MS 21608 for a linguistic profile, and the furthest west that it was possible to locate the language of the manuscript was Shropshire.[36] This borders Wales and such a location could explain the kind of balancing act that emerges with the two epitaphs on Llywelyn ap Gruffydd. Nevertheless, this picture of the language of NLW MS 21608 may not be complete, and the question reflects one of the problems with the LALME as we have it. We can only test new texts against the data that the LALME provides, and it is sadly lacking for Wales. There are only nine linguistic profiles for the whole of Wales (eight of them mapped).[37] Two are from Ruthin and one from south Denbighshire, and NLW MS 21608 shares a number of features with these three linguistic profiles within close proximity to each other in north Wales. The data available in the LALME, however, were not enough to make a judgment about whether NLW MS 21608 could have been compiled in Ruthin, as seems a possibility in the light of evidence for the integration in the Middle Ages of English and Welsh peoples in Ruthin.[38] This specific issue points to the need for a much fuller survey of the linguistic features of Middle English in Wales. It may not be possible to locate precisely the origin of every manuscript of known Welsh provenance that contains instances of Middle English, but it would nevertheless be useful to have data about the features of Middle English used in Wales, and in different parts of the Wales. It may well be that NLW MS 21608 was, in fact, compiled in Wales, possibly in Ruthin, and that its distinctly anti-Lancastrian stance, especially for the reign of Henry IV, is an expression of Welsh discontent.[39]

In addition to the main linguistic question referred to here, there is good reason to explore more fully the use, function, and status of Middle English within Wales. Did English language culture from England have a profound impact on Welsh culture through its language, or did Wales develop its own English language culture to run parallel with its Welsh language culture? This issue invites wider exploration, but, as a final point of reference, it is useful to turn to Humphrey Llwyd's *Cronica Walliae*, completed in 1559.[40] This is a translation and compilation in English drawn from Welsh language historical writing covering the princes of Wales from Cadwaladr Fendigaid to Llywelyn ap Gruffydd. It is the earliest English language chronicle produced in Wales to deal with this subject, and it ends with this sentence: "After this there was nothing done in Wales worthy memory, but that is to bee redde in the Englishe Cronicle." It is most likely that the "Englishe Cronicle" is the Middle English *Brut*, of which there were at least thirteen printings between 1480 and 1528.[41] Llwyd's statement concerning the significance of the "Englishe Cronicle" for an understanding of Welsh history and his decision to use English for his *Cronica Walliae* are intriguing, for he was one of the chief architects of one of the most significant political acts concerning the Welsh language in the sixteenth century. He was MP for Denbigh and in this capacity he guided through Parliament the legislation of 1563 that authorized the translation into Welsh of the Bible and the *Book of Common Prayer*.[42] Llwyd sees the value of both languages; he is bilingual but this does not mean that he has compromised his Welsh identity: Welsh is the chief language of the nation but English has a function within the context of Wales. Something of that same understanding is evident, implicitly or explicitly, in the Welsh manuscripts that contain Middle English.

Notes

1. The manuscript is described in J. Gwenogvryn Evans, *The First Portion of the Welsh Manuscripts at Peniarth, Towyn, Merioneth*, Report on Manuscripts in the Welsh Language, vol. 1, part 2 (London: Historical Manuscripts Commission, 1899), 373–74. See also Dafydd Jenkins, ed. and trans., *The Law of Hywel Dda: Law Texts from Medieval Wales*, The Welsh Classics (Llandysul: Gomer Press, 1986).

2. The full text of the charm in Aberystwyth, National Library of Wales MS Peniarth 39 is printed in William Marx, *The Index of Middle English Prose, XIV: Manuscripts in the National Library of Wales/Llyfrgell Genedlaethol Cymru, Aberystwyth* (Cambridge: D. S. Brewer, 1999), 30. The text is item 54 in R. E. Lewis, N. F. Blake, and A. S. G. Edwards, *Index of Printed Middle English Prose* (New York and London: Garland, 1985), but the occurrence in MS Peniarth 39 is not noted.

3. On the issue of the nature and extent of the use of English in medieval Wales, see Llinos Beverley Smith, "The Welsh Language before 1536," in *The Welsh Language before the Industrial Revolution*, ed. Geraint H. Jenkins,

A Social History of the Welsh Language (Cardiff: University of Wales Press, 1997), 15–44, and Alan R. Thomas, "English in Wales," in *The Cambridge History of the English Language, vol. V: English in Britain and Overseas*, ed. Robert Burchfield (Cambridge: Cambridge University Press, 1994), 94–147, at 94–98, 107–10.

4. See note 2.

5. Julia Boffey and A. S. G. Edwards, *A New Index of Middle English Verse* (London: British Library, 2005).

6. For a summary of the history of the foundation of the National Library of Wales/Llyfrgell Genedlaethol Cymru and its manuscript collections see the Introduction to Marx, *Index, XIV*, xiii–xx, which draws on a range of work published by members of the staff of Llyfrgell Genedlaethol Cymru. See also Ceridwen Lloyd-Morgan, "Medieval Manuscripts in the National Library of Wales," in *Sources, Exemplars, and Copy-Texts: Influence and Transmission*, ed. William Marx, *Trivium* 31 (1999): 1–12.

7. Marx, *Index, XIV*, 57–58.

8. Marx, *Index, XIV*, 19–27.

9. Daniel Huws, *Medieval Welsh Manuscripts* (Cardiff: University of Wales Press and the National Library of Wales, 2000; repr., 2002). See also Chaps. 1 and 2 by Huw Pryce and Daniel Huws respectively, in Philip Henry Jones and Eiluned Rees, eds., *A Nation and Its Books: A History of the Book in Wales* (Aberystwyth: National Library of Wales, 1998), 1–39.

10. Evans, *First Portion of the Welsh Manuscripts at Peniarth*, 323–25.

11. *The Elucidarium and Other Tracts in Welsh from Llyvyr Agkyr Llandewivrevi A.D. 1346*, ed. J. Morris Jones and John Rhys (Oxford: Clarendon Press, 1894), 5–76.

12. William Marx, "An Abbreviated Middle English Prose Translation of the *Elucidarius*," *Leeds Studies in English* 31 (2000): 1–53. The linguistic profile along with a discussion of language and localization appears on 3–5. Angus McIntosh, M. L. Samuels, and Michael Benskin, *A Linguistic Atlas of Late Medieval English*, 4 vols. (Aberdeen: Aberdeen University Press, 1986). (Henceforth LALME.)

13. Marx, "Abbreviated Middle English Translation of *Elucidarius*," 3–5. On "Ergyng," see Smith, "Welsh Language before 1536," 17–18; Geraint H. Jenkins, Richard Suggett, and Eryn M. White, "The Welsh Language in Early Modern Wales," in Jenkins, *Welsh Language before the Industrial Revolution*, 45–122, at p. 56; B. G. Charles, "The Welsh, Their Language, and Place-Names in Archenfield and Oswestry," in *Angles and Britons*, ed. J. R. R. Tolkien, T. H. Parry-Williams, Kenneth Jackson, B. G. Charles, Nora K. Chadwick, and William Rees (Cardiff: University of Wales Press, 1963), 85–110, at 87–96; Simon Meecham-Jones, chap. 2 in this volume.

14. *Index of Printed Middle English Prose*, item 460. See also Marx, *Index, XIV*, "Peniarth 12," 29, item 2.

15. Marx, *Index, XIV*, 31–34. The manuscript is described in Evans, *First Portion of the Welsh Manuscripts at Peniarth*, 389–99. There is a useful discussion of

Peniarth 50 in Manon Bonner Jenkins, "Aspects of the Welsh Prophetic Verse Tradition in the Middle Ages: Incorporating Textual Studies of Poetry from 'Llyfr Coch Hergest' (Oxford, Jesus College, MS cxi) and 'Y Cwta Cyfarwydd' (Aberystwyth, National Library of Wales, MS Peniarth 50)" (Ph.D. diss., University of Cambridge, 1990), 225–45.

16. Jenkins ("Aspects of the Welsh Prophetic Verse Tradition") does not specifically suggest Neath Abbey as the original home of the manuscript, but accepts arguments for its association with the region in which the abbey is situated. Evans (*First Portion of the Welsh Manuscripts at Peniarth*, 389–99) was the first to suggest Neath Abbey, and Ceridwen Lloyd-Morgan reports evidence that tends to support this view; see Ceridwen Lloyd-Morgan, "Prophecy and Welsh Nationhood in the Fifteenth Century," *Transactions of the Honourable Society of Cymmrodorion* (1986): 9–26, at 20 and note 26.

17. On Neath Abbey see David M. Robinson, *The Cistercians in Wales: Architecture and Archaeology 1130–1540* (London: Society of Antiquaries, 2006), 261–67; on the Cistercians in Wales see Robinson, *Cistercians in Wales*, 19–36, and Janet Burton, "*Homines sanctitatis eximiae, religionis consummatae*: The Cistercians in England and Wales," *Archaeologia Cambrensis* 154 (2005): 27–49. On the Cistercians as patrons of Welsh literature see Smith, "Welsh Language before 1536," 23 and note 28.

18. Margaret Enid Griffiths, *Early Vaticination in Welsh* (Cardiff: University of Wales Press, 1937), 195–213; Lloyd-Morgan, "Prophecy and Welsh Nationhood," 10; Glanmor Williams, "Prophecy, Poetry and Politics in Medieval and Tudor Wales," Chap. 3 of *Religion, Language and Nationality in Wales* (Cardiff: University of Wales Press, 1979), 71–86. Also Elizabeth Schoales, "Praise and Propaganda: Prophetic Poetry in Wales to 1400" (Ph.D. diss., University of Wales, Lampeter, 2003).

19. Peniarth 50, item 16 in Marx, *Index, XIV*, 33–34.

20. Lloyd-Morgan, "Prophecy and Welsh Nationhood," 18–20.

21. Marx, *Index, XIV*, 32–33.

22. Lloyd-Morgan, "Prophecy and Welsh Nationhood," 20.

23. On Jones see Nesta Lloyd, "A History of Welsh Scholarship in the First Half of the Seventeenth Century, with Special Reference to the Writings of John Jones, Gellilyfdy" (D.Phil. diss., University of Oxford, 1970).

24. Marx, *Index, XIV*, 38–39. The manuscript is described in J. Gwenogvryn Evans, *The Second Portion of the Welsh Manuscripts at Peniarth, Towyn, Merioneth*, Report on Manuscripts in the Welsh Language, vol. 1, part 3 (London: Historical Manuscripts Commission, 1905), 1036–38.

25. Ralph Higden, *Polychronicon*, 9 vols., ed. Churchill Babington and Joseph Rawson Lumby, Rolls Series (1865–86), 5: 215, 421, 329–37; 8: 61–65.

26. Peniarth 215, item 1 in Marx, *Index, XIV*, 38.

27. Aberystwyth, National Library of Wales MS 3041, item 17 in Marx, *Index, XIV*, 10.

28. Higden, *Polychronicon*, Book I, Chap. 60 (2: 173–75).

29. NLW 3041, 213, noted in item 17, Marx, *Index, XIV*, 10.

30. W. D. Brie, ed., *The Brut or the Chronicles of England*, EETS os 131 and 136 (London: Trübner, 1906, 1908; repr., in one volume, 2000). Lister Matheson, *The Prose Brut: The Development of a Middle English Chronicle* (Tempe, AZ: Medieval and Renaissance Texts and Studies, 1998). *Prose Brut*, 290–93 has comprehensive details on NLW 21608 and its place in the textual tradition of the *Brut*. The manuscript is described in William Marx, ed., *An English Chronicle 1377–1461*, Medieval Chronicles 3 (Woodbridge, Suffolk: Boydell and Brewer, 2003), xv–xxii.

31. The first edition of an Anglo-Norman version of the *Brut* has recently been published: see Julia Marvin, ed., *The Oldest Anglo-Norman Prose Brut Chronicle: An Edition and Translation*, Medieval Chronicles 4 (Woodbridge, Suffolk: Boydell and Brewer, 2006).

32. On the additions to the version of the *Brut* witnessed in this manuscript see William Marx, "Aberystwyth, National Library of Wales, MS 21608 and the Middle English Prose Brut," *Journal of the Early Book Society* 1 (1997): 1–16.

33. The epitaphs appear on fol. 88v of NLW 21608. They are printed in Marx, *English Chronicle*, 16–17, with the Latin text from the *Polychronicon*.

34. NLW 21608, fol. 8v; see Marx, *English Chronicle*, xviii. The reading in the inscription "wythout the preiudyce" is a legal term with the sense "without causing harm to persons or property."

35. Marx, *English Chronicle*, xviii.

36. Marx, *English Chronicle*, xviii–xxii.

37. LALME 3: 677–81. Two are from Ruthin (Denbighshire) (LPs 1288, 1289) with a third from south Denbighshire (LP 1363), one from Montgomeryshire (LP 436), and four are from Monmouthshire (LPs 7271, 7240, 7250, 1365). The unmapped linguistic profile is LP 1364 from Carmarthen. See also "Key Map 2," 2: 384.

38. R. Ian Jack, "Welsh and English in the Medieval Lordship of Ruthin," *Denbighshire Historical Society Transactions* 18 (1969): 23–49.

39. Marx, *English Chronicle*, li–lv.

40. Humphrey Llwyd, *Cronica Walliae*, ed. Ieuan M. Williams (Cardiff: University of Wales Press, 2002).

41. Matheson, *Prose Brut*, xxxiii–vi.

42. The importance of this legislation and Llwyd's role in securing its passage through Parliament are referred to a number of times in Jenkins, *Welsh Language before the Industrial Revolution*; see Jenkins, Suggett, and White, "Welsh Language in Early Modern Wales," at 81–83, Peter R. Richards, "Tudor Legislation and the Political Status of 'the British Tongue,'" 123–52, at 141–45, and Glanmor Williams, "Unity of Religion or Unity of Language? Protestants and Catholics and the Welsh Language 1536–1660," in Jenkins, *Welsh Language before the Industrial Revolution*, 207–33, at 213.

CHAPTER 2

WHERE WAS WALES? THE ERASURE OF
WALES IN MEDIEVAL ENGLISH CULTURE

Simon Meecham-Jones

L'oubli et, je dirais même, l'erreur historique
sont un facteur essentiel de la création d'une nation.[1]

The representation of Wales in Medieval English culture was created as, and
has remained, a discourse shaped from the repetition of (often artful) forgettings and historical errors, repeated to sustain complex and sometimes mutually
contradictory ideological agendas. In the medieval period, these forgettings and
errors had become crystallized into a consensus of accepted, albeit contradictory,
propositions, significantly derived and certainly sustained by the texts of three of
the most talented and influential mythmakers of the medieval period—Gildas,
Bede, and Geoffrey of Monmouth. The four central elements of this consensus
might be classified as the discourse of Britishness, the discourse of authority, the
discourse of peripherality, and the discourse of unequal value.[2] To varying
degrees, the application of these four premises has determined both the constitutional status of Wales within Britain following the arrival of the Angles and
Saxons, and the level of social and cultural respect accorded to Wales within
British life ever since. The crucial importance of studying how such premises
were formulated and promoted in the medieval period to describe the status of
Wales as a conquered and colonized subject lies in the continuing persistence of
these discourses, through a combination of intellectual inertia and the embedding
of privilege, to the point where they have become all but invisible, but remain
potent. The relationship of Wales, England, and Britain is still set in forms shaped
by the presumptions created to justify the priorities and circumstances of a
medieval war of colonization.

William the Conqueror's policy of granting exceptional powers of jurisdiction
and conquest to the Marcher lordships in the lands adjoining Wales had decisively

altered the military balance of strength; after this a new intensification of the process of cultural invasion began, set on dissolving and absorbing the inconvenient consequences of the existence of Wales. It was to provide a key concern for writers in the twelfth century, a concern witnessed indirectly in the texts of William of Malmesbury, William of Newburgh, Henry of Huntingdon, and their fellow chroniclers, and with greater imaginative force, though scarcely more intellectual clarity, in the more varied and original literary oeuvres of Walter Map and Giraldus Cambrensis.[3] Despite its subtle and elusive ideological complexity, the trans-European post-Galfridian elaboration of the Arthurian matter of Britain similarly presumed and (however consciously) served to promote the idea of Wales as a lesser political designation that had always existed within the greater British polity—a presumption for which no supporting evidence survives. Whether the developing Arthurian canon adapted and infused new meaning into surviving traces of Brythonic myth and tradition[4] or whether, as Knight has argued, "the freedom fighter was constructed in British Latin and the lordly, if haunted monarch developed in Europe-wide languages,"[5] the popularity of the Matter of Britain functioned to entitle the English Crown to disguise its newness with the historical vestments of a mythical British identity. It was political need that drove the "vigorous historiographical action" through which the British past was reimagined in support of the Anglo-Norman present.[6]

The process of absorbing the land of Wales into an English political superstructure seems to have represented so obvious a conclusion, for English medieval writers, and for later historians and literary critics commenting on their work, that the lack of any reflection by medieval authors on the processes of subjugation and colonization being undertaken in Wales has gone unremarked.[7] In the case of Wales (though not so of Ireland) Southern appears to be striking a paper tiger in mocking those who have questioned the processes of "imperial" seizure by church and state (though, with an ambiguous silkiness of expression, he evades expressing any opinion on the rightness, rather than the likelihood, of what he describes):

> this has given rise to much incredulity among modern scholars, but in fact—as with Wales—the authority of the Norman king over these areas was a fairly obvious first step in establishing uniformity of ecclesiastical discipline throughout the whole area of the British Isles, which archbishops of Canterbury, notably once more St Anselm, believed to have been put under their jurisdiction.[8]

The absorption of the Welsh church into the centralized discipline of the Roman Church certainly caused the destruction of many of the characteristics and practices of a venerable and distinctive Celtic Christian tradition and, although the replacement was, for the most part, achieved peacefully, it is doubtful whether it would have happened when it did without at least the threat of superior civil force. The related, in some sense parallel, military incorporation of Wales into a constitutional projection of Britishness was to prove far more problematic intellectually, as it was to prove militarily. In seeking to resolve the incompatible demands of the colonial project, the medieval conception of three patterns of nationhood—of England, Wales, and Britain—needed to draw fully upon the resources of forgetting, and of being reconciled to historical error (whether fallacy or misrepresentation), which Ernest Renan described as being essential to the creation of a nation (see epigraph). But the verb "to forget" has many shades of meaning: "to lose remembrance of," "to cease to retain in one's memory," "to omit or neglect through inadvertence," and even "to neglect wilfully, take no thought of, disregard, overlook, slight."[9] It is in this last category of definition that we should look to understand the "forgetting" that characterized both the relationship of medieval England and the Welsh nation, and the literary record of that relationship which has perpetuated that "forgetting."

It might be said that this forgetting takes three forms. The first concerns the crucial but overlooked importance of the push into Wales for the development of the English monarchy. The post-Conquest incursion into Wales inevitably produced immense political, economic, and constitutional consequences, creating models of military and social organization, into which the English Crown and its aristocratic warrior class were bound for nearly five hundred years. Even after Henry VIII abolished the Marcher lordships in 1536, these patterns, and the myths of cultural self-definition, which were developed to justify them, remained significant, and perhaps they still are.

The second form of forgetting concerns the virtual absence from the English medieval literary tradition of any overt reference to events in Wales. Despite the long history of English involvement in Wales, references in Middle English texts other than historical chronicles to Welsh history, or to English history in Wales, are scarce in number, and even the appearance of Welsh places and Welsh people are remarkably rare in English medieval culture. Despite the wealth of material made available in Latin during the twelfth century by Walter Map and Giraldus Cambrensis, Welsh narrative motifs were rarely adapted into English and Anglo-Norman forms. It might seem that the Arthurian canon offers a qualification to this absence but, apart from the difficulties in recovering to what extent (if at all) the Arthurian tradition reworked existing Brythonic sources, English medieval Arthurianism appears to have derived its material through French "intermediary" texts.[10] Where it does seem possible that Welsh models underlie non-Arthurian texts, as in Judith Weiss's suggestion that the exile of Gruffudd ap Cynan in Dublin provided a prototype for part of the career of Horn in the *Romance of Horn*, the model appears in a heavily disguised form, shorn of all its Welsh connections.[11]

This reluctance to make use of Welsh material can be demonstrated in every period of medieval literary culture in England, and in every language tradition. It is true at both a courtly and a popular level, both during and after the period of the conquest of Wales. In the productive decades of the great names of Ricardian literature in English, the absence of any notice of Wales is painfully apparent. Gower, in over 30,000 lines of the *Confessio Amantis*—which he describes as "A bok for Engelondes sake"[12]—mentions Wales not at all, and in a vast compendium of stories, draws nothing from Welsh tradition. Throughout his career, Chaucer makes a single direct mention of Wales,[13] though it is possible that *The House of Fame* offers a more reflective, if concealed, comment on the predicament of Wales.[14] In *Piers Plowman* Langland placed into the mouth of *Animus* a puzzling reference to Augustine's supposed conversion of England and Wales:

> Al was hethynesse som tyme Engelond and Walis,
> Til Gregory garte clerkes to go here and preche.
> Austyn [cristnede the kyng at Caunterbury],
> And thorugh miracles, as men mow rede, al that marche he tornede
> To Crist and to Cristendom,...[15]

It is hard to imagine that Langland, as a Malvern man, did not have some ideological intent to account for this historically absurd representation of familiar events.[16] Maybe his perception of the lawlessness of his native March inspired an ironic wordplay in the reference to an earlier "marche" being turned to Christ. The same aggressive and ideological word play surfaces also in Langland's depiction of the repulsive figure of covetousness, dressed in a wretched tabard of Welsh flannel:

> But if a lous couthe lepe the bettre
> She sholde noght wa[ndr]e on that Welche, so was it thredbare![17]

However, it is clear that in Langland's vision of universal history, there is no place for Wales to exist, except through its relationship with England.

If Langland's manipulation of the historical record is both overt and awkward, the same ideological pressures, and the same processes of neglect and elision, characterize the record of more popular forms also. Despite the length of the conflict (from the defeat of Gruffudd ap Llywelyn in 1063 to the end of the Glyn Dŵr campaign around 1413, English troops were engaged in Wales for more than three-hundred and fifty years), there are no surviving romances set during the wars in Wales, nor is there a tradition of popular songs celebrating victories there. Though the Parliamentary Rolls series includes some lyrics on the death of Edward I, there are no surviving lyrics celebrating his triumphs in Wales, and none of his battles against the Welsh seem to have inspired an equivalent to the anonymous poem on the Battle of Lewes (1264).[18] This absence is the more curious since the borderlands of the Welsh March have been identified as the place of origin for many of the most important and innovative texts written in Middle English—*Ancrene Wisse*, *Piers Plowman,* the *Harley Lyrics*, and the poems of London, British Library MS. Cotton Nero A. x. Many recent critical readings have made much of the shaping influence on these texts of their origins in a "frontier" society. But the features of the frontier stretched beyond the physical uncertainty of living in an area prone to military adventures: in Rees Davies's words "the March was more than a frontierland of armies; it was also a frontierland of peoples."[19] The energy expended by the Marcher Lords in seizing lands in Wales created a Marcher society characterized by (perceived) racial and linguistic difference, as Welsh-speaking people from the Welsh kingdoms and *cantrefi*[20] were brought together with English-speaking border peoples and a diversity of immigrants from elsewhere in England, the French possessions of the English Crown and Flanders, variously monolingual or multilingual in Middle English, Anglo-Norman or Picard, French or Flemish, under a single authority. The result was a complex overlapping pattern of partial, functional, and full multilingualism, both promoting and reflecting a pattern of intense cultural contact. But the pattern of conquest and appropriation in the March ensured that Welsh functioned as a crucial linguistic and cultural substrate in the development of Marcher culture.

An important witness of this is provided by the history of the district of Ergyng (in some records spelled as Erging), now known by its English name of Archenfield, and confirmed in its place within the English county of Herefordshire by the Act of Union of 1536. Ergyng is first recorded as a "Late British" kingdom, occupying territory in what later became the Welsh county of Monmouthshire and the English county of Herefordshire. The *Book of Llandaf* paints Ergyng as an important religious center in the period before Augustine's conversion of the English, particularly through the ministry of Saint Dyfrig, who appears to have been active in the fifth century in what might now be described as the South Herefordshire region of Ergyng.[21] In the pre-Conquest period, the shifting political fortunes of the Welsh Royal houses led to Ergyng being joined (variously) with the Welsh kingdoms of Glywysing, Gwent, and Morgannwg, while depredations by the Saxons from the kingdom of Mercia led to a diminution of territory. Though parishes of Ergyng (as Archenfield), such as Garway and Kilpeck, are catalogued in the *Domesday Book*, the classification notes the mixed nature of the community, and the survival of Welsh legal customs, guaranteed by Edward the Confessor after the defeat of Gruffudd ap Llywelyn:

> In Wormelow Hundred
> St. Peter's of Gloucester holds "Westwood," the head of this manor. King Edward held it. 6 hides. One of these has Welsh customs, the others English.[22]

Long after the greater part of Ergyng had been absorbed into the Marcher Lordship of Hereford, it remained a substantially Welsh-speaking area, and Welsh remained a spoken language in some parts of Herefordshire not merely post-Conquest, but for many generations after the Act of Union of 1536. Llinos Beverley Smith notes that

> ...in the late fourteenth century the parishioners of the parish of Garway in Archenfield maintained that their parish priest was unable adequately to minister to their needs "for he knew no Welsh and many of them had no knowledge of English."[23]

The persistence of Welsh as a vernacular in fourteenth-century Hereford, indeed the extent to which it appears to be considered wholly unremarkable,[24] provides a useful reminder of the deep Welsh/Brythonic roots of much border/Marcher culture that have generally left few observed traces in the records except when, as here, observed through the medium of Latin or French culture. It might be supposed that the speaking of Welsh was limited to the lower social orders of a feudal society, but the true situation was more complex, not least because of intermarriage between Welsh *uchelwyr* [nobles, gentry] and English landowning families. It is certainly possible, for example, that Owain Glyn Dŵr ended his days in South Herefordshire, living with his daughter and her family by marriage, the Scudamores, at Kentchurch or Monnington in the Golden Valley. An aristocratic/gentry interest in Welsh literature offers the most plausible explanation for the survival of one of the great treasures of Welsh medieval literature, the *Red Book of Hergest*. Though the manuscript that contains important witnesses for the texts of the *Mabinogion* (as well as much else, including the important historical source the *Brut y Tywysogion*) is known to have been commissioned at Ynystawe near Swansea,[25] it now bears the name of the Hergest estate[26] near Kington in Herefordshire, with which it was associated and which Daniel Huws describes as "its late medieval home."[27]

There are other physical traces of this profound cultural contact—from the Welsh place-names of villages in northwest Herefordshire[28] to the possible "Celtic" influence on the designs and motifs of the fascinating and distinctive Herefordshire school of Romanesque church design and decoration[29]—but for the most part it has been an unspoken and disregarded characteristic, albeit a stubbornly persistent one. For Raymond Williams, brought up in an "Anglicized" border village just across the Welsh border but in what was also once a part of Ergyng, even in the early twentieth century the contact and conflict between the dominant and anglicizing British culture and the awareness of a disregarded Welsh culture was crucial in shaping his sense of identity, and of his relationship to the models of power:

> You must remember I was born on the border, and we talked about "the English" who were not us, and also "the Welsh" who were not us.... But then I found to my surprise that many things I had thought were rather local to that border area, which was now Anglicized Wales, were really only problems that existed in much of the rest of Wales.[30]

Though the situation in the medieval March was complicated by the mixed authority of English as a language of power and a language of record compared to the recognized cultural superstrate languages of Latin and Anglo-Norman, there can be no question that the unresolvable contention between promoted and suppressed cultures characterized every element of Marcher society, to the extent that it seems reasonable to claim that the authors of *Ancrene Wisse* and *Sir Gawain and the Green Knight*, as much as Raymond Williams, were educated within what might be described as "the Welsh penumbra." Indeed many of the Marcher texts reveal evidence of penumbral qualities. It has long been accepted, for example, that *Ancrene Wisse* and the texts of the Katherine group show some lexical influence from Welsh, characteristics that have proved persuasive in locating the origin of the texts to Herefordshire:

> It was evidently a dialect of the Welsh Marches, for its vocabulary includes three distinctive words of Welsh origin: cader "cradle" in *Ancrene Wisse* and *Hali meiðhad*; genow "mouth" in *Ste Margarete*; and keis "satellites, henchmen" in *Sawles Warde*.[31]

A case could also be made for some lexical influence from Welsh on the vocabulary of the *Harley Lyrics*,[32] *Pearl,* and *Sir Gawain and the Green Knight.* The latter memorably includes a description of a journey through Wales, as Gawain travels from Camelot in search of the Green Knight, and this journey has been accorded a significant role in a number of recent readings of the poem.[33] Nonetheless, Gawain's journey is striking primarily because it has so few analogues in English medieval literature. One might expect Arthurian texts, in particular, to be full of Welsh locations and situations, but references prove to be both sparse and limited in their scope.[34] Often such references as do occur have the effect of taking us further away from the topography or history of real Wales. Some of the strangest of these penumbral transformations occur in the Anglo-Norman romances of Hue de Rotelande [Hugh of Rhuddlan]. Though probably written in a Norman settlement in Wales, Hue's romance of *Ipomedon* describes events in the distant Mediterranean settings of Sicily and Calabria, yet it also contains references to life in the March.[35] Cartlidge has recently drawn attention to the curious scene in which a foe of Ipomedon named Leander is identified with a defeated Welsh prince Rhys, but the details given of Rhys's career as an initially successful military leader subsequently decisively overthrown by the English are wholly incompatible with the life story of the most prominent Rhys of Hue's own time.[36]

If Hue's tactic is to assimilate elements of the locale in which he lived into the matrix of romance fantasy, his idiosyncratic response to his situation as a Norman or Englishman in Wales must be considered to be an exceptional case.[37] Generally the preferred stylistic tactic is silence. This unwillingness to engage with the physical or political reality of the relationship of "Englishness" (however defined) and Wales is the more striking when we compare it to the representation of other cultures and other conflicts in medieval English texts. There is something curious in the abiding popularity of Charlemagne romances in a country that (relatively) soon lost most of its French possessions.[38] Though Hardman has argued that "It is not as odd as it may seem...that an English readership at the time of the Hundred Years War should have been able to identify with the forces of a King of France as Christian Emperor in the romances of Charlemagne" since "Edward III implicitly declared himself the rightful heir of Charlemagne,"[39] that offers no explanation for the apparent evocation of motifs derived from the Charlemagne and pseudo-Turpin traditions at the expense of motifs derived from England's more immediate engagement—in waging intermittent war on its Western flank for more than two hundred years.[40] It might be overstating the case to suggest that the avoidance of Welsh topics reveals a distinct lack of pride in what was being done, but it does seem that the legendary past of the matter of France offered a subject less likely to raise disturbing questions. The same conclusion might be drawn also from the popularity of what Rouse, following Frantzen and Niles, has termed the "Anglo-Saxonism" of the insular romance form (though recollections of the pre-Norman past also played a role in bolstering the Anglo-Norman speaking elite's claim to legitimacy as rulers).[41] Similarly, romances like *Horn* and *Havelok* show no reluctance to deal with the Scandinavian past—whether because Norman culture claimed an ancestral kinship with that culture, or because Norse military force was deemed to be no longer a threat to the English Crown after the defeat at Stamford Bridge.

The puzzle is deepened when one considers the literary fecundity of the March. Michelle Warren, in arguing the proposition that "Arthurian historiography...was written most often and most emphatically in relation to boundary pressures," offers the conclusion that "Arthurian historiography took shape as a form of border writing."[42] But the border anxieties she describes, and the "pressures of border formation" existed not merely along the disputed Welsh/English border, but throughout the areas of Wales and the Welsh penumbra. The patterns of English encroachment and settlement in Wales inevitably created enduring divisions between English subjects and Welsh others, establishing frontiers throughout Wales between peoples who perceived themselves, or were perceived to be, distinct from their neighbors. The most celebrated of the English plantations in Wales was set up by Henry I in South Pembrokeshire, in which Flemish and English settlers were settled in the fertile farmlands of South Pembrokeshire and the coastal belt of southern Carmarthenshire. This created an Anglophone colony, "separated" from its Welsh-speaking neighbors by what has become known as the Landsker line, a line of more than fifty castles and fortifications, from Laugharne, through Narberth, Llawhaden, Wiston, and Haverfordwest to the castle at Roch. The line represented a psychological fissure more than a true military frontier, but the result was a severe and lasting cultural separation between the two halves of Pembrokeshire. Though the initial racial separation has long been forgotten, the idea of Pembrokeshire as two distinct and separated communities remains strong. But this act of plantation was exceptional in creating so substantial and clearly defined an enclave—a colony described as "Transwalliana" by George Owen (of Henllys, north of the line) in 1603[43] and, for many generations, popularly referred to by the English equivalent of his description as "Little England Beyond Wales"—though the tag seems to have fallen out of favor in the past twenty years.

More common was the setting up of garrison towns at strategic points (particularly harbors), with a settlement of (generally) English-speaking townspeople gathered around the castle, and enjoying certain rights and privileges granted by charter, and denied to their Welsh-speaking and disenfranchised neighbors, living in the adjoining country. Barrow describes the process of settlement and plantation that formed a key element of Edward I's policy of encastellation:

> All the northern castles were conceived as joint military and urban settlements. Adjacent to each castle there was founded a "free borough,"

peopled by incoming English merchants, who were usually granted the liberties of Hereford.[44]

The policy implanted institutional structures and new loyalties—the town of Laugharne proudly preserves the forms of a civic government by a portreeve with a council of aldermen and burgesses derived from a charter granted by Edward I in 1290. The result of this policy of colonization was to make every settlement in Wales a border—of language, "race," and jurisdiction—creating lasting separation between those who identified themselves with the colonizing power, and those who were outside its concern and beyond its protection. The charters for the town of Kidwelly show the persistence of the designation of areas of the borough as an "Englishry" and a "Welshry" well into the early modern period. Often this separation was realized as a border between the urban and the rural—and this pattern of differentiation was to prove enduring. Writing of Welsh life in the period from the 1880s to the First World War in her novel *Traed Mewn Cyffion* [Feet in Chains],[45] Kate Roberts depicted a separation between the inhabitants of the town of Caernarfon, whose aspirations were formed with reference to England and English-speaking culture, and the Welsh-speaking rural culture of the town's hinterland—a separation that derived from, and perpetuated, a social pattern developed six hundred years earlier.

Maybe the "border pressures" resulting from this day-to-day confrontation of cultures were too intense, too pungent, to be addressed directly through the genres—of romance, lyric, and drama—available to medieval writers. Instead the discomfort resulting from this contestation of proximity was diffracted into the elusive speculative geometry of the Arthurian tradition. Nonetheless, that the failure of writers in the Welsh penumbra, if not further afield, to engage with topics related to Wales and the wars in Wales, has been overlooked as an important, indeed defining, characteristic of English medieval literary production by successive generations of critics studying the canon of Middle English texts is itself curious, and a little disturbing. The centuries-old maintenance of this critical blind spot must be considered the third stage of the process of forgetting. It is a forgetting derived sometimes from the political preoccupations later critics brought with them to the study of medieval texts, and sometimes to the persistence and continuing potency of ideological constructs developed to deflect attention from the true nature of the colonial project in Wales.

It was the efforts of Loomis in focusing critical attention on the possible "Celtic" origins of many themes and motifs in European medieval literature that came closest to shaking, for a time, that consensus,[46] though the drawing of elements from anthropology, post-Jungian psychology, and ideas of primitivism led to both his work, and the thesis of "Celtic" origins becoming discredited in academic circles, and increasingly relegated to nonscholarly texts, of the kind found in bookshops in Glastonbury. More surprisingly, Loomis's efforts to posit "Celtic" culture as a primary source of European culture paradoxically marked Welsh and Irish cultures as being "past" and therefore in some way "spent" or superseded even in medieval literature—a vein of ore from which Chrétien, Thomas, Geoffrey of Monmouth, and the *Gawain*-poet could fashion works of value. The effect of Loomis's studies served (unconsciously) to divert attention away from the conspicuous absence of *contemporary* Welsh places, Welsh people and events in Wales in English medieval literature—an absence that demands explanation. Often it has seemed as if English writers (and critics studying the works of English writers) have regarded the engagements in Wales as being undeserving of comment, perhaps unconsciously applying to the history of English armies in Wales the judgment of Craterus in Walter of Châtillon's *Alexandreis* that some conflicts are unworthy of commemoration:

> Gloria quantalibet uili sordescit in hoste.
> Indignum satis est ut consumatur in illis
>   Gloria uel uirtus.[47]

> [However great it may be, glory loses its luster when the enemy is of poor quality. It is sufficient indignity that glory and valour are being wasted on those people.][48]

Of course, the proof of the "poor" quality of the resistance is demonstrated by the many generations it took to establish English control in Wales, a length of resistance despite the material inequality of forces that has often been overlooked. Marjorie Chibnall, for example, makes no comparison between the length of time it took to achieve the subjugation of Wales and William the Conqueror's relatively speedy securing of the Kingdom of England—a comparison that is made by John Davies, who reminds us that "The Normans won England after barely four years of campaigning" where though "by 1090, it seemed that the whole of Wales would be subject to them...that did not happen."[49] Rather Chibnall ascribes the slow progress in Wales to (merely?) practical constraints:

> That the conquest took more than two hundred years to complete was due partly to Norman methods of settlement, partly to the geographical and political condition of the region.[50]

The imprecision of her formulation—"the geographical and political condition of the region" effects (no doubt unconsciously) a historical foreshortening in which the considerable efforts and planning required to achieve each stage of the conquest are obscured. In place of the uneven and frustrating conquest by attrition over a number of generations, the process has become overlaid with a cloak of inevitability and apparent ease that distorts the historical record. That the details of phrasing can be so misleading, even in the work of as thorough and detailed a scholar of Norman history as Chibnall, provides a warning of the extent to which the struggle between the power of England and the (inconsistent) resistance of Wales has been fought, not merely in arms, but in the more devious contentions and ambushes of verbal engagements in the languages of authority.

What must be recognized is the enduring strength and longevity of concepts and descriptions applied by the English chroniclers to justify English actions in

Wales. One recurring ideological construct is that of the military capture and colonization as a process of the "pacification" of Wales. It is an idea that has reappeared persistently through accounts of Welsh history well into the twentieth century,[51] from Burke's pointed use of the term to denounce the denial of constitutional rights in medieval Wales,[52] to Edwards' account of the decisive victory at Maes Madog in 1295: "A month after the victory, Edward [I] was moving along that road to complete the pacification of Wales."[53] The choice of the word "pacification" is both striking and significant because it translates the identical choice of the same verb in its Latin form in a number of the chronicles contemporary with the drawn out process of conquest. It is a key term, for example, in the account of King Stephen's worthy toil in Wales presented in the twelfth-century chronicle the *Gesta Stephani*:

> nec solum ad Angliam, immo et ad Waloniam pacificandam multum sudoris, multum et pecuniarum impendere.

> [He spent much sweat, and likewise much money, to pacify not only England but also Wales.][54]

In its careful rhetorical placing, the chronicler insists on the equivalence of King Stephen's right to enforce a pacification on his subjects in England and in Wales. The text proposes an equivalence that has no demonstrable jurisprudential basis. King Stephen's right and duty to pacify England derives from his succession to the throne of King Henry I, a succession that is itself contested. But Stephen had no "subjects" in Wales, except for the subjects of the English throne, whose rights in Wales required justification—which is precisely what the chronicler seeks to conceal or deny. In adapting and perpetuating a verb from chronicle sources such as the *Gesta Stephani*, Edwards and his predecessors implicitly endorse the ideological construction of the text—that King Stephen could attempt to "pacify" the Welsh because they *should* have recognized his right to be considered "their master":

> in dominos suos Walenses mortale semper odium spirantes

> [the Welsh, who always cherished a deadly hatred of their masters.][55]

It does not suit the chronicle's purpose to ask by what right or power such mastery had been claimed, imposed, or deserved, but those are precisely the questions that twenty-first century readers, not beholden to accept the self-aggrandizing fictions of a twelfth-century faction, should bring to such texts.

In a much-quoted passage, the chronicler of the *Gesta Stephani* tells:

> Fuit eodem in tempore Ricardus filius Gisleberti in Walonia, uir sincera generositate insignis, cognatis et hominibus fultus ditissimis, terris et castellis heredatus innumeris, qui omnes affines suos fide habens confœderatos, obsidibus uero obstrictos, pacis eam multimodæque fecunditatis adeo reddidit affluentem, ut secunda esse Anglia perfacile crederetur.[56]

[At this time there was in Wales a certain Richard fitz Gilbert, a man
distinguished for his truly noble birth, supported by very wealthy relations
and vassals, endowed with countless lands and castles, who since he had all
his neighbours leagued with him by compact and likewise bound by giving
hostages, made the country so to abound in peace and varied prosperity
that it might very easily have been thought a second England.]

The chronicle tells us about his countless lands and castles, but not how, or how
recently, those lands had been acquired. Fitz Gilbert's father Gilbert fitz Richard
had been granted the lordship of Ceredigion by Henry I as recently as 1110,
following the confiscation of the demesne from Owain, son of Cadwgan ap
Bleddyn, whose crimes against the royal dignity consisted primarily of having
slept with the Princess Nest, a Welsh princess married to Gerald of Windsor
(from which marriage she was the grandmother of Giraldus Cambrensis) but
whose illegitimate children included Henry fitz Henry, a son of Henry I.[57]
The processes of appropriation and patronage are screened from view in the
more dignified phrase "terris et castellis heredatus innumeris" [endowed with
countless lands and castles] but the phrase is itself willfully misleading. The
inheritance of castles and nonroyal fortifications did not follow the rules of
automatic transmission, since the right to maintain such fortifications derived
from a personal grant from the king, which expired on the holder's death and
(at least in theory) required the confirmation of a new grant from the king to
the heir. Far from being embedded by generations of inheritance as the text
appears to suggest, the de Clare family were relative newcomers to Ceredigion,
while Richard fitz Gilbert held his castles on the sufferance of King Stephen,
whose disputed claim to the throne he sought to promote—support that was
rewarded with the lordship of Pembroke. Where the text seems to offer a vision
of the family carrying out their civic duties as if a twelfth-century equivalent of
blue-helmeted peacekeepers containing unrest in a turbulent war zone, it seeks
to obscure the links between their conduct and the family's need to safeguard
their swiftly amassed financial assets. Because they spring from an unquestion-
ing acceptance of the ideological priorities of their patron class, chronicles such
as the *Gesta Stephani*, and the *Histories* of William of Newburgh, Robert of
Torigni, and William of Malmesbury, display how the practice of the conceal-
ment of inconvenient detail develops from a form of (sometimes conscious)
forgetting into a means for the transmission of "l'erreur historique."

The heavy burden of ideological expectation carried in that one word
"pacification" can be seen as representative of the extent to which the nature of
the relationship between Wales and England has become encoded, and at times
obscured, in the specific details of the language used by medieval sources and
not challenged by subsequent readers. Though historians and critics could now
be expected to be sensitive to the ideological implications of such terms, the
obscuring shadows of such presumptions have not been banished. Traces of such
ideas, not overturned but suppressed through politeness, still haunt the discourse.
There is, for example, a suggestive uncertainty of phrasing in Chibnall's account

of the upbringing of Orderic Vitalis in Shropshire, an ambiguity that allows the idea of the "pacification" of Wales to be reinscribed:

> The first ten years of his life were passed in the region that he later described as "the remote parts of Mercia"; a county on the borders of Wales, only very recently pacified, and in the throes of great social and religious change.[58]

Both Wales and Shropshire could be said to have been "in the throes of great social and religious change," which makes it hard to be certain whether it is Shropshire or Wales that Chibnall describes as being "only very recently pacified." But whatever her intention, the placing of Wales and Shropshire in adjacent clauses reproduces precisely (though no doubt unconsciously) the illusion of the interchangeability of their constitutional status and condition that the author of the *Gesta Stephani* had sought to promote.

Of course, the very fact that the relationship under discussion is described as being that between Wales and England rather than between *Cymru* and England is a pointer to the relative success of the opposing sides in this interpretative contention.[59] It is easy to underestimate the many levels of symbolic and ceremonial value invested in a name, which render the act of naming a crucial signifier of (relative) status. The importance of such naming was recently reaffirmed, for example, in Greece's prolonged veto on the European Union's recognition of one of the republics of Yugoslavia under the name Macedonia, also the name of a region within Greece, and a name of iconic significance because of its association with the world-conquering Alexander. Though it was argued that recognizing Macedonia under this name might encourage claims on the sovereignty of Greek Macedonia, it was scarcely credible that a small and economically backward newly established state could be expected to offer any serious threat to the territorial integrity of Greece, even if the will existed for such a challenge. But it was not to be borne that the name of Alexander's kingdom should be claimed by a people outside Greece—a diplomatic impasse only resolved by the prefixing of Macedonia's name with the qualifying initials F. Y. R. ("former Yugoslav Republic of").

Similarly, in naming their Western neighbor "Wales" (or variations of its Latin form *Wallia*), English writers sought to mark out its defeated status—even before that defeat was established. It was a point not lost on Giraldus, who pointedly avoids the term *Wallia* in favor of *Cambria*.[60] As with the name of the country, so also the name of its people. That an invading people should get to fix the name of their (more) indigenous enemies with a word meaning "foreigner" continues to rile, as in Raymond William's rhetorical questioning:

> Why do they [the English] call the most identifiably British people in the island by the old English name for foreigner?[61]

For Abulafia, also, the term "Welsh" is one marked with disdain:

> A term that constantly describes those who speak distinctive languages is "Welsh," *w-l-s, g-l-s*: all it means is "foreigners," whether applied to

Galicians in Iberia, Galicians in Poland, Wallachians in Romania, Vlachs in Greece, Welshmen in western Britain, foreign moneyers at the *Vlašky dvůr* (*Welsches Hof*) at Kutna Hora in Bohemia, or Walloons in Flanders; each time it is the same word, which the "foreigners" then to some extent adopted to describe themselves (though not completely: Wales remains *Cymru* in the eyes and ears of its Celtic-speaking inhabitants).[62]

For John Davies, the term need not carry such demeaning associations, and he offers the possibility of a more neutral meaning:

It is often claimed that the word "Welsh" is a contemptuous word used by Germanic-speaking peoples to describe foreigners. Yet a glance at a dictionary of any of the Teutonic languages will show that this is not its only meaning. "Welsh" was not used by Germanic speakers to describe peoples living to the east of them; to the English *wealh-stod* meant an interpreter, but they had a different word for a translator from Danish. It would appear that "Welsh" meant not so much foreigners as peoples who had been Romanized.[63]

It is a useful corrective to the (forgivable) temptation to draw always the worst conclusion, but also it reminds us what a great distance of time and ideological interpretation must be inferred to any valuation of a specific writer's use of the word. Davies' reminder of the link between Welshness and Romanization reflects an association that may have carried some weight in Anglo-Saxon England, but that is rarely attested in Middle English constructions of the Welsh as *barbari* [barbarians]. Only in the Arthurian canon does the association of Britishness with the Roman past remain influential, whether through the (occasional) identification of Camelot with Caerleon/The City of the Legions, or the development of the myth of Arthur's conquest of Rome, and the patterning of his achievements on those of Macsen Wledig.

But the associations with Romanization or Britishness tended to reinforce the idea of Welshness as a relict identity—diminished from its mightier British past. Huw Pryce has shown how the self-identification of the Welsh as *Cymry* rather than *Brython* established itself in Welsh literate circles in the twelfth century, arguing that "the Latin terminology to express Welsh national identity: *Britannia, Britanni,* and *Britones* no longer provided adequate Latin equivalents for the vernacular term Cymry."[64] In the work of English writers of the same period, the nuances of the contrast are employed to (an alternative) ideological effect. In the letters of John of Salisbury, differential value is expressed through the use of the terms "Welsh" and "British." When, in 1166, warriors in north Wales inflicted an unexpected defeat on Henry II, who was at that time in dispute with the ecclesiastical authorities, John of Salisbury allows them the dignity of being named Britons:

Circumferat quis oculos mentis et intueatur quot et quales aduersarios ei Dominus suscitauerit ex quo aduersus Deum in depressione ecclesiae erexit

calcaneum suum, et plane mirabitur et, si prudens est uenerabitur iudicium
Dei qui non imperatores, non reges, non principes nationum ut ipsum
domaret elegit, sed extremos hominum, Britones Niuicollinos, primo.[65]

[Let anyone turn his mind's eye to view the number and the quality of the
enemies which the Lord has raised against the king and, if he is wise, filled
with reverence for God's judgement: for he has chosen not emperors or
kings or the princes of the nations to quell him, but chose first the remotest
of men, the Welsh {sic} of Snowdon.]

When railing against the immorality and insubordination of the Welsh, in a letter
to the Pope, written before 1161, John invokes the full majesty of his position
in his call for the Welsh to be brought to heel, and here it is as *Walenses* that he
berates them:

Et patentibus litteris uestris communiter ad episcopas Angliae, Waliae,
Hiberniae, Scotiae destinatis praecipiatis, quatinus quod nos, urgente
necessitate episcopi apud nos exultantis, canonice statuemus in Walenses,
ipsi ratum habeant et sententiam nostram firmiter obseruent.[66]

[And by letters patent to charge the bishops of England, Wales, Ireland,
and Scotland to regard as ratified whatever we, in view of the urgent need
of the bishop now an exile in our house {Bishop Maurice of Bangor} may
canonically decree against the Welsh, and firmly to obey our sentence.]

No word demonstrates more clearly the difficulty of recovering the nuances
with which key terms became ideologically invested. Pryce has argued strongly
that to interpret "the rebranding of *Britannia* with the label of *Wallia*" as a
sign of "the imposition of alien concepts of identity upon the Welsh would
be an oversimplification."[67] Nonetheless he concedes that "both Geoffrey
[of Monmouth] and Gerald share an assumption that there was something pejorative
about the Latin terms Wallia and Walenses (and variants thereof)" to the extent
that "both writers hinted that this 'Welsh' terminology itself carried the stigma
of barbarism."[68] It may well be that Pryce is correct in his judgment that "if the
Welsh accepted English terms of identity, . . . it is highly unlikely that they did
so reluctantly or saw themselves as thereby surrendering cherished notions of
identity in the face of pressure from outside,"[69] but it is clear, also, albeit with the
clarity that derives from hindsight, that, in accepting such terms, Welsh writers
were, however willingly, ceding ground in the textual contestation between
two politico/cultural traditions that accompanied the acts of warfare. Imposing
a name has long been recognized as a fruitful strategy in the establishment
of an intellectual ascendancy, and that is what was achieved, despite Giraldus'
attempted promotion of the ideologically less tainted alternative "Cambria."
To use the term "imposition" suggests a degree of coercion and intent that
the evidence cannot support, but it is important to remember the disparity of
access to material and cultural resources, which powers less direct patterns of
coercion. In particular, Pryce examines many "Cambro-Latin" sources from

the twelfth century, but it is important to note how many of these sources are clerical, and to recall how heavily implicated the church, in furtherance of its own jurisdictional and economic interests, was in the project of the incorporation of Wales into the English monarchy.[70] It is surely no coincidence that the shift Pryce describes in terminology from British to Welsh in the early twelfth century coincides with a period in which the Metropolitan see of Canterbury was very active in securing its unquestioned control over the church in Wales, particularly with regard to church appointments and church property. Rather than a planned imposition, what we see at work is a strategy more subtle though no less effective. The promotion of the term Wales and the rejection of Cymry and Cambria provide a fine example of the extent to which the writers of what might be called the "English discourse" succeeded in setting the linguistic agenda through which the Welsh campaigns were understood. If the erasure of Wales in medieval English literature has been so long unnoticed by critics, the reason lies in the continuing effectiveness of this setting of the agenda to justify English involvement—setting in place a series of interpretive models that continue to determine the ways in which subsequent generations have perceived and discussed the history of medieval Wales.

Following in the hermeneutic wake of William of Malmesbury, "second generation" chronicles[71] like the *Gesta Stephani*, the *Vita Edwardi Secundi* and the *Histories* of John of Worcester, William of Newburgh, and Henry of Huntingdon[72] extract maximum effect from each of the four of the key elements of the English depiction of the Welsh in the historical records—the discourse of authority, the discourse of Britishness, the discourse of peripherality, and the discourse of unequal value. None of these were in themselves original, recalling, developing, or mutating themes and ideas from Bede, Gildas, and pseudo-Nennius,[73] and the categories were to some degree mutually supportive. In John of Salisbury's formulation "extremos hominum" (remotest of men) we see an example of the frequently repeated implicature suggesting a link between the (perceived) geographical peripherality of the Welsh and their status as a people of lesser value. But there were irreconcilable contradictions embedded within the application of the four heads of argument, which became apparent when as disinterested scholars analyzing after the event, we consider the responses medieval English texts offer to the two crucial questions that demand an answer—why were the English in medieval Wales, and by what right did they justify their activities there?

To pose these questions is not to raise anachronistic concerns. Whether or not phrased in that form, there can be no doubt that the first question was raised by many at the time, in England and the March, as well as in Wales, while the search for an answer to the second question takes us closer to the nature of Angevin literature and historiography—as, in great part, a literature of justification. Overtly, in the histories and more elliptically in the romances (with their repeated motifs of exile, dispossessed heirs, and the return of order),[74] Angevin writers used the organizing powers of literary texts to create a model that demonstrated, paralleled, and justified the exercise of providence that had given the Normans control, first of the English throne and a wealth of lands in France, then Wales, then (more precariously) a toehold in Ireland. So cumulatively persuasive were these exercises in justification to prove that, to a remarkable degree, they still condition the answers offered to the two questions raised above.

It is the question of authority—by what right the English Crown justified its activities—that medieval studies has failed to pursue. But the answer matters, not because it might be considered to have some practical implications for contemporary politics, but because it is impossible to understand English medieval culture without knowing how the kings, churchmen, warriors, and intellectuals who urged the intervention in Wales, fought for it and profited by it, would have answered the question. The simplest recourse would be to have admitted the colonization of Wales was authorized and supported only by the authority bestowed by superior force—that the English were there simply because they could be, without fear of being expelled by force.

But throughout the chronicle sources festers a nagging anxiety about the perceived legitimacy of what was being done and a determination to assert the justice and legality of the process, made more pressing by the fact that the assertion proved fiercely difficult to sustain. One possible means of justification lay in the claiming of Welsh territories through the Norman practice of awarding "swordland"— that is, that a warrior could claim whatever territory he conquered.[75] Though this theory might be attractive in justifying the capture of lands from pagans in the north and east of Europe, its limitations were painfully apparent as a means of establishing the legitimacy of military operations that served to dispossess an existing population of observant fellow Christians. In their descriptions of the wildness and remoteness of Wales, the chronicles seem tempted by the fiction that Wales could be considered as *terra vacua* [unpopulated or unclaimed land] but the fiction was insufficiently reassuring. John of Worcester is typical in his praise of such tactics in the "distant" past, and his applauding of the marauding Anglo-Saxon monarchy suggests a little nostalgia that such behavior in his own day was obliged to be disguised by strategies of justification:

[603] Rex fortissimis et glorie cupidissimus, Æthelfryð plus omnibus Anglorum primatibus gentem Brytonum uastauit, pluresque terras eorum, exterminatis uel subiugatis indigenis, aut tributarias genti Anglorum, aut habitabiles fecit.

[Aethelfrith, the most vigorous of kings and the most desirous of glory, more than any other English ruler ravaged the race of Britons, and made more of their lands tributary to, or ready for settlement by, the English when he had exterminated or subjugated the inhabitants.][76]

Ironically, there were areas of upland Wales—on the slopes of Plynlimon or in the Brecon Beacons around Llyn-y-fan—that might plausibly be considered *terra vacua*, but it was not these difficult terrains that the settlers coveted and wished to make "ready for settlement by the English." Looking at the map of English seizure in the first fifty years following the Norman Conquest, it is the rich farmlands of Dyffryn Clwyd, the Vale of Usk, the Vale of Glamorgan, Gower, and South Pembrokeshire that were the desired prizes, while the relatively unpopulated uplands were left within the relict rump of territory known as *pura Wallia* ["true" Wales][77]—those unexploitable areas of Wales over which the English felt no pressing temptation to claim authority.

The myths of justification that were developed both reflect, and are vitiated by, the inherent contradictions of Norman rule in Wales. Rees Davies perhaps does the invaders an injustice in claiming that "In so far as we can hope to penetrate their thought-world, we can rest assured that they would have no qualms about the prospect or propriety of domination."[78] The literary record suggests a far more unstable certainty of title—though perhaps this is less concerned with "the prospect or propriety of domination" than with how that domination might be perceived. In the reign of Edward I, the king's determination to use whatever scant records, including the literary fictions of the Arthurian tradition, to justify his rule in Wales reveal clearly that for Edward it was not enough to exercise rule—he required that rule to be perceived as being exercised with clean hands, however tenuous the precedents for his claims might be. His determination to impose this view of his claims on Wales and Scotland has been well described by Rees Davies:

> ...the English kings saw the relationship, *and wanted it to be seen*, as approximating the status, responsibilities, and obligations of the princelings of Wales to those of the major barons of England. In much the same manner, of course, they manipulated their terminology and the historical evidence *vis-à-vis* the king of Scots in the 1290s, and with devastating results. The total breakdown in Anglo-Scottish relations from 1296 was a consequence of the determination of Edward I unilaterally to impose his view of the world and of the relationships of power on the Scots. He had succeeded triumphantly in Wales and there was every reason to believe (until 1306) that he would succeed in Scotland.[79]

Davies highlights the crucial importance of the manipulation of language as a weapon of war between England and Wales: "We need to sensitize our historical imaginations to the manipulation, be it conscious or otherwise, of language in this respect,"[80] and, indeed, he asserts the primacy of this tactic; but in doing so he offers an important warning for both historians and literary critics with regard to the continuing effectiveness of the tactics employed:

> His success in both countries was founded on the manipulation of the past and of language in the service of his own power. Historians have too often taken him at his own word.[81]

The "manipulation of the past" was necessary to establish a generally shared belief that English rule in Wales was long-standing and long accepted by the Welsh. The formulation of conventions of diplomacy in the modern period has given rulers an elegant solution to the dilemma Edward (and his predecessors) faced, in the development of two forms of acknowledgment of political control—in the recognition of de jure and de facto authority. When in 1990 a military dictatorship overturned the result of a national election in Burma and imposed a military junta, many countries refused to accept the military leadership as the de jure rulers of the country.[82] Nonetheless, it would be absurd to deny that the military exercises de facto control over the country so even the harshest critics of the regime concede de facto recognition of its authority. Similarly, there can be no question that English rulers exercised de facto control over areas of Wales, perhaps during the reign of Alfred and certainly during the reign of Æthelstan. The myth promoted by William of Malmesbury in ink, and by Henry I and Edward I by force, was to interpret these sporadic de facto events as proof of a greater de jure entitlement to the domination of the Welsh.

Since no compelling evidence was available to sustain this view (unless one counts the variants of the Arthurian myth which, though they usually promote the idea of the Britishness of Wales, have little to say on the subject of Welsh submission to the English), the favored tactic was simply to present it as fact. Thus William of Malmesbury presents the Welsh as fractious and ungrateful servants, to be brought back into line: "The Welsh were in constant revolt, and King Henry maintained pressure on them by frequent expeditions until they surrendered."[83] The chosen verb "to rebel" suggests strongly that the Welsh were challenging a lawful—that is a de jure—authority, creating a slippage within the text that obscures the origin of this "lawful" authority that seems to have no jurisprudential justification beyond the fist of superior force. Once the coercive and potentially misleading force of William's language is acknowledged, then it becomes a matter of concern that medievalists have generally not questioned its validity or avoided the terms he offers. Thus Chibnall remarks: "...his determination to assert effective authority hardened into a resolve to replace disloyal Welsh leaders by Norman lords wherever possible."[84]

There is no questioning in this statement by whose judgment the Welsh leaders might be considered "disloyal." Maybe terms like "disloyal" and "rebel" should always be placed in inverted commas in discussions of medieval Wales, if critics and historians are to maintain a disinterested and appropriately skeptical attitude to historical claims of dominion. Even after the Statute of Rhuddlan in 1284 imposed an institutional framework of governance to solidify English de facto rule in Wales, there is a case to be made for reserving some distance from too ready an acceptance of the lawful authority of what was enacted. Writing of the early fifteenth century, Paul Strohm comments that "Oldcastle was, for example, active against the Welsh rebels in the period between 1403 and 1408 when the prince served as Lieutenant of the Marches of Wales."[85] Though his description of the participants in the campaigns of Owain Glyn Dŵr as "Welsh rebels" captures both Oldcastle and his prince's sense of their opponents defying legal authority, it loses one level of nuance—in so far as to have written it as Welsh "rebels" would have signaled that the "rebels" did not believe themselves to be rebels or that they owed any duty of allegiance to a foreign crown. Though it may seem pedantic, there is much to be said for mediaevalists using such small signs as a means of marking out their unwillingness to be complicit in the perpetuation of a colonialist discourse.

This ambiguity of jurisdiction was to pose severe historiographical problems for the post-Conquest Norman kings, contending with the changed circumstances of an increasingly centralized state, and the increasing reliance on textual records to support their actions. It is clear that the narrative created to justify their rule, and to effect a reconciliation between the subject English and a recently disembarked Anglo-Norman elite was based around the imagery of continuity—of a class of new rulers governing in the old ways, according to the old laws. For Cannon, "the fundamental principle of such history is . . . what Geoffrey, Wace, and Laȝamon also believe: that the ancient law is the modern law because neither successive kings nor foreign conquest have ever altered a timeless custom."[86] A key figure in this narrative of succession is that of Edward the Confessor, the point of contact between the Saxon past and the Norman present, and the cult of Saint Edward was to be vigorously promoted, functioning more as a political than as a spiritual exemplum. Cannon notes how "at precisely the moment which threatened the most dramatic change, William the Conqueror sought to moderate his position by claiming the Anglo-Saxon law as his own."[87] But the relationship of Wales to the English throne was nowhere secured within the law of King Edward and the instability of the relationship(s) threatened to obstruct the efforts of the Norman and Angevin kings, in Baswell's perceptive phrase, "to construct a narrative of just dominion in England."[88]

One of the most frequent responses to the Welsh in medieval English texts is an expression of impatience—the Welsh are an inconstant people, changeable, not to be relied upon, and apparently incapable of seeing when they were beaten. For the author of the *Gesta Stephani*, the Welsh are a people "consuetudine bellantium, fide semper et locis instabilium" [accustomed to war, volatile always in breaking their word as in changing their abodes].[89] For Edward I, as for William of Malmesbury, any Welsh defeat should have resulted in an act of submission that bound the heirs of the defeated to all eternity. But there was no single constitutional structure to witness or enforce such obligations—nor did Welsh legal systems place the same faith in binding precedent as English Common Law. Rather, the fissiparous nature of medieval Welsh politics, with its shifting territorial boundaries, divergent rules of succession, and absence of any institutions invested with central authority made it impossible for Welsh rulers to enter into obligations that bound their successors. Isolated compromises, whether Hywel Dda's attendance on Æthelstan or Rhys ap Gruffudd's rapprochement with Henry II were, in Welsh eyes, merely that—discrete events, which had no coercive or predictive power over future conduct.

In 1971 Raymond Williams raised, perhaps with apprehension, the question "Who speaks for Wales?" (see note 30). Paradoxically it was the fact that there was no one person, one king, one native church, or one venerable institution to speak for medieval Wales that rendered the Norman project of appropriation and absorption so slow, so painful, and so (relatively) unsuccessful—a lack of success proved by the fact that both the idea of Wales as a nation and the Welsh language as a first language have survived, battle-weary, and a little shot-over, into the twenty-first century. Viewed from across the cultural divide, the perceived changeability and instability of Welsh culture seems to have appeared threatening to a political system in the process of devising a remarkably effective system of land tenure and inheritance to entrench landed privilege. Some hint of the frustration created by contact with the different social values and structures of Wales can be seen in the Statute of Rhuddlan, the act of 1284 in which Edward I annexed the land of the kingdom of Gwynedd and created an English principality of Wales, organized into counties and hundreds on the English model. Having fought a lengthy and ruinously expensive campaign to subdue Llywelyn ap Gruffudd, Edward I's pride and need to be perceived as righteous would not let him acknowledge the annexation as a new achievement. Instead, the Act talks of Wales as having always been an English feudal possession—promoting a myth of the consolidation of power that Edward knew to be unproveable precisely at the moment when (the English) Parliament was claiming for itself the powers Edward claimed were his birthright as king of England:

> Divine providence, which is unerring in its dispositions, among other gifts of its dispensation with which it has deigned to honour us and our kingdom of England has now of its grace wholly and entirely converted the land of Wales previously subject to us by feudal right with its inhabitants into a dominion of our ownership, every obstacle being overcome, and has annexed and united it to the crown of the said kingdom as a constituent part of it.[90]

The "manipulation of the past and of language" that so concerned Rees Davies in his account of Edward's campaign is here so blatant and so self-serving as to be embarrassing and maybe a little sinister. In the face of the determined manipulation of the historical record of the relationship of England and Wales by the highest authorities in the English monarchy, it is only fair to acknowledge the potential dangers medieval English writers faced in raising the subject of the Welsh people and events in Wales in their texts. That may be one explanation for the scarcity of Welsh themes, but it is an insufficient one. Whether the erasure of Wales resulted from indifference, ignorance, or an aversion fostered by the perceptions of Welsh "otherness" (for which we might blame Giraldus Cambrensis and Walter Map, amongst others) or perceived Welsh inferiority (for which Gillingham lays the blame on William of Malmesbury),[91] it is remarkable how accurately the literary record mimics the political development of the relationship between England and Wales.

Whether in the complaints of William of Malmesbury and William of Newburgh against the barbarity of a people who have the temerity to resist English incursion, to Edward I's vision of Wales as, by right, a feudal possession of England, medieval English culture formulated a confident and unquestioned vision of Wales as a subject territory in an enforced political union of unequal respect. But the projection of authority was made possible only by conscious processes of historical falsification and linguistic distortion that imbued the relationship of England and Wales with a poisonous, because unspoken, distrust. In an imposed culture of unequal respect it is, paradoxically, those with the power who might have cause to fear literature's ability to explain and reveal the insubstantial foundations of their authority. It is scarcely surprising, then, that, in its revealingly eloquent silence about the momentous events underway in Wales, English medieval literary culture demonstrates the paralyzing sterility that results from that fear.

Notes

1. Ernest Renan, "*Qu'est-ce qu'une nation?*" (Lecture at the Sorbonne, Paris, 1882), quoted in Ernest Gellner, *Culture, Identity and Politics* (Cambridge: Cambridge University Press, 1987), 6.
2. These patterns of imposing meaning on Wales are discussed in the introduction.
3. See W. A. Davenport, "Sex, Ghosts and Dreams: Walter Map (1135?– 1210?) and Gerald of Wales (1146–1223)," in *Writers of the Reign of Henry II*, ed. Ruth Kennedy and Simon Meecham-Jones (New York: Palgrave Macmillan, 2006), 133–50.
4. The most substantial survey of this question is offered in *The Arthur of the Welsh: The Arthurian legend in Medieval Welsh Literature*, ed. Rachel Bromwich, A. O. H. Jarman, and Brynley Roberts (Cardiff: University of Wales Press, 1991).
5. Stephen Knight, review of Oliver Padel, *Arthur in Medieval Welsh Literature* (Cardiff: University of Wales Press, 2000), in *Speculum* 78 (2003): 241–42. Knight's insistence that the figure of Arthur be read as "a construction of Latin discourse" offers a difference of emphasis rather than a contradiction of Padel, who concludes that Arthur enjoys "a place...hardly a major one" in Welsh heroic legend (Padel, *Arthur in Medieval Welsh Literature*, 60).
6. Michelle R. Warren, *History on the Edge: Excalibur and the Borders of Britain 1100–1300*, Medieval Cultures 22 (Minneapolis: University of Minnesota Press, 2000), xi.
7. Carpenter and Colls both raise the possibility that "such a conquest was [not] necessarily inevitable," though without suggesting how the consequences of English ambition and overwhelming military superiority might have been averted; see David Carpenter, *The Struggle for Mastery Britain 1066–1284*, Penguin History of Britain, vol. 3 (London: Allen Lane Penguin, 2003), 525; Robert Colls, *Identity of England* (Oxford: Oxford University Press, 2002), 35–36.
8. R. W. Southern, *Scholastic Humanism and the Unification of Europe Vol. II: The Heroic Age* (Oxford: Blackwell, 2001), 171. The importance of Southern's analysis of post-Conquest historiography has been acknowledged by Michelle A. Warren: "As R. W. Southern first suggested, the cultural traumas of Norman colonization focused attention on the near and distant past, as both dominant and dominated groups defended their collective identities and sought therapeutic cures for alienation in history" (Warren, *History on the Edge*, xi).
9. *The Oxford English Dictionary* lists as alternative definitions for "forget" (s.v. *forget*, v): "to lose remembrance of, to cease to retain in one's memory, to omit or neglect through inadvertence, to neglect willfully, take no thought of, disregard, overlook, slight."
10. The truth of the claims by Geoffrey of Monmouth and Chrétien de Troyes to have taken their material from old British books has occupied generations

of critics, but the failure to recover any manuscripts that might have been Geoffrey's "Vetustissimus liber" has left the argument inconclusive at best.

11. Judith Weiss, "Thomas and the Earl: Literary and Historical Contexts for the *Romance of Horn*," in *Tradition and Transformation in Medieval Romance*, ed. Rosalind Field (Cambridge: D. S. Brewer, 1999), 1–14, at 1–6; see also M. Dominica Legge, *Anglo-Norman Literature and Its Background* (Oxford: Clarendon Press, 1963), 99. If Weiss and Legge are correct in their suggestion that the romance was first presented in Dublin in 1170, in the presence of Henry II and an expeditionary force of Normans from West Wales who have in recent years been described as "Cambro-Normans," that may explain the otherwise unexpected use of a (presumably) recognizable Welsh narrative model.

12. John Gower, Prologue to the *Confessio Amantis*, line 24, in *The Works of John Gower: The English Works*, ed. G. C. Macaulay, 2 vols. (Oxford: Clarendon Press, 1901), 1: 2, p. 2

13. Two harsh accounts of Chaucer's attitude to the non-English inhabitants of Britain are offered by Cohen and Bowers: Jeffrey Jerome Cohen, "Postcolonialism," in *Chaucer an Oxford Guide*, ed. Steve Ellis (Oxford: Oxford University Press, 2005), 448–62; John M. Bowers, "Chaucer after Smithfield: From Postcolonial Writer to Imperialist Author," in *The Postcolonial Middle Ages*, ed. Jeffrey Jerome Cohen (Basingstoke: Palgrave Macmillan, 2000), 53–66.

14. Simon Meecham-Jones, "English Gaufride and British Chaucer?" forthcoming.

15. *Piers Plowman*, Passus XV, lines 441–45; see *William Langland: The Vision of Piers Plowman (B Text)*, ed. A. V. C. Schmidt, Everyman's Library (London: Dent, 1978), 191.

16. Emily Steiner offers a reading of Passus XV as an exercise in "radical historiography" in which English history is shaped to offer a model of "historical exemplarity"; Emily Steiner, "Radical Historiography: Langland, Trevisa, and the *Polychronicon*," *Studies in the Age of Chaucer* 27 (2005): 171–212. One price to be paid, though, for this "definition of Englishness" is the need to obscure the distinct history of England's neighbor.

17. *Piers Plowman*, Passus V, lines 194–95; see Schmidt, ed., *Piers Plowman (B Text)*, 48.

18. London, British Library MS Harley 978, fol. 107; see C. L. Kingsford, ed. and trans., *The Song of Lewes* (Oxford: Clarendon Press, 1890).

19. R. R. Davies, *Lordship and Society in the March of Wales 1282–1400* (Oxford: Clarendon Press, 1978), 2.

20. *Cantref* the basic Welsh territorial administrative unit; see A. D. Carr, *Medieval Wales* (New York: Palgrave Macmillan, 1995), x.

21. *The Text of the Book of Llan Dâv*, ed. J. Gwenogvryn Evans (Oxford: Oxford University Press, 1893); E. D. Jones, "The Book of Llandaff," *National Library of Wales Journal* 4 (1945–46): 123–57; Wendy Davies, "St Mary's Worcester and the Liber Landavensis," *Journal of the Society of Archivists* 4

(1972): 459–85; Wendy Davies, "Liber Landavensis: Its Construction and Credibility," *English Historical Record* 88 (1973): 335–51; Wendy Davies, "Braint Teilo," *Bulletin of the Board of Celtic Studies* 26 (1975): 123–37; Wendy Davies, *An Early Welsh Microcosm*, Studies in History 9 (London: Royal Historical Society, 1978); Wendy Davies, *The Llandaff Charters* (Aberystwyth: National Library of Wales, 1979).

22. *Domesday Book, Vol. 17, Herefordshire*, ed. Frank and Caroline Thorn (Chichester: Phillimore, 1983), 181a.

23. Llinos Beverley Smith, "The Welsh and English Languages in Late-Medieval Wales," in *Multilingualism in Later Medieval Britain*, ed. D. A. Trotter (Cambridge: D. S. Brewer, 2000), 7–21, at 12.

24. In his examination of multilingualism in Herefordshire, Michael Richter recounts a miracle worked by Thomas Cantilupe, a deceased Bishop of Hereford, recorded in a manuscript now in the Vatican Library, MS Vat. Lat. 4015. After a miraculous cure, a formerly mute beggar is discovered (according to the testimony of some of the witnesses called by a papal delegation sent to investigate Cantilupe's claims to canonization) speaking fluently in both English and Welsh. His purported words are represented in an inaccurate but recognizable form in the manuscript, presumably by a non-Welsh-speaking cleric; see Michael Richter, "Collecting Miracles along the Anglo-Welsh Border in the Early Fourteenth Century," in Trotter, ed., *Multilingualism*, 53–61; Michael Richter, *Sprache und Gesellschaft im Mittelalter: Unterzuchen zur mündlichen Kommunikation in England von der Mitte des elften bis zum Beginn des vierzehnten Jahrhunderts*, Monographien zur Geschichte des Mittelalters 18 (Stuttgart: Anton Hiersemann, 1979).

25. The contents of the manuscript are described by Daniel Huws, *Medieval Welsh Manuscripts* (Cardiff: University of Wales Press and National Library of Wales, 2000), 82–83.

26. Hergest was the seat of one branch of the Vaughan family, members of which are recorded as patrons of Welsh poets of the fifteenth century such as Guto'r Glyn and Lewys Glyn Cothi.

27. Huws, *Medieval Welsh Manuscripts*, 80. There was also a second important Welsh language manuscript, the *White Book of Hergest*, which contained poetry by Lewys Glyn Cothi and twenty-seven poems by Dafydd ap Gwilym. The manuscript was destroyed in a fire at a bookbinder's in London in 1810, but fortunately transcriptions had already been made of its contents; see Huws, *Medieval Welsh Manuscripts*, 96.

28. These survive in three forms. Some retain their original Welsh form, for example, Llanover, Pontrilas, and Pencraig. Kentchurch and Dewchurch retain their ecclesiastical allegiance to the Celtic saints St. Cein and St. Dewi, though the place-names have been translated—the form Llankeyne is recorded as late as the fifteenth century. Then there are the place-names that witness translinguistic incomprehension—from Moccas (from the Welsh Moch-rhos, literally the pig's heath) to Bredwardine (from the Welsh Brodorddyn).

29. See Malcolm Thurlby, *The Herefordshire School of Romanesque Sculpture* (Logaston: Logaston Press, 1999).

30. Raymond Williams, "Marxism, Poetry, Wales," interview with *Poetry Wales* 1977, repr. in *Who Speaks for Wales? Nation, Culture, Identity*, ed. Daniel Williams (Cardiff: University of Wales Press, 2003), 81–94, at 87.

31. E. J. Dobson, *The Origins of Ancrene Wisse* (Oxford: Clarendon Press, 1976), 115–16.

32. A. T. E. Matonis, "The Harley Lyrics: English and Welsh Convergences," *Modern Philology* 86.1 (1988): 1–21.

33. For example, Patricia Clare Ingham, *Sovereign Fantasie: Arthurian Romance and the Making of Britain* (Philadelphia: University of Pennsylvania Press, 2001); Sylvia Federico, *New Troy: Fantasies of Empire in the Late Middle Ages* (Minneapolis: University of Minnesota Press, 2003).

34. These are considered in more detail by Tony Davenport and Cory Rushton in chaps. 7 and 9.

35. *Ipomedon, poème de Hue de Rotelande (fin du XIIe siècle)*, ed. A. J. Holden, Bibliothèque Française et Romane, serie B: 17 (Paris: Klincksieck, 1979).

36. Introduction, *Boundaries in Medieval Romance*, ed. Neil Cartlidge (Cambridge: D. S. Brewer, 2008), 6–7.

37. At what point English people ceased to differentiate between the "Norman" elite and the English people has been a subject of much debate. Gillingham, Ian Short, and Hugh Thomas each suggest that the distinction is not considered meaningful by the middle decades of the twelfth century; see John Gillingham, *The English in the Twelfth Century* (Woodbridge: Boydell, 2000); Ian Short, "*Tam Angli quam Franci*: Self-Definition in Anglo-Norman England," *Anglo-Norman Studies* 18 (1995): 153–75; Hugh M. Thomas, *The English and the Normans* (Oxford: Oxford University Press, 2003). Chibnall offers a similar judgment: "Only in the later eleventh and early twelfth centuries was it possible to consider the colonisation and settlement as a movement of the 'Norman people.' By conquering England they had taken part in an enterprise that was to change their character and help to form a new 'English people' "; Marjorie Chibnall, *The Normans* (Oxford: Blackwell, 2000), 86. An alternative reading is offered by Elaine Treharne, who argues that critics should reconsider "the obfuscation of the English and their literary output...by those historiographers of the late eleventh and twelfth centuries whose allegiance was to the Normans"; Elaine Treharne, "Periodization and Categorization: The Silence of (the) English in the Twelfth Century," in *New Medieval Literatures* 8, ed. Rita Copeland, Wendy Scase, and David Wallace (Turnhout: Brepols, 2007): 248–75, at 254.

38. The full extent of English literary involvement in the Charlemagne tradition is considered by Marianne Ailes and Phillipa Hardman in Cartlidge, *Boundaries*, 43–56.

39. Phillipa Hardman, "The *Sege of Melayne*: A Fifteenth Century Reading," in Field, ed., *Tradition and Transformation*, 71–86, at 75.

40. A full bibliography of the "Pseudo-Turpin Chronicle" is provided by Shepherd in his introduction to *Turpines Story*; see Stephen H. A. Shepherd, *Turpines Story a Middle English Translation of the Pseudo-Turpin Chronicle*, EETS os 322 (2004), lvii–lix.

41. Robert A. Rouse, *The Idea of Anglo-Saxon England in Middle English Romance* (Cambridge: D. S. Brewer, 2005); Allen Frantzen and John D. Niles, *Anglo-Saxonism and the Construction of Social Identity* (Gainesville: University of Florida Press, 1997).

42. Warren, *History on the Edge*, esp. x and xii.

43. George Owen, *A Description of Pembrokeshire*, ed. H. Owen (London: Honourable Society of Cymmrodorion, 1892).

44. G. W. S. Barrow, *Feudal Britain* (London: Edward Arnold, 1967), 366.

45. Kate Roberts, *Traed Mewn Cyffion* (Llandysul: Gomer Press, 2001); Kate Roberts, *Feet in Chains*, trans. John Idris Jones (Bridgend: Seren, 2002).

46. R. S. Loomis, *Celtic Myth and Arthurian Romance* (New York: Columbia Press, 1927); R. S. Loomis, ed., *Arthurian Literature in the Middle Ages: A Collaborative History* (Oxford: Clarendon Press, 1959).

47. Marvin L. Colker, *Galteri de Castellione Alexandreis* (Padua: In aedibus Antenoreis, 1978), *Alexandreis* 9: 542, 249.

48. Translation from R. Telfryn Pritchard, *Walter of Châtillon the Alexandreis* (Toronto: Pontifical Institute of Medieval Studies, 1986), 214.

49. John Davies, *The History of Wales* (London: Allen Lane Penguin, 1993), 106.

50. Chibnall, *Normans*, 65.

51. Amusing examples of the trope, and of the twists of logic needed to deploy it, can be found, for example, in Bernard Bolingbroke Woodward's *History of Wales*, a highly detailed and extensive history dedicated to the purpose that "Wales may receive into her heart, such good as her subjugation by England was intended to convey to her"; Bernard Bolingbroke Woodward, *The History of Wales from the Earliest Times, to Its Final Incorporation with the Kingdom of England* (London: Virtue, 1853), 586. Though it is (presumably) inconceivable that critics or historians could seek to revive (without careful qualification) the imagery of pacification, it is still current in the descriptions of military analysts. Asprey uses the "pacification of Wales" as an example in his account of guerrilla warfare; Robert B. Asprey, *War in the Shadows: The Classic History of Guerilla Warfare from Ancient Persia to the Present* (London: Little Brown and Company 1994), 39–43.

52. Edmund Burke, *Speech on Conciliation with America*, ed. Hammond Lamont (Boston: Athenaeum Press, 1903), 42–46.

53. J. G. Edwards, "The Battle of Maes Madog and the Welsh Campaign of 1294–5," *English Historical Review* 153 (1924): 1–12, at 12.

54. *Gesta Stephani*, ed. and trans. K. R. Potter, rev. R. H. C. Davis (Oxford: Clarendon Press, 1976), Book I, Chap. 7, 14–15.

55. Potter and Davis, eds., *Gesta Stephani*, Book I, Chap. 7, 14–15.

56. Potter and Davis, eds., *Gesta Stephani*, Book I, Chap. 9, 16–17.

57. The forfeiture of Owain's lands is described more thoroughly in *Brut y Tywysogion*, ed. Thomas Jones (Cardiff: University of Wales Press, 1955), 34.

58. *The Ecclesiastical History of Orderic Vitalis, Volume I*, ed. and trans. Marjorie Chibnall (Oxford: Clarendon Press 1980), 2.

59. The words *Cymru* and *Cymry* are believed to derive from the Brythonic word *combrogi* (which means "fellow countrymen," or sometimes in the early texts, "kinsmen"). Exactly the opposite idea is expressed in the words *Welsh* and *Wales*, derived from the Saxon *wealh* [foreigner].

60. Brynley Roberts argues: "He [Gerald] uses consistently the name *Kambria*, refuses to accept Gwalia, but neither does he use *Britones* which was the historically loaded term which the Welsh used for themselves"; see Brynley F. Roberts, "Gerald of Wales and Welsh Tradition," in *The Formation of Culture in Medieval Britain*, ed. Françoise H. M. Le Saux (Lampeter: Edwin Mellen Press, 1995), 129–47, at 146. Bartlett similarly notes Gerald's distaste for the English-derived form, which seems to stem from his awareness of the different nuances of power embodied in each name; see Robert Bartlett, *Gerald of Wales, 1145–1223* (Oxford: Clarendon Press, 1982), 185.

61. Williams, *Who Speaks for Wales?* 64.

62. David Abulafia, "Introduction," 1–26, in *Medieval Frontiers: Concepts and Practices*, ed. David Abulafia and Nora Berend (Aldershot: Ashgate, 2002), 23.

63. Davies, *History of Wales*, 71.

64. Huw Pryce, "British or Welsh? National Identity in Twelfth-Century Wales," *English Historical Review* 116 (2001): 775–801, at 799. *Cymry*— the plural of *Cymro* [Welshman]—is used to mean both "Welshmen" and "Wales" in this period. The familiar modern spelling of *Cymru* as a distinct word to represent "Wales" is first recorded in 1536.

65. *The Letters of John of Salisbury, in Two Volumes*, ed. W. J. Millor and C. N. L. Brooke (Oxford: Clarendon Press, 1979), 2: 106–9. In their translation, Millor and Brooke rendered *Britones* as "Welsh" which, though it might avoid some misunderstanding, distorts the nuance of John's very conscious choice of word. It is, at best, a backhanded compliment by John, since their success is compared to the biblical example of *latrunculos et seruos abiectos* [petty thieves and low slaves] who rose against Solomon.

66. Millor and Brooke, eds., *Letters of John of Salisbury*, 1: 136–37.

67. Pryce, "British or Welsh?" 116, 800.

68. Pryce, "British or Welsh?" 116, 785.

69. Pryce, "British or Welsh?" 116, 796. An alternative reading of the change is offered by Michael Richter, "The Political and Institutional Background to National Consciousness in Medieval Wales," in *Nationality and the Pursuit of National Independence*, ed. T. W. Moody, Historical Studies 11 (Belfast: Appletree Press, 1978): 37–55.

70. The crucial role of the church in encouraging English expansionism is highlighted by Chibnall and Flanagan; Marjorie Chibnall, *Anglo-Norman*

England, 1066–1166 (Oxford: Blackwell, 1986); Marie Therese Flanagan, *Irish Society, Anglo-Norman Settlers, Angevin Kingship* (Oxford: Clarendon Press, 1989).

71. "Second generation" in the sense that it draws heavily on the model of William of Malmesbury's *Gesta*; see William of Malmesbury, *Gesta Regum Anglorum: The History of the English Kings*, ed. and trans. R. A. B. Mynors, rev. R. M. Thomson and M. Winterbottom, 2 vols. (Oxford: Clarendon Press, 1998–99).

72. Potter and Davis, eds., *Gesta Stephani*, Book I, Chap. 7; *The Chronicles of John of Worcester Vol. II*, ed. R. R. Darlington and P. McGurk (Oxford: Clarendon Press, 1995). William of Newburgh, *Historia rerum Anglicarum, The History of English Affairs*, Book I, ed. with trans. and commentary by P. G. Walsh and M. J. Kennedy (Warminster: Aris & Phillips, 1988); Henry, Archdeacon of Huntingdon, *Historia Anglorum: The History of the English People*, ed. and trans. Diana Greenway (Oxford: Clarendon Press, 1996).

73. Dumville has convincingly shown that the identification of the author of the *Historia Brittonum* with the figure of Nennius, which appears in some (though not the earliest) of the texts must be discounted. However, since medieval writers believed the *Historia* to be the work of Nennius, the term Pseudo-Nennius to describe the author has been coined. D. N. Dumville, "'Nennius' and the *Historia Brittonum*," *Studia Celtica* 10.11 (1975–76): 315–22; D. N. Dumville, "The Corpus Christi 'Nennius,'" *Bulletin of the Board of Celtic Studies* 25 (1974): 369–80.

74. The nature of Angevin literature as a literature of justification is discussed in Simon Meecham-Jones, Introduction, in Meecham-Jones and Kennedy, *Writers of Reign of Henry II*, 1–24, at 11–22. A valuable study of the theme of exile in the romances is provided by Rosalind Field, "The King Over the Water: Exile-and-Return Revisited," in *Cultural Encounters in the Romance of Medieval England*, ed. Corinne Saunders (Cambridge: D. S. Brewer, 2005), 41–54.

75. Bartlett characterizes the process as a crucial element of the "aristocratic diaspora" across Europe from the tenth to the thirteenth century; Robert Bartlett, *The Making of Europe: Conquest, Colonization and Cultural Change, 950–1350* (London: Allen Lane Penguin, 1994), 24–59.

76. *The Chronicles of John of Worcester Vol. II*, ed. R. R. Darlington and P. McGurk (Oxford: Clarendon Press, 1995), 73–77.

77. The term *pura Wallia* presents considerable difficulties of nuance in translation. Lewis and Short's *A Latin Dictionary* (Oxford: Clarendon Press, 1975) offers as a range of meaning for *purus* "clean, free from dirt or filth, pure, unstained, undefiled." The use of this adjective to describe unconquered Wales presumably infers that *pura Wallia* is unadulterated by foreign influence, but the choice of it in preference to *vera* [true] or even *barbara* [barbarous] while suggesting a pose of impartiality, remains striking.

78. R. R. Davies, *Domination and Conquest: The Experience of Ireland, Scotland and Wales 1100–1300*, Wiles Lectures 1988 (Cambridge: Cambridge University Press, 1990), 4.

79. R. R. Davies, *The King of England and the Prince of Wales, 1277–84: Law, Politics and Power* (Cambridge: Department of Anglo-Saxon, Norse, and Celtic, 2003), 13.

80. Davies, *King of England*, 13.

81. Davies, *King of England*, 13.

82. Burma also provides a telling example of the power and importance of names. The governments of the United Kingdom and the United States refuse to accept the authority of the military regime to rename the country Myanmar, and use the form "Burma" in official material; the European Union uses the form "Myanmar/Burma," while those (relatively few) governments that have granted full recognition use the form "Myanmar." The same awareness of the political implications of choosing a particular form can also be seen in media usage—as a matter of policy, the *BBC* and *The Wall Street Journal* use "Burma," while *CNN* and *The Economist* use "Myanmar."

83. William of Malmesbury, *Gesta Regum Anglorum*, 2: 727.

84. Chibnall, *Anglo-Norman England*, 45.

85. Paul Strohm, *Sir John Oldcastle: Another Ill-Framed Knight*, The William Matthews Lectures (London: Birkbeck College London, 1997), 14.

86. Christopher Cannon, *The Grounds of English Literature* (Oxford: Oxford University Press, 2004), 71.

87. Cannon, *Grounds of English*, 58.

88. Christopher Baswell, "King Edward and the Cripple," in *Chaucer and the Challenges of Medievalism: Studies in Honor of H. A. Kelly*, ed. Donka Minkova and Theresa Tinkle (Frankfurt am Main: Peter Lang, 2003), 15–29, at 21.

89. Potter and Davis, eds., *Gesta Stephani*, Book I, Chap. 7, 14–15.

90. *English Historical Documents Volume III*, ed. Harry Rothwell (London: Routledge, 1996), 422.

91. Gillingham, *English in the Twelfth Century*, 8–9.

CHAPTER 3

THE LICHFIELD/LLANDEILO GOSPELS REINTERPRETED

Michelle P. Brown

Scholarship concerning the great Gospelbooks that are amongst the leading cultural monuments of the "Insular" period of British and Irish history, ca. 550–850, has grown apace during the course of the past century and a half. It has been interlaced with a reawakening of regional and national identities and with a developing sense of the value of such cultural artifacts as iconic rallying points. The pendulum of intellectual debate has accordingly swung wildly between extremist positions in which swathes of interrelated materials have been claimed as entirely the product of one nation or another, within this cluster of isles. Thus the Hiberno-Saxon Gospelbooks, notably the Book of Durrow, the Book of Kells, the Durham Gospels, the Echternach Gospels, and the Lindisfarne Gospels have generally been claimed for England and Scotland by Masai, Kendrick, Bruce-Mitford, and Julian Brown and for Ireland by Henry, William O'Sullivan, Daibhi Ó Croinin, and Bernard Meehan. Others, such as George Henderson, Nancy Netzer, and myself, have adopted a more nuanced approach, favoring a spread of production centers across all three areas at a time when their religious cultures often collaborated in the shared work of conversion and construction, the very term "Insular" serving as a convenient shorthand to obviate the necessity of drawing arbitrary national distinctions.[1]

In recent years, cultural restitution claims have assumed a political vogue as part of the bargaining currency in campaigns for regional economic redevelopment and as a means of mobilizing local public awareness and support. The stakes are high, for these works of the past can affect the lives of the present in very potent ways. Nor are these confined to the secular sphere and the creation of jobs in areas in need of regeneration, for the cultural heritage of faith is also deployed in the contemporary ministry and witness of Christian churches and as a means of capturing flagging public attention and a share of the tourist market.

In the face of such agendas North East England agitates for the return of the Lindisfarne Gospels from the British Library, Scotland calls for the repatriation of the Book of Deer from Cambridge University Library, the Manx Chronicle Liberation Front besieges the British Library, and Trinity College Library in Dublin is lobbied for the return of the Book of Kells to the town of that name at the same time that its ancient Market Cross has had to be removed to Dublin because of damage from tourist coaches. Such an impetus is often encountered as a predictable reaction to centralization and as an adjunct to moves toward greater local autonomy. Not surprisingly then, Wales also has its own book held captive in the bondage of Babylon—the St. Teilo or Llandeilo Gospels. Llandeilo Fawr lies at the heart of Carmarthenshire, whose rural and industrial livelihoods have been hard hit in the current age with its electronic trading and service industries. Its church was once the center of the paruchia of Saint Teilo, a friend of Wales' sixth-century patron saint, Dewi (David) and now participates in the cultural revival of this attractive little market town with it music festival and its new heritage/community center imaginatively constructed within the church building.

The manuscript in question is an eighth-century Insular Gospelbook now in Lichfield Cathedral Library, MS 1, which is more commonly known as the Lichfield Gospels or St. Chad Gospels. Situated in the heart of the Black Country, this gem of a cathedral—which has been lesser known that many of its counterparts because of its now depressed industrial hinterland—is itself gripped by a sense of spiritual and cultural renewal and is mounting its own funding bid to establish enhanced facilities for the display and interpretation of its ancient treasures and contemporary artworks.

Both centers have played a vital role in helping to ensure the precious survival of this unique witness to a former age, in which both places enjoyed prominence. Both have sought to advance their claims over those of the other. These have revolved around the question of where the book originated, rather than acknowledging that it has had a relationship with both and that, as with people, the biography of a book is defined by the multiplicity of places it has been and people it has known and not just by where it was born. To address this and to open up the book to a wider audience, a collaboration between the two churches was negotiated, with myself mediating on behalf of the British Library, to apply the library's award-winning "turning the pages" technology to the manuscript so that it could be explored via installations at both sites. The Gospelbook had been on loan to the library for its exhibition "Painted Labyrinth: The World of the Lindisfarne Gospels" during 2003 and had been digitized while there, by the kind permission of the Dean and Chapter of Lichfield Cathedral. The collaboration was a highly successful and productive one and the electronic touch screen version of book (displaying its most significant openings) was installed at both churches in 2006. The book was now to meet more people than ever before.

So, what do we know of this particular book's biography, or provenance?[2] The first evidence we have of its whereabouts date to around a century after it was made, by which time it was in Wales where, from the mid-ninth to mid-tenth centuries a number of documents, subscriptions, and attestations were inscribed in its margins and other blank spaces. These indicate that it served during that time as the Book of the High Altar or oathbook of St. Teilo's Church. The Lindisfarne Gospels, which was made on Holy Island around 710–21, served a similar function as the Book of the High Altar of medieval Durham,[3] and British Library, Royal MS 1.B.vii, had a record of the manumission of slaves entered into a blank column in order to commemorate the accession of King Athelstan, who presented the book to Christ Church Canterbury where the transaction was solemnized by its enshrinement in an ancient copy of Scripture that had been made in the mid-eighth century (around the same time as the Lichfield/Llandeilo Gospels).[4] The additions to the latter are in Latin and Welsh and include the earliest examples of both Welsh handwriting and of the written Welsh language. It is therefore a major monument of early medieval Welsh culture and history.

Although the texts of some of these documents may date back to the eighth century and were copied into the book retrospectively, the earliest ones to be recorded in it directly at the time relate to Gelhi (Gelli), son of Arihtiud, and his family. In the mid-ninth century a Welsh scribe penned in Latin, in a prominent blank space at the end of St. Matthew's Gospel (page 141), a document known as the "Surexit" inscription. This records that Gelhi did a deal with one Cingal and swapped his best white horse for the book; he subsequently presented it to the altar of St. Teilo at Llandeilo Fawr. An earlier document relating to his family was also transcribed below, on the same page. It asserted that they were not guilty of misrepresentation in a case brought against them by one Tutbulc of contested ownership of a parcel of land in Tyr Telych that was thought to be gold-yielding. This is the oldest surviving original document in Welsh. Perhaps Gelhi's magnificent gift to the church was intended to clinch the matter once and for all and to exonerate him from any wrongdoing, symbolized by his oath, taken upon a venerable copy of sacred text. These transactions were probably the first of many to be legitimized by swearing oaths on this very Gospelbook, rather as we still swear in court upon texts representing whichever creed we subscribe to. The Pater Noster was likewise inscribed at the end of St. Mark's Gospel and was used in solemnizing oaths, for the land deals transacted around Llandeilo during the ninth and tenth centuries were inscribed nearby in Welsh and Latin (on pages 216–17), and in the margin around the miniature depicting St. Luke (page 218) a Latin manumission was added, granting liberty to Bleiddudd ap Sulren. This was one of the earliest such documents freeing slaves in the post-Roman world.

Gelhi won fame by his donation, for the spiritual kudos accrued by such acts of redemption and restitution of books was even greater than the worldly PR equivalent afforded to the modern local politicians who front cultural restitution campaigns. The Armenian church, the first to have officially accepted Christianity, viewed the redemption from captivity of sacred books taken by pagan desecrators as an act that earned tremendous benefits for the soul and numerous inscriptions in books record such acts.[5] Another example from closer to home is that of the Stockholm Codex Aureus,[6] a mid-eighth-century Kentish Gospelbook that contains a marginal inscription recording that it was ransomed in return for gold from pagan Viking forces a century later by Ealdorman Ælfred of Kent and his wife, Werburgh, and was presented by them for the good of

St. Luke evangelist miniature with manumission added in the margin in ninth-century Wales Chad/Lichfield/Llandeilo Gospels (Lichfield Cathedral Library, MS 1, page 218)

their souls to the altar of Christ Church Canterbury. The potential parallel with the case of the Lichfield/Llandeilo volume is an obvious and persuasive one and suggests that Gelhi was likewise redeeming a sacred book that had been taken from mother church by attackers and was restoring it for spiritual gain, and public legitimization of his family's property claims, to the church—not necessarily to the center from which it had been taken, but rather to that which was most significant to him, Llandeilo, the mother church of a leading churchman, St. Teilo, and one of the most important religious communities in early medieval Wales. Notes in the margins of the manuscript reveal that at this time it was the seat of a "Bishop of Teilo" named Nobis and that it had extensive land holdings. Its oathbook was obviously much prized, for not only does it contain the aforementioned documents and the cross-shaped marks and names of many local worthies, but the church still houses two portions of fine ninth-century stone crosses, the interlace designs on one of which display the influence of the book's cross-carpet page. This was a glorious age for Llandeilo and its environs, for it lay in the lea of Dynevor, craggy seat of King Hywel Dda (ca. 887–950), Wales' famous lawgiver who, like his English counterpart, Alfred the Great, codified and formalized the Welsh lawcodes. Little wonder then that there should have been a venerated oathbook on the nearby altar of St. Teilo in the authoritative sacred presence of which such laws were enacted and witnessed.

If the Gospelbook did fall into the hands of Cingal and then Gelhi in the aftermath of raids upon the church, then the Viking upheavals of the first half of the ninth century are most likely to have been the cause, although the internecine raids conducted by the English and the Welsh, in both directions across Offa's Dyke, cannot be ruled out either.[7] In the absence of evidence indicating that Llandeilo Fawr had itself been subject to such despoliation, it is perhaps unlikely that the book was being returned to its earlier home. It could just as well have come into Wales from England, which was experiencing tremendous upheaval, with people and artifacts from the Midland kingdom of Mercia fleeing westward and southwestward into territories unoccupied by their Viking invaders.[8] Alternatively, Viking activity on the Welsh seaboard could have afforded opportunity for the book to have been traded, having been looted from any number of English, Scottish, or Irish monasteries. For important though the book undoubtedly was in early medieval Wales, the possibility that it was originally made there does not seem a plausible one, for the reasons that follow.

The Welsh church had long-established traditions of its own and a venerable history of Christian scholarship that produced figures of the stature of Gildas who exerted such a formative influence upon British and Irish thought.[9] It must have produced many books prior to the mid-ninth century, but the only one that is thought to have survived, although many early documents are preserved in later medieval copies in works such as the Book of Llandaff, is the Hereford Gospels.[10] This is essentially a provincial reflection of the Hiberno-Saxon mainstream while the other surviving examples of Welsh script and decoration that have survived carved upon stone and metalwork indicate that the styles and traditions of late Roman Britain remained overwhelmingly influential, as they did in the fields of document production and law. It was in the perpetuation and reinvention of British antiquity that early medieval Wales excelled, while the distinctive and highly polished forms of calligraphy and illumination to be found in Hiberno-Saxon books (of the sort made in Irish, Scottish, and Northumbrian scriptoria) tend to be echoed only as provincial variants. Striking and moving though Welsh sculptures such as the Margam and Nevern crosses are, they lack the disciplined design and technical precision of the Northumbrian Acca cross, the Ruthwell

and Bewcastle crosses, of the Pictish Aberlemno Churchyard cross-slab or the
Nigg cross-slab, or the Irish Tullylease cross-slab or the Ahenny, or Iona high
crosses. There is no reason, judging from the extant examples of Welsh script,
to think that Welsh books would have been any more closely related to their
Hiberno-Saxon counterparts, had they survived.

Wales did not contain monasteries that were attached to the *paruchia* of
St. Columba, which had exerted such a powerful formative influence upon
parts of Ireland, Scotland, and Northumbria (and thereby its daughter houses in
England, such as Lindisfarne's foundations of Lastingham and Lichfield). Yet the
Lichfield/Llandeilo Gospels are a prime example of Hiberno-Saxon book production and display a particular close reliance upon the Lindisfarne Gospels, one
of the great cult books of the Columban and Cuthbertine federations. Indeed,
the designs of the Lichfield/Llandeilo Gospels' carpet page, the decorated incipit
pages that open each Gospel (three remain) and the Chi-rho that introduces
the Nativity in Matthew's Gospel, are so indebted to those of the Lindisfarne
Gospels that it is highly likely that the artist of the former was allowed to study
the openings of the great cult book of St. Cuthbert's shrine on Holy Island at
first hand. He devised his own formulae to replicate the overall design of these
pages without having to emulate the meticulous, time-consuming detail of
Lindisfarne's zoomorphic interlace and La Tène spiralwork—an artistic shorthand that is highly effective and aesthetically pleasing in its own right. Yet look
closely and all the major elements of the Lindisfarne Gospels' designs are there;
in the Chi-rho page, for example, the star still appears behind the "X," announcing
Christ's birth, and the flamboyant curved panels of spiralwork, resembling great
metalwork escutcheons, still adorn the head and foot of the letter, while its body
is filled with interlaced wildfowl who are the first cousins of their Holy Island
predecessors.

Such privileged access to the major openings of what must have been one
of the most renowned books of the age suggests that the Lichfield/Llandeilo
Gospels were probably being made in their turn as the focal point of an important church, perhaps itself the home of the shrine of a leading saint, which was
most likely also a member of the Columban *paruchia*. The rest of the book's
illuminated pages, which depict the evangelists Mark and Luke and their sym-
bols (damage to the front and back having occasioned the loss of Matthew and
John), are not modeled on those of the Lindisfarne Gospels, however. Mark,
with his Roman tonsure, short hair, and stylized, rectilinear throne with its
zoomorphic terminals, recalls elements from the harping David in the Durham
Cassiodorus (which has not been firmly localized but that is generally attributed
to Northumbria or southern Scotland).[11] His leaping lion symbol resembles that
in the Lindisfarne Gospels, however, while his angular throne is from the same
school of furniture-making as that occupied by King David in the Cassiodorus
and by Matthew's symbol, the man, in the Echternach Gospels, a volume associated with the Irish-Northumbrian mission to what is now Luxembourg.[12]
The image of St. Luke in the Lichfield/Llandeilo Gospels has similar stylized
tubular drapery to that of his counterpart, St. Mark, which resembles that in

Carpet page preceding St. Luke's Gospel Chad/Lichfield/Llandeilo Gospels (Lichfield Cathedral Library, MS 1, page 220)

the Echternach Gospels and which was probably ultimately derived from highly stylized figures on Coptic textiles, but his luxuriant, flowing locks of hair and his Osiris-like pose, holding rod and staff in Pharaonic Old Testament fashion, have more in common with details from the Arrest miniature, the St. John/Majesty miniature and the Temptation miniature in the Book of Kells, the Columban cult book par excellence. The calligraphic, rounded half-uncial script of our volume is closely based upon what Julian Brown termed the "reformed" half-uncial that was perfected in the Lindisfarne Gospels around 720 and that was still practiced by the scribes of the Book of Kells around 800, but it is laid out in long lines in single columns, as in most of the great Insular Gospelbooks, rather than Jerome's "per cola et commata" arrangement in which line length serves to clarify sense and sentential that was employed in the Lindisfarne Gospels.[13] Nor is its Latin text the excellent version of Jerome's Vulgate edition that was copied at Wearmouth-Jarrow from a Neapolitan exemplar and subsequently used on Holy Island as the exemplar for the Lindisfarne Gospels, but rather a "mixed Celtic" text in which Vulgate and Old Latin readings merged, of the sort favored throughout the rest of the Columban federation and its Gospelbooks.[14]

The conclusion to be drawn then from the physical appearance and textual contents of the Lichfield/Llandeilo Gospels is that its affinities lie firmly within the Columban orbit and indicate privileged access to the Lindisfarne Gospels on Holy Island—in mid-eighth century—a generation after that book was made—combined with influences from other Northumbrian and Irish manuscripts and the sort of text favored in other centers in those regions (linked primarily by St. Columba's mission and those of his followers) rather than the avant-garde Vulgate edition circulated from Wearmouth-Jarrow. This Hiberno-Saxon cultural orbit is not known to have embraced Wales, which had its own well-developed traditions, to such a significant extent. The center for which the Lichfield/Llandeilo Gospels were made was most likely a daughter house of the Columban federation that adhered to its more traditional textual use.

One further piece of evidence that argues strongly against a Welsh origin is the use of Germanic runes. The display script of the Lindisfarne Gospels blended Roman and Greek letter forms with angular letters that evoked the wooden epigraphic origins of the Germanic runic alphabet. The Lichfield/Llandeilo Gospels went a step further and introduced actual runic letters, the equivalents of their Latin counterparts. The use of runes on the Ruthwell cross, located in the ancient British kingdom of Rheged in southwestern Scotland that had been annexed by Anglian Northumbria during the early eighth century when this striking monument was erected, has been interpreted as an overt statement of English political and cultural supremacy.[15] It is, surely, unthinkable that any self-respecting Welsh artist-scribe would have willingly introduced the visual cultural indicators of an alien nation whose territorial incursions were being actively resisted by Wales at the time that the book was made.[16]

It is, therefore, improbable that the book was made in Wales. It has suffered heavy losses: the back portion containing the end of St. Luke's Gospel and the whole of St. John's is missing and was probably ripped away; the front of the volume lacks prefatory matter, canon tables, and a St. Matthew miniature and commences with the decorated incipit of his Gospel. The Matthew incipit is badly worn, to the point of near illegibility, although what remains is clearly modeled upon the corresponding "Liber" page of the Lindisfarne Gospels. The discoloration and wear indicates that this page probably served as the book's outer cover for a time. During the ninth century someone attempted to improve the

Decorated Chi-rho Chad/Lichfield/Llandeilo Gospels (Lichfield Cathedral Library, MS 1, page 5)

appearance of what was now the frontispiece by reasserting some of the details of the design and filling the bow of the "b" with a pellet design, resembling Viking age metalwork, in black and white pigments. The likely scenario suggested by these features is that the book was subjected to spoliation between the time it was made, in the mid-eighth century, and the ninth century and torn asunder, perhaps to remove a treasure binding. The Book of Kells was likewise stolen from the shrine of St. Columba at Kells later in the Middle Ages and later found abandoned in a ditch—without its precious binding.[17] It was probably taken from the Columban house for which it was originally made, perhaps during the Viking raids of the ninth century, and was brought to Wales, where it was redeemed for the Christian church by Gelhi and installed as the oathbook of St. Teilo during the golden age of Welsh lawgiving.

By the mid-tenth century the ascendancy of Llandeilo was in decline and the book was taken out of Wales. The continued insertion of marginal inscriptions and documents shows that it was taken to Lichfield Cathedral. The earliest inscription names "Wynsige presul" who was probably the bishop of Lichfield of that name who came into office in 963. In the lower part of page 141, beneath the documents relating to Gelhi and his family, a late tenth-century Anglo-Saxon hand inscribed a series of Old English names, some incorporating Greek letters, that probably commemorate notable deceased members of the Lichfield community. The book has remained there for over a millennium, save for a short time in the seventeenth century when it was removed by Precentor Walter Higgins to escape the ravages of iconoclast Roundheads during the sieges of Lichfield in 1643–46. It was returned by the Duchess of Somerset in 1673 and is still used at the installation of Lichfield's bishops.

It has often been asserted, most frequently by representatives of Lichfield Cathedral, that the Gospelbook was at Lichfield earlier in its history, before it was taken into Wales. Such claims have not really rehearsed the arguments in support of the premise, or against it. However, a piece of evidence has just come to light that might lend them credibility. In 2004 what is thought to be the shrine of St. Chad was excavated under the crossing of the Cathedral by Cathedral Archaeologist Warwick Rodwell.[18] Carefully deposited in a pit beside it were fragments of a fine sculpture of an angel, carved around 800, which probably formed half of an Annunciation panel on the gable end of a stone house-shaped shrine. This is likely to have been an enhancement to the original seventh-century wooden house-shaped shrine of St. Chad to which Bede refers in the *Historia Ecclesiastica*,[19] added at a time when Lichfield was temporarily elevated to the status of England's third archbishopric, at the center of the powerful kingdom of Mercia.[20] Chad was one of the four Northumbrian brothers who trained on Holy Island and who were sent as missionaries to South Yorkshire and Southumbria. He established his *cathedra* at Lichfield in 667 and died there in 672. His shrine became an important focus of pilgrimage and, like the shrine of St. Cuthbert on Holy Island, would in its heyday have had a great Gospelbook displayed on its altar—the equivalent of the Lindisfarne Gospels. What more fitting than that the cult book of St. Chad should have paid tribute, in its visual allusions, to the great treasure of his home monastery, or that its wider cultural influences should have come from the Columban *paruchia* from which they both, ultimately, hailed, or that its text should have been that in general use in such circles, rather than a "new" edition introduced to Holy Island via Wearmouth-Jarrow? This is all circumstantial evidence, of course, but Lichfield certainly fits the bill as the sort of center for which the Lichfield/ Llandeilo Gospels would have been made.

To return to the Lichfield angel. The damage it sustained was inflicted during the ninth century, probably at the time that Lichfield was taken by the Vikings. At sometime between the mid-ninth century raids and before the cathedral was revived during the early tenth century the shrine was despoiled and broken and someone carefully gathered up some fragments of its sculpture and buried them in the hypogeum of the shrine itself, placing them face downward on a rubble core. This recalls Jewish practice in which any flawed ritual objects and texts were ritually deposited in a Genizah room, rather than being dishonored by being thrown away.[21] This respectful act ensured the rare survival of the pigments with which the sculpture was originally painted. These are a symphony of purple, pink, white, and black—a palette that does not recommend itself for use on stone, unlike more primary or earth-based colors. This unusual palette finds its closest parallel in the decorated pages of the Lichfield/Llandeilo Gospels. I have suggested elsewhere that its use may recall not only the Late Antique and Byzantine practice of inscribing sacred text upon purple pages, summoning up the color symbolism associated with the imperial dignity—"born to the purple," but also Bedan exegesis. In his Commentary on the Tabernacle Bede compares the shades of purple, lilac, and white of the textiles in the Holy of Holies of the Temple of Jerusalem to the aspirations of the souls of the just.[22] Might the distinctive coloration of the Gospelbook have been intended to recall such thought, and if it graced the church containing St. Chad's shrine, might this also have been reflected on the sculptures that were added to the shrine half a century later, around 800, so that the two visible manifestations of sanctity complemented one another?

Another book that was made at Lichfield in the early ninth century, the prayerbook of Bishop Æthelwald of Lichfield (818–30) that is known as the Book of Cerne due to its provenance after it was evacuated from Viking-held Lichfield, also paid tribute to earlier monuments of the cathedral.[23] For its St. John miniature features a resplendent purple, white and black eagle symbol that is the closest stylistic parallel for the Lichfield angel and that recalls the appearance of the earlier Gospelbook.[24] The Lichfield angel and the Book of Cerne together show that Lichfield was not only an important ecclesiastical focus but that it was also a major artistic center during the Insular period. It would undoubtedly have possessed impressive biblical and liturgical manuscripts and, although it cannot be conclusively proven, one of these was probably the Lichfield/Llandeilo Gospels.

We do not know how this Gospelbook traveled between Wales and England, whether as diplomatic gift between kings or clerics, or as the booty of Vikings or other raiders. What we do know is that it played an important role in the lives of the communities of both Lichfield and Llandeilo and in the cultural history of early England and Wales. Such books were made to speak to all; they are not the sole property of any one place in which they have rested during their journeys—they transcend regional and temporal considerations and in a spiritual and cultural sense they belong to us all.

Notes

1. For an overview of the various scholarly debates, see Michelle P. Brown, "Fifty Years of Insular Palaeography, 1953–2003: An Outline of Some Landmarks and Issues," in *Archiv für Diplomatik. Schriftsgeschichte Siegel- und Wappenkunde*, ed. W. Koch and T. Kölzer (Köln: Böhlau, 2004): 277–326.

2. On the Lichfield Gospels' provenance, see J. J. G. Alexander, *Insular Manuscripts, 6th to the 9th Centuries*, A Survey of Manuscripts Illuminated in the British Isles 1 (London: Harvey Miller, 1976), no. 21. See also D. Jenkins and M. E. Owen, "The Welsh Marginalia in the Lichfield Gospels. Part I," *Cambridge Medieval Celtic Studies* 5 (1983): 37–66, and "The Welsh Marginalia in the Lichfield Gospels. Part II: The 'Surexit' Memorandum," *Cambridge Medieval Celtic Studies* 7 (1984): 91–120.

3. On the Lindisfarne Gospels (British Library, Cotton MS D.iv), see Michelle P. Brown, *The Lindisfarne Gospels: Society, Spirituality and the Scribe* (London: British Library and Toronto: University of Toronto Press, 2003).

4. Brown, *Lindisfarne Gospels*; R. G. Gameson, "The Royal 1.B.vii Gospels and English Book Production in the 7th and 8th Centuries," in Richard Gameson, ed., *The Early Medieval Bible*, Cambridge Studies in Palaeography and Codicology (Cambridge: Cambridge University Press, 1994), 24–52. For details of both volumes, see Alexander, *Insular Manuscripts*, nos. 9 and 20.

5. Vrej Nersessian, *Treasures from the Ark: 1700 Years of Armenian Christian Art*, British Library Exhibition Catalogue (London: British Library, 2001); Roger Wieck, ed., *Treasures in Heaven: Armenian Art, Religion and Society*, Exhibition Catalogue, Pierpont Morgan Library (Princeton: Princeton University Press, 1994).

6. Stockholm, Kungliga Biblioteket MS A.135; see Alexander, *Insular Manuscripts*, no. 30.

7. Wendy Davies, *Wales in the Early Middle Ages*, Studies in the Early History of Britain (Leicester: Leicester University Press, 1982).

8. On the evacuation of books from Mercia see Michelle. P. Brown, *The Book of Cerne: Prayer, Patronage and Power in Ninth-Century England* (London: British Library and Toronto: University of Toronto Press, 1996); Simon Keynes and Michael Lapidge, trans. and eds., *Alfred the Great: Asser's Life of King Alfred and Other Contemporary Sources* (Harmondsworth: Penguin, 1983); Helmut Gneuss, *Books and Libraries in Early England*, Variorum Collected Studies (Aldershot, Hants: Variorum, 1996).

9. David N. Dumville and Michael Lapidge, eds., *Gildas: New Approaches*, Studies in Celtic History 5 (Woodbridge, Suffolk: Boydell and Brewer, 1984).

10. Hereford Cathedral Library, MS P.I.2; see Alexander, *Insular Manuscripts*, no. 38.

11. Durham Cathedral Library, MS B.II.30, see Alexander, *Insular Manuscripts*, no. 17; Richard N. Bailey, *The Durham Cassiodorus*, Jarrow Lecture Series,

Newcastle upon Tyne, 1978, repr. in *Bede and His World: The Jarrow Lectures, 1958–93*, vol. 2, ed. Michael Lapidge, Variorum Collected Studies (Aldershot, Hants: Variorum, 1994); Michelle P. Brown, "'Excavating' Northumbrian Manuscripts: What Can They Tell Us?" in *New Directions in Northumbrian Archaeology* S. Newton et al., ed. (forthcoming).

12. Paris, Bibliothèque Nationale de France MS lat. 9389, see Alexander, *Insular Manuscripts*, no. 11.

13. In T. D. Kendrick, T. J. Brown, R. L. S. Bruce Mitford et al., *Evangeliorum Quattuor Codex Lindisfarnensis*, 3 vols. (Olten and Lausanne: Urs Graf, 1956–60); Brown, *Lindisfarne Gospels*.

14. Patrick McGurk, *Latin Gospel Books from A.D. 400 to A.D. 800* (Paris and Brussels: Aux Éditions Érasme, 1961), no. 16; Brown, *Lindisfarne Gospels*.

15. Fred Orton and Ian Wood, with Clare A. Lees, *Fragments of History: Rethinking the Ruthwell and Bewcastle Monuments* (Manchester: Manchester University Press, 2007); for an alternative interpretation of these pieces in a monastic context, see Éamonn Ó Carragáin, *Ritual and the Rood: Liturgical Images and the Old English Poems of the Dream of the Rood Tradition* (London: British Library and Toronto: University of Toronto Press, 2005).

16. On Anglo-Welsh relations during this period, see Davies, *Early Medieval Wales* and David N. Dumville, *Britons and Anglo-Saxons in the Early Middle Ages*, Collected Studies Series (Aldershot, Hants: Variorum, 1993).

17. Dublin, Trinity College Library, MS 58; see Peter Fox, *The Book of Kells*, 2 vols., facsimile (Lucerne: Faksimile Verlag, 1990); Alexander, *Insular Manuscripts*, no. 52.

18. See Warwick Rodwell, "Lichfield Cathedral: Archaeology of the Nave Sanctuary," *Church Archaeology* 7–9 (2003–5), 1–6 and front cover; see also notices in *Current Archaeology* 205 (2005): 3211–12 and *British Archaeology* (2006): 6–7.

19. On Chad and his mission, see *Bede's Ecclesiastical History of the English People: With Bede's Letter to Egbert and Cuthbert's Letter on the Death of Bede*, trans. Leo Sherley-Price; rev. R. E. Latham; intro. and notes by D. H. Farmer (London: Penguin, 1990), 42, 181–83, 196–97, and 206–11.

20. On early Lichfield and its place within Mercian history, see Michelle P. Brown and Carol A. Farr, eds., *Mercia, an Anglo-Saxon Kingdom in Europe* (Leicester: Leicester University Press, 2001); Nicholas Brooks, *The Early History of the Church of Canterbury: Christ Church from 597 to 1066*, Studies in the Early History of Britain (Leicester: Leicester University Press, 1984); Ann Dornier, ed., *Mercian Studies* (Leicester: Leicester University Press, 1977); Ian W. Walker, *Mercia and the Making of England* (Stroud: Sutton, 2000).

21. On the Cairo Genizah, founded in 882, see Michelle P. Brown, ed., *In the Beginning: Bibles before the Year 1000* (Washington, D. C.: Freer/Sackler, 2006).

22. Bede, *De Tabernaculo*, Book II; see Dom David Hurst, ed., Bede, *De Templo et De Tabernaculo*, *Corpus Christianorum Series Latina* 119a

(Turnhout: Brepols, 1969); for discussion of this point, see Michelle P. Brown, *Lindisfarne Gospels*, 277 and *Book of Cerne*, 123–24. For a Raman laser analysis of the pigments used in the Lindisfarne Gospels and other books of the period, see Brown, *Lindisfarne Gospels*, 275–99 and Appendix I. The purple pigment in the Lichfield/Llandeilo Gospels is likely, by analogy, to be an organic pigment extracted from a plant such as turnsole (crozophora tinctoria) that can range from red to blue depending on the amount of acidity or alkalinity that is added. Initial research by Emily Howe of Birmingham Museum Services indicates that the purple pigments on the angel sculpture are probably metal oxides, more suitable for application to stone than the manuscript equivalents.

23. Cambridge, University Library, MS Ll.1.10; see Michelle P. Brown, *The Book of Cerne: Prayer, Patronage and Power in Ninth-Century England* (London: British Library and Toronto: University of Toronto Press, 1996); Alexander, *Insular Manuscripts*, no. 66.

24. Michelle P. Brown, "The Lichfield Angel and the Manuscript Context: Lichfield as a Centre of Insular Art," *Journal of the British Archaeological Association* 160.1 (2007): 8–19.

CHAPTER 4

"FEORRAN BROHT": EXETER BOOK RIDDLE 12 AND THE COMMODIFICATION OF THE EXOTIC

Peter Robson

Je ne suis pas une femme, je suis un monde.

Flaubert, La Tentation de Saint Antoine

In the past ten years, the Exeter Book's hitherto somewhat overlooked Riddle 12 has become rather a cause celebre in the realm of Old English poetic scholarship, thanks to the combination of its apparently sensational, and salacious, subject matter with critical issues of class, sex, and gender. Riddle 12 is something of a peculiarity among its fellows and is consequently quite difficult to classify as a particular type or subgenre of riddle. The problem arises from the fact that the riddle seems to fall neatly into two halves, the first, running from lines 1 to 7a, taking the form of the classic "speaking subject" riddle, in which the subject of the enigma invites us to speculate on its identity, and the second, running from lines 7b to 15b, which seems to include a second layer of riddling, this time of the double entendre type. The first part of the riddle involves the subject, in this case, an ox, describing its uses before and after death:

> fotum ic fere   foldan slite
> grene wongas   þenden ic gæst bere
> gif me feorh losað   fæste binde
> swearte wealas   hwilum sellan men
> hwilum ic deorum   drincan selle
> beorne[e] of bosme   hwilum mec bryd triedeð
> felawlonc fotum.[1]

[On foot I go   tear up the earth
green fields   when I bear a spirit
if life slips from me   I bind tight
dark *wealas*   sometimes better men
sometimes to the brave   I give drink
to men from my bosom   sometimes the bride treads me
very proud with feet.][2]

This first part of the riddle opens with a series of relatively straightforward descriptions of the uses of the ox: ploughing green fields, when alive, and after death providing leather, for the making of bonds, a drinking bottle, and shoes, or perhaps a skin floor covering. We shall worry the bone of the troublesome *wealas* later, and attempt to establish whether it is intended to convey the idea of Welshmen, slaves, or indeed both; but for the moment it is worth noting that the riddle to this point is reasonably unremarkable, and falls comfortably within the bounds of the standard "speaking subject" riddle. The second part of the riddle, however, that has excited a great deal of critical attention is much less easy of interpretation, to the point that it is even rather less than clear what aspect of the riddle's solution is intended to be revealed/concealed by the lines in question:

hwilum feorran broht
wonfeax wale   wegeð ond þyð
dol druncmennen   deorcum nihtum
wæteð in wætre   wyrmeð hwilum
fægre to fyre   me on fæðme sticaþ
hygegalan hond   hwyrfeð geneahhe
swifeð me geond sweartne   saga hwæt ic hatte
þe ic lifgende   lond reafige
ond æfter deaþe   dryhtum þeowig

[sometimes brought from afar
a dark-haired *wale*   lifts and presses me
a stupid drunk maid   in the dark nights
wets me in water   sometimes warms me
fairly by the fire   me into the depths thrusts
the high-spirited hand   shakes me about
turns me through the black   say what I am called
who in life   plunders the land
and after death   serve men.]

The second part of the riddle differs from the first in the obvious manner that it seems to contain only one description of an item pointing to the solution, the role of which the speaker takes, whereas, as we have seen, the first part contains four such descriptions. This is in itself enough to indicate that we are in a somewhat different area here, and alert us to the difference in nature between these lines and those that precede them. The devotion of thirteen half-lines to this extended description is enough to make the second part of Riddle 12 stand almost as a riddle in its own right, and it is certainly the case that this section is extremely enigmatic of interpretation. As we will see, scholarly attention has focused on the interpretation of the item being described in these lines, and on the action being performed by the *wonfeax wale*, as well as on the social and ethnic identity of this character. The existence of the "subriddle" in the second half of Riddle 12 has made it difficult to approach the poem as a whole, for the whole does not fit neatly into the class of double entendre riddles in which the last thirteen half-lines would seem to be most at home.

These introductory remarks have drawn attention, not least by the decision to lay the text of the poem out in two halves, to a perceived discontinuity in the riddle text. The overall aim of this chapter, however, is quite the opposite: to attempt to synthesize these interpretations of the second part of the riddle, and to attempt to explain the cultural work that is effected by the riddle as a whole, drawing jointly on discourses of gender, class, ethnicity, and sexuality as they are represented in these thirty enigmatic half-lines.

The Background of Vocabulary: Wealas and the Welsh in Old English

One of the signal pleasures of the Anglo-Saxon language is, it is worth remembering, its remarkable economy, which in poetic terms is capable of surpassing the sum of its parts and creating a detailed web of reference and allusion; trains of memory and significance sparked by a single word. This feature is also perhaps the most dangerous potential stumbling block for a translator, however, as the likelihood of seizing on precisely the right nuance for a particular occurrence of one word, in context, can never be quite certain. It is precisely this problem we come up against when examining this riddle, in the case of the repeated word *wealh*. And this is a significant word in the riddle, especially in the context of this chapter, for without it, and without the meaning we choose to assign to it, an analysis of Riddle 12 would have no place in this collection. Not for the first time, and assuredly not for the last, the most basic interpretation of an Old English poem is contingent on a single word.

It may be worth, then, exploring the potential significances of the word *wealh*, and establish whether they can shed any light on our reading of the riddle as a whole. Bosworth and Toller cite two basic meanings for the unadorned *wealh*: "foreigner," and most specifically a British Celtic foreigner, and "slave."

Margaret Lindsay Faull provides perhaps the most extensive account of the semantic territory covered by Old English *wealh*, covering the territory of ethnic designation, class designation, and the verbal and adjectival forms such as *wealian* and *wealhwordum* that I will discuss below.[3] Interestingly, Faull also deals with the incorporation of the term into Old English proper names, often among the aristocracy, arguing that this may initially have signaled mixed parentage, but that later the usage became indiscriminate. If we wished to distance ourselves from the idea that *wealh* must always signify a Welshman and/or a slave, Old English proper name usage would provide usable evidence for this.

Where we begin to enter more interesting territory, however, is with compound words containing the *wealh* element, of which Bosworth and Toller list six, as follows: *wealhbasu*, a color word meaning "foreign" scarlet; *wealhafoc*, a type of bird of prey; *wealhnutu*, a "foreign" nut, or, more helpfully, a walnut; *wealhmore*, a "foreign" root, *wealhland*, meaning a foreign land, and sometimes specifically Normandy; and, finally *wealhword*, which the dictionary translates as a "wanton word." This last definition seems to be categorically removed from the others, as it appears not to involve a conception of "foreignness," but instead to involve a different sense of outsidership.

Bosworth and Toller translate *wealhword* as "wanton word." The use of "wanton" as a defining word proves somewhat frustrating. Though it be undeniably polite, it offers little idea of what the lexicographer believes the Old English to mean. The context offered for the usage of the term is as follows, in a fragment that follows a tenth-century Latin penitentiary: "Ic eom ondetta ðæt ic onfeng on mine muð wealworda" [I confess that I have allowed wonton words into my mouth].[4] The very presence of the concept of "wanton words" in a penitentiary tells us that they are indeed sinful, and worthy of confessing, and it is tempting to think of them as possibly sexual in nature, but unfortunately the penitentiaries do not make their nature clear.

Whether or not *wealhword* is related to our usage of *wealh* may be in dispute, but what is indisputable is that it does relate to *wealian*, which Bosworth and Toller define as "to be bold, wanton." Bosworth and Toller's definition of *wealhword* as "wanton word" tells us as much about the Victorian values of the lexicographers as it does about the Old English word, for it is left entirely to the reader of the dictionary to decide what sort of wantonness is under discussion, and to decide whether the Old English word is to be considered in a sexualized context or not. While it is of interest to a historian of nineteenth-century morals, the entry is singularly unhelpful as far as a tight understanding of the word in context goes. The context for *wealian* is revealing, as it occurs in Ælfric's Sermon on Ash Wednesday:

> He cwæð þæt he nolde ond wealode mid wordum, and sæde þæt he wolde his wifes brucan on unalyfedum timan.[5]
>
> [He said that he would not {go to the Ash Wednesday service}, and spoke shamelessly, and said that he would use his wife at the forbidden time.]

Ælfric's use of *wealian* tends toward a suggestion that the *wealhwordum* in this context would be constituted by the man's promise that he will violate accepted conduct by continuing to have sexual relations with his wife during the period the church forbids it. This tends to suggest that words that vaunt unlawful, perhaps one might say wanton, sexual desires of this kind are among the category of things covered by the conception of otherness delineated under *wealh*. It is far from the scope of this article to make claims for the etymological relationship between the verb *wealian* and the noun *wealh*,[6] but what we can claim is that the terms are sufficiently similar as to be mutually evocative.

The compound words that make use the *wealh* component seem to be related principally to conceptions of foreignness, descriptions of items, and concepts that come from abroad, or at least are not native to Anglo-Saxon England. The conception of these items seems to be entirely unrelated to perceptions of the British, and the items in question, walnuts, exotic birds, and dyes seem to imply an origin much further afield than the Welsh marches. Where we find the *wealh* component in relation to a specific non-English country, it refers, not to Cambria, but to Normandy. It begins to seem, therefore, that we must factor this sense of the word into our reading of the riddle, and begin to stray a little from our initial conception of slaves and Welshmen into the realm of the exotic. The lexis of this individual word, we can see, is polysemous, and we must be careful to bring all the potential nuances of *wealh* to bear on our reading of the riddle.

The use of the term *wealh* in Riddle 12, then, requires exposure to all the elements considered above before we can begin to unravel the set of thoughts and ideas it evokes. A reading that takes on board only the conception of slavery, and/ or of Welshness, will be the poorer for missing out on the possibilities that the term can evoke a nonspecific "exotic" foreignness, as related to imported commodities such as scarlet dyes and foreign foodstuffs. Likewise, the possibilities offered by the parallels to *wealian* and *wealhwordum* seem to point to an association with transgressive language and behavior that is certain to affect a reading of the riddle. So, far from solving the problems presented by the question of how to read the riddles' uses of *wealh*, an examination of the vocabulary background of the word has opened new issues to be dealt with. Whether the word first means Welshman or slave, and thus whether Welshmen are slaves, or slaves Welshmen, becomes colored by the possibilities of meaning offered by other instances of the term in compound usage. While we might have thought of the problem as being one of identity, and whether we are really dealing with real Welshmen in this riddle, the intervention of these other instances forces us to consider the term as potentially multifaceted, partaking of slavery, of Celtic ethnicity, and of a generic alterity both in terms of origin and conduct. While a few pages ago we might not have considered Welshness as constituting a particularly "exotic" category, in the sense in which we use the word, it certainly seems that in the Old English vocabulary, exoticism may well be one of the meanings that comes under the *wealh* spectrum.

It ought to be the case in normal speech and writing that context should make everything clear, and allow us to establish without thinking that aspect of an unclear piece of vocabulary to prioritize. In dealing with Old English, however, none of us, however skilled, can have the native-speaker insight that allows such automatic editing to take place. This lack on the one hand can create problems of interpretation, but on the other hand leads to the examination of subtleties of meaning, and for anyone attempting a critical analysis is both a curse and a blessing. This is especially true in the case of riddles, where it can be taken for granted that the subject will be possessed of more than one character, and where the two potential solutions to the riddle must be borne in mind simultaneously.

Riddle 12: A Critical History

The first major article to make an attempt to read Riddle 12 cogently as something more than a curiosity is John Tanke's attempt to examine the intersecting ideologies that limit and describe the female figure of the final section of the poem.[7] Relying on a conception of Riddle 12 as a double entendre riddle, Tanke suggests that the function of the text is to play innocent and obscene interpretations of the enigma against one another, for the purpose of comic and social relief. For Tanke, the genre of the double entendre riddle is the ridicule of the law, as socially prescribed, in order to attain a comic effect by revealing the sexual desires that lie beneath the constructed norm, creating a "liberating" effect. However, asks Tanke:

> What do we make of the fact that the figure whose representation elicits this laughter is herself a slave? That the figure used to ridicule the law is herself ridiculed? If the double-entendre facilitates a liberation of repression, does this liberation also depend on the enslavement of the "dark-haired servant woman"? If so, then the riddlers' ostensibly antagonistic relationship to the law is again called into question, for they would seem to be invoking the law even as they ostensibly flout it. In fact our reading of Riddle 12 will suggest that their interest is not to flout the law at all, but rather to get the *wale* to flout it for them.[8]

Tanke's thesis on the latter part of Riddle 12 suggests that the casting of a marginal character as the one who violates accepted sexual conduct serves the purpose of providing a release from repressive sexual mores, while delegating responsibility for the release to one who is placed so low that the writ of acceptable behavior need not include her. Tanke accepts that the riddle does not deal with female sexuality in a healthy, representative manner, and points out that the female figure is portrayed in a manner in which she is circumscribed by the discourses of race, class, and gender:

> I have endeavoured to show that, far from accurately representing the margins of Anglo-Saxon society, Riddle 12 makes their very marginality a prime feature of its rhetoric. The intersecting and mutually reinforcing margins of race, class, and gender leave their traces in the *wonfeax wale* as a literary figure. This figure is the locus of an extraordinary and paradoxical fantasy: that of a subject so enslaved to the law that she is capable of toppling it.[9]

The implication of Tanke's remarks, however, still runs along the lines of arguing that the riddle performs the function, at some level, of flouting the "law," even though the transgression is committed on the riddler's, and the audience's, behalf. Tanke's reading of the riddle is essentially based on the perception that the double entendre riddle functions in a particular manner: it reveals the sexual thoughts of men, creating humor by exposing them to public view. While Tanke modulates this view by taking into account the intersection of prescriptive discourses that inhabit this riddle, what he does not do is to explain where the joke lies in all this.

According to Rudolf Gleissner, the defining characteristic of the double entendre riddle is the ridicule of established conduct, which he refers to as the "law":

> The joke, in order to be understood and in order to function properly, needs the law, which it opposes and assaults. On the other hand, there must already be a certain detachment from the established law, which allows it to be ridiculed.[10]

For Tanke, this distance is provided in our riddle by the persona of the female speaker, whose lowly social position, combined with her sex and her ethnicity, is sufficient to distance her both from us, and from the "law," so that transgression may be accomplished without concern for reproach. His application of Gleissner's thesis to Riddle 12, however, does not go so far as to engage with the possibility that Riddle 12 is not a double entendre riddle at all, in the sense that Gleissner suggests.

Of course, Riddle 12 is predicated, like all riddles, on the notion that the central figure is not what it appears to be; it would hardly be a riddle if it were not. Likewise, the section that deals with the *dol druncmennan* and her activities with what may or may not be a leather bottle, appears to contain exactly the sort of sexual conundrum one might expect from a riddle of the double entendre type. However, the approach taken by Tanke is relevant only to *part* of this riddle, and a similar imbalance exists in the approaches of Higley and Rulon-Miller. The inconvenient presence of the first half of the poem, which emphatically does not deal with sexual double entendre, makes the interpretation of the second half of the poem, and indeed the poem as a whole even more troublesome than it otherwise might be.

Most riddles of the double entendre type function in a manner in which a simple object is described in terms that obscure its true identity, and present it in a sexualized light. In Riddle 12, however, not only is the object somewhat odd, being at once a living creature and a material for manufacture, but the extended description is fragmented into five parts, the last of which appears to be highly obscure: a riddle that requires solving in its own right before application to the main solution. The central object of the riddle, the Ox, is not presented, as are the Onion or the Key in Riddles 25 and 44, as a "double exposure," which shows at once a sexualized and an "innocent" object. It is rather the action performed with or on the object that is presented in a sexualized manner. In the Onion riddle, we are presented with an obvious sexualization of the riddle's subject, in which the Onion appears as a phallus, growing erect and perhaps ejaculating under the ministrations of a woman, whereas in Riddle 12 the object remains passive, and is not itself sexualized in any way. The Ox takes on the role first of itself, alive, and then of its uses after death in the leather trade: thongs for binding, a drinking vessel, shoes, or perhaps a hide carpet, and finally what may be (once again) a leather bottle.

Ann Harleman Stewart's reading of the Exeter Book's sexual riddles points out that the "Onion" riddle itself

> ...not only adorns its careful balancing act with [...] a series of tiny subplots—but also leads up to the surprise of a slapstick conclusion. It is comic rather than crude, ribald rather than lascivious, with a sort of affectionate ridicule that is the opposite of prurience.[11]

Indeed, the description of a series of tiny subplots leading to a slapstick conclusion could fit very well to our riddle, and certainly the shape-shifting nature of the Ox-Leather ranks with the most inventive of the Old English riddles, but it is certainly worth noting that the cloaking of the sexualized onion is of a different order from the representation of the Ox-Leather, which is not clouded in obscurity, willing us to misread, but rather being employed usefully, as the riddle points out: *þe ic lifgende lond reafige, ond æfter deaþe dryhtum þeowig.* It is the human "user" of one part of the riddle who is sexualized, rather than the object, and the double entendre, such as it is, centers on the action performed rather than on the object itself. Stewart expresses doubt about the inclusion of Riddle 12 in the genre of double entendre riddles in which Tanke would like to place it, considering it at best a "borderline case,"[12] and perhaps we would do best to agree. Certainly, the classic form of the sexual double entendre riddle is not the form of Riddle 12, which has a far broader scope.

Of course, Tanke and Stewart are at odds in their readings of the riddle's sexuality (if we can legitimately apply Stewart's reading to this semiexcluded text), and Tanke's conception of the construction of sexual ideology through the employment of marginalizing discourse could hardly be less compatible with Stewart's vision of a liberated sexuality that is the "opposite of prurience."

If we are to adduce a double entendre in Riddle 12, then it is not the one that functions in the healthily "ribald" manner that Stewart suggests. It is difficult to quantify the values placed on terms such as "ribald" and "lascivious," and harder still to know how to decide whether an Old English audience would have considered a riddle one rather than another of these things. Indeed, the interpretation of the various aspects of the double entendre present in the Onion riddle that Stewart discusses could lead to quite different conclusions from the exposition of healthy sexuality that Stewart adduces, dependant on the interpreter's point of view. The riddle's final clause, in particular, is clear as far as the "Onion" side is concerned, but rather less so as regards the "obscene" interpretation, which includes a number of possibilities, some of which would certainly fall into the categories of both comedy and crudity.[13]

We may not, then, wish to draw ourselves into a situation in which this "must" be read as a double entendre riddle, and may prefer to think of it as a riddle *with* doubles entendres. Doing so liberates us from the constraint of having to follow Gleissner's "laughter" line, and to search for the manner in which the riddle's exposition of sexuality provides release from the strictures of morality.

Nina Rulon-Miller's interpretation of Riddle 12 differs from Tanke's explication of the riddle in that she denies the presence of the sort of comic release that Tanke finds in the text. Asking "What's so funny about female masturbation?"[14] Rulon-Miller embarks on an exploration of the riddle in which she finds that the sexual act performed, rather than providing comic relief "elicits its narrator's sneer" and by extension, ours.

The heart of Rulon-Miller's interpretation of the riddle is her suggestion that the precise nature of the "innocent" interpretation of the riddle can be identified as the *cuir bouilli* method of leather production, in which the leather is soaked, moulded, and then dried over a fire, before being finished with resin, beeswax, and soot.[15] The identification of precise versions of the innocent and obscene solutions to the riddle enable Rulon-Miller to suggest a response to Tanke's question of why the woman is condemned, suggesting that the intersection of class, gender, race, and lack of propriety are coupled with the guilt of the narrator at having "allowed himself to indulge in and share an act of imaginative voyeurism of which he is ashamed."[16] For Rulon-Miller, the subject of the poem is less to do with the contrast Tanke adduces between liberated and restrained sexuality, but rather to do with manner in which the characters of the riddle, the Ox, the *wealas*, the *wale,* and the narrator himself, are all "bound and fettered, they are 'slaves to God' and 'live under the yoke of the Rule,'" quoting the Benedictine *Regularis concordia.*

While Rulon-Miller's attempt to provide a cogent reading of the entire riddle is useful, the adduction of "fettered desire" as a secondary solution does not entirely embrace all the figures of the riddle, and does not attempt to rationalize those characters that are not obviously "bound" in this way.

Sarah Higley's reading of the riddle suggests as Tanke does, to an extent, that the riddle is essentially in intersection of discourses, creating a marginalized figure in the form of the *dol druncmennan.* Higley, however, comes closest to the suggestion that the concentration on this portion of the riddle can be misleading to an interpretation of the whole, and closest to the suggestion that the poem may be genuinely racist in tone. Higley draws a comparison between Riddle 12, and a figure that appears in Walter Hilton's *Scale of Perfection*, noting that the two figures seems to betray similar concerns:

> Although *The Scale of Perfection* post-dates the Exeter Book by several hundred years, I find its preoccupation with a mysterious dark idol, emblem of self and sinfulness, to be peculiarly resonant with the distracting, mysterious, and dark body of the *wale*, perhaps reflecting a corresponding Anglo-Saxon fear of foreign faces, foreign colouring and the foreign terrain of female sexuality.[17]

The presentation of the distracting image that interferes with the contemplation of Christ in Walter Hilton's *The Scale of Perfection* as a dark image redolent of Outremer exoticism and indicative of racial prejudices provides Higley with a new way of examining the *wale* as she appears in Riddle 12. From this perspective, she may function as representative of Anglo-Saxon worries regarding the epitome of alterity presented by the sexually active foreign woman, who, as we have already seen, is a highly marginalized figure. What Higley does not pursue, however, is the possibility that the alterity of the figure may imply not only a fear of otherness, but also an explicitly sexual desire, which seeks to subsume and rationalize the unfamiliar by exploiting it sexually.

On the other hand, Higley's linking of the two figures allows her by analogy to view the woman of the riddle as a counterpart to the interfering image in Hilton:

> Innuendo raises questions about the central and the peripheral, the subject and the margin. The joke of the riddle is that it makes us compromise our sense of the order of things: what should be peripheral (what the woman is doing instead of what the solution to the riddle is) becomes central, causing us to contemplate something that we, pious monks that we are, would do better to ignore. [...] the final joke may be that the clues to the prurient meanings of these riddles are not nearly so well-organized as the clues to the innocent readings, and we are getting into a sweat over "nought." Again, I am reminded of that "murk ymage" of Hilton's, that *sweartne*, that abject thing that is nothing and that will draw us away from divine contemplation, that reveals the wrong text, [...] yet which demands our examination and handling because of what it reveals to us about ourselves, as much as what it suggests about medieval xenophobia and misogyny.[18]

Higley's conclusion is interesting in that it takes account of the existence of the remainder of the riddle, which Tanke does not engage with, and suggests the possibility that the distraction provided by the brief aside on masturbation may well function, for us, as the "joke" of the riddle, in that we engage so strongly and exclusively with the "controversial" and "problematic" section of the text that we lose perspective in dealing with the remainder.

Bearing these interpretations in mind, let us go on to discuss the manner in which these intersections of class, gender, sexuality, and race do intersect in the riddle, and what this might suggest about the overall nature of the discourse of which the riddle is a part.

Sex and Alterity: A New Reading of Riddle 12

Given the amount of thought devoted to Riddle 12 in the discussions recounted above, and the seemingly universal agreement that there is a connection displayed in the riddle between gender, ethnicity, and sexuality, it seems remarkable that no proposition has been made regarding the manner in which this connection takes place, and most interestingly, the cultural work that such connections perform. In what follows, it is our aim to consider the possibility that these intersections, and their cultural work might interestingly be considered from a colonialist perspective, and analogized with later forms of discourse that are clearly delineated in the relationships between Europe and the Orient. If we can usefully apply the ideas of domination, racism, and nationalism that Edward Said adduces in his study of the European construction of "Orientalism" to the manner in which the Anglo-Saxon poet deals with a race subject to his own, we may be able to gain a clearer idea of the type of cultural effect achieved by the poem as a whole.

Of course, what Said proposes in regard of Orientalism—an entire structure of scholarship, education, and literature subtly dedicated to assertion of the primacy of Europe over its Eastern neighbors—is a very great deal more than we can expect to find in the Anglo-Saxons' approach to their British neighbours and subjects, and certainly more than we can hope to find in a single Old English poem of uncertain date, authorship, and even content. However, what we can expect to find in Anglo-Saxon literature, and in our poem, is an approach to and thus description of the British.

Anglo-Saxon literature does not shy away from dealing with the British, and indeed, as Nicholas Howe has argued, the presentation of the British in Bede's *Historia ecclesiastica*[19] provides a key part of his construction of the Anglo-Saxon migrations as a function of the divine will. Likewise, Alcuin refers to Bede in his description of the fall of Britain, which he uses as a mirror for the Viking sack of Lindisfarne in 792, urging moral reflection and reform as remedies against succumbing to the same fate as the British. This model, of using the British as a structure for Anglo-Saxon identity, as a group to define oneself against, may be helpful to our reading of the poem, for within the poem itself, the British figures represented, the *swearte wealas* (line 4) and the *wonfeax wale* (line 8), are distinguished by contrast with the non-British, presumably Anglo-Saxon figures that appear alongside them, the *sellan men* of line 4 and the *bryd* of line 6. In the first case, an explicit judgment is made on the relative qualities of the subjects, the *wealas* are clearly delineated as inferior to the *sellan men*, who may also be bound by the leather, as well as to the *deorum* to whom the riddle subject serves drink. The inferiority is clearly expressed along racial lines, with the darkness as a marker of difference. The inferior status accorded to the captives is not the result of subject status alone, as the likewise-bound *sellan men* indicate, but due specifically to their status as outsiders. Likewise, the *dol druncmennan* of line 9 is characterized by the racial signifier of her dark hair, as well as the designation *wale*, and is implicitly contrasted with the *bryd* of line 6, to whom no such epithets are applied.

The characterization of the British figures in the poem relative to their non-British counterparts must be important to any reading of this riddle, as the obvious juxtaposition of the two sets of characters demonstrates. In particular, the representation of the sexual activity of the British woman in the second part of the riddle has much to tell us about the manner in which this writer chooses to present the British, and it is at this point that some of Said's conception of the manner in which Orientalist writers present "oriental" women could be adduced as a model of the type of discourse in operation.

According to Said, for the Orientalist writer, "the Orient seems to suggest not only fecundity but sexual promise (and threat), untiring sensuality, unlimited desire, deep generative energies,"[20] and it is this approach to Oriental sexuality that allows the writer to construct an idea of the oriental woman as an object of Western sexual attention. According to Tanke's thesis on the riddle, the location of sexual activity is transposed from the mainstream to the margin in this poem, in a sense revealing the "shadow" of the Anglo-Saxon gaze, and allowing the exploration of taboo sexuality through the exploitation of a marginal figure. The revelation of sensuality and desire in this marginal figure, however, would seem to correspond as well to a thesis of objectification and erotic fantasy as to one that suggests the use of the figure to express hidden desires on the part of the audience.

Said suggests that "the association is clearly made between the Orient and the freedom of licentious sex,"[21] and it would seem to be the case here also that an association is made between the woman's subject and foreign status and her irrepressible sexual energy. The association between the woman's own darkness and the *sweartne* through which she sweeps the object in question is unavoidable: the woman herself is dark, she pursues her action in the *deorcum nihtum*, and the final activity described involves the introduction of yet another layer of darkness, which forms the sexual heart of the riddle. The sexuality represented in this riddle is very far from the healthy, open sensuality that Stewart finds in the double entendre genre, but is rather hidden, furtive, and compulsive in nature, and the interest of the poet appears prurient, rather than affectionate. The description of the woman as *dol druncmennan*, a stupid, drunken servant girl, denies the woman responsibility for her actions, in a manner that incriminates rather than absolves her from responsibility. Said cites Gustave Flaubert, writing to long-term correspondent Louise Colet that "the oriental woman is no more than a machine: she makes no distinction between one man and another man,"[22] suggesting a sexuality that is not subject to control, but is reprehensible for this, and dehumanizing, rather than a cause for celebration. The characterization of the girl in our poem as stupid and drunken encourages us to view her as similarly mindless and dehumanized, an object freely available for our contemplation and, indeed, exploitation.

If we view the woman of the poem as a "machine," whose stupid, drunken erotic act dehumanizes and objectifies her, then it could be tempting to view such a description as a function of a discourse that is geared toward a construction of Welshness, or foreignness, that involves the treatment of the woman as a sexual commodity. The view that we take of the woman in this poem is, at least partially, conditioned by the manner in which the poet presents her as marginal and disenfranchised, as lower class, and as stupid and drunk. It is also, however, conditioned by our appreciation of the lexis of the term *wealh*, however, which, as we have seen, cannot reasonably be restricted to Welshness, or even slavery. If we are to include the possible connotations of the word that we have explored above—of *wealh* as redolent not just of marginality, but of outright outsidership, foreign, and exotic—then we gain a different perception of the sort of sexual strategy in employment here. If we can read the woman as partaking of a category of objects of foreign origin, exotic dyes, birds, and foodstuffs, then we can begin to consider the riddle as a different sort of sexual game from that suggested by Tanke, one less of subversion than of erotic fantasy, in which the servant girl's masturbation becomes a commodification of the exotic, valuable for its use in creating an image of the woman as an object for sexual exploitation. The transformation of the woman into a representation of the British in general, mindlessly sexualized and subject to their own stupidity as much as English hegemony, fits happily with the view expressed in Said that orientalist discourse, in its treatment of women, offers the sort of view expressed by Flaubert in his description of the Queen of Sheba as a world, rather than a woman.[23]

The remainder of the riddle fits well into this conception of the text as part of a "colonial" Anglo-Saxon discourse relating to the circumscription of the British, with the bound passivity of the *swearte wealas* of line 4 functioning as a parallel to the enslavement of the woman to her own sexuality. The role of the riddle's subject, the leather itself, seems to be the subjection of the British characters, binding the one, and sexually enslaving the other. On the other hand, the relation of the ox-leather to the non-British characters is one of servitude, ploughing the land in lines 1–2, serving drink in line 5, and providing material for shoes, or a carpet in lines 6–7. The ox-leather functions as servant to the Anglo-Saxon characters, and master to the British, ensuring supremacy and highlighting the comparison between servant and master. If, like Sarah Higley, we can be free to impose a contemporary para-solution to the riddle, which she does in her reading of our pursuit of the "wrong" reading, then perhaps from this point of view we could suggest that the leather may represent, for us, the discourse that the poem employs in circumscribing the British and liberating the English.

Notes

I am indebted to the Lomers discussion panel, before which I presented a version of this chapter in 2005, for their fascinating and inspiring comments on potential readings of Riddle 12, and particularly for an encouraging response to the idea of the riddle as a tool of Anglo-Saxon "colonial" discourse.

1. W. S. Mackie, *The Exeter Book*, EETS os 194 (London: Oxford University Press, 1934), 45.

2. My half-line by half-line translation is intended as a gloss to the Old English for reading purposes, rather than an ideal interpretation, and attempts to be as "open" as possible.

3. M. L. Faull, "The Semantic Development of Old English *Wealh*," *Leeds Studies in English*, n.s. 8 (1974): 20–44.

4. H. Logeman, "Anglo-Saxonica Minora," *Anglia* 9 (1889): 98; H. Logeman, "Anglo-Saxonica Minora," *Anglia* 11 (1989): 98, line 37. See also Faull, "Semantic Development," 34. The dictionary supplement records a second example, in Logeman, "Anglo-Saxonica Minora," 101, in which the text

is the same as that quoted above. The two manuscripts in question (British Library Cotton Vespasian D. 20 (fol. 87) and British Library Cotton Tiberius C.1 (fols. 159b–161b) both include penitentiaries in Old English. The two texts are substantially very similar, and in the case of this phrase, identical.

5. W. W. Skeat, ed., Aelfric's Lives of Saints, 2 vols., EETS os 76, 82, 94, 114 (London: Trübner, 1881–85. 1890–1900). 1: 48–49.

6. Again, see Faull, "Semantic Development."

7. J. W. Tanke, "*Wonfeax Wale*: Ideology and Figuration in the Sexual Riddles of the Exeter Book." In *Class and Gender in Early English Literature*, ed. B. J. Harwood and G. R. Overing (Bloomington and Indianapolis, Ind.: University of Indiana Press, 1994), 22.

8. Tanke, "*Wonfeax Wale*," 30.

9. Tanke, "*Wonfeax Wale*," 39.

10. Reinhard Gleissner, *Die "Zweideutigen" Altenglischen Rätsel des Exeter Book in Ihrem Zeitgenossichen Kontext* (Frankfurt am Main: Peter Lang, 1984), 14. Translation in Tanke, 29.

11. Ann Harleman Stewart, "Double Entendre in the Old English Riddles," *Lore and Languages* 3.8 (1983): 42.

12. Stewart, "Double Entendre," 45.

13. Possibilities include the presence of tears from exertion, pain, or pleasure; and the possibility that the wetness stems from the penis itself, rather than the woman, which is what I assume Stewart suggests by a "slapstick conclusion."

14. N. Rulon-Miller, "Sexual Humour and Fettered Desire in Exeter Book Riddle 12," in *Humour in Anglo-Saxon Literature*, ed. J. Wilcox (Cambridge: D. S. Brewer, 2000), 99.

15. Rulon-Miller, "Sexual Humour," 118–21.

16. Rulon-Miller, "Sexual Humour," 123.

17. Sarah L. Higley, "The Wanton Hand: Reading and Reaching into Grammars and Bodies in Old English Riddle 12," in *Naked before God: Uncovering the Body in Anglo-Saxon England*, ed. B. C. Withers and J. Wilcox (Morgantown, W. Va.: West Virginia University Press, 2003), 31.

18. Higley, "Wanton Hand," 51.

19. Nicholas Howe, *Migration and Mythmaking in Anglo-Saxon England* (Notre Dame, Ind.: University of Notre Dame Press, 1989).

20. Edward W. Said, *Orientalism* (Harmondsworth: Penguin, 1978), 188.

21. Said, *Orientalism*, 90.

22. Gustave Flaubert to Louise Colet, quoted in Said, *Orientalism*, 187.

23. Gustave Flaubert to Louise Colet, quoted in Said, *Orientalism*, 187.

CHAPTER 5

"BY THE AUTHORITY OF THE DEVIL": THE OPERATION OF WELSH AND ENGLISH LAW IN MEDIEVAL WALES

Sara Elin Roberts

In his Hartwell Jones Memorial Lecture of the Honourable Society of Cymmrodorion in 1961, T. Jones Pierce set out an imaginary scenario where Welsh law had continued to develop, and was recognized alongside English and Scots law in the House of Lords:

> ...the potentialities of Welsh law in the thirteenth century suggest that we could have ended with three systems of jurisprudence in these islands. In which case we might today have had a distinguished specialist in Welsh law sitting alongside his English and Scottish brethren (as Lord of appeal in ordinary) in the supreme court of the United Kingdom.[1]

It would have been a third kind of law—as well as the Scottish civil law tradition, and the common law tradition in England, Welsh law would have contributed a *volksrecht* system, a law derived from the people.[2] The scenario set out by Jones Pierce would have been fantasy even by the end of the Tudor period, and the use of Welsh law in the courts in Britain was abolished with the Acts of Union in 1536. But up until then, Welsh law was in use in Wales, and it existed as a separate law, distinct from both English common law and Canon Law.

Welsh Law, or the Law of Hywel [*Cyfraith Hywel*], is attributed to King Hywel ap Cadell, or Hywel Dda (Hywel the Good) d. 949 or 950. It survives in around 40 manuscripts, dating from the mid-thirteenth to the early fifteenth century.[3] Although the manuscripts are later in date, some parts of the law contained in them may be much earlier, but it is uncertain what link, if any, Hywel Dda had personally with the law. He may have had a role to play in developing some aspects of legal activity in Wales, possibly influenced by Athelstan in England, but there is no historical evidence to link Hywel Dda to the Welsh laws.[4] The prologue to the Welsh lawbooks gives a story describing how he gathered together the nobles and learned men, lay and ecclesiastical, to the White House (taken to be Whitland) and together they discussed and brought the laws into order.[5] The prologues emphasize that the meeting was reforming existing law. This was probably an attempt to give the law a royal and ecclesiastical link, particularly as Welsh law was often under attack by the Norman clerics.[6]

The manuscripts can be separated into four redactions, or groups. Each manuscript of Welsh law is different, although the witnesses in each redaction have more in common with one another, showing similarities in both order and type.[7] The Welsh law manuscripts known at the time were edited by Aneurin Owen in 1841 and published as *Ancient Laws and Institutes of Wales*.[8] Owen gave each manuscript a letter from the English alphabet as an identifier, and the manuscripts are still referred to using those sigla. The Welsh redactions were named by Owen after geographical areas, but Wade-Evans' suggestion to name the redactions after figures given prominence in the prologues of each redaction was deemed more accurate, and so they are named Cyfnerth (Cyfn), Blegywryd (Bleg), and Iorwerth (Ior).[9] Cyfnerth has seven manuscripts, and is perhaps the loosest grouping of the three redactions, although some subgroups can be found within the seven manuscripts.[10] Cyfn is often seen to be the oldest redaction of the three, although the manuscripts are later in date than some of those in the Ior redaction. The eight manuscripts in the Ior redaction may reflect the law in Gwynedd during the reign of the two Llywelyns (Llywelyn ap Iorwerth, ca. 1194–1240 and Llywelyn ap Gruffudd, 1246–82),[11] particularly Llywelyn ap Iorwerth, and the eight manuscripts form a close group, unlike those in Cyfn and Bleg.[12] There is also a concise, perhaps revised version of the Ior redaction in one manuscript, called Llyfr Colan.[13] The largest group is Bleg, consisting of thirteen manuscripts, fairly close in order and content, but further split into two groups.[14] The Bleg texts are from south Wales, and several of the later manuscripts show signs of editing, and often contain additional material in the form of a "tail," appended to the main Bleg text. This additional material was often taken from the other redactions, but some of it may be early, and it could also contain oral sources and legal rules in the forms of triads, some models of pleadings and material for training lawyers, and fifteenth-century Welsh laws.[15] This additional material is often of practical use, and may reflect the law in action.[16] Aneurin Owen put the material found in these tails in his second volume, calling it the "Anomalous Laws."

The Latin texts of the Welsh laws are often omitted from discussions on the redactions, but rather than being a separate group, there are five groups of the Latin texts. They were probably originally translations from some sort of Welsh legal text, and Latin D was then translated back into Welsh to form the Bleg texts.[17] The Latin texts are not entirely in Latin, but are peppered with Welsh words, perhaps because there was no Latin word for some Welsh legal concepts. Latin D, in particular, has long sections left in Welsh.[18]

The law as found in the redactions and in the manuscripts can be separated into sections consisting of chapters or tractates. The order of the tractates vary in the manuscripts, and the tractates—and even material within the tractates—can be a mixture of early and late additions. The Ior manuscripts have a triadic arrangement—the laws of court, the laws of country, and the judges' test book—but this division is not found in the Bleg and Cyfn manuscripts. However, in those manuscripts, the laws of court and the laws of country are distinct.

The System of Law

Although there are archaic elements in the lawbooks, the law was a sophisticated and highly developed system, with the lawbooks created by the lawyers for their own use. It was a compensation-based law.[19] In a hierarchical society, each person had a life value, *galanas*, that was to be paid to the family if the person was killed; it was calculated on a sliding scale according to status. A woman's value was calculated according to her husband's status, or for an unmarried woman, her father's. Women were not entitled to hold land or speak in court. Aliens, people from outside Wales, had very low status and few rights in medieval Welsh law. Similar to the life value, *galanas*, each person had *sarhaed*, an injury value, which was priced at half of a person's *galanas* and was an additional payment for a deliberate injury—the word *sarhaed* means insult. Only with accidental injuries and deaths would the injury or life value be paid without the *sarhaed* payment. In Welsh law, the emphasis was on taking responsibility for actions, and this included vicarious liability: a father was responsible for the actions of his underage son, and the owner was responsible for any damage caused by his/her animals.

A fact about Welsh law that is often seen as surprising is that the death penalty was only used for certain cases of theft, and was not applied in cases of homicide. Instead, Welsh law had a complicated *galanas* system. The word *galanas* can mean the act of homicide, or the payments for that act, and also a person's life value; in medieval Welsh poetry it is often used to refer to a disaster or lamentable death in general. The *galanas* system was developed as a way of avoiding revenge killing and blood feud as an extended compensation structure. In the event of a killing, the dead person's *galanas*, or life value, would have to be paid. Rather than the killer taking this fully upon himself, the obligation to pay was divided between his extended family, up to the third cousin, and payment was made in turn to the dead man's whole family, up to the same degree of relationship. The theory was that everyone in the family would have paid the price for a killing, and everyone in the victim's family would receive compensation. Although the rules for paying *galanas* are set out in the lawbooks, it is uncertain to what extent they would have been followed.[20]

Theft was considered to be more serious than homicide in Welsh law as it was a stealth act. As a stealth act undermined society, certain cases of theft were punishable by death.[21] *Galanas*, theft, and arson are the three major crimes in Welsh law, and are called "The Three Columns of Law." The section of the

Three Columns of Law on arson is shorter than those for *galanas* and theft, and rather than concentrating on deliberate acts of arson, more emphasis is put on who takes responsibility for the damage caused by accidental fires.

The Three Columns of Law is usually the first part of the "laws of country" in the Bleg and Cyfn lawbooks. The other main part is the laws of court, a long section detailing the situation in the royal court—the twenty-four officers and their rights and responsibilities, including their seating position in the court during a major feast and payments due to and from them by virtue of their role.[22] The laws of court were already rather archaic by the thirteenth century and it is unlikely that the rules were observed to the letter—although this can be said for many sections of Welsh law—but it does offer an idealized picture of the royal court in Wales.[23] The laws of country concentrate on what could be called more practical law—the Three Columns of Law being the main part of the criminal law system—but also included in the laws of country were detailed laws on contract and suretyship, with the surety as a person to guarantee and enforce a contract or debts. A surety would be used for any relationship of obligation. Several sections discuss responsibility in communal agricultural situations: there are laws on corn damage, a section on joint plowing, and injuries to animals. Land law, however, is seen as a separate entity: it sets out the details of how to conduct cases for lands, and how to claim land in law, and also lists the different tenures in Welsh law.[24]

The law of women has been much discussed, and it is an interesting section of Welsh law.[25] It sets out the status of women, and deals with marriage, divorce, and children. There were several different unions recognized in Welsh law, varying from the casual to full legal marriage, and marriage changed in status after seven years. After this period, the couple could separate, and all of their goods would be divided, following the rules set out in the lawbooks, and excluding the land. If a couple separated with just cause before seven years were up, the woman received various payments set out at the beginning of the marriage—marriage was a contract, and both sides had certain obligations or payments, one of them being the woman herself.[26] Often seen as a subsection of the law of women, the section on children covers paternity, how to claim or deny a child as one's own, and how to deal with offences by children under the legal age of fifteen.

The judges' test book or *Llyfr Prawf*, only found in the Ior redaction, is usually cited as the section a lawyer would need to know in order to practice Welsh law.[27] It consisted of the value of wild and tame, which gives a price for every animal and object, essential for paying compensation. The value of wild and tame is included in the other redactions, as was the other section in the test book in Ior—the Three Columns of Law. Ior also has collections of *damweiniau*, sentences starting "if it happens...," giving exceptions to the rules found in the tractates, which were possibly exercises for training lawyers.[28] The *damweiniau* appear to have been preferred to triads in the north; Bleg and Cyfn texts usually include a large collection of triads, mnemonic lists, absent from the Ior redaction.

English Influence on Welsh Law, or Vice Versa

This brief overview of Welsh law demonstrates that it was separate from English law, and was a native Welsh system developed perhaps in an insular way, without too much borrowing from other traditions. Several of the concepts found in Welsh law are unique, and the Latin manuscripts leave certain terms in Welsh, possibly because they could not be translated. The most obvious of these terms is perhaps *galanas*, which is left in the original today— the word "homicide" does not cover all aspects of the Welsh term and is therefore insufficient.[29] Often it was not the actual concept that would not translate, but certain nuances within one legal concept. In the medieval Welsh law of theft, distinction was made between stealing, which was taking something without the owner's knowledge or permission, and borrowing something without consent, which would not necessarily count as theft.[30] In the Welsh laws, there was a term for the latter act—*anghyfarch*, but even today, that idea cannot be expressed in a concise way in English law, and the phrase "taking without consent" is used in that situation with motor vehicles—for example, in cases of joyriding—the closest thing to medieval Welsh *anghyfarch*, its verbal form being the rather ridiculous "twocking."[31]

However, that is not to say that there were no influences whatsoever on the Welsh laws, nor similarities with other legal systems. Naturally, some legal concepts are basic—punishing a wrongdoer or compensating someone who has suffered a loss—and often primitive, and similarities do not prove that there was any borrowing.[32] Wales in the Middle Ages was not immune to external influences, and Welsh law was no exception to this. Unsurprisingly, perhaps, culture and society looked primarily to the Celtic west, and medieval Welsh law and early Irish law have a great deal in common.[33] Although Welsh and English law in the Middle Ages appear to be too different for overlap, there is evidence that there was some borrowing, perhaps at a very early period. Several English loanwords can be found in the Welsh laws, but interestingly, they are mainly found in the laws of court, describing the royal court and its functions—archaic and probably obsolete by the thirteenth century.

One of the members of the royal family, and one of the main people in the Welsh royal court, was the king's heir apparent, and the Welsh term is *edling*. This term derives from the Old English *aetheling,* used in English to denote any relative of the king.[34] Another English loanword is found as the name of one of the main officers of the court. The *distain* was originally the person in charge of the king's meals (in the illustration in Peniarth MS 28, he is pictured holding a dish),[35] but the office developed to become some sort of chief minister or advisor—Ednyfed Fychan was the *distain* for Llywelyn ap Iorwerth, and wielded great power; he was also an ancestor of Henry VII.[36] The word *distain*, however, is from old English *dishthegn* (dish + thegn), who was a steward or table servant.[37]

Apart from the loanwords, tracing elements of Welsh law that were influenced by English law is almost impossible, due to the nature of the development of Welsh law. It is difficult to set even a vague date on individual tractates, let alone the laws as a whole that are broadly dated from the mid-thirteenth century to the mid-fifteenth century, and it may be the case that individual sentences in the tractates date from different periods.

There is some evidence also that the Welsh princes would have a say in the Welsh laws. The king or lord was the chief person in Welsh law, and the king was called upon to act as a supreme judge in some cases, for example, land law. In the Ior redaction, Bleddyn ap Cynfyn, fl. 1064–75, who ruled Gwynedd and Powys, is named as someone who changed two sections of Welsh law.[38] Furthermore, the Ior redaction that, according to internal evidence, was being adapted by the law-yers may have been changed as the political situation in north Wales developed. In the thirteenth century, Gwynedd was the dominant dynasty in Wales, and the emphasis on royal rights found in the laws of court in Ior may reflect the rise of royal power in Gwynedd under Llywelyn ap Iorwerth.[39] Also, in the Ior laws of court, more emphasis is given to the role of the queen, and she has more officers and they have more rights than in the Bleg and Cyfn texts. Llywelyn ap Iorwerth was married to Joan, daughter of King John of England, a political player in her own right, unlike other Welsh princesses, and these adaptations to the Ior laws of court may reflect her influence.[40] The thirteenth-century Ior lawtexts may also be a reaction to English law, and may demonstrate an attempt to emulate the establishment of lawbooks in England. The Ior manuscripts are the earliest of the Welsh law manuscripts, and English influence may be the reason; however, very few Welsh manuscripts of any genre survive before the mid-thirteenth century, so there seems to have been a tradition of producing manuscripts in Wales at that time. English influence on the Welsh laws is, therefore, hard to prove, but there is some evidence that Hywel Dda was a regular visitor to the court of Athelstan, and may have been given particular respect in his court.[41] At that early stage, at least, the channels were open, and these links with Athelstan may also be the reason why Hywel Dda's name, as opposed to any other Welsh prince, was chosen as the one that would give Welsh law royal credibility.

Welsh law was not a static thing—each lawbook is a little bit different, and the lawyers were also editors, and would change and add sections to reflect practice in their time. Iorwerth ap Madog is named in the prologue to the judges' test book in the redaction now named after him—Iorwerth—as being the person who gathered together the material in the judges' test book.[42] His material came from "books" written by other lawyers—Cyfnerth ap Morgenau, Gwair ap Rhufawn, Goronwy ap Moriddig, and other unnamed books, including an "old book of the White house."[43] While the naming of famous lawyers in the prologues to the lawbooks was common, and much of the prologues may be fiction, in this case, there is evidence for Iorwerth ap Madog's existence. Elsewhere, Iorwerth's grandfather is named (Rhawd), and Dafydd Jenkins demonstrated that Iorwerth ap Madog was from the family of Cilmin Droetu in north Wales.[44] Another of the people named in the prologue to the test book has a redaction named in his honor—Cyfnerth ap Morgenau is the same person after whom Llyfr Cyfnerth was named. He was also from the same family of poets and lawyers, and was a cousin of Iorwerth's grandfather, Rhawd.[45] There appears to be no evidence for the other names found in the list.

Although the Welsh lawbooks were written in Welsh, with perhaps the lawyers themselves as the intended audience, that is not to say that there was no knowledge at all of Welsh law in England. For a start, it was known to the English kings, who, perhaps to their dismay, were aware that they had no rights of jurisdiction over the Welsh people, at least until the conquest of Wales in 1282. The famous clause 56 of Magna Carta states this fact clearly: "English law shall apply to land holdings in England, Welsh law to those in Wales, and the law of the Marches to those in the Marches."[46] But apart from being aware of the Welsh laws, some interest was shown in the content of the laws, if not for the best of reasons. Much has been said about the three Welsh redactions, but there was a fourth redaction, written in Latin. Assuming that the Welsh lawyers practiced through the medium of Welsh—the model pleadings, including formulae for what should be said in legal cases, are written in Welsh in the Welsh manuscripts—these Latin lawbooks must have been written with a wider audience in mind, and there is evidence that one of these manuscripts at least reached that wider audience.

The Latin Texts

Hywel Emanuel, in his study of the Latin texts, made it clear that the Latin texts are not the poor relation of the Welsh texts, but have great significance for the history of Welsh law.[47] Several of the manuscripts are early, and although they were probably derived from existing laws in Welsh, there is no extant early Welsh lawtext from which they are immediately derived. Emanuel suggested that Peniarth MS 28, the earliest of any of the Welsh lawtexts, written in Latin, was conceived in the time of Rhys ap Gruffudd, ruler of the kingdom of Deheubarth, in the time of the Norman incursions into Wales.[48] The Normans were more successful in south Wales than in the north, and Emanuel's theory was that Rhys ap Gruffudd would have felt the need to foster the Welsh laws, and emphasize their "genuineness and antiquity" against the Normans, who had their own system of law.[49] In order to demonstrate the value of the Welsh laws, however, they would have to have been legible to the Normans, and therefore a Latin version was produced. Rhys ap Gruffudd was Justice of South Wales on behalf of Henry II, which suggests interest in the laws, and like Bleddyn ap Cynfyn, he is named in the lawtexts as someone who adapted sections of Welsh law.[50] Several of the Anglo-Saxon laws were translated into Latin, and there are also Anglo-Norman lawbooks in Latin, so there were precedents for Latin legal texts, and there may also have been an element of elevating the status by having a text in Latin.[51]

Aberystwyth, National Library of Wales MS Peniarth 28, in Latin, the oldest Welsh law manuscript in either language, is also important for its illustrations found throughout the text—rare for a Welsh manuscript.[52] However, it also contains information that has some bearing on events in Welsh history. Daniel Huws demonstrated that the manuscript has the pressmark of St. Augustine's abbey in Canterbury.[53] Peniarth MS 28 was at Canterbury by the fourteenth century, and it was probably there earlier than that, for the use of a certain Archbishop John Pecham.[54] The mid-thirteenth century was a troubled time

for the kingdom of Gwynedd, when Llywelyn ap Gruffudd, the ruler, was
under pressure from Edward I. Edward invaded Wales in 1277, and rather more
successfully in 1282, culminating with the conquest of Wales. John Pecham was
archbishop of Canterbury 1279–92, and played a crucial role in the negotiations
between the King of England and the Prince of Wales. Although there were
several complaints on both sides during the dispute, one factor was a legal matter
that arose in Arwystli, a commote in mid-Wales, and whether Welsh law or
English law should be used to settle the matter.[55] Pecham studied the Welsh laws,
and his conclusions were not favorable, to say the least: the laws were in part
written by the Devil himself.[56] From a Norman point of view, the laws would
have been contrary to Canon law, and certain aspects in particular—allowing a
married couple to separate, and allowing illegitimate children to inherit in cases
where the father had acknowledged them—would have seemed immoral.[57] The
prologues to the Welsh lawbooks are an attempt to justify the laws in the eyes of
the church—they refer to Hywel Dda gathering clergy as well as learned laymen
to put the laws in order, and some texts even mention a pilgrimage to Rome,
giving the laws Papal justification.[58] Pecham was not to be swayed. Interestingly,
Peniarth MS 28, which was in the library at Canterbury, has several notes in
the margin, marking significant points—mainly in the laws of women, the very
source of Pecham's condemnation.[59] Pecham's comments gave Edward I some
justification for conquering the immoral Welsh.

The "Hybrid Society" in the March of Wales[60]

Following the conquest in 1282, Edward I issued the Statute of Rhuddlan,
which, amongst other things, established courts imposing English law in Wales
for criminal cases. The use of Welsh law was allowed to continue for civil procedures. It appears that during this period, English law became popular in Wales
for civil cases too, but the use of Welsh law was not officially abolished until
Henry VIII passed the Acts of Union in 1536. The period between the conquest
of Wales and the Acts of Union is an interesting one as far as the law is concerned,
and aspects of both Welsh and English law were used in cases in various parts of
the country.[61] The principality of Wales, once subject to one law, that of Hywel
Dda, became more similar to the situation in the March of Wales. In addition
to giving the Welsh the right to use Welsh law, and the English the right to
use English law, clause 56 of Magna Carta also states that the law of the March
is to be applied in the March.[62] The March of Wales was the border area conquered in part by the Normans following 1066, and each lordship was governed
separately by its lord—famously, the king's writ did not run in the March. The
March was a mixture of Welsh and English—in some lordships, the population
was separated into Welshries and Englishries and followed their appropriate laws
(Dyffryn Clwyd is one example), but in other lordships, the population would
be mixed, and often the laws would be mixed too.[63] R. R. Davies discussed the
law of the March fully, and although there was never a written lawbook or document outlining exactly what the law of the March was, it was clearly a mixture of
Welsh and English law, with the lords often cherrypicking the most advantageous

parts of both codes.[64] Land law was one part of Welsh law that survived, as land holding is often a conservative element in a society. Other areas also occur in the records, and there are cases of Welsh compurgation being used rather than a jury.[65] Records sometimes refer to the law of the March, but evidence of what exactly this was is hard to find, partly due to the paucity of court rolls and the brief nature of those documents.

The Legacy of Welsh Law

Along with Welsh law, following 1536, English law was to apply in the March as well, but unsurprisingly, it is in this area that the occasional survival of customs or laws are found following the Acts of Union. Survivals include a case for land in Caeo, Carmarthenshire, in 1540, which follows the rules and quotes sections from the lawbooks.[66] Although the law of the March was also abolished in 1536, the legal principles behind Welsh law were still used in the March, and there are examples of legal cases combining both Welsh and English legal elements.[67] The *dadl croes* from Brycheiniog is a procedure for claiming land, in Welsh, found in a manuscript of Welsh poetry mainly by Hywel Dafi, possibly in the hand of the poet himself.[68] It combines Welsh and English legal concepts in one document, and is interesting as it shows that the law was flexible—the case could be settled in a number of different ways.[69] Welsh law manuscripts were still being written in this period, and those manuscripts often include practical sections of law. Some of those manuscripts may have been an attempt to gather as much legal material together as possible, perhaps so that people could have the option of using aspects of Welsh law, but it is uncertain to what extent those manuscripts were actually used in the courts. Aberystwyth, National Library of Wales MS. Wynnstay MS 36 is a beautiful manuscript from the beginning of the fifteenth century, and although it contains a great deal of later material, it was clearly intended for a library and did not see heavy use, although it was copied in full, twice.[70] Unfortunately, it may be the case that some of these later manuscripts were merely a swansong, or an attempt to preserve the material before it disappeared for good. It is possible to trace developments in Welsh law due to the different redactions and manuscripts, and this has some importance on the picture it gives us of society, although dating any changes is challenging; Jenkins states that part of what makes Welsh law valuable is the evidence for how the jurists applied the principles of the law to meet new situations.[71] Jenkins, as a lawyer, sees the skill of his medieval Welsh predecessors.

After 1536, only one or two cases were heard using Welsh law, and the use of Welsh law effectively came to an end. Jones Pierce's imaginary vision of the three laws of Britain together in the House of Lords was most definitely his own imagination, and no part of Welsh law was ever knowingly incorporated into modern English law. (The fact that some aspects of Welsh law might be useful in English law today is a topic for another discussion!) Sections of Welsh law were archaic and not observed in the Middle Ages, so Jones Pierce's grandiose claim would have been unlikely to have been substantiated. However, some of the concepts of Welsh law were basic and general, and some survive informally, in market places or folk memory. The influence of Welsh law in England was minimal, but in Wales it was crucial: the lawbooks were far more than legal documents. They are a large part of the surviving Welsh language manuscripts from the Middle Ages, and are significant prose texts, full of technical and everyday medieval Welsh vocabulary. The law gave the Welsh language, to some extent, a dignity, and several of the legal terms are part of the native vocabulary rather than being English or Latin borrowings; the Welsh laws may also have contributed to the survival of the Welsh language.[72] Welsh law was also a great unifier for the "politically fragmented" Welsh people during the Middle Ages,[73] and although the Law of Hywel played its part in the conquest of 1282, it was the one institution that applied to every Welshman.

Notes

1. T. Jones Pierce, "The Law of Wales—The Last Phase," in *Medieval Welsh Society: Selected Essays by T. Jones Pierce*, ed. J. B. Smith (Cardiff: University of Wales Press, 1972), 369–89, at 379.

2. Dafydd Jenkins, "The Significance of the Law of Hywel," *Transactions of the Honourable Society of Cymmrodorion* (1977): 54–76, at 63.

3. Dafydd Jenkins, ed. and trans., *The Law of Hywel Dda: Law Texts from Medieval Wales*, The Welsh Classics 2 (Llandysul: Gomer Press, 2000), xxi.

4. Jenkins, ed. and trans., *Law of Hywel Dda*, xi–xvi.

5. Jenkins, ed. and trans., *Law of Hywel Dda*, xiii; for an example of a prologue, see page 1.

6. Huw Pryce, *Native Law and the Church in Medieval Wales* (Oxford: Oxford University Press, 1993), 71–72.

7. Jenkins, "Significance of the Law of Hywel," 74.

8. Aneurin Owen, ed., *Ancient Laws and Institutes of Wales, Comprising Laws Supposed to Be Enacted by Howel the Good, etc.*, 2 vols. (London: Eyre and Spottiswoode, 1841).

9. Arthur W. Wade-Evans, ed., *Welsh Medieval Law Being a Text of the Laws of Howell the Good Namely, the British Museum Harleian MS 4353 of the 13th Century/with Translation, Introduction, Appendix, Glossary, Index and a Map* (Oxford: Clarendon Press, 1909), vii–x; T. M. Charles-Edwards, *The Welsh Laws*, Writers of Wales (Cardiff: University of Wales Press on behalf of the Welsh Arts Council, 1989), 17–21.

10. Charles-Edwards, *The Welsh Laws*, 20–21.

11. For a discussion on the reign of both Llywelyns, see Kari Maund, *The Welsh Kings: The Medieval Rulers of Wales* (Stroud: Sutton, 2000), 113–28 and 129–48.

12. Jenkins, "Significance of the Law of Hywel," 75; Charles-Edwards, *The Welsh Laws*, 38.

13. Dafydd Jenkins, ed., *Llyfr Colan: y Gyfraith Gymreig yn ôl Hanner Cyntaf Llawysgrif Peniarth 30*, History and Law Series 19 (Cardiff: Board of Celtic Studies, University of Wales Press, 1963).

14. Charles-Edwards, *The Welsh Laws*, 20–21.

15. Christine James, "Tradition and Innovation in Some Later Medieval Welsh Lawbooks," *Bulletin of the Board of Celtic Studies* 40 (1993): 152–54.
16. James, "Tradition and Innovation," 156.
17. Jenkins, "Significance of the Law of Hywel," 74; Hywel David Emanuel, "The Book of Blegywryd and Ms. Rawlinson 821," in *Celtic Law Papers: Studies Presented to the International Commission for the History of Representative and Parliamentary Institutions*, ed. Dafydd Jenkins (Brussels: Éditions de la Librairie Encyclopédique, 1973), 163–64.
18. Hywel David Emanuel, ed., *The Latin Texts of the Welsh Laws*, History and Law Series 22 (Cardiff: Board of Celtic Studies, University of Wales Press, 1967), 53.
19. Jenkins, ed. and trans., *Law of Hywel Dda*, xxx–xxxi.
20. R. R. Davies, "The Survival of the Bloodfeud in Medieval Wales," *History* 54 (1969): 343–57.
21. Jenkins, ed. and trans., *Law of Hywel Dda*, xxx.
22. The laws of court have been discussed in full in Thomas Charles-Edwards, Morfydd E. Owen, and Paul Russell, eds., *The Welsh King and His Court* (Cardiff: University of Wales Press, 2000).
23. See David Stephenson, "The Laws of Court: Past Reality or Present Ideal?" in Charles-Edwards, Owen, and Russell, eds., *Welsh King and His Court*, 400–414.
24. Charles-Edwards, *The Welsh Laws*, 27.
25. See Dafydd Jenkins and Morfydd. E. Owen, eds., *The Welsh Law of Women: Studies Presented to Professor Daniel A. Binchy on His Eightieth Birthday 3 June 1980* (Cardiff: University of Wales Press, 1980).
26. Jenkins, "Significance of the Law of Hywel," 69.
27. Charles-Edwards, *The Welsh Laws*, 30–31.
28. Charles-Edwards, *The Welsh Laws*, 49–53.
29. See Emanuel, ed., *Latin Texts of Welsh Laws*, 121–24, where various words in the Three Columns of Law (including the title) have been left in Welsh in the Latin text.
30. Jenkins explains and translates *anghyfarch* as "surreption"; see Jenkins, ed. and trans., *Law of Hywel Dda*, 282.
31. Section 12 of the Theft Act 1968. With thanks to Timothy Petts for referring me to this, and also to the common usage of twocking. *Twoc* is listed in the *Oxford English Dictionary* as a slang word.
32. Jenkins, ed. and trans., *Law of Hywel Dda*, xxxiii.
33. Jenkins, ed. and trans., *Law of Hywel Dda*, xxxiv.
34. R. C. Stacey, "King, Queen, and *Edling* in the Laws of Court," in Charles-Edwards, Owen, and Russell, eds., *Welsh King and His Court*, 47.
35. Daniel Huws, *Peniarth 28: Darluniau o Lyfr Cyfraith Hywel/Illustrations from a Welsh Lawbook* (Aberystwyth: National Library of Wales, 1988), Figure 6 and note.
36. A. D. Carr, *Medieval Wales*, British History in Perspective (London: Palgrave Macmillan, 1995), 68.

37. *The Blackwell Encyclopaedia of Anglo-Saxon England*, ed. Michael Lapidge, John Blair, Simon Keynes, and Donald Scragg (Oxford: Blackwell, 1999), 444; it is possible that the English dishthegn also developed to be a higher ranking office.
38. Jenkins, ed. and trans., *Law of Hywel Dda*, 98, 165.
39. Stacey, "King, Queen, and *Edling*," 51.
40. Jenkins, ed. and trans., *Law of Hywel Dda*, 220; Stacey, "King, Queen, and *Edling*," 55.
41. Maund, *The Welsh Kings*, 47–49.
42. Jenkins, ed. and trans., *Law of Hywel Dda*, 141.
43. Jenkins, ed. and trans., *Law of Hywel Dda*, 141.
44. Dafydd Jenkins, "A Family of Welsh Lawyers," in *Celtic Law Papers*, 123–33, at 125.
45. Jenkins, "Family of Welsh Lawyers," 124.
46. Magna Carta, Clause 56.
47. Emanuel, ed., *Latin Texts of Welsh Laws*, 1.
48. Emanuel, ed., *Latin Texts of Welsh Laws*, 11.
49. Emanuel, ed., *Latin Texts of Welsh Laws*, 11.
50. Maund, *The Welsh Kings*, 107; Emanuel, ed., *Latin Texts of the Welsh Laws*, 64.
51. Emanuel, ed., *Latin Texts of Welsh Laws*, 12.
52. Huws, *Peniarth 28*, Introduction.
53. Daniel Huws, *Medieval Welsh Manuscripts* (Cardiff: University of Wales and the National Library of Wales, 2000), 169.
54. Huws, *Medieval Welsh Manuscripts*, 172.
55. J. Beverley Smith, *Llywelyn ap Gruffudd: Tywysog Cymru* (Cardiff: University of Wales Press, 1986), 337–340.
56. Emanuel, ed., *Latin Texts of Welsh Laws*, 71–2.
57. Pryce, *Native Law and the Church*, 71–72.
58. Pryce, *Native Law and the Church*, 72.
59. Huws, *Medieval Welsh Manuscripts*, 172.
60. The appropriate description "hybrid society" is used by R. R. Davies, *Lordship and Society in the March of Wales* (Oxford: Clarendon Press, 1978), 9–10.
61. Pierce, "The Law of Wales," 379–80.
62. Magna Carta, Clause 56.
63. R. R. Davies, *Lordship and Society*, 9–10; R. R. Davies, "The Law of the March," *Welsh History Review* 5 (1970–71): 156 and 25–26.
64. R. R. Davies, "The Twilight of Welsh Law 1284–1536," *History* 51 (1966): 137, citing Paul Vinogradoff and Frank Morgan, eds., *Survey of the Honour of Denbigh, 1334,* Records of the Social and Economic History of England and Wales (London: Milford, 1914), 313–14.
65. Davies, "Twilight of Welsh Law," 154–56; Davies, "Law of the March," 17–18.
66. Pierce, "The Law of Wales," 370–72.

67. Sara Elin Roberts, "Legal Practice in Fifteenth-Century Brycheiniog," *Studia Celtica* 35 (2001): 307–323.
68. Roberts, "Legal Practice," 307–309.
69. Roberts, "Legal Practice," 316–17.
70. Sara Elin Roberts, "Creu trefn o anhrefn: gwaith copïydd testun cyfreithiol," *National Library of Wales Journal* 32 (2002): 397–420.
71. Emanuel, ed., *Latin Texts of Welsh Laws*, xxxv.
72. Emanuel, ed., *Latin Texts of Welsh Laws*, xxxvi.
73. Emanuel, ed., *Latin Texts of Welsh Laws*, xxvi.

CHAPTER 6

TREVISA'S TRANSLATION OF HIGDEN'S POLYCHRONICON, BOOK I, CHAPTER 38, DE WALLIA: AN EDITION

Ronald Waldron

Higden tells us in his Second Preface to the *Polychronicon* [Chronicle of Many Times] that the first of the seven books "describes places and countries and lands all over the world," while the subsequent six books contain an account of the conduct and deeds of the six ages of man from the creation to "our time" (i.e., the fourteenth century). For Higden the world is no flat earth, but a sphere, precisely 20,040 miles in circumference, in which the three continents of Asia, Africa, and Europe are surrounded by the great Ocean, which "embraces all the earth like a garland." He intended that every copy of the *Polychronicon* should have as a frontispiece a *mappa mundi*, like the famous Hereford one, and some extant copies do have this. The first book (after a discussion of the location of the Earthly Paradise) describes the inhabited world, starting with India in the Far East and moving westwards through Asia Minor, the Middle East, and North Africa, to Western Europe, homing in, in Chapters 32–60, on Ireland and *Britannia*, a term he uses interchangeably with *Anglia* to refer to England alone, as well as for the whole complex of regions later called the British Isles.

The almost exclusive sources for Chapter 38, *De Wallia*, the chapter on Wales and its inhabitants, were the *Itinerarium Kambriae* and *Descriptio Kambriae* of Gerald de Barry (Giraldus Cambrensis).[1] Higden's method may be characterized as one of drastic condensation. Under four *tituli*—the origin of the name, the qualities of the country, the manners of the inhabitants, and the marvels—he compresses Gerald's two prose treatises into 410 lines of verse.

One of the few passages where Higden attempts to encapsulate an extended treatment in his verse, using much of the vocabulary of Gerald's original, is the description of Goldcliff in Monmouthshire and the thoughts the description gives rise to about minerals and mining (Lat. 225–44, ME 237–66). His

usual method, however, is to pare everything down to brief comments, omitting almost all of Gerald's anecdotal amplification. For instance, in relating the
marvels of Brecknock Mere,[2] he confines himself to two features: the changes
in the appearance of the lake and the miraculous birds that will sing only at the
command of the rightful lord of the district, omitting the story Gerald tells about
a Welsh nobleman in the time of Henry I whose lordship was vindicated by the
singing birds against the claims of two Normans.

Higden does not tell us why he chose to compose this chapter (uniquely) in
Latin verse—in four-stressed rhymed couplets. The most plausible explanation
is that in the fourteenth century, Wales was regarded by the English (even in an
age of general credulity) as supremely a land of divination, romance, and fantasy, and hence a subject more suitable for verse than sober prose. Trevisa follows
Higden and translates the chapter into rhymed English couplets of rough-and-
ready tetrameter lines. If we juxtapose Trevisa's low opinion of poetry and poets,
as expressed elsewhere in his translation of the *Polychronicon*,[3] with the pejorative
comment he interpolates in lines 321–46 of the English version here, it is evident
that he too thought that verse was eminently suitable for at least some of material
of *De Wallia*, because of its incompatibility with reason and doctrine.

If the two English writers can be accused of presenting an unflattering picture of the Welsh, it must be admitted that the attitude of Gerald himself is
ambiguous—and avowedly so. While he is enthusiastic about the scenery and
natural resources of his native country, and appreciative of such characteristics
as the native wit and eloquence, the musical accomplishment, and the piety of
his fellow countrymen, he is equally condemnatory of what he sees as their per-
fidiousness, their internecine quarrelsomeness and greed for property. In fact the
Descriptio is organized partly as a list of pros and cons, and ends with strategies
on the one hand for the effective conquest of the Welsh and on the other hand
for their continued resistance to English rule. While there is an overt stance of
objectivity in Gerald's attitude to the Welsh, its complexity undoubtedly reflects
his own mixture of social identities. Though three parts Norman and only one
quarter of Welsh ancestry—on the Welsh side, through his mother Angharad,
the granddaughter of Rhys ap Tewdwr, the king of South Wales who died in
1093—Gerald was second cousin to the then Lord Rhys, prince of South Wales.
He was also an archdeacon in the church in Wales and, though at one stage chap-
lain to the Archbishop of Canterbury, contended and traveled for many years
to restore (as he saw it) the metropolitan status of St. Davids, with himself as its
archbishop, consecrated by the Pope, and hence on a par with Canterbury. It is
thus possible to detect a strain of aristocratic and ecclesiastical superiority in his
strictures on Welsh manners, coexisting with pride in his country of origin.

Higden's summary treatment of Gerald's descriptions has an overall trivial-
izing effect. The throwaway style conveys belittlement of the characteristics that
Gerald admires. For instance, the belief of the Welsh in their Trojan ancestry is
reduced to satirical comment on their ability to take pride in family relations
however distant (Lat. 176–79, ME 187–90) and on their preference for flat loaves
of bread (Lat. 120–24, ME 127–30). He makes their reverence for the clergy and
their awe of (ecclesiastical) staves and bells look like superstition, rather than

genuine religious devotion (Lat. 180–83, 381–90, ME 191–94, 439–48), while their reputation for generous hospitality is given a reverse implication in Trevisa's translation of *Taxando porciunculas / Seruans sibi reliquias* (Lat. 144–45) as:

A deleþ hys mete atte meel
& 3eueþ euerych man hys deel,
And al þe ouerpluse
A kepeþ to hys oune vse. (ME 153–56)

Recent improvements in the brutish manners of Britons (Lat. 188–91, ME 199–202) are complacently (*þat ys knowe as cleer as ly3t*) attributed to social intercourse with *Saxons*.

Both Higden and Trevisa were undoubtedly pandering to English prejudices toward the Welsh and, given the later popularity of the *Polychronicon* in both its Latin and English forms (Trevisa's translation was printed by Caxton in 1482),[4] it is a fair assumption that the *De Wallia* chapter continued to reinforce those prejudices in the centuries during which travel between the two countries was far from easy.[5]

The text of Chapter 38 of Book I of Higden's *Polychronicon*[6] is edited here from Oxford, New College Library MS 152 (Ox), now in the Bodleian Library, with collation of Glasgow, University Library, MS Hunter 223 (Hu), for the lines 1–58 (after which there is a gap in this manuscript extending beyond the end of the chapter), and Princeton, University Library MS Garrett 152 (Ga). The ME text is edited from London, British Library, MS Cotton Tiberius D VII (C), dated *s.* xiv/xv, with collation of five other manuscripts of Trevisa's translation: Glasgow, University Library, MS Hunter 367 (G), dated *s.* xv med, London, British Library, MS Stowe 65 (S), dated *s.* xv in, Princeton, University Library, MS Taylor 6 (T), dated *s.* xv 3, London, British Library, MS Harley 1900 (H), dated *s.* xv in, and London, British Library, MS Additional 24194 (A), dated *s.* xv 1. The sigla given here are also used in my edition of Book VI, which may be consulted for a fuller description of the manuscripts and their relationships.[7] Capitalization and punctuation are editorial and abbreviations are expanded silently, common abbreviated words (e.g., *wt*, *þt*) to a form preferred by the scribe when the word is written out in full. Emended (altered or supplied) letters and words are enclosed in square brackets: [ ]. An isolated obelus, †, in the text indicates emendation by omission. Angle brackets, < >, on the other hand, enclose parts of the text that are not clearly legible or are lost from the copy text but that can be confidently supplied from other manuscripts. Only substantive variants are noted in the apparatus, and peculiarities of the text (corrections, insertions, etc.) are generally noted only for the base manuscript of each text, Latin and Middle English.

Polychronicon, Book I, Chapter 38
Oxford, New College MS152, fols. 27rb–29rb

De Wallia

Libri cursus nunc Cambriam
Prius tangit quam Angliam;
Sic propero ad Walliam,
Ad Priami prosapiam;
Ad magni Iouis sanguinem,   5
Ad Dardani progeniem.
Sub titulis hijs quatuor
Terre statum exordior:
Primo de causa nominis,
Secundo de preconijs,   10
Tandem de gentis ritibus,
Quarto de mirabilibus.
De racione nominis
Hec terra que nunc Wallia
Quondam est dicta Cambria   15
A Cambro bruti filio,
Qui rexit hanc dominio,
Set post hec dicta Wallia
A Gwalaes reginula,
Regis Ebranci filia,   20
Ad hec nupta confinia;
Seu a Gwalone procere,
Rupto soni caractere,
Reperies ad litteram
Denominatam Walliam.   25
Cuius circumferencia,
Quamuis sit minor Anglia,

1. Libri] *3-line capital* L.

Polychronicon, Book I, Chapter 38
MS. London, British Library MS Cotton Tiberius
D. vii, fols. 35v–37v

De Wallia: The contr<y> Walis

Now þe book takeþ an hond
Wales tofor Engelond;
So y take my tales
& wende in to Wales,
To þat noble brood   5
Of Priamus hys blood,
Knowelech for to wynne
Of gret Iupiter hys kynne.
For to haue yn muynde
Dardanus hys kynde.   10
Yn þis foure titles y fynde
To telle þe staat of þe londe.
Cause of þe name y schal telle
& þanne preise þe lond welle.
Þanne y schal w<r>yte wiþ my pen   15
Al þe maners of þe men.
Þanne y schal fonde
To telle meruaylles of þe londe.
De ratione nominis
Wales now hatte Wallia
And som tyme heet Cambria,   20
[For Camber,] Brut hys sone,
Was prynce & þar dude wone.
Þanne Wallia was to meene
For Gu[a]lai[s] þe qu<een>e,
Kyng Ebrancus hys chylde,   25
Was wedded þuder mylde;
And of þat lord Gwalon
Wiþdraweþ lettres of þe soun,
And put to l, i, a,
& þou schalt fynde Wallia.   30
And þey þis lond
Be wel lasse þan Engelond,

4. wende] wende forth A.   11. þis] these G.   12. þe(2)] þat STHA.   13. telle]
preceded by fynde *crossed through and underdotted* H.   18a. **de r(ati)one no(min)**
is] *om.* G.   19. *Lines 19 and 20 inverted in* C. now] *om.* T   20. somtyme]
sumtyme it ST.   21. For Camber] GSTHA, *om.* C (*scribe's omission: no space for
loss of text*).   24. Gualais] GSTHA, gulaic? C (*edge split with loss of letters*).   26.
mylde] ful mylde G.   29. l. i. a.] l. i. & a. A.   31. þey] þei3 þat A.

Par tamen glebe gloria,
In matre et in filia.
De patrie preconijs.   30
Terra fecunda fructibus,
Et carnibus, et piscibus,
Domesticis, siluestribus,
Bobus, equis, et ouibus;
Apta cunctis seminibus,   35
[fol. 27va]   Culmis, spicis, graminibus,
Aruis, pratis, nemoribus,
Herbis gaudet, et floribus;
Fluminibus et fontibus,
Conuallibus et montibus;   40
Conualles pastum proferunt,
Montes metalla conferunt;
Carbo sub terre cortice,
Crescit viror in vertice;
Calcem per artis regulas   45
Prebet ad tecta tegulas.
Epularum materia
Mel, lac, et lacticinia,
Mulsum, medo, seruisia,
Habundat in hac patria;   50
Et quicquid vite congruit
Vbertim terra tribuit.
Set ut de tantis dotibus
Multa claudam sub breuibus
Stat h[e]c in orbis angulo   55
Ac si Deus a seculo
Hanc daret promptuarium
Cunctorum salutarium.
Hec Wallia diuiditur

45. regulas] *otiose macron above* as.   50. Habundat] Abundant Hu.   55. hec] Hu,
Ga; hoc Ox.   58. salutarium] *end of text for this chapter in MS Hunter 223.*

As good glebe ys on as oþer,
Yn þe douȝter & þe moder.

De patrie preconijs

Þey þ<at> lond be luyte,   35
Hyt ys fol of corn & of fruyte
And haþ greet plente ywys
Of flesch & of fysch,
Of <bes>tes ta<m>e & wylde,
Of hors, scheep, & oxen mylde,   40
Good lond for al seedes,
For corn, herb[es], <and grasse> þat <spredes.>
[Þar buþ wodes & medes,
Herbes & floures þar spredes.]
Þar buþ ryuers & welles,   45
Valeys & eke hulles.
Vales bryngeþ forþ voode
& hulles metayl goode.
Col groweþ vndur londe
& gras aboue at honde.   50
Þar leome ys copious
& sclattis for hous;
Hony, mylk, & whyte
Þar ys deynte & noȝt lyte.

[fol. 36r]   Of bragot, meod, & ale   55
Ys gret plente in þat vaale.
And al þat neodeþ to þe lyue
Þat lond bringeþ forþ fol ryue.
Bote of [gret] ryches for to drawe
& close meny in schort sawe,   60
Hyt ys in a corner smal,
As þey God furst of al
Made þat lond so feele
To be celer of al heele.
Wales ys deled by   65

---

32. wel lasse] lasse wel G, full l. T.   34a. **de patrie p(re)conijs**] *om.* G.   36.
of(2)] *om.* GST.   38. of(1)] Both of GA; of(2)] *om.* G.   42. herbes] STHA, herb
CG; and] *om.* T.   43. Þar buþ wodes & medes] GSTHA, *om.* C.   44. Herbes &
floures þar spredes] GSTHA (þar] þat GS), *om.* C.   46. eke] also A, *om.*
GSTH.   47. Vales] Valeis GSTHA.   48. goode] riȝt goode A.   50. at] at þe
GA.   52. sclattis] sclattes also A.   54. Þar ys] was there T.   56. þat] the T.   58.
fol] *om.* G.   59. gret] GSTHA, *om.* C.   60. & close] *om.* A; close] clothes G; in]
in a A.   61. a] *om.* GT.   64. celer] celerere T; al] *om.* ST.

Amne qui T[i]wy dicitur,   60
Northwalos ab Australibus
Scindit certis limitibus;
Austrina pars Demetria,
Secunda Venedosia;
Prima sagittis preualet,   65
Hastis secunda preminet.
In hoc pr[o]cinctu Wallie
Tres olim erant curie:
Ad Kaermerthin primaria,
In Anglesey set alia,   70
Tercia in Powisia,
Pengwern, que nunc Salopia.
Septem quondam pontifices,
Nunc quatuor sunt presules;
Quondam suis principibus   75
Parebant, nunc Saxonibus.
De incolarum ritibus
Conuictus huius patrie
Differt a ritu Anglie,
In vestibus, in victibus,   80
In ceteris quampluribus.
Hijs vestium insignia
Sunt clamis et camisia,
Et crispa femoralia,
Sub ventis et sub pluuia.   85
Plura non ferunt tegmina,
[fol. 27vb] Quamuis brumescat Borea.
Sub istis apparatibus,
Spretis lintheaminibus,
Stant, sedent, cubant, dormiunt,   90
Pergunt, pugnant, prosiliunt.
Hij sine supertunicis,
Collobijs et tunicis,
Capis, tenis, capucijs,

60. Tiwy] Tiwi Ga; Twy Ox.   67. procinctu] Ga; precinctu Ox.

A water þat hatte Twy:
Norþ Wales fram þe souþ
Twy deleþ yn place fol couþ.
Þe souþ hatte Demecia,
& þe oþer Venedocia.   70
Þe furste schoteþ & arowes beres,
Þoþer deleþ al wiþ speres.
Yn þis Wales, houȝ hyt be,
Were som tyme courtes þre:
At Kaermarþyn was þat on,   75
& þat oþer was yn Mon;
Þe þridde was yn Powysy,
In Pengwern, þat now ys Schroysbury.
Þar were bischoppes seuene,
& now buþ foure euene,   80
Vndur Saxons al at hond,
Som tyme vndur princes of þat lond.

De incolarum ritibus

Þe maner lyuyng of þat lond
Ys wel dyuers fram Engelond,
Yn mete & dryngk & cloþing,   85
[&] meny oþer doyng.
A buþ cloþed wonder wel
Yn a scheurte & a mantel,
A crisp breche wel vayn,
Boþe in wynd & in rayn.   90
Yn þis cloþing a buþ bold,
Þey weder be ryȝt cold;
Wiþoute scheetes alway
Euer more in þis aray
A goþ, fyȝteþ, pleyeþ, hoppeþ, & lepeþ,   95
Stondeþ, sytteþ, eteþ, liggeþ, & slepeþ;
Wiþoute sorkot, goune, cote, & kurtille,
Wiþoute gipon, tabard, cloke, & belle,
Wiþoute lace & chaplet, þat heer lappes,
Wiþoute hoodes, hat, & cappes.   100

---

70. oþ(er)] north G.   72. þoþ(er)] And þe oþere A, & þat oþer H.   73. þis] *om.*
HA.   74. were] Wre A.   75. was] *followed by* & *above line* S.   78. now ys] is
now ST.   82a. **de incolarum ritibus**] *om.* G.   84. wel] full T.   85. &(2)] &
in T.   86. &] GHA, & in ST, in C.   88. Yn] & ST; &] & in H.   90. in(2)] *om.*
G.   92. Þey] Thoȝ the GSTHA.   95. A] He T.   96. eteþ] *om.* HA; slepeþ]
clepiþ ST.   97. sorkot] sourtat ST; &] *om.* A.   99. þat] þat þe G.   100. hat]
hattes G, hiȝte T; &] or A.

Nudatis semper tibijs,   95
Vix aliter incederent,
Regi licet occurrerent.
Hastis, sagittis breuibus
Concertant in confljictibus,
Validiores pedites   100
Ad pugnam sunt quam equites.
Hijs silue sunt pro turribus,
Paludes pro aggeribus:
Fugam vt pugnam capiunt,
Cum opertunum senciunt.   105
Hos dicit Gildas fragiles,
Et nec in pace stabiles;
Cuius causa si queritur,
Mirum nequaquam cernitur
Si gens expulsa satagat   110
Vt expulsores abigat.
Set frustra hijs temporibus,
Succisis iam nemoribus,
Cum sint circa maritima
Firmata castra plurima.   115
Gens diu famem sustinens,
Communem victum diligens,
Cocorum artificia
Non querit ad edulia;
Nam panem ordeacium   120
Edit et auenacium,
Latum, rotundum, tenuem,
Vt decet tantum sanguinem.
Raro frumento vescitur,
Vix furni flammis vtitur;   125
Hijs pultes ad legumina
Pro epulis acr[u]mina,

---

97. Regi licet] Licet regi Ga.   101. sunt] *at end of line, marked for transposition.*   106. Hos] H *altered from* B?   108. causa si] si causa Ga.   127. acrumina] ("pungent foods"); acrimina Ox, agruminia Ga.

Þus arayed goþ þe segges,
& alwey wiþ bare <le>gges.
A kepeþ non oþer goyng,
Þey a mette wiþ þe kyng.
Wiþ arwes & schort speres   105
A fyȝteþ wiþ ham þat ham deereþ.
A fyȝteþ betre, ȝef hyt neodeþ,
Whan a goþ þan whan a rydeþ.
Yn stude of castel & tour
Hy takeþ wode & mareys for socour.   110
Whanne a seþ þat hyt ys to do,
In fiȝtyng a wol be ago.
Gildas seiþ a buþ variable
In pees, & noȝt stable.
Ȝef me axeþ why hyt be,   115
Hyt ys no wonder for to se
Þey men yput out of londe
To put out oþere wolde fonde.
Bote al for noȝt at þis stonde,
For meny wodes buþ at grounde,   120
And apon þe se among
Buþ castels ybuld fol strong.
Þe men may dure long onete
& loueþ wel comyn mete;
Þay con ete & be mery   125
Wiþoute gret kywery.
Þay eteþ breed, cold & hoote,
Ymad of barlych & of ote:
Brood cakes, round & þynne,
As wel semeþ so gret kynne.   130
Seelde a eteþ bred of wheete,
& seelde a doþ ouenes heete.
Þay habbeþ gruwel to potage,
& a leek hys kyn to companage;

---

101. þe] þes ST; segges] gegges SA.   102. legges] *edge split with loss of letters,*
C.   103. A] He A; goyng] thyng A.   104. a] he A; mette] amette T, mete
GSHA.   105. &] & with T.   107. hyt] *om.* T.   108. whan a] if he T.   110.
wode] wodes ST.   111. a] he T; seþ] saith GT; þat] *om.* GH.   112. a] he
T.   113. Gildas] Gilda G.   114. noȝt] no þing A.   115. me axeþ] men axen
T, men axeþ H.   116. to] þe H.   117. of] of that T.   120. at] at þe GS.   123.
þe] þen G; onete] in heete T.   126. gret] any gret G, any T, *om.* S.   128.
Ymad] *om.* HA.   132. a doþ] he doth T; ouenes heete] oues ete HA.   133. Þay
habbeþ] He hath T.   134. a leek hys] al like is GST; kyn] kynde H.

Butirum, lac, et caseus
Oblongus et tetragonus.
Hec sunt eorum fercula,   130

Que prouocant ad pocula
Medonis et seruisie,
Quibus instant cotidie.
Vinum putant precipuum
Quanto sit magis rubeum.   135
Potando gens hec garula
Vix cessat fari friuola.
[fol. 28ra]   Ad mensam et post prandium
Sal porri sunt solacium.
Set et paterfamilias   140
Hoc reputat delicias,
Caldarium cum pultibus
Dare circumsedentibus,
Taxando porciunculas,
Seruans sibi reliquias.   145
Hoc eis nocet nimium
Ad carnis infortunium,
Quod contra iussum fisicum
Edunt salmonem calidum.
Domos demissas incolunt,   150

Ex virgulis quas construunt
Distantibus limitibus,
Non prope ut in vrbibus.
Cum deuastarint propria,
Vicina querunt atria;   155
Edentes quod inueniunt,
Post hec ad sua redeunt;

154. deuasterint] deuasterunt Ga.   157. hec] hoc Ga.

Also botre, mylk, & chese   135
Yschape euelonge & cornerdwyse.
Suche messes a eteþ snel,
& þat makeþ ham dryngke wel
Meode & ale, þat haþ myȝt;
Þaron a spendeþ day & nyȝt.   140
Euer þe redder ys þe wyn
Hy holdeþ hyt þe more fyn.
Whanne a dryngkeþ atte naale,
A telleþ meny lewed tale;
For whanne dryngke ys an handlyng,   145
A buþ al fol of jangglyng.
Atte mete, & after eke,
Hare solas ys salt & leke.
Þe housebond in hys wyys
Telleþ þat a gret pryys   150
To ȝeue a caudron wiþ gruwel
To ham þat sitteþ at hys meel.
A deleþ hys mete atte meel
& ȝeueþ euerych man hys deel,
And al þe ouerpluse   155
A kepeþ to hys oune vse.
A eteþ hoot samon alway,
Þey fysyk hote nay;
Þarfore a habbeþ wo
& myshappes also.   160
Hare hous buþ lowe wiþal,
Ymad of ȝerdes smal,
[fol. 36v]   Noȝt, as in cyte<ys, nye>,
Bote <fer atw>ynne & noȝt to<hyȝ>.
<Whanne> al ys yete þat was at home,   165
Þanne to here <neyȝh>bors wol þay roome
An<d> ete what hy may fynde & se,
& þanne turne hoom aȝe.

136. euelonge] endlong H.   137. a] he T; snel] swelle G.   140. þaron] There
inne A; a] he T.   143. a] he T.   144. a] he T; meny] many a TA.   145. ffor] ff
retouched? C.   145. an] in G.   147. Atte] At G.   152. hys] here T.   153. atte]
at G.   154. euerych] ech ST.   156. vse] house A.   157. *In STHA, lines 157 and
158 are copied after 160.* A] He T; hoot] but G.   158. þey] alþouȝ H; hote] hiȝte
T; sigge HA   159. a habbeþ] he hath T; a] þe G.   161. hous] houses GH.   162.
of ȝerdes] with yardes G.   163–80. *Ultra-violet light used,* C.   165. þat was] *om.*
HA.   166. roome] come G.   167. hy] y ST.   168. aȝe] ayein T.

Vitam ducentes ocio,
Sopori, et incendio.
Mos cunctis est Walensibus   160
Aquam dare hospitibus;
Si primo pedes lauerint,
Pendunt quod bene venerint.
Ita quieti victitant
Quod raro bursam baiulant.   165
Hijs pecten et peccunia
Pendent ad femoralia;
Et cum abhorrent nimium
Ani pudendum sonitum,
Mirum quod ante ostium   170
Habent latrinas sordium.
Choro, lira, et tibijs
Vtuntur in conuiuijs,
Set elatis funeribus
Clangunt caprinis cornibus.   175
Extollunt Troie sanguinem,
De quo ducunt originem.
Propinquos satis reputant
Quos centum gradus separant.
Sic preferunt se ceteris,   180
[Fau]ent tamen presbiteris,
Et summi Dei famulos
Venerantur vt angelos.
Hos consueuit fallere
Et ad bella impingere   185
Merlini vaticinium,
Et frequens sortilegium.
Mores brutales Britonum
[fol. 28rb]   Iam ex conuictu Saxonum
Commutantur in melius,   190

166. peccunia] pccunia.   175. Clangunt] Clangant Ga.   181. Fauent] RS, MS
B; Parent Ox, Parent se Ga.

Þe lyf ys ydul þat hy ledes,
In brennyng & slepyng & such dedes.   170
Walyschmen vseþ wiþ here my3t
To wasche here gystes feet any3t;
3ef a wassheþ here fet, alle & some,
Þanne þey knoweþ a buþ welcome.
A ly<bbeþ> so eslych in a rout,   175
Þat selde a bereþ pors ab<ou3>t;
At here breech, out & at hoome,
Hy honge<þ> boþe money & come.
Hyt ys <won>der a buþ so heende,
& hateþ a crak <of þe> neþer ende,   180
And wiþ core
Makeþ here worderobe atte dore.
A habbeþ in gret mangery
Harp, tabour, & pyp for mynystracy.
A bereþ forþ cors wiþ sorowe gret,   185
& bloweþ loude hornes of <geet>.
A preyseþ fast Troian hys blood,
For þarof come al here brood:
Ny3 kyn a wol be,
<Þey3> a passe an hondred gre.   190
Aboue oþer men a wol ham dy3t,
& worschipeþ preostes <wiþ †> hare my3t:
As angels of heuene ry3t
A worschipeþ seruauntis of God almy3t.
Ofte <g>yled was þis brood,   195
& 3ernede batail al for wood,
For Merlyns prophecy,
& ofte for sortilegi.
Bestial maners of Britons,
For company of Saxons,   200
Buþ yturnd to betur ry3t;

---

170. slepyng] scleynge ST.   171. wiþ] with al G.   172. any3t] at ny3t.   173. a]
he HA.   175. so] *om*. GT.   177. here] here ougne T.   180. þe] here S.   181.
And] R G; wiþoute] STHA, wiþ C; core] lore T.   183. a habbeþ] And hath T;
mangery] maistry G.   184. for] and G.   185. cors] corses G, the cors T.   186.
of] al of T.   187. Troian hys] troian GHA.   188. come] cometh T.   189.
a] he T.   190. a] he A; gre] degre G.   191. a] he T.   192. wiþ] GSHA, wiþ
al CT.   194. A] þe G; seruauntes] s(er) *retouched* C..   195. gyled] beguiled
T.   196. 3ernede] 3erneth T, serued G.   199. Bestial] Best in HA.

Vt patet luce clarius.
Ortos et agros excolunt,
Ad opida se conferunt,
Et loricati equitant,
Et calceati peditant,   195
Vrbane se reficiunt,
Et sub tapetis dormiunt;
Vt iudicentur, Anglici
Nunc pocius quam Wallici.
Hinc si queratur racio   200
Quiecius quam solito
Cur illi viuant hodie,
In causa sunt diuicie,
Quas cito gens hec perderet,
Si passi[m] nunc confligeret.   205
Timor dampni hos retrahit,
Nam nil habens niil metuit.
Et, ut dixit Satiricus,
Cantat viator vacuus
Coram latrone, tucior   210
Quam phaleratus dicior.
De terre mirabilibus
Ad Brehnoc est viuarium
Satis habundans piscium,
Sepe coloris varij   215
Comam gerens pomarij,
Structuras edificij
Sepe videbis inibi.
Sub lacu cum sit gelidus,
Mirus auditur sonitus.   220
Si terre princeps venerit,
Aues cantare iusserit,
Statim deproment modulos,
Nil concinunt ad ceteros.

205. passim] Ga; passi Ox.   207. niil] nichil, *with* ch *subpuncted.*
223. deproment] RS depromunt.

Þat ys knowe as cleer as lyȝt.
Þay teleþ gardyns, feld, & dounes,
& draweþ ham to gode tounes.
Þay rydeþ yarmed as wol God,   205
& goþ yhosed and yschod,
And sitteþ fair at here mele,
& slepeþ in beddes fayr & feele.
So þay semeþ now <yn> muynde
More Englysch þan Walsch kynde.   210
Ȝef me axeþ why a doþ now so
More þan a wer ywond to do,
Þay lyueþ yn more pees
By cause of here ryches;
For he<re> catel scholde slake   215
& hy vsede ofte wrake.
Drede of lost of here good
Makeþ ham now stylle of mood.
Al yn on hyt ys ybroȝt:
Haue no þyng & drede noȝt.   220
Þe poet seiþ a sawe of preof:
Þe footman leer syngeþ tofor þe þeof,
And ys wel bolder on hys way
Þan þe horsman ryche & gay.

De terre mirabilibus
Þar ys a pool at Bregheynoc,   225
Þaryn of fysch ys meny a flok.
Ofte a changeþ hys hu on cop,
& bereþ aboue a gardyn crop.
Ofte tyme, how hyt be,
Schap of hous þar þou schalt se.   230
Whan þe pool ys frore, hyt ys wonder
Of þe noyse þat ys þarvnder.
Ȝef þe prince of lond hoote,
Bryddes syngeþ wel mury note,

203. Þay teleþ] He delueth T; feld] feldes GT. 205. Þay] He T. 207. here] *om.*
G. 208. feele] wele A. 209. þay] it T; yn] *edge split with loss of letters,* C. 210.
More] more in ST; Walsch] W. in G. 211. me] men T; a] he T. 212. a] he
T. 218. stylle] milde T. 224a. **de t(er)re mirabilibus**] *om.* G. 226. of
fysch ys] is fysch G; fysch] fisshes T. 230. þar] *om.* G. 231. is] is no T. 232.
noise] voiȝs ST. 233. of] of þe G. 234. wel] full T, wiþ A.

Iuxta Caerlion menia,   225
Ad duo miliaria,
Stat rup[e]s fulua nimium
Contra solarem radium,
Quam Goldeclif gens nominat,
Vt aurum quia rutilat;   230
Nec frustra fit in rupibus
Flos talis sine fructibus,
Si foret qui penitima,
Terre venas et viscera,
Transpenetrare sedula   235
Nouisset arte preuia.
Occulta latent plurima
Nature beneficia,
Que, actenus incognita,
[fol. 28va]   Humana pro incuria,   240
Per posterorum studia
Patebunt sub noticia;
Quod antiquis necessitas
Hoc nobis dat sedulitas.

---

227. rupes] Ga, RS; rupis Ox.   228. inibi] ibi *crossed through before it*.   231. fit]
sit Ga. rupibus] ruptibus *with* t *subpuncted*.   233. foret] floret *with* l *subpuncted*.
penitima] ffinitima Ga.

As mury as þay can, 235
& syngeþ for non oþer man.
Bysides Kaerleon,
Twey myle fram þe toun,
Ys a rooch wel bry3t of leeme
Ry3t a3enes þe sonne beme; 240
'Goldclyf' þat rooch hy3te,
For a schyneþ as gold fol bry3te.
Such a flour in stoon ys no3t
Wiþoute fruyt, <&> hyt were sou3t,
[3if me couþe by crafte vndo 245
Þe veynes of þerþe & come þerto.]
Meny benfys of kynde
Buþ now yhud fram mannes muynde,
And buþ onknowe 3et
For defaute of mannes wyt. 250
Gret tresour ys hud in grounde,
& after þis hyt schal be yfounde
By gret study & bysynes
Of ham þat comeþ after vs.
Þat old men hadde by gret neode 255
We habbeþ by bysy dede.
Tre<uysa>: Yn bokes3e may rede
Þat kynde fayleþ no3t at neode.
Whan no man hadde craft <i>nmuynde,
Þanne of craft halp God & kynde. 260
Whanne no techare was yn londe,
Men hadde craft by god hys sonnde.
Hy þat hadde craft so þenne
Tau3te forþ craft to oþer menne.
Som craft þat 3et com no3t in place 265
Som man schal haue by god hys grace.
[fol. 37r]   **R(anulphus):** An ylond ys, wiþnoyse & stryf,

---

239. wel] full T.   242. fol] *om.* G.   245–46. 3if…þerto] GSTHA, *om.*
C.   252. after] *retouched* C.   258. no3t at] at no T.   259. *Edge split with loss*
of one letter, C.   262. craft] craftes T.   265. þat 3et com no3t] come not yet
G.   266. man] men A.

Itidem in South Wallia   245
Apud Kaerdif est insula,
Iuxta Sabrinum pelagus,
Bar[ri] dicta antiquitus
In cuius parte proxima
Apparet rima modica,   250
Ad quam si aurem comedes,
Sonum mirandum audies;
Nunc quasi flatus follium,
Nunc metallorum sonitum,
Cotis ferri fricamina,   255
Fornacis tunc incendia.
Set hoc non est difficile
Ex fluctibus contingere
Marinis subintrantibus
Hunc sonum procreantibus.   260
Apud Penbrok est regio,
Quam demonum illusio
Vexat iactando sordida
Et exprobrando vicia,
Que nullis valet artibus   265
Fugari neque precibus;
Quod, quando terram agitat,
Casum gentis pronosticat.
Ad Cr[ucm]aur in Westwalis
Est tumulus mirabilis   270
Que se conformem cuilibet
Aduenienti exhibet;
Vbi si arma integra
Reliquantur in vespera,
Confracta proculdubio   275
Reperies diluculo.
Ad Neuyn in Northwallia
Est insula per modica,
Que Bardi[s]eya dicitur;
A monachis incolitur;   280
Vbi tam diu viuitur
Quod senior premoritur;
Ibi Merlinus conditur
Siluestris, ut asseritur.
Duo fuerunt igitur   285

248. Barri] Ga; Baru Ox.   265. Que] (sc. *illusio*) Qui Ga. nullis] nullus
Ga.   268. gentis] Ga; nentis Ox.   269. Crucmaur] RS; Crucman Ga, Cronaur
Ox.   279. Bardiseya] Ga; Bardineya Ox.

Yn West Wales at Kaerdyf,
Fast by Seuarn stronde;
Barry hy3t þat ylonde.   270
Yn þe [hider] syde in a chyne
Þou schalt hyre wondur dyne,
And dyuers noyse also,
3ef þou putte þyn ere þarto.
Noyse of leues & of wynde,   275
Noyse of metayl þou schalt fynde;
Frotyng of yr & whestons þou schalt hyre,
Hetyng of ouenes þanne wiþ fuyre.
Al þis may [wel] be
By wawes of þe se   280
Þat brekeþ yn þare
Wiþ such noyse & fare.
At Penbrook in a stude
Feendes doþ ofte queede,
And þroweþ foul þing ynne,   285
& despiseþ also synne.
Noþer craft ne bedes may
Do þennes þat sorowe away;
Whanne hyt greueþ þat place so,
To þe men hyt bodeþ wo.   290
At Crucmar, in West Waal,
Ys a wondur buryal:
Euerych man þat comeþ hyt to se
Semeþ hyt euene as moche as he.
Hool wepon yleft þar a ny3t   295
Schal be ybroke ar day ly3t.
At Nemyn in norþ Wales,
A lytul ylond þar ys
Þat hatte Bardysey;
Monkes woneþ þar alwey.   300
Men lyueþ so longe in þat hurste
Þat þe eldeste deyeþ furste.
Me seiþ þat Merlyn yburyed þar ys,
Þat heet also Siluestris.
Þar were Merlyns tweyne   305

---

268. at] and A.   271. hider] GSTHA, *om.* C.   272. wondur] a wondre GTA.
274. þarto] to STHA.   277. Frotyng] Fretyng G.   279. wel GSTHA, *om.*
C.   282. wiþ] þat maketh G.   284. Feendes] Fendeþ A.   287. Noþer] An
othir T.   289. þat place] *om.* HA.   291. Crucmar] crucynar ST.   292. buryal]
buryals GSTHA.   293–95. hyt to se...yleft] *om.* ST.   293. Euerych] ech
ST.   295. yleft] *om.* HA.   297. Nemyn] neuyn G.   303. Me seiþ] Men seien T.

Merlini, ut conicitur,
Vnus dictus Ambrosius,
Ex incubo progenitus
Ad Kermerthyn Demecie
Sub Vortigerni tempore;   290
[fol. 28vb]   Qui sua vaticinia
P[ro]flauit in Snowdonia
Ad ortum amnis Conewey
Ad cliuum montis Eryry
(Dineys-Embreis, ut comperi,   295
Sonat collem Ambrosij),
Ad ripam quando regulus
Vortiger sedit anxius.

289. Demecie] *third minim of* m *above line with caret.*
292. Proflauit] Ga; perflavit Ox.

& propheciede beyne.
On hy3t Ambros Merlyn,
& was ygete by goblyn,
Yn Demecia at Caermarthyn
Vndur Kyng Vortigern. 310
He tolde out hys prophecy
Euen in Snawdony,
Atte heed of þe water of Conewey,
In þe syde of Mont Eryry —
'Dynas Embreys' a Walysch 315
'Ambros hys hulle' an Englysch.
Kyng Vortigern saat on þe water syde
& was wel fol of wo;
Þan Ambros Merlyn prophecyede
Tofor hym þar ry3t þo. 320
Treuisa: What wy3t wolde wene
Þat a vend my3t now gete chylde?
Som men wol mene
Þat a may no werk such wylde.
Þat fend þat goþ a ny3t, 325
Wymmen wel ofte to gyle,
'Incubus' hatte by ry3t.
On gyleþ men oþer whyle:
'Succubus' ys þat wy3t.
God graunt vs no such vyle. 330
Who þat in here my3t
Comeþ wondur hap schal he smyle.
Wiþ wondur dede,
Boþe men & wymmene seede
Fendes wol kepe 335
Wiþ craft, & bryng in on heepe.
So fendes wylde
May make wymmen bere chylde;
3et neuere in muynde
Was chyld of fendene kynde. 340
For wiþoute eye

---

306. beyne] vein T, ful euen G.   307. Ambros] ambros and GSTHA.   308.
by] of A.   312. in] into T.   314. of] of þe G.   315. Embreys] *om.* G.   316.
Ambros hys] Ambros GH.   319. prophecyede] p(ophesied so A.   320. þar]
om. H; ry3t þo] *om.* T.   321. wy3t] witte H.   322. my3t now] now mi3te ST;
now] *om.* G; gete] gete a GST.   323. wol] wolde GSTA.   324. werk such] such
werke GST.   325. any3t] in ny3t G.   326 wel] ful TA; to] *om.* G; gyle] begile
A.   327. hatte] hette he G.   328. On gyleþ] And gileþ A, Begileth G.   329.
ys] hatte ST.   330. no] now ST.   332. wonder] vnder G; he] *om.* STA.   339.
neuere] venerie T.   340. of fendene] of fendes A, of the fendes T.

Est alter de Albania

Merlinus, que est Scocia;   300
Repertus est binomius
Siluestris Calidonius;
A silua Calidonia,
Qua promsit vaticinia;
Siluestris dictus ideo,   305
Quod consistens in prelio
Monstrum videns in aere
Mente cepit excedere,
Ad siluam tendens propere,
Arthuri regis tempore;   310
Prophetauit apercius
Quam Merlinus Ambrosius.
Sunt montes in Snowdonia
Cum summitate nimia,
Ab ymis vsque † verticem   315
Vix transmeantur per diem,
Quos Cambri vocant Eryry,
Quod sonat montes niuei;
Hij Wallie pecoribus

315. vsque] Ga; v ad Ox.   316. transmeantur] transmeatur Ga.

Þar myȝte child non such deye.
Clergy makeþ muynde
Deþ sleþ noȝt fendene kunde,
Bote deþ slouȝ Merlyn: 345
Merlyn was ergo no goblyn.

R(anulphus): Anoþer Merlyn, of Albanlond,
Þat now hatte Scotlond,
Hadde names two:
'Siluestris' & 'Calidonius' also   350
Of þat wode Calidoni,
For þar a told hys prophecy,
And het 'Siluestris' as wel,
For whanne a was yn † batel,
And syȝ aboue a gryslych kunde,   355
[A] ful anon out of hys muynde,
And ne more bode
Bote ran to þe wode.

Treuisa: Siluestris ys 'wood'
Oþer 'wyld of mood'   360
Oþer elles
'Þat at wode a dwelles'.

R(anulphus): Siluestris Merlyn
Tolde prophecy wel fyn,
And prophecyede fol suyr   365
Vndur Kyng Arthuyr,
Ooponlych, noȝt so clos
As Merlyn Ambros.
Þar buþ hulles in Snawedoni
Þat buþ wondurlych hyȝ   370
Wiþ heythe as gret way
As a man may go a day
And hatte 'Eryry' a Walyshe
'Snowy hulles' an Englysch
Yn þeose hulles þar ys   375

342. child non such] no such child ST.   344. fendene] fendes A.   345. Bote]
om. H.   346. *line om.* G.   347. R/] *om.* GSTA   350. Calidonius] canydonius
ST.   352. þar] þat A.   353. as] also as G.   354. yn] GA, yn a CSTH (*above
line, same hand* C)   356. A] & CGSTHA.   357. ne] made no GSTHA; bode]
aboode H.   358. ran] ran anone H.   360. wyld] while H.   362. at] at þe GA;
a] *om.* GST.   363. R/] *om.* GA.   364. wel] full T.   365. fol] wel G.
373. a] *om.* T.   374. an] in G.

Sufficerent in pascuis;   320
In horum summo vertice
Sunt duo lacus hodie,
Quorum vnus eraticam
In se concludit insulam,
Ventis hinc inde mobilem,   325
Ripis approximabilem,
Ita vt armentarij
Mirentur se clam prouehi.
Dat alter lacus perchios,
Trutos omnes monoculos;   330
Quod reperitur hodie
In Mulwellis Albanie.
Ruthlan in confinibus
Tegengil est fons modicus,
Qui non marinis moribus   335
Die b[i]s vndat fluctibus,
Set vndis crebro deficit,
Vndis vicissim sufficit.
In Monia Northwallie,
Que Anglesey est hodie,   340
Est lapis, sicut didici,

[fol. 29ra]   Concors humano femori;
Qui, quantolibet spacio
Asportetur ab aliquo,
Nocte per se reuertitur.   345
Hoc comperit, ut legitur,
Hugo comes Salopie
Henrici primi tempore;
Probandi causa lapidem
Ligauit ad consimilem   350
Magnis cathenis ferreis,
Et proiecit in fluctibus;
Qui tamen sub diluculo

321. summo] sompno Ga.   328. se] sic Ga.   330. Trutos] turtros Ga (t[2] *above line*).   337. Die bis] RS; Diebus Ox, Ga.

Lese ynow for al bestes of Wales
Þeose hulles on cop beres
Twey gret fysch weres
Conteyned in þe on pond
[Meoueþ wiþ þe wynd] an ylond   380
As þey a dude swymme
& ney3heþ to þe brymme
So þat herdes habbeþ gret wondur
[fol. 37v]   & wene þat þe world meoueþ vnd[er]
Yn þe oþer ys perch, trou3tes, & oþer fys<ch>,   385
& <e>uerich ony3ed ys.
<So fareþ> as wel
In Albania þe mylewel.
Yn Ruthlond by Tegengil
Þar ys a lytul wyl   390
Þat floweþ no3t alway,
As þe se twyes a day,
Bote som tyme a ys dry<3e>
& som tyme al fol vp by þe y3e.
Þar ys in Northwallia,   395
In Mon þat hatte Angleseya,
A ston acordyng wel ny3
As hyt were a mannes þy3.
Hou3 fer euer þat ston
Be ybore of eny man,   400
Any3t a goþ hoom hys way.
Þat he fond by asay,
Huwe erl of Schroysbyry,
Yn tyme of þe furste Henry.
For he wolde þe soþe yfynde,   405
Þat ston to a noþer he gan bynde
Wiþ gret cheynes of yre,
& threw al yfere
Ybounde at on heepe
Ynto a water deope.   410

---

376. ynow] *om.* G; bestes of] *om.* A.   377. þeose hulles] þis hill A; on] on þe
A.   380. Meoueþ wiþ þe wynd] HA, wiþ þe wynd meoueþ CGST; an] eny
ST.   384–86. *Edge split with loss of letters,* C   385. trou3tes] turturs ST.   386.
& euerich ony3ed] on euery side A; euerich ony3ed] euerychone ete G; euerich]
ech ST.   389. Yn] Biside G; by] in G; Tegengil] Tetengill T.   393. *Edge split
with loss of letters,* C.   394. al] *om.* ST; fol] fille T; vp] *om.* GH.   396. In Mon] a
man T.   398. þy3] fre3 G.   400. man] moon A.   401. Any3t] At ny3t G.   403.
erl] þe Erle HA.   404. furste] first kyng GST.   405. soþe] south G.   408. al]
hem al G; yfere] in fyre GA.   410. a] *om.* T.

Visus est loco pristino.
Hunc semel quidam rusticus   355
Ligauit suis cruribus;
Statim femur computruit;
Lapis ad locum redijt.
Si opus fiat Veneris
Iuxta procinctum lapidis,   360
Lapis sudorem faciet,
Et proles non proueniet.
Est rupes audiencium,
Sic dict[a] per contrarium;
Vbi, si sonum feceris   365
Cornu vel exclamaueris,
Hac parte non percipitur
Sonus, qui illac editur.
Est alia et insula
Huic loco contigua,   370
Set heremitas continet,
Quorum si quisquam dissidet,
Statim se mures congregant;
Escas eorum deuorant.
N[ec] cessat hec molestia,   375
Donec cesset discordia.
Sicut hic et Hibernica
Gens extat malencolica,
Sic sancti huius climatis
Propositi sunt vindicis.   380
In hac quoque prouincia,
Hibernia, et Scocia,
Campane sunt et baculi
Ornatu sub multiplici,
Tam digni proculdubio   385
In clero et in populo,
Quod vereantur hodie

364. dict] RS; dictud Ox, Ga.   375. Nec] Non Ox.

Ʒet amorowe þat ston
Was yseye erlych in Mon.
A cherl huld hym sylf fol slyʒ
& bond þat ston to hys þyʒ.
Hys þyʒ was roted ar day   415
& þe ston went a way.
Ʒef me doþ lechery
Nyʒ þat ston by,
Swoot comeþ of þe ston,
Bote chyld comeþ þar non.   420
Þar ys a rooch wel wondyrly:
'Þe rooch of huyryng by contrary'.
Þeyʒ þar crye eny a man yborn,
& blowe also [wiþ] horn,
Noyse þat ys þar ymad þey þou abyde   425
Þou schalt huyre noon in þis syde.
Þar ys anoþer ylond
Fast by Mon at hond;
Hermytes þar buþ fol ryue.
Ʒef eny of ham doþ stryue,   430
Al þe muys þat may be gete
Comeþ & eteþ al here mete;
Þanne ceeseþ neuer þat wo,
Ar þe stryf ceese also.
As men in þis lond   435
Buþ angry as in Irlond,
So seintes of þis contray
Buþ also wre[tt]hfol alway.
Also in þis lond,
Yn Irlond, & in Scotlond,   440
Boþe belles & staues
In worchip men haues,
And buþ worschiped so þenne
Of clerkes & lewed menne
Þat men dredeþ also   445

---

415. ar day] ariday S, it it was daie T.   417. me doþ] men do T.   418. by] faste
by A.   419. Swoot] Souc G.   421. wel] full T.   424. also] as loude G; wiþout]
with an G.   426. huyre noon] anon T.   427. anoþer ylond] anyer londe
G.   428. at] at þe GA.   429. ryue] GSTHA, fol ryue C.   435. in] of T.
438. wretthfol] ST, wrecchfol CGHA.   439. and 440. *in reverse order in*
G.   441. Boþe] Beþ H.   442. In] þat in H.   444. Of] with G, *om.* A; &] & of
STH, and with G.   445. men] man T, *om.* HA; dredeþ] e(1) *retouched?* C.

Periurium committere
Tam super horum alterum
Quam super euuangelium.   390
Ad Basingwere fons oritur,
Qui sacer vulgo dicitur;
[fol. 29 rb]   Et tantis bullis scaturit,
Quod mox iniecta reicit;
Tam magnum flumen procreat,   395
Vt Cambrie sufficiat.
Egri qui dant rogamina
Reportant medicamina.
Rubro guttatos lapides
In scatebris reperies;   400
In signum sacri sanguinis
Quem Wenefrede virginis
Guttur truncatum fuderat.
Qui scelus hoc patrauerat,
Ac nati et nepotuli,   405
Latrant, vt canum catuli;
Donec sancte suffragium
Poscant ad hunc fonticulum,
Vel ad vrbem Salopie,
Vbi quiescit hodie.   410

400. scatebris] scatabris Ga.

To swere on eny of þo,
Staf oþer belle,
As hyt were þe gospelle.
At Basyngwere ys a welle
Þat sacer hyȝt as men doþ telle.   450
Hyt springeþ so strong, as men may se,
What ys cast yn hyt þroweþ aȝe.
Þar of springeþ a greet strond;
Hyt were ynow for al þat lond.
Syke † at þat plas   455
Habbeþ boþe hele & gras.
Yn þe wulmes ofter þan ones
Ys founde reed splekkede stones,
Yn tokon of þe blood reed
Þat þe mayde Wenefreed   460
Schad at þat put
Whanne here þrote was ykut.
He þat dude þat dede
Haþ sorowe on hys seede;
Hys children at al stoundes   465
Berkeþ as whelpes of houndes,
Fort þay praye þat mayde grace,
Ryȝt at þat welle place,
Oþer yn Schroysbury strete,
Þar þat mayde resteþ swete.   470

446. on] be TA; of] *om*.G.   449. Basyngwere] Basyngwerke GH, basyng wher
T.   451. strong] sore A, fast G; men] man T.   452. þroweþ] turneth G; aȝe]
ayeine T.   454. þat] þe G.   455. Syke] HA, Syke men CGST.   457. ofter
þan] after þen G.   458. Ys] beþ H; splekkede] spekeled G, sprekled H, plekked
A.   461. þat] þe G.   467. Fort þay] For þy A.   468. þat] þe G.

Commentary

Lat. 1–25, ME 1–30. From *Descr.* 1: 7 (RS, 178–79; Thorpe, 231–32). However, Higden may have taken some names directly from Geoffrey of Monmouth, *Historia Regum Britanniae*, 2: 1–8 (for *Ebrancus*—there spelt *Ebraucus*—and *Galaes*, see Geoffrey of Monmouth, *History of the Kings of Britain*, trans. Sebastian Evans, rev. Charles W. Dunn [London: Dent, 1963], 29–34). Higden's *Gwalone* apparently derives either from Gerald's rejected *Walo* (RS, 179; Thorpe, 232) or directly from Geoffrey's suggested eponym *Gualo* (*Historia Regum Britanniae*, 12: 19, Evans, trans. 263–64). Gerald was aware (Thorpe, 232) that the English name for Wales actually came from the OE *wealas* "foreigners," and resented it as a barbarism, but Higden ignores this identification.

Lat. 23. *caractere*] The reading in MS B of the RS edn. is *carcare*, which yields the meaning "when the prison of the sound is broken." This looks more plausible as Higden's original reading, though, against this, HM 132, Higden's autograph manuscript, has *charactere*. Trevisa is certainly translating a text with *charactere*.

Lat. 26–58, ME 31–64. From *Itin.* 1: 2 (RS, 33; Thorpe, 93); *Descr.* 1: 6 (RS, 176–78; Thorpe, 230).

Lat. 50. *Habundat*] The singular verb in Ox and Ga (subject *materia*, 47) is more likely to be original than Hu's *Abundant*.

Lat 55. *hec*] The reading of Hu and Ga (against Ox: *hoc*) agrees with an understood *Wallia* (cf. *hec Wallia* 59).

Lat. 59–66, ME 65–72. *Itin.* 1: 4, 2: 5 (RS, 54, 123; Thorpe, 112–13, 181); *Descr.* 1: 6 (RS, 177; Thorpe, 230–31; By "twy" Higden and Trevisa must mean the River Dovey, Gerald's "Dewi").

Lat. 67–76, ME 73–82. Castles/courts: *Itin.* 1: 10 (RS, 80–81; Thorpe, 139), *Descr.* 1. 4 (RS, 169–70; Thorpe, 223–24) (Dinevor=Carmarthen). Bishoprics: *Itin.* 2: 1 (RS, 105; Thorpe, 164), *Descr.* 1: 4 (RS, 169–70; Thorpe, 224).

Lat. 77–97, ME 83–104. On the mode of dress of the Welsh, see *Descr.* 1: 10 (RS, 184; Thorpe, 237).

ME 89. *vayn*] There is nothing corresponding to this word in the Latin; "vain, useless" would be contradicted by 91–102; so perhaps it is Trevisa's distortion of *fyn* "fine" for rhyme.

ME 95. Trevisa's *A* is plural ("they"—cf. the Latin version), but the scribe of T has understood it as singular and copied it as *He*. He leaves the *-ep* verbal endings (normal in Trevisa's dialect for 3 pl. present tense), which he usually changes to *-en* when he recognizes them as plural.

Lat. 98–105, ME 105–12. For these general features of Welsh life, cf. *Descr.* 1: 8 (RS, 180–81; Thorpe, 234).

Lat. 106–15, ME 113–20. Gildas on cowardice and perfidy in the Welsh: see *Descr.* 2: 2, 3 (RS, 207–11; Thorpe, 257–60).

Lat. 112–15, ME 115–22. Castle-building is one of the procedures recommended by Gerald, in the twelfth century, to "any prince who is really determined to conquer the Welsh and to govern them in peace"; *Descr.* 2: 8 (RS, 218; Thorpe, 267). Higden, in the fourteenth century, is able to observe that the policy has been successful.

Lat. 116, ME 123. The ability to endure hunger is a claim made for the Welsh a number of times by Gerald, e.g., in *Descr.* 1: 9, 2: 3, 10 (RS, 182, 210, 226; Thorpe, 235, 260, 273).

Lat. 117–75, ME 124–86. The domestic and social habits of the Welsh are the subject of Gerald's Chap. 10 of *Descr.* 1 (RS, 182–84; Thorpe, 236–37), but Higden distorts some of Gerald's observations and apparently introduces some pejorative ones of his own, such as the alleged custom of siting the privy just outside the front door of the house (Lat. 170–71).

Lat. 130–37, ME 137–46. Gerald alludes to the drunkenness and greed of the Welsh in times of plenty, in contrast to their abstinence and frugality in times of scarcity (*Descr.* 2: 5 [RS, 212–13; Thorpe, 262]); Higden generalizes the negative judgment. I have not found this comment on wine in Gerald; in fact the passage reads like a stereotypical condemnation of the drinking habits of a neighboring people—cf. *Polychronicon*, Book VI, Chap. 9: on the Danes: *a natura potatores fortissimi*, and Hamlet's reechoing of the theme in *Hamlet*, Act I, scene iv:

> This heavy-handed revel east and west
> Makes us traduced and tax'd of other nations.
> They clepe us drunkards, and with swinish phrase
> Soil our addition...

Lat. 160–63, ME 171–74. Gerald's ambiguous *si pedes ablui permiserint* is taken by Higden to mean that the guests (the implied subject of *lauerint, pendunt,* and *venerint*) wash their own feet. Trevisa's translation, on the other hand, implies that he understood that the host washes the guests' feet.

Lat. 173–74, ME 183–84. Gerald's four chapters on Welsh eloquence, poetry, and music (*Descr.* 1: 12–15 [RS, 186–94; Thorpe, 238–46]) are here reduced to one perfunctory couplet.

Lat. 176–79, ME 187–90. Trojan ancestry and pride of family: *Descr.* 1: 15, 17 (RS, 193–94, 200; Thorpe, 245–46, 251).

Lat. 180–83, ME 191–94. Respect for the priesthood: *Descr.* 1: 18 (RS, 203; Thorpe, 253).

Lat. 181, ME 192. Trevisa's *worschipeþ* translates Lat. *fauent* rather than *parent* ("obey"). *Fauent* is the reading of MS B collated by the RS editor, and is adopted here as a conjectural emendation.

Lat. 184–87, ME 195–98. For Merlin and other soothsayers, see *Descr.* 1: 16 (RS, 194–200; Thorpe, 246–51).

Lat. 188–205, ME 199–218. This passage on the improvement in the manners of the Welsh (here attributed to contact with the English and greater commercial prosperity) is original with Higden and relates to the fourteenth-century situation, as Higden saw it.

ME 192. The metrically superior reading of GSHA suggests that the *al* of CT is scribal.

ME 205. *as wol God*]. The phrase puzzled Higden's first RS editor, Babington, who notes: "The text seems corrupt." In the context of Welsh "barbarism" and English "civilization," however, the phrase probably expresses the conviction that everything in which the English differ, even military dress, can be characterized as the will of God.

Lat. 206–11, ME 219–24. The reasonable argument that the contemporary more peaceful stance of the Welsh is an effect of their greater material prosperity is followed, rather illogically, by the topos of the superior contentment and security of the poor compared to the wealthy.

Lat. 214–410, ME 225–470. Higden finds ample material to illustrate the marvels of Wales in Gerald's account of the 1188 journey through Wales of Archbishop Baldwin to recruit support for the Third Crusade.

Lat. 214–24, ME 225–36. The description of Brecknock Mere (also known as Llangorse Lake) is at *Itin.* 1: 2 (RS, 33–36; Thorpe, 93–96).

Lat. 225–44, ME 237–66. The account of Goldcliff, including Gerald's speculation on mineral deposits in the earth, is from *Itin.* 1: 5 (RS, 56–57; Thorpe, 115–16). The passage runs as follows in Gerald's Latin prose:

> Non procul inde [i.e., from Caerleon] stat rupis marina, Sabrinis supereminens fluctibus, quae Anglorum lingua Goldclive vocatur, hoc est, rupis aurea; eo quod aurei coloris saxa praeferat sole repercussa, miro fulgore rutulantia.
>   Nec mihi de facili fieri persuasio posset,
>   Quod frustra tantum dederit natura nitorem
>   Saxis, quodque suo fuerit flos hic sine fructu. [unidentified quotation—perhaps original to Gerald]

si foret, qui venas ibidem, et penitima terrae viscera, arte praevia transpenetraret; si foret, inquam, qui de petra mel eliceret, et oleum de saxo. Multa nimirum occulta latent naturae beneficia, quae, per incuriam hactenus incognita, posterorum educet cura propensior et diligentia. Nam sicut antiquos in humanae vitae commodis inveniendi viam ipsa necessitas urgens edocuit, sic junioribus industria sedula plurimum contulit, et ingenii perspicacioris acumen multa modernis aperuit. Quoniam, ut ait poeta, duas inventionum istarum causas assignans:

> Labor omnia vincit
> Improbus, et duris urgens in rebus egestas. (Virgil, *Georgics*, 1: 145–46)

Lat. 245–60, ME 267–82. For Barry, see *Itin.* 1: 6 (RS, 66–67; Thorpe, 125). It is not clear to me why Trevisa translates Higden's *South Wallia* as "West Wales."

Lat. 261–68, ME 283–90. On the activities of devils in Pembroke, see *Itin.* 1: 12 (RS, 93–94; Thorpe, 151–52).

Lat. 265–68. The construction seems to be: "an apparition . . . which is not able to be banished by any skills or prayers."

Lat. 269–76, ME 291–96. The miraculous tumulus at Crug Mawr is referred to by Gerald at *Itin.* 2: 3 (RS, 118; Thorpe, 177).

ME 297. Nefyn, Caern., is meant (cf. the Latin text), but Trevisa appears to have understood Nemyn; it is corrected later to Neuyn only by the scribe of G.

Lat. 277–312, ME 297–368. On Bardsey Island, see *Itin.* 2: 6 (RS, 124; Thorpe, 183–84). A longer discussion of the two Merlins, on which Lat. 299–312 is based, occurs in *Itin.* 2: 8 (RS, 133–34; Thorpe, 192–93).

Lat. 313–32, ME 369–88. Gerald's chapter on Snowdonia, from which these details come, is *Itin.* 2: 9 (RS, 135–36; Thorpe 194–95).

ME 317–20. These lines rhyme, exceptionally, abab. The scribe of A (who copies the text as verse) appears to have tried to reform them into two couplets, so:

> Kyng fortigern sat on
> þe water side & was wel ful of woon
> þanne Ambrose merlyn p(ro)phesied so
> To fore hi(m) þere riȝt þoo

ME 257, 321, 359: *Treuisa*; 267, 347, 363: *Ranulphus*. Throughout the *Polychronicon*, Higden uses the initial R (for *Ranulphus*) to signal the interpolation of an opinion or observation of his own into what is presented overall as a compilation of other writers' work. Trevisa adopts this custom for his own ME interpolations (labelled *Treuisa*) in his translation of Higden's chronicle. These are sometimes (as in the case of lines 359–62) definitions aimed at his English readers, or additional doctrinal comments (as in 257–66). Quite frequently an interpolation takes the form of a correction of what he perceived as a doctrinal error on Higden's part, as in lines 321–46 here. Normally he copies the rubric *Ranulphus* from his copy text. In this chapter, however, where the three instances of *Ranulphus* are not copied from the Latin, he appears to be using the rubric to signal the end of his own interpolation and the resumption of translation from Higden's Latin.

ME 388. *mylewel*] "mulvel"; see OED s.v. mulvel, where it is defined as "cod." Thorpe (195) translates Gerald's *Mulvelli* (pl.) (RS, 136) as "mullet." Higden's *In Mulwellis* (Lat. 332; RS edn. variants: *Mulwelles*, *Mulwelle*) suggests he thought it was a place-name.

Lat. 333–38, ME 389–94. The spring at Rhuddlan is mentioned in *Itin.* 2: 10 (RS, 137; Thorpe, 196).

Lat. 339–62, ME 395–420. The miraculous homing stone of Anglesey: *Itin.* 2: 7 (RS, 128; Thorpe, 187–88).

Lat. 363–68, ME 421–26. *Itin.* 2: 7 (RS, 128; Thorpe, 188).

ME 424. *wiþ*] The reading of all the ME manuscripts collated (except G—a mid-fifeenth-century manuscript) is *wiþout*. This could be either a mistranslation (cf. Latin text) or early scribal error. The emendation gives the benefit of the doubt to Trevisa.

Lat. 369–80, ME 427–38. This story of the island of Ynys Lannog is also from Gerald's chapter on Anglesey (RS, 131; Thorpe, 190), as is the remark about the proneness of the Welsh and Irish (and their saints!) to be angry and vindictive (RS, 130; Thorpe, 189). Higden has already used this observation (from Gerald's *Topographia Hibernica*, 2: 55) in his earlier chapter on Ireland (*Polychronicon*, Book I, Chap. 36).

Lat. 381–90, ME 439–48. Gerald mentions this characteristic of the Welsh, Scots, and Irish in *Itin.* 1: 2 (RS, 27; Thorpe, 87), and (of the Welsh specifically) in *Descr.* 1: 18 (RS, 203; Thorpe, 253).

Lat. 391–410, ME 449–70. Gerald briefly mentions Basingwerk Priory in *Itin.* 2: 10 (RS, 137; Thorpe, 196) as the place where the Archbishop and his entourage spent one night before crossing the Dee to Chester, but says nothing about St. Winefred. Higden, the monk of Chester, was evidently acquainted with what for him was a local legend, and introduces it as a fitting conclusion to his chapter on Wales.

Lat. 391, ME 449. *Basingwere*] for *Basingwerk* (apparently Higden's error, uncorrected by Trevisa).

Notes

1. Contrary to his usual practice, Higden gives no sources for this chapter in the body of the text. His list of sources in Chap. 2 of Book I, however, mentions three works of Giraldus: *Topographia Hiberniae*, *Itinerarium Wallie*, and *Vita Regis Henrici Secundi*. It may be that he mentally subsumed the *Descriptio Kambriae* (which he certainly used, as the Commentary section will show) under the second of these. The two works of Giraldus that Higden used for this chapter are specified in the Commentary section as *Itin.* and *Descr.*, referring to the Latin texts as edited by James F. Dimock (London: Longmans, Green, Reader, and Dyer, 1868) Rolls Series [RS] 21, vol. 6, and the English translations by Lewis Thorpe in *Gerald of Wales, The Journey through Wales and the Description of Wales* (London: Penguin, 1978).
2. Latin lines 213–24, Thorpe, *Gerald*, 93–96.
3. "*Treuisa*. God woot what þis ys to mene, bote poetes in here manere of speche feyneþ as þey euerych kunde, craft & lyuyng hadde a dyuers god, euerych fram oþer." Trevisa clashes again with Gerald in the same chapter,

where he objects to the qualification "...ȝef hyt ys leuefol for to trowe" after Gerald has stated that "Yn þis Caerleon was Amphibalus ybore þat taughte Seint Albon. Þar þe messagers of Rome come to þe gret Arthure hys gret courte." Trevisa: interpolates: "ȝef Gerald were in doute wheþer hyt were leuefol for to trowe hyt oþer no, hyt was noȝt fol gret redynesse to wryte hyt in hys bokes as som man wolde weene. For hyt ys a wonder sweeuon ymet for to wryte a long story to haue eueremore in muynde and euere haue doute ȝef hyt be a mysbeleeue. Ȝif alle hys bokes were such, what loore were þerynne, and namelych whyle a makeþ noon euydence for nernoþer syde noþer telleþ what him meoueþ so for to sygge" (*Polychronicon*, I: Chap. 48: MS Cott. Tib. D. vii).

4. On this subject see A. S. G. Edwards, "The Influence and Audience of the *Polychronicon*: Some Observations," *Proceedings of the Leeds Philosophical and Literary Society: Literary and Historical Section* 17 (1980): 113–19.

5. Trevisa's complicity in Higden's pejorative picture of the Welsh is further evidence that, though a Cornishman, he felt no personal affinity with Celtic Britain nor any wish to vindicate its legendary history as related by Geoffrey of Monmouth. See John E. Housman, "Higden, Trevisa, Caxton, and the Beginnings of Arthurian Criticism," *Review of English Studies* 22 (1947): 209–17, and my reply in *Notes and Queries* 234 (1989): 303–7.

6. The standard edition, *Polychronicon Ranulphi Higden Monachi Cestrensis; together with the English Translation of John Trevisa and of an Unknown Writer of the Fifteenth Century*, ed. Churchill Babington and Joseph R. Lumby, 9 vols., Rolls Series 41 (London: HMSO, 1865–86), is referred to here as "RS edn." The text of Trevisa's translation in that edition is based on Cambridge, St. John's College MS 204, in Book I collated solely with London, British Library MS Add. 24194, which I have collated as MS A for the present edition of Chap. 38. I have demonstrated elsewhere (see note 7) that the St. John's MS is a direct or indirect copy of A. Therefore, although the text of Chap. 38 in the RS edn. has been collated for the purpose of the present edition, it has been unnecessary to cite variants from that edition.

7. Ronald Waldron, ed., *John Trevisa's Translation of the "Polychronicon" of Ranulph Higden. Book VI*, Middle English Texts 35 (Heidelberg: C. Winter, 2004).

CHAPTER 7

WALES AND WELSHNESS IN MIDDLE
ENGLISH ROMANCES

Tony Davenport

On the face of it Wales would seem to be a perfectly suitable and available setting for medieval romance. In the late twelfth century, when romance first seems to have developed distinct forms, there were existing literary images of Wales that might have acted as background to stories of adventure and quest. One of these is the strand of supposed British history found in Geoffrey of Monmouth, which identified Wales mainly with the past. Geoffrey closes his chronicling of the kings of Britain with the dominance of the Saxon invaders, who

> ...landed in parts of Northumbria and occupied the waste lands from Albany to Cornwall. There was no inhabitant left alive to stop them, except for a few little pockets of Britons who had stayed behind, living precariously in Wales, in the remote recesses of the woods...As the foreign element around them became more and more powerful, they were given the name of Welsh instead of Britons: this word deriving either from their leader Gualo, or their queen Galaes, or else from their being so barbarous.[1]

This picture readily merges with scenes from the *Vita Merlini*, Geoffrey's portrayal of a composite Scottish/Welsh Merlin progressing from madness—the result of battle trauma as it would now be seen—to wisdom as a hermit in the woods, prophesying and lamenting:

> O madness of the Britons...they engage in civil wars and battles between relatives...The Welsh shall attack the men of Gwent and afterwards those of Cornwall, and no law shall restrain them. Wales shall rejoice in the shedding of blood. O people always hateful to God, why do you rejoice in

bloodshed? Wales shall compel brothers to fight and to condemn their own relatives to a wicked death . . . Segontium and its towers and mighty palaces shall lament in ruins until the Welsh return to their former domains.[2]

So Merlin combines characterizing the Welsh as violent among themselves, with Wales as a ruined, lost civilization, waiting for the return to a former glory. By the end this has advanced to prophecies of the eventual return of the united Britons from Wales, Cornwall, Brittany, Scotland, Cumbria to peaceful possession of their land. Just as influential as the figure of Merlin is the role of the forest as the landscape of escape and suffering, to recur in the stories of Tristram, Lancelot, Ywain, and Perceval; the forest tradition already exists before medieval times, but it becomes particularly associated with the legendary history of Britain, whether as the primal landscape for the settlement of the country by Albin and her sisters or for tales of the Celtic otherworld.[3] Hence the image of Wales at the wild edges of civilization, a place of fighting and civil war, looking for a return to past greatness and independence.

On the other hand, a more factual, if erratic, literary picturing of Wales is found in the writings of Gerald de Barri (i.e., Gerald of Wales, but his Norman name is a better indicator of his cultural situation). Superficially at least he is more realistic and scientific. *The Journey through Wales* was based on actual travel: the expedition with Archbishop Baldwin in 1188 to recruit men from Wales for the Third Crusade, which took about five weeks, made a complete circuit of the country; the account gives an idea of the different regions, princedoms, and towns at the time.[4] The *Description of Wales*—about natural features, history, social customs, national characteristics—was based on personal observation, though it includes borrowed, unsubstantiated material; it was first written in 1191 but subsequently revised. There is plenty of story material in Gerald's *Journey*, since he enlivens his account of each region with wonders and anecdotes, and there is plenty of thematic material in the *Description*, in which Gerald includes more generalizations about Welshness. An example of plot-material, occurring in Book I, Chapter 2 of the *Journey*, when they have reached Brecknock, is the story of the Norman Bernard of Newmarch's son, Mahel, who gave his mother's lover a beating as he left the mother's house one night; the mother, named Nest (or Agnes by the English), took revenge by falsely telling Henry I that Mahel was not Bernard's son, thus denying him his inheritance. Family history such as this seems much closer to raw material for a writer than, say, the Breton ballads that Marie de France claims as her source. Stories of saints, devils, and faithful dogs, descriptions of Roman ruins, abbeys, and rivers create an impression of interesting variety in the life, landscape, and history of Wales. There are some intriguing passages on language, despite the fact that Gerald's attempts at comparative philology are amateurish and simple and that he specifies only commonplaces of vocabulary, place-name elements, and so on, though he does correct Geoffrey's etymologies for Wales and Welsh by relating them to the Saxon *wealh*, "foreign." Most interesting are his examples of clashes of language, as in the story of Henry II arriving from Ireland in Cardiff and challenged in English (Gerald actually says "quasi Teutonice") by a tall man in a white habit who preaches against misuse of the Sabbath. In French ("lingua Gallica"), Henry tells Philip de Mercros, the soldier who is holding the rein of his horse, to ask "this rustic" if he is dreaming, which the soldier then does in English ("Anglice"). More interesting now than the actual warning to Henry to mend his ways is the bilingual maneuvering, with further complexity added by Gerald's recording the incident in Latin.[5] In this instance, the Welsh language is not mentioned, though presumably among the bystanders there were Welsh speakers, as well as those conversant with English and French. Welsh is involved in the case of a similar confrontation, when Henry II was again arriving from Ireland, this time at St. Davids: a Welsh woman threw herself at his feet as he was walking in procession with the clergy toward the cathedral, complaining about the bishop in Welsh; her words are explained by an interpreter; she is then "driven away by those who understood the Welsh language" and she exits, repeating "the well-known fiction and prophecy of Merlin" that a King of England after conquering Ireland would die when he returned to St. Davids as he crossed the stone bridging the river Alun. (Henry defies the prophecy and crosses.)[6] It is such cultural clashes and mixtures that one might have expected to turn up in romance tales of travel and border-crossing, but which romances are very apt completely to ignore.

The Description of Wales is more concerned with social ethnography, the nature, manner, and customs of the Welsh people, alongside passages about nature, such as the habits of beavers. Here is a characteristic passage:

> In Wales no one begs. Everyone's home is open to all, for the Welsh generosity and hospitality are the greatest of all virtues. They very much enjoy welcoming others to their homes. When you travel there is no question of your asking for accommodation or of their offering it; you just march into a house and hand over your weapons to the person in charge. They give you water so that you may wash your feet and that means that you are a guest.[7]

Gerald seems to have thought of himself as drawing up a balance sheet, since his second book concentrates on the less good aspects of the Welsh:

> Although they have no conception of honour themselves, the Welsh, like all barbarous peoples, want more than anything else to be honoured. They respect and revere honest dealing in others, although they lack it them-selves. As a race they are mercurial and unreliable. The moment they show signs of rebellion, no mercy should be shown to them and they must be punished immediately...The prince or governor must never entrust his capital or chief stronghold to the Welsh, for, however friendly they appear, a people which is held in subjection is always plotting treachery.[8]

However, since this passage appears, *mutatis mutandis*, also in *The Conquest of Ireland*, Book II, Chapter 39, one can see it as part of Gerald's generalizing about Welsh and Irish, as he does in his description of musical instruments, skills and techniques, and the section on guerrilla warfare and how to govern rebellious countries.

Between them Geoffrey and Gerald are indicators of the sorts of material available to romance writers that one might expect to recognize in non-Welsh texts. These include the ideas of remoteness and wildness, which make suitable settings for lonely upbringings, interludes of madness, fighting encounters, vengeful brothers, as well as instances of a distinct society and language, of borders to cross, and of separate traditions and history.

When one turns to romance roughly contemporary with Gerald's writings, one finds in the most important collection of early romances after Chrétien, the *Lais* of Marie de France (some of which at least were written in England, though not in English), that Wales can occur as a setting, most particularly in *Milun*. The story is of illicit love and a concealed pregnancy and birth; the hero is a knight born in South Wales whose reputation as a noble, bold, and courtly fighter, attracts a rich nobleman's daughter; she offers herself to him as his love and is just as enterprising when it comes to hiding the resulting pregnancy and arranging for their son to be taken to Northumbria to be brought up by her sister. Since Milun is forced to go abroad to seek fame and fortune as a mercenary, his love has little choice but to marry the rich man her father finds for her. For the next twenty years Milun and his beloved exchange messages by means of a trained swan, alternately starved and fed by the two, so that it goes to and fro between them. They are at last brought together by their son who identifies his father after breaking off a fight with him at a tournament in Brittany, when he sees the gray hair beneath his helmet.

There are several interesting features in the poem, including the identification of the place where hero and heroine live and the antithesis between Wales and Northumbria as mutually exclusive areas of knowledge. The most unusual narrative motif is the appearance of a swan as love-messenger. Constance Bullock-Davies argued that the swan, which is outside the range of literary convention as a go-between, was a literal link to South Wales and that the details given of the odd process (the starving/feeding routine) betokens truth to nature.[9] She localizes the story to Gwent, with reference particularly to the natural breeding-ground for swans in the marshy lands south or southwest of Caerleon, from the mouth of the River Rhymney to Portskewitt, an area that was a tidal flat until the eighteenth century. There are a number of details that, she suggests, "it is difficult to account for in other than factual terms" and concludes that the motif is "obviously meant to be part of an identifiable background."[10]

The translators of Marie's *Lais* distinguish between those set almost entirely in Brittany or Normandy, which "could well have been written in France,"[11] and those either with travelling heroes or set in Britain. In *Guigemar* the hero sails from Brittany to a destination that could be Cornwall or South Wales; in *Eliduc* the hero sails to Devon and the lay mentions Totnes and Exeter; *Lanval* is set in Carlisle; *Chevrefoil* takes place in Cornwall and mentions Tintagel, though we are told that Tristram, like Milun, was born in South Wales. *Yonec* is nearest to *Milun*, a tragic version of the secret son story, beginning in Caerwent, where a rich old advocate imprisons his young wife in a tower; she is magically visited there by a knight who arrives in the form of a hawk to love her and beget a son upon her. The old man and his spying sister discover the secret and bring about the knight's death. The story ends twenty or so years later in Caerleon, when the hawk-knight's tomb is visited by the old man, his wife, and her son, named Yonec, and the history thereby revealed; the lady dies after handing his father's sword to Yonec, who kills his stepfather and becomes the region's lord. Marie is less detailed about circumstances in this tale of love and magic, specifying only the situation of Caerwent on the River Duelas and the fact that formerly the river was navigable as far as the city. In Caerleon she describes simply a castle and an abbey with a tomb.

Apart from what these British settings imply about the author's own life, making it likely that Marie settled in Britain and introduced places she had visited or heard about into her tales, they suggest that for a French-speaking writer at the time, Wales was as potentially interesting and central to contemporary ideas of chivalric fiction as other settings. The rarity of similar appearances of Wales in romance texts written in English marks a different attitude. Even a text that in French had a significant role for Welshness might lose it in translation, as is the case in *Sir Perceval of Galles*, the English version of Chrétien's Grail romance.[12] In the French text the hero's being "gallois" is a meaningful identification of character, even if apparently in a mainly negative sense, as Rupert T. Pickens demonstrates in his discussion of the poem.[13]

> Galois sont tot par nature
> Plus fol que bestes en pasture;
> Cist [i.e., Perceval] est ausi come une beste.
>   (243–45)

By the standards of the Arthurian court, to be Welsh is to be uncivilized and stupid, and yet that court is itself exposed to irony and moral judgment in the poem, so that the hero's simple courage and expertise with his Welsh javelin, and his rough peasant dress assert the strengths of his Welsh origins. Chrétien's comparison of *gallois* and *courtois* virtually disappears from the English poem, just as the Grail theme does. The English Perceval is a comically "wild" boy, referred to only a couple of times as "of Galles," and retaining from his Welsh origins only his forest upbringing. The emphasis is on the hero's innocence: the idea of cultural Welshness is replaced by a biblical primitiveness.[14] Interestingly *Sir Perceval of Galles* is in some respects closer to the Welsh *Peredur* from which the identification of Welshness with stupidity and barbarity has been removed for obvious reasons.[15]

It is not until the fifteenth century that one encounters a romance in English that has Wales as its setting throughout. This is *Sir Cleges*, surviving in two manuscript versions, in Bodleian Library MS Ashmole 61 and National Library of Scotland MS Advocates 19.1.11.[16] It is set in the past and deliberately evokes a nostalgic sense of the life of long ago and the ancestors "þat before vs were"; to this end the king on the throne is Uther Pendragon, so that simple domestic virtues are celebrated as belonging to pre-Arthurian times. Sir Cleges and his wife,

Dame Clarys, are exemplars of an old-style lordly generosity, especially in
their Christmas feasts, when they reward minstrels as well as their tenants,
guests, and visitors, and distribute alms to the poor. Cleges, we are told, acted
"As he hade ben a kynge." As a result he is reduced to poverty; all his manors
have to be sold until he has only the house in which he lives frugally with his
wife and two young children. The first dramatized scene is of husband and
wife at Christmas time, living "by Cardyff syde," that is, outside the walls of
the town where Uther presides over his court. Hearing the music and dancing
of others as he walks about, Cleges laments in remembering the "myrth he
was wonte to hold," but his wife cheers him, urging him to be satisfied with
what he has and they go in to the meal she has prepared; afterward they play
with their children, attend evensong, and go to bed contented, rising early to
go to church, where Cleges prays for the safety of his family and Dame Clarys
for the comfort of her husband. The main event in this partly pious romance
is the miracle of a cherry-tree fruiting at Christmas, and the miracle, like the
homely scene before it, is set in domestic simplicity: Cleges goes to the garden
and offers thanks to God, kneeling beneath the cherry-tree; as he rises he
grasps the bough and finds leaves and fruit. At first fearing that this is a sign
of more grievance to come he again is rallied by the ever-cheerful wife, who
proposes that he should go to Cardiff next day with a basket of the fruit as a
gift for the king.

> Tomorrow to Cardyff I will go
>   After your entent.
>   (239–40)

So, on Christmas morning with his elder son he sets off.

The narrative now turns in the direction of fabliau and satire as Cleges has
to face three challenges at the gates of the palace: first the porter, seeing a man
in poor clothing, threatens violence, demanding a third share "Off þat the kyng
wyll gyff þe / Wheþer it be syluer or gold" (287–88); Cleges is forced to consent.
Then follows the doorkeeper/usher; again threats of violence shift at the sight of
the cherries into a demand for a third of any reward; Cleges "wiþ heuy chere"
accedes. The steward in turn repels Cleges as "Cherle!" sees the cherries and
demands his third. Cleges ponders on his situation:

> Myselue I schall haue nothyng,
> For my traueyll schall I not gete.
>   (351–52)

At last he is in the king's presence and the gift is made; the king makes a
present of the cherries to the Cornish lady who is to be his wife and who is his
Christmas guest (an interestingly different view of the relationship between
Arthur's parents) and cherries are served to all in the hall. Cleges, as ever ready
gloomily to think that all has been in vain, when offered by Uther anything

he wishes as a reward, "Wheþer it be lond our lede, / Or oþer gode," asks only for twelve strokes:

> With my staff to pay þem all,
> Myn aduersarys in þis hall.
>
>   (430–31)

Uther repents of his offer but Cleges persists, the blows are delivered to steward, usher, and porter, and when Cleges is given the opportunity to explain, the company laughs, and the king's minstrel explains that "thys pore man" is Sir Cleges, a former knight, "A man of hye stature." Uther rewards him with "All þat longes to a knyght" and the castle of Cardiff itself, makes him his steward, sends a gold cup to Dame Clarys and makes the son a squire. So the poem ends with prosperity restored and the goodness of the knight and his wife praised.

Sir Cleges may be enjoyed and dismissed as a light-hearted Christmas game, though it earns admiration for its ingenuity in combining elements from several different genres; balancing the pious miracle, itself handled with convincing simplicity, and the fabliau comedy of the encounters with porter, usher, and steward, shows unusual poise, and the domestic realism of the scenes between Cleges and his wife provides the most touching and sympathetic picture of family life in Middle English romance. The miracle echoes the Cherry-Tree Carol's story of Mary and Joseph and some miracles of saints,[17] though none is an exact match and the image of the Christmas cherries is uniquely expressive of the theme of the blessedness of the poor, good man, a theme found in different forms in other romances, such as Sir Amadace and Sir Launfal. In no romance, however, is there a more vivid contrast than in Sir Cleges between poverty and riches, the rich man in his castle, the poor man at his gate.

> Syr Cleges and hys son gent
> The ryght wey to Cardyfe went
>   On Crystenmas Day.
> To þe castell-ȝate þei com full ryght,
> As þei wer to mete dyght,
>   At none, þe soth to sey.
> As Sir Cleges wold in go,
> Yn pore clothyng was he tho,
>   In a simple aray.
> The porter seyd full spytously:
> "Thow schall withdraw þe smertly,
>   Y rede withoute deley.
>
> Els be God and Seynt Mary,
> Y schall breke þi hede smertly,
>   To stonde in begers route.
> Yff þou draw any mour inwerd,
> Thow schall rew it afterwerd;
>   Y schall þe so cloute."

"Gode sir," seyd Sir Cleges tho,
"Y pray ȝou, late me in go;
   Thys is withouten doute.
The kyng I haue a present browȝt
Fro hym þat made all thinge of nouȝt;
   Behold and loke aboute!"
             (253–76)

The humiliation of Cleges at the gates of Uther's court may be read as a contrast between Welsh and English manners, even if Uther is historically a fellow-Briton. There is some bite added to the story of the shared blows if one attributes a touch of nationalism to the encounters.[18]

Cleges is rewarded at the end for generosity, not only restored to favor and recompensed but made master of Cardiff Castle; one could think of it as an illustration of Gerald de Barri's identification of hospitality as a particularly Welsh virtue. This is a tale from long after Prince Llewelyn, perhaps after the rebellion of Glyn Dŵr, and it may be that history makes it more likely that one should read the position of Cleges as that of an English marcher lord but it is more satisfying to think of him as a native of Cardiff who is for once allowed to get his own back.[19]

Otherwise Wales is mentioned surprisingly little in Middle English narratives—surprisingly because romances are so geographically varied, and tend to use the hero's crossings of borders as stages in his adventures; one might therefore expect more use of identifiable boundaries within Britain, at least for those heroes whose ancestry was not continental. There are a few notable occurrences. First to come to mind is likely to be the hero in *Sir Gawain and the Green Knight*, as he rides "þurȝ þe ryalme of Logres" by a specified route:

Til þat he neȝed ful neghe into þe Norþ Wales.
Alle þe iles of Anglesay on lyft half he haldez,
And farez ouer þe fordez by þe forlondez,
Ouer at þe Holy Hede, til he hade eft bonk
In þe wyldrenesse of Wyrale...

             (697–701)

There has been plenty of debate about the details but it is clear that a journey north from a southwestern Camelot is likely to pass through Wales, and it sounds as if Gawain is following Gerald de Barri's route up the west coast and then east along the north coast, crossing the Conwy and Clwyd rivers where they flow into the sea, then through St. Asaph to Holywell, along the Dee estuary, crossing the Dee before Chester; however, the text famously assumes that the reader knows more about the crossings into the Wirral than has proved to be the case in modern times. It is interesting that Gawain finds himself "in contrayez straunge" (line 713) only after he has left Wales behind and passed into an anonymous landscape of mountain, stream, and forest.[20] This sort of "normal" appearance of Wales as part of a likely journey away from the Arthurian court serves to highlight the extraordinary and implausible geography of many romances involving traveling heroes and heroines. *Guy of Warwick* begins in England with references to Warwick, Oxford, Buckingham, Wallingford, but Guy is soon off to France, Germany, Constantinople; later after killing a dragon in Northumbria, he stays in England only long enough to marry and beget a child before setting off for Alexandria. *Bevis of Hamtoun* has a home base in Southampton but the hero is soon whisked away to "Ermonie," "Mombraunt," Cologne, and though there are later localized London references, there is no sustained likelihood in the geography. The Constance story might be expected to provide likely ports of call and, indeed, in the version in *Emaré*, the heroine's first unsteered voyage from Rome brings her "into a lond / That hyghth Galys"; this is usually taken to be Galicia in Spain, but could be read as Wales, since it is just as likely a place to which to drift in an open boat and rather more likely than Northumbria, which is where Constance comes to shore in the retellings by Chaucer and Gower. The source for both was the life of Constance written by Nicholas Trivet, who at least took note of the linguistic problem inherent in these tales of more than one country and culture to the extent of making Constance an accomplished polyglot who could address the inhabitants of Northumbria "en Sessoneys [Saxonish]."[21] Chaucer is alerted by this to take note of some of the multicultural aspects of the tale; he both explains how she made herself understood and varies the passage in Trivet/Gower where Bishop Lucius has to be sent for to come from Bangor to baptize those converted by Constance:

> The constable of the castel doun is fare
> To seen this wrak, and al the ship he soghte,
> And foond this wery womman ful of care;
> He foond also the tresor that she broghte.
> In hir langage mercy she bisoghte,
> The lyf out of hir body for to twynne,
> Hire to delivere of wo that she was inne.
>
> A maner Latyn corrupt was hir speche,
> But algates therby was she understonde...
>
> This constable and Dame Hermengyld, his wyf,
> Were payens, and that contree everywhere;...
>
> In al that lond no Cristen dorste route;
> Alle Cristen folk ben fled fro that contree
> Thurgh payens, that conquereden al aboute
> The plages of the north, by land and see.
> To Walys fledde the Cristyanytee
> Of olde Britons dwellynge in this ile;
> Ther was hir refut for the meene while.
> (Man of Law's Tale, 512–46)

John Burrow has written about Chaucer's reference to the form of Latin in use as a lingua franca,[22] and it seems an appropriate corollary to this awareness on

Chaucer's part that he should supply an explanatory note on the Northumbria/ Wales antithesis in terms of religion; Geoffrey of Monmouth's legendary history is given a new gloss. This is in fact Chaucer's only use of the word "Wales," though in *The House of Fame* his reference to the bard Glasgerion shows some knowledge of Welsh traditions and a Welsh or Irish source has been claimed for the whirling house of twigs described there. Similarly one can find scattered mentions of Wales in Laȝamon, Langland, *Morte Arthure*, Malory, but actual visits to Wales are scarce. However, there is a small group of English romances in which Wales is part of the hero's adventurous progress. First comes the story of Horn.

The Anglo-Norman *Romance of Horn*, composed by one of the ubiquitous Thomases of the twelfth century, perhaps a native English speaker, or at least someone who knew enough English to engage in wordplay on his hero's name and use some English terms, could (according to the argument of Judith Weiss and others) have been intended for an audience in Dublin at Christmas 1171 consisting of Henry II, Richard fitz Gilbert, earl of Clare (known as Strongbow) and other Anglo-Norman barons brought to Ireland at the request of the King of Leinster.[23] If so, it would place the poem at the heart of the conflicting interests described by Gerald de Barri in his *Expugnatio Hibernica (The Conquest of Ireland)*. Gerald's cousin, Raymond le Gros, was Strongbow's constable and Gerald wrote of his and his Norman uncles' deeds in Ireland with pride (and presumably with some knowledge). Gerald's modern biographer, Robert Bartlett, expresses the complex ethnic, linguistic and political intermesh by suggesting that

> . . . the invasion of Ireland [i.e., by Henry II] in 1169 and the subsequent settlement exported the whole chequered society of South Wales into a completely different racial and linguistic framework.[24]

And he quotes a charter issued in the name of Raymond le Gros which is addressed to:

> . . . all present and to come, French, English, Flemish, Welsh and Irish.[25]

(The Flemish are included because Henry I had settled Flemish craftsmen in Pembrokeshire and Flemish was still spoken there in the twelfth century.)

So *The Romance of Horn* possibly had as its context an extremely complex language and social mixture. It is interesting in the light of what Gerald has to say about Welsh and Irish music-making, their variety of instruments and technical skills, that the *Romance of Horn* contains a remarkably lengthy, detailed passage about harp-playing, far more specific and technical about tuning the instrument than is the norm in minstrel narratives.

The story is one of a young hero forced into exile, who travels to another country where he helps the king and gains the love of the king's daughter before returning to his own homeland to win back his own rights. He then has to rescue his bride from a forced marriage before marrying her himself. Perhaps in some lost original version of the tale only two countries were involved, the hero's homeland and the kingdom where he finds his bride, but already by the time the Anglo-Norman poem was composed it has become three countries. It begins in an unnamed realm (later referred to as Suddene and usually understood as some part of England, although the historical material of the plot has been transmuted into fighting between Christians and Saracens), then moves to Brittany where Horn and Rigmel fall in love, and then, when Horn loses the favor of King Hunlaf, to Ireland where a second princess falls in love with him.

Weiss's argument, referred to above, is that Thomas's reasons for introducing a story of a Breton who came to seek his fortune in Ireland, helps the king there, and after the male heir has been killed, nearly marries the king's daughter and acquires the kingdom, are the parallels to the career of Strongbow. After Henry II had refused to allow him his father's title as Earl of Pembroke, he was asked for help by the King of Leinster, with the promise of his daughter's hand and the kingdom after the king's death as inducements. Strongbow therefore followed his Welsh allies to Ireland in 1170 and helped to quell the king's enemies (Irish, Norse, and Danes), married the King of Leinster's daughter but needed the help of Henry II to quell rebellion when the King of Leinster died and Strongbow tried to take over power. Thus there may well be particular political point in the mixture of countries in the Anglo-Norman *Romance of Horn*, rather than just the romancer's desire for duplication and introducing as many lovelorn princesses as possible. But does the political point survive in the several English versions of the story?

The best-known English version *King Horn* was composed at least fifty, perhaps as much as a hundred years, later and famously confuses things by increasing the use of fictional place-names like those detective stories of the 1930s and beyond set in Loamshire or whatever. The story begins in Suddene (variously identified in modern times as Cornwall, the Isle of Wight, the Isle of Man, South Dean in Roxburghshire, etc.) and moves to Westernesse (read as the Wirral, Brittany, Cumbria, Cornwall, Galloway—why not Wales?) and then to Ireland. The poem has nearly always been seen as a blurring of the story's historical origins into folktale: the Saracens perhaps taken over from the chansons de geste,[26] are again the enemy both in Suddene and in Ireland, and the continuous crossings of water and repetitions of action seem less significant as geographical strategies and more part of a pattern of growing up and fulfilling the idea of heroism on the part of Horn; the nebulous geography adds to the suggestive poetic and psychological power of the tale.

However, something different occurs in the other (almost certainly fourteenth-century) English treatment of the material, *Horn Childe and Maiden Rimnild*. This text is preserved in the Auchinleck Manuscript,[27] and so can be associated with early fourteenth-century taste for romances about wandering heroes, such as *Guy of Warwick*, and for Breton lais. The action is far more traceable on a map (and the Saracens have disappeared as have most of the sea-crossings). The story begins in northern England ("From Humber norþ") where Horn's father Haþeolf is king; this realm is attacked by marauders from

Denmark who come to "Clifeland by Teseside," fight on Allerton Moor; later Haþeolf goes hunting on Blakey Moor (between Whitby and Pickering), holds a feast at Pickering whence his knights ride to York. He is there attacked by three Irish kings after they have ravaged Westmorland; the knights are summoned to Stainmore (possibly a reminiscence of the Battle of Stainmoor in 954) where Haþeolf is killed. The Irish return to Ireland leaving the opening for an earl from Northumbria to take over Haþeolf's territory and force the king's young son, Horn, and his eight companions to take flight with Horn's tutor. Nothing else in the poem is as detailed in its geography as this opening section, which makes clear the Yorkshire perspective of the composition of the work, but the narrative continues to make sense in terms of place.

The action moves to southern England where King Houlac takes in Horn and his company and Horn and Rimnild fall in love. The companions gradually disperse; two of them go to France and settle there, two to Brittany, leaving behind four—two who are faithful to Horn, two who betray him by telling Houlac that Horn has seduced his daughter, which leads to Horn's banishment. It is, however, again on horseback rather than by sea that the hero takes flight and, adopting a new name, Godebounde, arrives in Wales to take service with the king and to "win gold and fe."

In Wales there are two episodes. First, as he rides through a forest, Horn has to prove his prowess when challenged by an armed knight:

> To Wales Horn com atte lest...
> Þurth a forest as he schuld fare,
> An armed kniзt mett he þare,
> & bad Horn schuld abide,
> To зeld his harneise lesse & mare,
> Oþer iuste, wheþer him leuer ware:
> "Þe lawe is nouзt to hide."
> & Horn of iusting was ful fain
> & seyd to þe kniзt oзain,
> "Ful leue me were to ride."
>   (611, 613–21)[28]

Second, the knight tells Horn of the Welsh king and an eight-day tournament at the Welsh court:

> Our kinges name is Elidan:
> In al Wales is þer nan
> So strong a man as he;
> While þe seuen days be gan,
> Euerich day wiþ sundri man,
> Iusting bedes he þe;
> Þe eiзten day, be þou bold

(ʒif þou þe seuen days mai hold)
Þe king þan schaltow se
Com rideand on a stede broun
Wiþ a soket of feloun, [a deadly spearhead]
Forto win þe gre...

(646–57)

The forest and mountain setting and the nature of the two actions could be
taken as the poet's simple equation of Wales with the commonplaces of fictional
chivalry, but there is more to both episodes. As Robert Rouse has pointed out,
Horn's encounter with the knight who bars the road marks a crossing from an
area of English law into one of Welsh law.[29] Horn attempts to assert his right to
free passage: "Ful leue me were to ride," but the Welsh knight ignores this and
simply charges Horn who accepts the lawlessness of the place by fighting back
and winning. There would seem to be a clear opposition between the England
of King Houlac where Horn has been taught "Þe lawes boþe eld and newe"
(line 274) and the apparent lawlessness of Wales. The description of Elidan's rule
is of a regime based solely on martial force. Maldwyn Mills suggests that the
custom of the hero having to fight with all the king's vassals in succession before
fighting the king himself may be a specifically Celtic motif, since it occurs also
in *Peredur*.[30] The court is given its own place and its independent identity emphasized in the hero's allying himself to the king's interests when he is accepted as a
vassal by Elidan.

Þe king at Snowedoun he fond þare,
Sir Elydan þat tide.
He iusted al þat seuen niʒt,
Eueri day wiþ sundri kniʒt:
He gat þe fairest pride;
Þe eiʒten day wiþ Elidan
(& wan her stedes euerilkan)
In herd is nouʒt to hide.

He smot þe king opon þe scheld:
Of his hors he made him held,
& feld him to þe grounde.
Swiche on hadde he founde seld,
Þat so had feld him in þe feld,
Bifor þat ich stounde.
Þe king asked him what he hiʒt,
& he him answerd anonriʒt,
"Mi name is Godebounde."
"Y wil þe ʒif gold & fe,
ʒif þat þou wil duelle wiþ me
Bi ʒere a þousand pounde."

(646–57, 661–81)

But the significance of the two episodes is perhaps not in any peculiar Welshness in the content, but rather in the simple plausibility of using Wales in such a story; it represents a crossing of boundaries and it functions as a stepping stone to the scenes in Ireland in both narrative and geographical terms. Elidan has to send Welsh knights to Ireland to help his son Finlak, and Horn accepts his responsibility as vassal. So the poem moves to its fourth location in Ireland, specifically 3olkil (most probably Youghal, near Cork), where Horn encounters King Malkan who had killed his father and so is able to exact revenge as well as fulfil his obligation to Elidan. The death of Finlak's sons in the battle and the love of his daughter, Acula, for Horn provide the narrative climax of these Welsh/Irish scenes, from which the poet has to wrench his story back to the threatened Rimnild and to return to England and eventually to Northumbria for the hero to win back his father's land.

This particular version of the Horn story probably came into being during the reign of Edward I (1272–1307) or Edward II (1307–27), but it is difficult to recognize any allusions to contemporary history; reference might be expected to, say, Edward I's campaigns against Prince Llywelyn (1276–77), or to the Statute of Wales (1284) that declared that "the whole of Wales shall be entirely annexed and united to the crown of our kingdom," or to Edward I's building of castles surrounding Snowdonia, or to the investiture of Prince Edward as Prince of Wales at Caernarfon Castle in 1301.Maldwyn Mills suggests that there might be historical allusions, perhaps to Rhodri Mawr, king of Gwynedd, who killed the Danish leader, Horm, in battle in 855 and who was forced by the Danes to take refuge in Ireland.[31] The Welsh scenes may simply be part of the pseudo-historical texture of the Horn story. However, Matthew Holford has argued more recently that there were closer contemporary resonances.[32] Making Horn a supreme fighter successively in England, Wales, and Ireland means that the poem is not just about the emergence of a sense of English nationhood, but about English power in the wider context of the British Isles, "a narrative about empire as well as nation."[33] This emphasis could have seemed necessary when the lordship over Ireland, Wales, and Scotland claimed by Edward I came under threat in the reign of Edward II. From a broader, literary point of view, the episode in Wales indicates that by the early fourteenth century Wales has a role in romance as a suitable wild place of forest and mountain or as a kingdom across a border where the laws and rules are different: romance needs to have a stock of such places as the setting of adventure. *Horn Childe* indicates that it was possible to compose a "traveling" hero's romance within the compass of England, Wales, Ireland, and that the adaptation of Anglo-Norman material might mean a plausible substitution of possible venues for fictional and exotic settings.

Something comparable happens in the English version of the Tristan story, *Sir Tristrem*, where part of the adaptation of the love story into a biographical, hero-focussed romance is to include a period in Wales for the hero.[34] Like *Horn Childe, Bevis of Hamtoun,* and *Guy of Warwick, Sir Tristrem* has an introductory story (of Tristrem's father, and the hero's birth) followed by journeys to foreign kingdoms and involvement with second heroines.

Wales is first mentioned in the poem in the feigned dialogue between Tristrem and Ysoude when they know that Mark is eavesdropping. Tristrem pretends to threaten to leave the court:

> Þou sinnest, leuedi, on me,
> Þou gabbest on me so.
> Mi nem nil me nouȝt se;
> He þreteneþ me to slo.
> More menske it were to þe
> Better for to do,
> Bi God in Trinite,
>   Þis tide;
> Or y þis lond schal fle
> Into Wales wide.
>   (2114–23)[35]

When Ysoude has by subterfuge proved her "innocence" in the trial by ordeal at Westminster, Tristrem does have to leave the court and go into exile and it is to Wales that he makes his way, deliberately seeking a fight in reaction to his loss of Ysoude.

> Tristrem, wiþouten wene,
> Into Wales he is;
> In bataile he haþ ben
> And fast he fraines þis
>   Riȝt þare:
> For he ne may Isoude kisse,
> Fiȝt he souȝt aywhare.
>   (2293–99)

There are several elements in the episode in Wales; first there is, as in *Horn Childe*, a king with a daughter. Then comes a giant, Urgan, besieging the king's tower in order to possess the daughter. The situation is readymade for the hero.

> In Wales þo was a king
> Þat hiȝt Triamour;
> He hadde a douhter ȝing,
> Was hoten Blauncheflour.
> Vrgan wiþ gret wering
> Biseged him in his tour
> To winne þat swete þing
> And bring hir to his bour
>   Wiþ fiȝt.
> Tristrem wiþ gret honour
> Bicom þe kinges kniȝt.
>   (2300–10)

Blaucheflour is, of course, Tristrem's mother's name; Urgan is the brother of Morgan, the killer of Tristrem's father, already slain by Tristrem. So Tristrem becomes, like Horn, the Welsh king's champion, defeats the giant, and would have won both Blaucheflour and Wales were he not committed elsewhere. Handing over Wales to Blaucheflour, Tristrem accepts only the whelp, Peticrewe, which he dispatches as a gift to Ysoude. The outcome of the Welsh adventure is that Tristrem is welcomed back into Mark's court and so it functions as a successful venture across the border in which the hero wins fame and fortune; the royal prince returns to his uncle's court with his reputation enhanced. It almost seems to belong to a different story, a succession of journeys, challenges, and conquests, like the romances of Bevis or Guy and, though it is the result of one of the gaps in the Auchinleck Manuscript,[36] it seems apt that the text does not get as far as the tragic ending. Wales functions here as a place to escape to, another realm where a hero who is spoiling for a fight to assuage his wounded feelings may find a legitimate cause for his valor. The alternative kingdom, later to be echoed in the kingdoms of Spain, where Tristrem again goes to seek fighting, and of Britanny where Tristrem actually marries the daughter of the court, acts as parallel and mirror to the court he has left.

The romance that ought to be a significant landmark in Middle English awareness of Wales is *Lybeaus Desconus*, a "son-of Gawain" romance that survives in an unusually large number of manuscripts,[37] both because it describes a classic chivalric journey that is mainly in Wales, and because it picks up some elements from the legendary history of Wales that Geoffrey of Monmouth transmits or creates.[38] A young knight builds up experience of many different types of adventure on his way to a quest from Arthur's court, here placed at Glastonbury, into unfamiliar territory: it makes most sense to understand this territory as central Wales. The quest is to Synadoune to rescue its lady; R. S. Loomis identified Synadoune with the ancient Roman city of Segontium, located at the base of Snowdon and connected in medieval times with many myths and legends.[39] From ca. 80–380 Segontium, a fort built on a hilltop above the site of modern Caernarfon was garrisoned by Roman troops; a smaller fort, of which some walls remain still, was built in the time of Constantius (292–304), the father of Constantine, on a cliff above the river. Roads led east to Chester, south to Carmarthen and Caerleon, parts of which are still known as Sarn Elen (Elen's Causeway). After the Romans left in the 380s the deserted fort may have been used by invading Britons from the north or left to decay. Segontium was named by Nennius, together with Caerleon and Caerwent, as one of the three ancient cities of Britain that were situated in Wales, and tells the legend that Constantine's son was buried there and that Constantine sowed there seeds of gold, silver, and brass so that no poor man should ever dwell there. It was to the name of Nennius that the idea became attached that the medieval Welsh princes were descended from Roman emperors and even that Saint Helena, the mother of Constantine, was Welsh. As was noted above, Geoffrey of Monmouth in his *Vita Merlini* has Merlin prophesy that the city (*urbs Sigeni*) shall lament in ruins until the Welsh return to their former power. Loomis linked the idea of the ancient city's ruins speaking to a later age of a past grandeur to Gerald de Barri's description of the vestiges of ancient splendor at Caerleon-on-Usk:

> Caerleon is of unquestioned antiquity. It was constructed with great care by the Romans, the walls being built of brick. You can still see many vestiges of its one-time splendour. There are immense palaces, which, with the gilded gables of their roofs, once rivalled the magnificence of ancient Rome... There is a lofty tower, and beside it remarkable hot baths, the remains of temples and an amphitheatre. All this is enclosed within impressive walls, parts of which still remain standing.[40]

With reference to the romances of the twelfth century and later, the argument runs that Segontium (Caer Seint, *urbs Sigeni*) is to be recognized in Anglo-Norman references to "la cité de Snauedun" in Gaimar, and to "le roi de Sinadoune" in the *Lai du Cor* and to Isneldoune in Béroul. The source of *Lybeaus Desconus*, Renaut de Beaujeu's *Li biaus Desconeus*, knows that the city was deserted but had an ancient marble palace, occupied by minstrels and by a hideous wyvern (really the queen in her enchanted form) that can be returned to human form only by the hero's kiss, and then only because he is the son of Gawain by a fairy. What appears as a ghost town in the romance was properly Senaudon, the capital of the ancient realm of Wales.

The Middle English version of the story cannot be said to realize in full the possibilities of this story material. Thomas Chester (the presumed author of this romance, and of *Sir Launfal* and *Octavian*[41]) turns the material into the classic pattern of a knight on the road; a better title might be "The Road to Synadoune." It begins in the manner of the story of Perceval with a bastard child, brought up nameless in the woods, winning his way to Arthur's court and so into the world of adventure. On the road with the messenger, Elene, and her accompanying dwarf, Lybeaus Desconus encounters a representative range of types of chivalric challenge: contentious knights, giants holding a maiden captive, a contest of beauty, a hunt, and an idyllic island, a kind of bower of bliss with another giant, another lady. After many delays the city itself is reached and proves another intriguing combination of challenges and bizarre images, with the inhabitants in wait with ordure with which to pelt any knight disgraced by being defeated by the steward, and then the enchanted hall where the queen is held prisoner by the two sorcerers, and finally a frightening Gothic scene in which a window falls from its frame and a winged serpent with a woman's face enters and approaches the hero to embrace and kiss him. Because Lybeaus Desconus is in reality the son of Gawain, his kiss can return the unnerving worm to her true form as the Queen of Synadoune. So a nameless hero finds his identity by rescuing a ghost city from its enchantment and "all þe people of þe toun" join in the celebrations.

Whether one can build this sequence of romance motifs into a national myth, let alone a treatment of real historical issues for Wales in the fourteenth century, is obviously debatable, but the theme is recognizably present within the material. Chester possibly knew enough about the legends to show deliberate intent in his naming of the messenger who comes to Arthur's court and who accompanies the hero on his much-interrupted journey, as Elene. Other Welsh signposts in the poem are the use of Cardiff as the setting for the beauty contest between Sir Gyfroun's lady and Elene,[42] and the names of the two enchanters who hold the Queen of Synadoune prisoner (Mabon/Maboun and Evrain/Irain).[43] No detailed description of Cardiff is given beyond bringing the two ladies "to toun," into the marketplace, "Amydward þe cyte," then shifting the scene to a field outside the town for the subsequent joust between Lybeaus and Gyfroun, and then returning "ynto þe toune" for the awarding of the prize of a gerfalcon to Lybeaus; when Arthur sends a hundred pounds as a reward for the hero's valorous deeds, Lybeaus holds a forty-day feast for "lordes of renoun." The use of a major town for a series of social events provides some plausible geographical solidity among the other, vaguer placings of adventures, "Be a castell aunterous" (279) or "In þat wylde forest" (545), though the focus remains on the continually interrupted and resumed journey as "euer þey ryden west / ... Toward Synadowne" (544–46). The narrative may therefore be construed as a combination of the familiar romance motif of a young hero's coming to maturity with the myth of the recovery of Wales's lost heroic past. The plot is colored by a strong moral pattern in that this romance is one of the few with a clear allegorical element. The hero is sidetracked on his journey by a sojourn in the mysterious Ile d'Or. It is to this setting, rather than the city of Synadoune, that Chester attributes something of the grandeur and the history of Gerald's Caerleon, when Lybeaus first approaches it:

> Lybaeus rod many a myle
> Among aventurus fyle
>   Jn Yrland and yn Wales.
> Hyt befell yn þe monþ of June,
> Whan þe fenell hangeþ yn toun,
>   Grene yn semely sales;
> Þys somerys day ys long,
> Mery ys þe fowles song
>   And notes of þe nyȝtyngales.
>
> Þat tyme Lybeaus com ryde
> Be a ryuer syde
>   And saw a greet cyte,
> Wyth palys prowd yn pryde
> And castelles heyȝ and wyde
>   Wyth gates greet plente.
> He axede what hyt hyȝt;
> Þe mayde seyde anon ryȝt,
>   "Syr, Y telle hyt þe:
> Men clepeþ hyt Yle d'Or,
> Her haþ be fyȝtynge mor
>   Þanne owher yn any countre."
>   (*Lybaeus Desconus*,
>   Cotton Caligula text, 1222–42)

Here the lady, Dame Amour, proves to be a sensuous enchantress, seducing Lybeaus Desconus, making him forget his quest until Elene confronts him and reproves him for his lack of honor and his shameful delay. The English version reduces the attention given to the episode, but Chester gives it a clearer place in the moral scheme by making it a single stage in his heroic progress, whereas Renaut takes his hero back to Dame Amour and leaves uncertainty as to which lady is the real heroine of the romance. Chester was a hackwriter but his habit of making an amalgam between his source material and a potpourri of episodes, images, and phrases drawn from popular romances in English develops his stories in a variety of ways. The idea of "wild Wales" is given a dramatically imagined quality of mystery and enchantment, and the sequence of adventures for the hero populates the country with an interesting mixture of opponents, allies, and beautiful women to attract and beguile him. The medley may be said to be the best Middle English version of the Wales of romance.

It is only in Welsh language texts that it was at all likely that writers would turn romance themes into expressions of Welsh anxieties about race and nationhood. From the perspective of those writing in English, it would seem that concern with crusading history and with English relations with France, together with negotiating the cultural transfer of texts written in French into a different idiom, all took precedence over the expression of political and linguistic tensions and accommodations within the British Isles. However, the texts discussed here suggest that a few writers of popular romance from the early fourteenth century on were beginning to include in stories of knighthood some chivalric adventures in knowable parts of Britain, rather than, or at least alongside, more fantastic venues. English awareness of Wales—its history, geography, and people—remains an underexplored literary area in the medieval period, but the glimpses given by a handful of romances are enough to incite speculation about its possibilities.

Notes

1. Geoffrey of Monmouth, *The History of the Kings of Britain*, trans. Lewis Thorpe (Harmondsworth: Penguin, 1966), 282–84.
2. *Vita Merlini*, trans. John Jay Parry, first published 1925 (University of Illinois Studies in Language and Literature), repr. in *The Romance of Merlin: An Anthology*, ed. Peter Goodrich (New York and London: Garland, 1990), Chap. 4, at 83.
3. See Corinne Saunders, *The Forest of Medieval Romance* (Cambridge: D. S. Brewer, 1993).
4. Geraldi Cambrensis, *Itinerarium Kambriae* and *Descriptio Kambriae*, ed. James F. Dimock, in *Giraldi Cambrensis: Opera*, ed. J. S.Brewer, J. F. Dimock, and G. F. Warner, 8 vols., RS 21 (London, 1861–91), 6: 3–152 and 155–227; trans. Lewis Thorpe as *The Journey through Wales* and *The Description of Wales* (Harmondsworth: Penguin, 1978).
5. *Journey through Wales*, Book I, Chap. 6.
6. *Journey through Wales*, Book II, Chap. 1.
7. *Description of Wales*, Book I, Chap. 10.

8. *Description of Wales*, Book II, Chap. 9.

9. Constance Bullock-Davies, "The Love-Messenger in *Milun*," *Nottingham Medieval Studies* 16 (1972): 20–27.

10. Bullock-Davies, "Love-Messenger," 27.

11. *The Lais of Marie de France*, trans. and ed. Glyn S. Burgess and Keith Busby (Harmondsworth: Penguin, 1986), 13.

12. Though one has to note that "Galles" included Strathclyde; hence Chrétien's *Yvain* begins at Arthur's court at Carlisle "in Galles," which becomes "Kerdyf" [Cardiff] in *Ywain and Gawain*, though later in the English romance the court has moved to Chester, and in any case the hero's actions occur in unnamed settings in forest, castle, and so on.

13. Rupert T. Pickens, *The Welsh Knight: Paradoxicality in Chrétien's Conte del Graal* (Lexington, Ky.: French Forum Publishers, 1977), 113–17.

14. See David C. Fowler, "*Le Conte del Graal* and *Sir Perceval of Galles*," *Comparative Literature Studies* 12 (1975): 5–20.

15. Keith Busby, "*Sir Perceval de Galles, Le Conte du Graal* and *La Continuation-Gauvain*: The Methods of an English Adaptor," *Études Anglaises* 31 (1978): 198–202, points out some other correspondences: "The corresponding part of the Welsh *Peredur*, however, is tinged with the kind of physical humour…that we find in the English poem" (200).

16. *Sir Cleges*, in *Middle English Humorous Tales in Verse*, ed. G. H. McKnight (Boston; London: D. C. Heath, 1913), 38–59, with notes at 71–80; quotations are from this text. The text of the poem in *The Middle English Breton Lays*, ed. Anne Laskaya and Eve Salisbury (Kalamazoo, Mich.: TEAMS, Medieval Texts, 1995), 367–407, has no significant differences in these passages.

17. As, for example, the story of Saint Gerard who produced cherries for a sick man in January. This and other miraculous appearances of fruit out of season were identified by Loomis; see C. Grant Loomis, "*Sir Cleges* and Unseasonable Growth in Hagiology," *Modern Language Notes* 53 (1938): 591–94.

18. There are many analogues to the story of the shared blows; the motif is found, for example, in *Gesta Romanorum*; others are listed in McKnight's edition of the poem. An unnoticed analogue, however, is in *Sir Tristrem*; when Tristrem is abducted as a boy, while playing chess on board ship, he is sought by the faithful Rohaud, "þat noble kniʒt," who follows the pilgrims who have taken Tristrem to Mark's court, and has to bribe his way, paying first the pilgrims, then the abusive porter: "Cherl! Go away / Oþer y schal þe smite / What dostow here al day?" (620–22), and then the usher.

19. John Hines suggests that *Sir Cleges* was influenced in its use of Cardiff as setting by the representation of the town in *Gereint* (personal communication).

20. Despite this, Patricia Clare Ingham, "'In Contrayez Straunge': Colonial Relations, British Identity and *Sir Gawain and the Green Knight*," *New Medieval Literatures* 4 (2000): 61–93, later adapted as Chap. 4 of

her book *Sovereign Fantasies: Arthurian Romance and the Making of Britain*
(Philadelphia, Pa.: University of Pennsylvania Press, 2001), argues that
"the poet's interest in Wales and a history of conquest" and "the otherness
of Wales" (116–17) play a significant role in the poem.

21. "E ele lui respoundi en Sessoneys, qe fu la langage Elda, come cele
    questoit aprise en diverses laungages...."; see W. F. Bryan and Germaine
    Dempster, *Sources and Analogues of Chaucer's* Canterbury Tales (Chicago:
    University of Chicago Press, 1941), 165–81, at 168.

22. John Burrow, "A Maner Latyn Corrupt," *Medium Aevum* 30 (1961):
    33–37.

23. The idea was first suggested by Mary Dominica Legge, "The Influence of
    Patronage on Form in Medieval French Literature," in *Stil-und-Formprobleme
    in der Literatur*, ed. Paul Böchmann (Heidelberg: Carl Winter, 1959), 136–41,
    but developed further by Judith Weiss, "Thomas and the Earl: Literary and
    Historical Contexts for the *Romance of Horn*," in *Tradition and Transformation
    in Medieval Romance*, ed. Rosalind Field (Cambridge: D. S. Brewer, 1999),
    1–13, esp. 2–7.

24. Robert Bartlett, *Gerald of Wales, 1146–1223* (Oxford: Clarendon Press,
    1982), 14.

25. Bartlett, *Gerald of Wales*, 14.

26. See Diane Speed, "The Saracens of *King Horn*," *Speculum* 65 (1990):
    564–95.

27. Edinburgh, National Library of Scotland, MS Advocates' 19.2.1, fols.
    317v–23v.

28. Quotations from the romance are from *Horn Childe and Maiden Rimnild,*
    ed. from the Auchinleck MS, National Library of Scotland, Advocates'
    MS 19.2.1, by Maldwyn Mills, Middle English Texts 20 (Heidelberg:
    Carl Winter, 1988).

29. Robert Rouse, "English Identity and the Law in *Havelok the Dane, Horn
    Childe and Maiden Rimnild* and *Bevis of Hamtoun*," in *Cultural Encounters
    in the Romance of Medieval England*, ed. Corinne Saunders (Cambridge:
    D. S. Brewer, 2005), 69–83, at 79.

30. Mills, ed., *Horn Childe*, 56–57.

31. Mills, ed., *Horn Childe*, 58–59.

32. Matthew Holford, "History and Politics in *Horn Childe* and *Maiden
    Rimnild*," *Review of English Studies* 57 (2006): 149–68.

33. Holford, "History and Politics," 160.

34. *Sir Tristrem* and *Horn Childe* both survive in the Auchinleck Manuscript
    and similarities between them have led to the suggestion that one
    influenced the other; see Mills, ed., *Horn Childe*, 55–56 and 69–70.

35. George P. McNeill, ed., *Sir Tristrem: A Scottish Metrical Romance*, Scottish
    Text Society (Edinburgh, 1886).

36. See note 27; the missing leaf would have been between fols. 321v and
    322r.

37. Six, including the well-known miscellany of popular pious and romance
    texts in London, British Library MS Cotton Caligula A. ii., and the

similar collection in Oxford, Bodleian Library MS Ashmole 61, where *Sir Cleges* is found.

38. *Lybeaus Desconus*, ed. Maldwyn Mills, EETS os 261 (London: Oxford University Press, 1969).

39. Roger Sherman Loomis, "From Segontium to Sinadon—The Legends of a *Cité Gaste*," *Speculum* 22 (1947): 520–33.

40. *Journey through Wales*, Book I, Chap. 5.

41. See Maldwyn Mills, "The Compositional Style of the 'Southern' *Octavian, Sir Launfal* and *Lybeaus Desconus*," *Medium Aevum* 31 (1962): 88–109.

42. Often understood in the past as Carlisle, but though "Karlille" occurs in one manuscript version (and "Cardigan" in another), the majority of spellings in the manuscripts ("Cardelof," "Karlof," "Cardeuyle," "Kardill") leave enough uncertainty for one to take the commonsense view that the road from Glastonbury to Snowdon is more likely to pass through Cardiff than Carlisle. See note on line 800 in Mills' ed., *Lybeaus Desconus*, at 222.

43. From names that occur in Welsh texts as the sons of Urien, though probably taken from Chrétien by Renaut; see Loomis, "From Segontium to Sinadon," 529.

CHAPTER 8

CROSSING THE BORDERS: LITERARY
BORROWING IN MEDIEVAL
WALES AND ENGLAND

Ceridwen Lloyd-Morgan

Despite the best efforts of specialists in Celtic studies over the past four decades, the temptation to characterize certain elements in Old French or Middle English romances and tales as "Celtic" seems still to be irresistible to many scholars.[1] The ancient and long-discredited attempts of R. S. Loomis and his followers to find a "Celtic" hero lurking behind every knight, or a Welsh or Irish text behind every narrative element, have not, apparently, lost their attraction. Nonetheless, we cannot ignore the supposedly Welsh setting of many French and English romances, and the high incidence of names of Welsh or Breton origin in such texts, most especially Arthurian narratives from Marie de France and Chrétien de Troyes to Thomas Malory. Teasing out the relationship between, on the one hand, extant sources in Welsh (or in other Celtic languages) and, on the other, highly literary texts produced in very different social, political, linguistic, and cultural circumstances cannot proceed without an understanding of those circumstances. The interface between Welsh material and that read in England, whether in French or in English, should be seen as a two-way process.

In the multilingual context that developed in the centuries following the Norman Conquest, it was inevitable that Anglo-Norman tales and romances and French texts of Continental origin would circulate side by side in England, even to the extent that copies of certain texts of Continental origin were produced on both sides of the Channel: the early thirteenth-century romance of *Perlesvaus* is just one example.[2] Many Middle English narrative texts, both Arthurian and non-Arthurian, derive from French originals, whether directly or indirectly. The question is whether certain elements within texts read in England, whether in English or in one of the varieties of French, might be characterized as "Welsh" or of Welsh origin and if so by what means they were sucked in to an English, Anglo-Norman, or French literary context.

It is, of course, thanks to Geoffrey of Monmouth's *Historia Regum Britanniae* and to the Norman-French version, the *Roman de Brut*, which Wace completed in 1155, that the Arthurian material came to be so widely disseminated in francophone circles. Without them, it is doubtful whether Chrétien de Troyes, in the late twelfth century, would have set so much of his work in the Arthurian world. It is Chrétien's influential works, especially the *Conte del Graal* or *Roman de Perceval*, that provided the starting point for the development in subsequent decades of a massive body of Arthurian tales and romances. Some of these, like Chrétien's own romances of *Perceval, Yvain,* and *Erec,* spawned versions in a staggering number of Western European languages, including the Welsh tales of *Peredur, Owein,* and *Geraint.* Even the more sprawling compositions of Chrétien's successors, such as the so-called Vulgate Cycle and the even more massive Post-Vulgate Cycle, were widely copied and read, eventually giving rise in their turn to translations and adaptations, including, in English, substantial portions of Malory's *Morte Darthur.* Characters in these French and English narratives often have their counterparts in Welsh tradition, some, though not all, of which can be shown to be older. As Rachel Bromwich has shown, however, the personal names are virtually always detached from the story material in which they are embedded in the Welsh sources, the bearers of those names being transformed by French authors' imaginations into literary constructs often very different from their counterparts in Wales.[3]

By the late twelfth century, thanks to Chrétien's influential *Conte del Graal,* Perceval's supposed Welsh identity and his epithet "li gallois" had been established, but comparison with the eponymous hero of the Welsh tale of *Peredur* reveals the immense gap between Welsh and continental perceptions of cultural identity and attributes. This is even more striking when we bear in mind the evident influence of the *Conte del Graal* on the surviving versions of *Peredur.* Similarly, although events in French Arthurian romances are often localized in what purports to be Wales, the geography, as indeed the descriptions of Welsh life and customs, undoubtedly owes more to French literary imaginations than to any historical or geographical reality.[4] The contrast could scarcely be greater between the Wales of such texts and that depicted in the Anglo-Norman *Fouke le Fitz Waryn,* first composed in the late thirteenth century on the Marches of Wales, by an author who evidently had firsthand knowledge of both geography and people.[5] Nonetheless, the translinguistic and transcultural migrations of continental French material were as important in Wales as in England. When fashion brought French Arthurian romances to Welsh audiences of the thirteenth century and beyond, characters corresponding to ones familiar in Welsh tradition could still be recognized despite their French trappings. They could thus be reinstated by translators or adapters into Welsh literary tradition, together with their new and often very different set of attributes and adventures.

The extent of the penetration of French, as well as English, culture within medieval Wales is not always fully appreciated, yet it is an essential component of the process of linguistic and literary interchange between all three cultures; an awareness of the nature and outcomes of this phenomenon is essential for understanding the context of production of texts and manuscripts, as well as for an informed reading of the texts themselves. In Wales, it is not usually possible to establish in specific cases whether access to French material came through the many direct contacts with the Continent or via England, or again through the Norman and English presence within Wales and along the border, or whether the medium of transmission was oral or written.[6] Important as the role of Breton *jongleurs* and of Welsh political, mercantile, and religious contacts with France may have been in facilitating two-way cross-channel cultural traffic, the inter-mingling of languages and cultures within Wales and along its borders is likely to have been equally if not more crucial in this process.

There can be little doubt that when two cultures come into contact through conquest, the conqueror's language and culture will leave its mark on indigenous traditions, and this process can be clearly observed in Wales from the eleventh century onward. The absorption of foreign influences and their marrying with Welsh forms of expression, whether intellectual, literary, or, indeed, in the visual arts, can be observed even before the eleventh century. This is no less than could be expected, given the position of Wales within Western European culture during the Middle Ages. While it is true that certain aspects of the culture of medieval Wales survived into the modern period, the post-Romantic idea(l) of a purely "Celtic," inward-looking society insulated from outside influences, bears little resemblance to reality. Belonging as it did to Western Christendom, Wales had long had access to the wider European intellectual tradition, an inheritance that can be observed not only in purely religious texts, but also, as Marged Haycock has revealed, in secular elements of continental origin in Early Welsh poetry.[7]

That Wales was open to external influences and ready to incorporate them promptly into its own culture is neatly illustrated by a copy of Bede's *De Natura Rerum*, made by a Welsh scribe in about 1100, and whose few remaining folios are now Aberystwyth, National Library of Wales, Peniarth MS 540.[8] The scribe was evidently a Welsh speaker, for in two passages he glossed in Welsh the Latin words for colors of the rainbow and for neap and spring tides. He adorned his manuscript with some fine monochrome initials in the Irish style, some with zoömorphic elements. These features point very clearly to the famous scriptorium established by Sulien (ca. 1010–91) at Llanbadarn Fawr in west Wales. Sulien, who had received much of his education in Ireland, passed on his skills to his four sons, notably the famous Rhigyfarch (1056?–99), whose achievements included the so-called Ricemarch Psalter.[9] But although the Irish influence evidently persisted after the death of Sulien's sons, in the next genera-tion our scribe had already fully absorbed new influences, looking east rather than west. That he should have access to Bede's *De Natura Rerum* and make a new copy is in itself worthy of note, but still more significant is that the script he chose was Caroline minuscule, a script popularized here by the Normans. This is a remarkably early example of Norman or French influence, given that the Normans' post-1066 westward push was not rapid, despite some pre-Conquest presence in the form of individual settlers and members of the merchant class, whose wares, it has been suggested, may perhaps be reflected in a small group of French loanwords in the early prose tales *Pedeir Keinc y Mabinogi* [The Four Branches of the Mabinogi].[10]

Nonetheless, the Norman advance, although piecemeal in terms of early Conquest, seems to have quickly led to Welsh access to a wider array of manuscripts and texts from the French *Sprachraum*. Since it was the borders and the southeastern and northeastern regions of Wales that first came under Norman control, offering as they did easier military access than did the more mountainous parts further west and inland, it is even more striking that our Bede manuscript should provide evidence of influence on scribal practice in west Wales as early as the turn of the twelfth century. Furthermore, this example predates the foundation by Normans of monasteries in Wales. The first of these new monastic establishments were Benedictine priories founded by Marcher lords in the south and southeast in the early aftermath of the Conquest and their culture reflected that of their founders.[11] Although the first Cistercian house, Tintern, was founded in 1131, this too had little contact with the Welsh-speaking population of *pura Wallia*. It was not until after the establishment of the Cistercian monasteries at Hendygwyn-ar-daf (Whitland) in 1151 and of Ystrad Fflur (Strata Florida) in Ceredigion, followed in subsequent years by many others in the Welsh heartlands, that a close relationship began to develop between these houses, founded directly from Cîteaux, and the local population and their native rulers. Eventually that relationship would lead to the Cistercians, who maintained regular contact with their French mother-houses, playing an important role in the development of manuscript production and of the written tradition of secular as well as religious texts. On the strength of its "monkish" poems, it has been argued that the oldest extant vernacular Welsh manuscript, the mid-thirteenth-century Black Book of Carmarthen, for example, may have been copied at Whitland.[12] One of the earliest copies of *Cyfraith Hywel*, the native Welsh laws, might perhaps also have been produced there, during the second half of the thirteenth century: its text indicates a southwestern origin.[13] It was almost certainly at Strata Florida that the earliest surviving, major compendium of secular and religious texts, the White Book of Rhydderch (Aberystwyth, National Library of Wales (henceforth NLW MSS Peniarth 4–5), was compiled in the mid-fourteenth century, as was, in part at least, the Hendregadredd MS (NLW MS 6680), which comprises the most important extant collection of poetry, on which work began sometime after 1282 and continued into the 1330s.

The history of the establishment of a Norman presence in Wales and its relationship with the native population need not be rehearsed in detail here. But its important consequences culturally cannot be underestimated. Perhaps the most significant was the influence on the ruling classes in Welsh rulers of the newcomers' language and their material, intellectual, and artistic culture. Although at first their increasing contact with Norman-French led to a thriving trade for professional interpreters, fluent in Welsh, French, and, indeed, English, Welsh lords and their officials soon began to gain fluency.[14] By the late twelfth century Gerald of Wales, himself the non-Welsh-speaking product of a mixed Welsh and Norman marriage, would note in his *Itinerarium Kambriae* that the prince Owain Cyfeiliog was able to converse fluently with Henry II.[15] By the thirteenth century there is little doubt that French was spoken at the court of the princes of the house of Gwynedd and it must surely have been the language of communication between Llywelyn ap Iorwerth (ca. 1173–1240) and his wife, Siwan or Joan, an illegitimate daughter of king John, after their marriage in 1205. After the loss of Welsh independence in 1282, the establishment by Edward I of a series of castles and fortified boroughs, such as those at Conwy and Caernarfon, opened up Gwynedd to new influences. By the fourteenth century French was frequently used for administrative and legal documents and was increasingly widely read by the educated laity. By the first half of the fifteenth century a poet educated outside Wales, perhaps at Oxford, could boast that he had mastered the language: Ieuan ap Rhydderch's claim comes in his *Cywydd y fost* [the boast poem], datable to ca. 1422, but his grasp of French, Latin, and English as well as his native tongue is confirmed elsewhere.[16] Linguistic skills brought with them valued access to *pethau dieithr* (line 28), lit. "foreign things," that is, knowledge from outside Wales, for Ieuan, on the one hand evidently in full command of native Welsh poetic skills parades his familiarity with a staggering range of academic subjects.

The impact on Welsh literature of the increasing accessibility of French material was considerable. Much has been published over the last decades on the secular, narrative literature of the fourteenth and fifteenth centuries, notably to the development of a substantial corpus of literature in translation, in the apparent absence of any new and original native prose compositions. Welsh versions appeared of French epics such as *La Chanson de Roland* and the *Pèlerinage de Charlemagne*, of Arthurian romances such as the *Perlesvaus* and *Queste del Saint Graal*, and of Anglo-Norman narratives of (according to inflexible modern categories) more intermediate genre, such as *Boeve de Haumtone*. The adaptation of these foreign narratives to fit more comfortably into native literary traditions, and a tendency to "mix and match" native and foreign elements in shorter, composite texts like the Welsh narrative of the *Birth of Arthur* probably first compiled at the end of the fourteenth century, or the mid-fifteenth-century *Darogan yr Olew Bendigaid,* suggest that those texts which survive in complete or almost complete form reveal only the tip of the iceberg of French literary penetration. Telltale details—a personal name here, a reference there to a specific event— can provide important, if tantalizing evidence of Welsh access to other French texts of which no full-scale translation has survived. It is from such evidence that we know that at least one copy of the *Prose Merlin* and *Prose Lancelot* were available to redactors in late fourteenth- and early fifteenth-century Glamorgan, for example.[17]

Documentary evidence of another kind pointing to the coexistence if not cohabitation of French and Welsh books in cultured circles is provided by the inventory of the goods of Llywelyn Bren, member of a Glamorgan gentry family who was executed in 1317 for treason after a failed rebellion which he had led, significantly, with a member of the Norman family of Mansel. The inventory notes that he owned "i. romanz de la rose, iii. livres Galeys, ii. autres lyvres," indicate that books in French and Welsh could rub shoulders in the private library of a Welsh-speaking gentleman in the early fourteenth century.[18] It has been suggested that the *Roman de la Rose* might have had some influence on the work of the celebrated poet Dafydd ap Gwilym, who was active at this same period, though this is impossible to prove, as is the direct influence of the French or Occitan traditions of love poetry, despite some general similarities.[19] Nonetheless, there is ample evidence of overlap between the Welsh and French-medium textual cultures. By the early fifteenth century Welsh manuscript compendia sometimes contain, at least to some extent, the same type of material as manuscripts produced for a family of Anglo-Norman descent.[20] Catalogues of the libraries of the Welsh religious houses are scarce, but it is worth noting that a number of those in the neighboring English counties held copies of secular French narratives, in some case texts of which Welsh versions survive. The catalogue of the Benedictine priory of Penwortham in Lancashire, an offshoot of the abbey of Evesham in Worcestershire, lists amongst its extensive French holdings *Boeve de Haumtone*, *Amis et Amiloun*, and a codex containing a "Mort de Arthur" and a "Sankreal." These were most probably the early thirteenth-century Vulgate *Mort le roi Artu* and *La Queste del Saint Graal;*[21] with the exception of the *Mort le roi Artu*, Welsh versions were produced of all these narratives, and there is some evidence that the *Mort* might also have been known to Welsh redactors in the later Middle Ages and the early sixteenth.[22] In the fourteenth century Glastonbury, a house with strong Welsh connections, had at least one copy, in an English hand, of the *Perlesvaus*, which was also translated into Welsh.[23]

Such overlap was not confined to secular narratives such as those already mentioned. The Welsh version of Walter of Henley's treatise on husbandry, translated in south-east Wales from an Anglo-Norman exemplar some time after the last quarter of the thirteenth century, shows that borrowing extended to functional texts, though in this instance a moral or homiletic purpose may also be involved.[24] Perhaps more unexpectedly, some religious texts were translated from Anglo-Norman rather than Latin originals, as recent work by Sarah Rowles on the sources of *Ystorya Adaf* (*Vita Adae et Evae*) has revealed. Although four manuscripts, of which the earliest, Aberystwyth, National Library of Wales, Peniarth MS 14, belongs to the second half of the thirteenth century, contain versions translated from Latin, that preserved in Aberystwyth, National Library of Wales, Llanstephan MS 27 (ca. 1400) was indisputably based on an Anglo-Norman version.[25]

Many of these translations, of both secular and religious material, were produced for lay patrons, most notably the brothers Rhys ap Thomas ab Einion, for whom Llanstephan 27 was produced, and Hopcyn ap Thomas ab Einion for whom that massive prose and verse compendium, the Red Book of Hergest (Oxford, Jesus College MS 111, currently held at the Bodleian Library), was compiled, as well as Welsh translations of Geoffrey of Monmouth, and of *La Queste del Saint Graal* and *Perlesvaus* (Library Company of Philadelphia, MS 8680, and Aberystwyth, National Library of Wales, Peniarth MS 11), amongst others. The evidence of manuscripts which can be traced to this Glamorgan family reveals that they or their translators and scribes had access to a startling range of texts and manuscripts.[26] The French or Anglo-Norman texts included, as well as those already mentioned, *La Chanson de Roland* and *Pèlerinage de Charlemagne*, and an Anglo-Norman version of *Boeve de Haumtone*, while even some of the Welsh material used, notably some of the religious poetry, came from as far afield as Anglesey, at the opposite end of the country.[27]

Foreign influence seems to have extended even to proverbs. Pioneering work by Richard Glyn Roberts has shown that many of the proverbs collected under the title *Madwaith Hen Gyrys o Iâl* and preserved in the Red Book of Hergest were not, as had usually been assumed, of purely native origin, but were probably borrowed from French or Anglo-Norman sources.[28] Although the Red Book of Hergest was copied some time between 1382 and about 1400, Roberts stresses that versions of this collection of proverbs are attested in extant manuscripts as early as the mid-thirteenth century.

The fact that Welsh poets from the twelfth century onward often incorporated proverbs of French or Anglo-Norman origin in their work raises interesting questions about their access to both French language and literature. Traditionally scholars have assumed that the Gogynfeirdd (poets of the native Welsh princes), worked in an oral context. But even if much of their work was first composed and transmitted orally, there can be little doubt that written copies existed long before the appearance of the earliest Welsh manuscripts now surviving, which do not predate the mid-thirteenth century. Moreover, French words were sometimes borrowed into Welsh remarkably early. To take one example, *rhamant*— though not with the modern meaning of "romance"—is attested in the elegy for Owain Gwynedd (d. 1170) composed by Cynddelw Brydydd Mawr (fl. ca. 1155–95).[29] Given that the first French texts to be described as *romans* were the *Roman de Thèbes*, apparently composed about 1150, and Wace's *Roman de Brut*, completed and offered to Aliénor d'Aquitaine in 1155, to find the term *rhamant* in Welsh in a poem presumably datable as early as 1170 is striking, if not remarkable, and indicates that Welsh literary circles were aware of the most recent developments in French literature. This short time gap is all the more striking because Cynddelw, in contrast to his younger contemporaries, tends to be a somewhat conservative poet, eschewing loanwords until they are well established. This may, however, reflect the taste of his audience and especially his patron or patrons, for under the rule of Llywelyn ap Iorwerth (ca. 1173–1240) the princely court of Gwynedd, with which Prydydd y Moch is associated, was more open to foreign influence than the court of Madog ap Maredudd in Powys, which was Cynddelw's home area. But borrowed vocabulary alone cannot show whether the medium by which a word was introduced was written or oral. Since the proverbs, many of which are found in French literary texts, suggest a greater, more specific French penetration, their presence in the poetry raises further questions about the poet's access to and use of written sources—a vexed question in itself. Although Richard Glyn Roberts is rightly cautious, he does not rule out the possibility that some of the poets had made use of manuscript collections of proverbs, which, as we have seen, contained items of French origin.[30]

If the borrowing of proverbs might derive from imported written collections, or indeed, from direct or indirect contact with speakers of French or Anglo-Norman, once again the French influence on the court of Llywelyn ap Iorwerth in northwest Wales could be significant. But another possible source is French literature, which had already left its mark on Welsh prose tales by the first half, probably by the first quarter of the thirteenth century. It is at this period, it is generally believed, that the three Welsh tales of *Peredur, Owein,* and *Gereint* were composed, inspired by the corresponding romances of Chrétien de Troyes, his *Perceval* (and its continuations), *Yvain,* and *Erec et Enide;* these three Welsh versions can be seen as precursors of the closer translations produced a little later. Proverbs are common in Chrétien's work and in other French narrative texts and if these were not the direct source for imported proverbs, they may at least have reinforced borrowings from elsewhere. The poets, especially those from the period after the Edwardian conquest of Wales, often evoke details from secular tales and compare their patrons to the heroes whose exploits were celebrated in them. In some cases such references can be linked to an extant translation, such as *Y Seint Greal,* the Welsh version of *La Queste del Saint Graal,* and *Perlesvaus.* But references are also made by the poets to other narratives of foreign origin, where there is no evidence that a Welsh version was ever made, Guy of Warwick being one important example.

It is possible, therefore, that the broad outlines, at least, of such tales were trickling down through oral tradition, perhaps deriving ultimately from a reading or performance from a written copy at one of the courts frequented by the poets on either side of the border, for the border provided a continuum, not a clear dividing line. Thus throughout the Middle Ages and even beyond, many parishes on the English side had substantial Welsh-speaking populations, representing all levels of society. In the mid- and late fifteenth century, for example, poets such as Lewys Glyn Cothi and Gutun Owain composed praise poetry and elegies for patrons in Herefordshire and Shropshire respectively.

Whether through written or orally transmitted sources, or, more likely, through both, French or Anglo-Norman left a significant linguistic legacy in Welsh. Predictably, many borrowings find their way into those texts translated or adapted from French sources, such as *Y Seint Greal.* But not all these borrowings were suggested by the French text used. Where copies of the Welsh redactor's source text(s) are still extant, not infrequently we find that the borrowed French word is not attested in that particular text, indicating that such words had already become embedded in the Welsh language, at the very least in the Welsh writer's social context and geographical area.[31] Not all these words survived the Middle Ages and in some cases it can be difficult to establish, in the absence of any clear phonological or morphological evidence, whether a French word was borrowed directly or via English.

Given that French or Anglo-Norman manuscripts found their way into Welsh hands, it is not surprising that the language does occasionally appear in Welsh manuscripts by the fourteenth century: about 1350, for example, French memoranda were added to the Book of Llandaf (Aberystwyth, National Library of Wales, MS 17110E), a Latin manuscript first compiled in the mid-twelfth century.[32] At the very end of the fourteenth century we find for the first time, in Cardiff, Central Library, MS 3.242 (olim Hafod MS 16) a volume containing a small amount of material in French as well as Welsh and Latin. Part of this manuscript belongs to the same group as the Red Book of Hergest, copied in Glamorgan in a scriptorium that produced a number of texts in translation as well as native Welsh material.[33]

Aberystwyth, National Library of Wales, Peniarth MS 7, a northwestern Welsh manuscript of ca. 1300, was bound in thirteenth-century fragments of the Anglo-Norman metrical romance *Berinus*, though these are probably not of Welsh origin.[34] This is particularly suggestive since the manuscript itself contains, amongst other texts, the earliest known version of the tale of *Peredur*, itself partly derived from French sources, including Chrétien's *Conte del Graal*, and Welsh prose versions of the Old French epic poems *La Chanson de Roland* and *Le Pèlerinage de Charlemagne*, and of the related chronicle of Pseudo-Turpin.[35] Although Anglo-Norman literary texts were undoubtedly composed and written down on the borders of Wales—as witness the late thirteenth-century *Fouke le Fitz Waryn*—it has not been possible to identify any manuscript entirely or mainly in Anglo-Norman that must have been composed in Wales. Neither do we yet have the evidence to demonstrate beyond reasonable doubt that any complete English manuscript was produced in Wales, whether written by a native speaker of English or a bilingual (or multilingual) Welsh scribe. The context in which manuscripts were used in Wales, whether they were in Welsh, Latin, French, or English, can be difficult to establish. Many Welsh manuscripts, which have only rarely retained their medieval bindings, yield few internal clues as to their origins or the milieu in which they spent their first centuries. Little is known of the contents of private libraries until much later, but it is striking that by the sixteenth century marks of ownership provide evidence of Middle English books in Welsh hands. Examples include a mid-fifteenth-century exemplar of Lydgate's *Life of Our Lady*, now NLW MS 21242C, which was in Welsh hands by the sixteenth century, and a copy of Chaucer's *Tretyse on the Astrolabe*, now NLW MS 3567B, was in the possession of John Edwards of Chirk, Denbighshire, as early as 1551. A late fifteenth-century copy of the English *Brut*, now NLW MS 21608, was in Welsh ownership in Rhuthun, Denbighshire early in the sixteenth century; although the present state of research precludes any definite conclusions about its origins, William Marx has suggested that we should not rule out the possibility that this manuscript was made for a member of the local merchant class.[36] Medieval French manuscripts have emerged from gentry libraries, but in the absence of any help-ful codicological or catalogue evidence we cannot be sure at what point they entered collections. Aberystwyth, National Library of Wales, Bettisfield MS 19, a fourteenth-century roll containing an Anglo-Norman Life of St. Melor, is a case in point. It is tempting to imagine that the unusual, presumably old-fashioned use of the roll format for a literary text could be an indication of local provenance. Bettisfield is in Flintshire, and it is significant, if predictable, that most surviving early examples of English books in Welsh hands come from the northeastern counties contiguous with England, for these Border regions, with their important market towns such as Chester, Shrewsbury, and Oswestry, would be obvious channels for transmission and interchange of both mate-rial and cultural goods. Nerys Howells has argued that Oswestry in particular played a key role in bringing poets like Dafydd ap Gwilym in the fourteenth century and Gwerful Mechain in the late fifteenth century into contact with outside influences, as well as opportunities for contact with other Welsh poets, on whichever side of the border they happened to be resident.[37]

Further research on the English spoken in Wales in the later Middle Ages might provide further clues, but it would not be unreasonable to suppose that by the fourteenth century, in the aftermath of the Edwardian conquest, manuscript production of some kind might be generated among the English-speaking communities planted in parts of Wales. Manuscripts in either Anglo-Norman or English might also have been produced within the Welsh-speaking communities just over the English border in Shropshire and Herefordshire. The first surviving trilingual manuscript to include English, Aberystwyth, National Library of Wales, Peniarth MS 50, containing mostly prophetic texts in prose and verse in Welsh, Latin, and English, was compiled in about 1445 in Glamorgan. The main hand is that of a certain David, whose name appears on page 114, and who, according to J. Gwenogvryn Evans, may have been associated with the Cistercian abbey of Neath.[38] Although Peniarth 50 contains no material in French, in at least one of his Welsh texts, *Darogan yr Olew Bendigaid*, the compiler made considerable use of French texts, especially Arthurian romances of the first quarter of the thirteenth century.[39]

In its use of English, however, Peniarth MS 50 reflects the beginning of an increasing trend, coinciding, no doubt, with the gradual demise of Anglo-Norman as a living language. Henceforth Welsh translators would increasingly target English rather than French texts, and by the beginning of the sixteenth century most new translations were based on English rather than French sources, many of them religious texts, and increasingly based on printed rather than manuscript sources. Examples include the Welsh *Dives a Phawper*, based on Henry Parker's English book published in 1493, and *Darn o'r Ffestial*, translated from the collection of homilies by John Mirk of Lilleshall in Shropshire that had been published by Caxton in 1483. Nonetheless, French texts continued to be read. The poet Lewys Morgannwg (fl. 1525–53) had had access to a manuscript of the *Perlesvaus*—perhaps the same one that had been the source of the second part of *Y Seint Greal* about 1400—for one of his poems includes details not found in the Welsh version, which has been abridged and edited in the translation process.[40] His contemporary, Elis Gruffydd, made use of a number of French texts, including romances of the French Vulgate Cycle such as the *Prose Lancelot*, as well as English texts from the Alliterative *Morte Arthur* to Caxton's *Chronicle* and John Rastell's *Pastyme of People*.[41] Elis Gruffydd spent more of his life in England and France than he did in Wales, and his residence first in London and later in Calais would have greatly facilitated his access to the wide range of sources on which he drew, but his practice of drawing on Welsh, Latin, French, and English sources is no different from that of his contemporaries and predecessors within Wales itself.

Linguistic and literary borrowing from French or Anglo-Norman was a common pattern in many Western European countries in the later Middle Ages, from Ireland in the west to Iceland in the north and to Italy and the Iberian peninsula in the south. The number of translations or adaptations of French narratives, whether chansons de geste, romances or other genres, into vernacular languages bears clear testimony to that. But the degree of interpenetration that occurred in the Welsh case was unusually high, thanks to the shared border with England.

That border could not and did not constitute a clear line between Welsh and Anglo-Norman settlement, language, culture, or political interests, but instead a broad area whose populations were mixed ethnically and linguistically and whose allegiances were varied and complex. Although there is more incontrovertible evidence of direct literary influence from Anglo-Norman and French in Welsh than vice versa, it is evident that borrowing was far from one-sided. Although many, varied channels could have been involved in the transmission of narrative materials of ultimately Welsh origin into French literary life, direct contacts between Anglo-Norman and Welsh individuals and communities must have played a significant, perhaps major part in that process. If writers speaking dialects of French were quick to see in those narratives and traditions potential grist to their literary mills, the Welsh were no less prompt to see the potential of importing or reimporting them and reworking them once more according to contemporary taste, needs, and political preoccupations.

Notes

1. So great has been the concern of many Welsh scholars that at the conference of the International Arthurian Society held at Bangor in 2002, Bill McCann, Helen Roberts and Sioned Davies held a roundtable discussion entitled "Find the Lady; the Search for Celtic Orgins," to air the problem. Several papers presented at the same society's conference in Utrecht in 2005 showed that their arguments had unfortunately fallen on deaf ears.

2. Oxford, Bodleian Library, Hatton 82, was copied by an Anglo-Norman scribe in the mid-thirteenth century and bears an Anglo-Norman ex libris inscription showing that it belonged to Bryan FitzAlan (d. 1306) of Bedale in Yorkshire. On the manuscript tradition of the romance William A. Nitze and T. Atkinson Jenkins, eds., *Le Haut Livre du Graal. Perlesvaus*, 2 vols. (Chicago: University of Chicago Press, 1932–7), 1: 3–7, 2: 3–24; William A. Roach, "A New *Perlesvaus* Fragment," *Speculum* 13 (1938): 216–20; Keith Busby, "A New Fragment of the *Perlesvaus*," *Zeitschrift für Romanische Philologie* 99 (1983): 1–12, and James P. Carley, "A Fragment of *Perlesvaus* at Wells Cathedral Library," *Zeitschrift für Romanische Philologie* 108 (1992): 35–57. The latter, a manuscript of the first half of the fourteenth-century, was copied from a continental exemplar by an English scribe who introduced many Anglo-Norman features to the language of the text (40).

3. Rachel Bromwich, "Celtic Elements in Arthurian Romance: A General Survey" in *The Legend of Arthur in the Middle Ages: Studies Presented to Armel H. Diverres*, ed. P. B. Grout, R. A. Lodge, C. E. Pickford, and E. K. C. Varty (Cambridge: D. S. Brewer, 1983), 41–55, and Rachel Bromwich, "First Transmission to England and France," in *Arthur of the Welsh: The Arthurian Legend in Medieval Welsh Literature,* ed. Rachel Bromwich, A. O. H. Jarman, and Brynley F. Roberts (Cardiff: University of Wales Press, 1991), 273–90.

4. These points were developed in a hitherto unpublished paper by Julianne Bruneau of the University of Notre Dame, Indiana, read at the conference of the International Arthurian Society at Utrecht in July 2005; a different approach is taken by Kristen Lee Over, *Literary and Cultural Identities in Medieval French and Welsh Arthurian Romance*, Studies in Medieval History and Culture (New York and London: Routledge, 2005).

5. The only extant witness is a prose version composed between during the period 1325–40, but a copy of the original verse narrative apparently of the late thirteenth century, survived into the sixteenth century; the original author was probably from Ludlow. See E. J. Hathaway P. T. Ricketts, C. A. Robson, and A. D. Wilshere, eds., *Fouke le Fitz Waryn* (Oxford: Blackwell, 1975), ix–xxxvii. On the unique manuscript, see also Jason O'Rourke, "British Library MS Royal 12.C. xii and the Problems of Patronage," *Journal of the Early Book Society* 3 (2000): 216–26.

6. On the types of contact, see, for example, Marie Surridge, "Romance Linguistic Influence on Middle Welsh," *Studia Celtica* 1 (1966): 63–92; Llinos Beverley Smith, "Yr Iaith Gymraeg cyn 1536," in *Y Gymraeg yn ei disgleirdeb,* ed. Geraint H. Jenkins (Cardiff: University of Wales Press, 1997), 15–44; see also Michael Richter, *Sprache und Gesellschaft im Mittelalter: Untersuchungen zur mündlichen Kommunikation in England von der Mitte des elften bis zum Beginn des vierzehnten Jahrhunderts* (Stuttgart: Hiersemann, 1979).

7. Marged Haycock, "'Some Talk of Alexander and Some of Hercules': Three Early Medieval Poems from the Book of Taliesin," *Cambrian Medieval Celtic Studies* 13 (1987): 7–38.

8. See Daniel Huws, "A Welsh Manuscript of Bede's *De Natura Rerum*," in *Medieval Welsh Manuscripts,* ed. Daniel Huws (Cardiff: University of Wales, with the National Library of Wales, 2000), 104–22.

9. Now Trinity College, Dublin, MS 50. See, for example, Huws, *Medieval Welsh Manuscripts*, 10 and references there given. Michael Gullick also confirms the date as the very beginning of the twelfth century (personal communication).

10. For general accounts of the Norman presence in Wales, see, for example, R. R. Davies, *Conquest, Coexistence and Change: Wales, 1063–1415* (Oxford: Clarendon Press jointly with [Cardiff]: University of Wales Press, 1987); on the loan words in the Four Branches, see Ifor Williams, ed., *Pedeir Keinc y Mabinogi* (Cardiff: University of Wales Press, 1974), xxxiv, and T. M. Charles-Edwards, "The Date of the Four Branches of the Mabinogi," *Transactions of the Honourable Society of Cymmrodorion 1970* (1971): 263–98, at 265–66.

11. See, for example, F. G. Cowley, *The Monastic Order in South Wales* (Cardiff: University of Wales Press, 1977), 9–17.

12. R. Geraint Gruffydd, "'Cyntefin Ceinaf Amser' o Lyfr Du Caerfyrddin," *Ysgrifau Beirniadol* 4 (1969): 12–26.

13. Now Aberystwyth, National Library of Wales, MS Peniarth 28: see Daniel Huws, "*Leges Howelda* at Canterbury," in *Medieval Welsh Manuscripts*, 169–76,

and Daniel Huws, *Peniarth 28. Darluniau o Lyfr Cyfraith Hywel/Illustrations from a Welsh Lawbook* (Aberystwyth: National Library of Wales, 1988).

14. Constance Bullock-Davies, *Professional Interpreters and the Matter of Britain* (Cardiff: University of Wales Press, 1996).

15. *The Journey through Wales and The Description of Wales*, trans. Lewis Thorpe (Harmondsworth: Penguin, 1978), 202–3; for Latin text, see *Giraldi Cambrensis Opera*, ed. James F. Dimock, 8 vols., Rolls Series (1868), 6: 144–45. That Owain's son Gwenwynwyn could likewise bridge the cultures is suggested by his presence in the Anglo-Norman *Fouke le Fitz Waryn* (see note 5).

16. For *Cywydd y fost*, see R. Iestyn Daniel, ed., *Gwaith Ieuan ap Rhydderch* (Aberystwyth: University of Wales Centre for Advanced Welsh and Celtic Studies, 2003), 3: esp. lines 25–28; see also notes at 139–47.

17. See, for example, Ceridwen Lloyd-Morgan, "Lancelot in Wales," in *Shifts and Transpositions in Medieval Narrative. A festschrift for Elspeth Kennedy*, ed. Karen Pratt (Cambridge: D. S. Brewer, 1997), 169–79, and J. H. Davies, "A Welsh Version of the Birth of Arthur," *Y Cymmrodor* 24 (1913): 247–64, and note 22 below. I am currently preparing a new edition and study of the "Birth of Arthur."

18. J. H. Matthews, *Cardiff Records, Being Materials for a History of the County Borough from the Earliest Times*, 6 vols. (Cardiff; London: By Order of the Corporation, 1898–1911), 4: 58.

19. Huw M. Edwards, *Dafydd ap Gwilym. Influences and Analogues*, Modern Languages and Literatures Monographs (Oxford: Clarendon Press, 1996), esp. at 158–65, 184–88, 202–44.

20. See, for example, Jason O'Rourke, "Political and Literary Culture in Wales and the English Border Country, 1300–1475" (Ph.D diss., Queen's University, Belfast, 1999), and Jason O'Rourke, "Imagined Histories: An English Prophecy in a Welsh Manuscript Context," *Journal of the Early Book Society* 5 (2002): 152–53.

21. Madeleine Blaess, "Les manuscrits français dans les monastères anglais au Moyen Âge," *Romania* 94 (1973): 321–58, at 341. It is worth noting that the catalogue of Lanthony abbey (Lanthony Secunda) in Gloucestershire, which was first founded in Breconshire, lists three French items, including two known in Wales, the *Elucidarium* and a Donatus (probably a French translation of the *Ars Minor*); cf. Blaess, "Les manuscrits français," 331.

22. Internal evidence in a number of Welsh texts of the fifteenth century suggests that a complete copy of the Vulgate Cycle was available to Welsh redactors. See Ceridwen Lloyd-Morgan, "Nodiadau ychwanegol ar achau Arthuriaidd a'u ffynonellau Ffrangeg," *National Library of Wales Journal* 21 (1980): 329–39, and Ceridwen Lloyd-Morgan, "*Darogan yr Olew Bendigaid*: chwedl o'r bymthegfed ganrif," *Llên Cymru* 11 (1981–82): 64–85. The Calais-based Welsh chronicler, Elis Gruffydd, may also have had access to a copy of the *Mort Artu*.

23. Carley, "A Fragment of 'Perlesvaus.'"

24. Alexander Falileyev, ed., *Welsh Walter of Henley*, Medieval and Modern Welsh Series 12 (Dublin: School of Celtic Studies, Dublin Institute for Advanced Studies, 2006), esp. xvii–xx; lxxxix–xc.

25. Sarah Rowles, "*Ystorya Adaf*: Golwg ar un o ffynonellau cyfieithwyr y chwedlau crefyddol," *Llên Cymru* 29 (2006): 44–63.

26. The range of material becomes ever more striking as new research brings to light still more evidence not only of translations but also familiarity with other nonnative texts for which full translations may never have been made. For general surveys of translations see, for example, Ceridwen Lloyd-Morgan, "French Texts, Welsh Translators," in *The Medieval Translator, II*, ed. Roger Ellis (London: Centre for Medieval Studies, Queen Mary and Westfield College, University of London, 1991), 45–63, and Morfydd E. Owen, "The Prose of the *Cywydd* Period," in *A Guide to Welsh Literature 1282–c. 1550*, ed. A. O. H. Jarman and Gwilym Rees Hughes, rev. Dafydd Johnston (Cardiff: University of Wales Press, 1997), 314–50.

27. Barry Lewis, "Llawysgrifau a Barddoniaeth Grefyddol yn y bedwaredd ganrif ar ddeg," *Cof Cenedl* 21 (Llandysul: Gomer Press, 2006), 31–62.

28. Richard Glyn Roberts, "Golygiad o dri fersiwn o *Madwaith Hen Gyrys o Iâl* ynghyd ag astudiaeth o'u ffynonellau a rhagarweiniad i'r traddodiad paremiolegol yn llenyddiaeth Gymraeg yr Oesau Canol" (Ph.D. diss., University of Wales, Bangor, 2006); Richard Glyn Roberts, "Y Traddodiad Paremiolegol yng Nghymru'r Oesau Canol. I. Rhai Diarhebion Cydwladol," *Dwned* 11 (2005): 19–33. Other proverbs, Roberts shows, were borrowed from English or Latin, while certain examples seem to be familiar throughout Western Europe.

29. Nerys Ann Jones and Ann Parry Owen, eds., *Gwaith Cynddelw Brydydd Mawr*, 2 vols., Cyfres Beirdd y Tywysogion [The Poets of the Princes Series] 3–4 (Cardiff: University of Wales Centre for Advanced Welsh and Celtic Studies, 1991–95), 2: 56, line 44. For further discussion of *rhamant* and its implications, see Ceridwen Lloyd-Morgan, "Medieval Welsh Tales or Romances? Problems of Genre and Terminology," *Cambrian Medieval Celtic Studies* 47 (2004): 41–58.

30. Richard Glyn Roberts, "Y Traddodiad Paremiolegol yng Nghymru'r Oesau Canol. II. 'y reyn oll sydd yn llawn diarebion,'" *Dwned* 12 (2006): 31–47, at 46.

31. See Ceridwen Lloyd-Morgan, "A Study of *Y Seint Greal* in Relation to *La Queste del Saint Graal* and *Perlesvaus*" (D.Phil. diss., Oxford, 1978), 64–70, 218–24.

32. Huws, *Medieval Welsh Manuscripts*, 3 note 1.

33. On Hafod 16, see J. Gwenogvryn Evans, *Report on Manuscripts in the Welsh Language*, 2 vols. (London, 1898–1910), 2: 318–20; Huws, *Medieval Welsh Manuscripts*, 60.

34. See Antoine Thomas, "Découverte de fragments d'un poème français inconnu sur Bérinus," *Journal des Savants* n.s. 20 (1922): 74–81; J. J. Jones, "Fragments of a French Romance," *National Library of Wales Journal* 1

(1939): 103–5, and Daniel Huws, "Y Pedair llawysgrif ganoloesol," in *Canhwyll Marchogyon: Cyd-destunoli* Peredur, ed. Sioned Davies and Peter Wynn Thomas (Cardiff: University of Wales Press, 2000), 1–9, at 2–5.

35. The manuscript also contains Welsh versions of apocrypha, translated from Latin sources, notably *Ystorya Adaf.* For a full list of contents see Evans, *Report on Manuscripts,* 1: 317–19.

36. William Marx, ed., *An English Chronicle, 1377–1461* (Woodbridge, Suffolk: Boydell and Brewer, 2003), xv–xxii.

37. Nerys Ann Howells, ed., *Gwaith Gwerful Mechain ac eraill* (Aberystwyth: University of Wales Centre for Advanced Welsh and Celtic Studies, 2001), 31–40.

38. Part parchment, part paper, this is also the earliest extant example of the use of paper in a Welsh manuscript. See Huws, *Medieval Welsh Manuscripts,* 17; Evans, *Report on Manuscripts,* 1: 389–99.

39. Ceridwen Lloyd-Morgan, "*Darogan yr Olew Bendigaid*: chwedl o'r bymthegfed ganrif," *Llên Cymru* 11 (1981–2): 64–85.

40. In his poem "Moliant Tomas ap Wiliam, Pen-rhos," see A. Cynfael Lake, ed., *Gwaith Lewys Morgannwg* (Aberystwyth: Cheltaidd, 2004), 144–46, 200–201, no. 37, line 40.

41. Ceridwen Lloyd-Morgan, "Welsh Tradition in Calais: Elis Gruffydd and His Biography of King Arthur," in *The Fortunes of King Arthur,* ed. Norris J. Lacy (Cambridge: D. S. Brewer, 2005), 76–91.

CHAPTER 9

MALORY'S DIVIDED WALES

Cory James Rushton

When Malory's Merlin prophesies that the young Arthur will "...be longe kynge of all Englond and have under his obeyssaunce Walys, Yrland, and Scotland, and moo reames than I will now reherce," he is reinforcing Malory's adherence to a long-standing English tradition: Arthur, originally a Celtic king and a Briton (admittedly a loaded and ambiguous term), is now a king of "Englond" who dominates England's Celtic neighbors.[1] Many scholars of Malory's text are relatively content to leave the matter there: whatever Malory says can either be traced to some other and earlier text, or if it cannot be so traced, the absent text can be assumed. It is true that Malory is a repository of earlier traditions, but he also has a mind of his own. While this chapter will focus on Malory's view of the Welsh (and, by association, the Cornish), Malory's method can be seen at work in his depiction of Camelot's Scottish faction; Malory emphasizes the Scottish nature of Gawain's followers in his final two books, an emphasis probably meant to echo earlier depictions of the dangerous Scot: the rebel king Lot, nearly the ruler of Britain, and the treacherous and ambitious Scots of the *Tristram*.[2] Malory's Welsh are more difficult to track, in part because the Scots are emphasized in exactly those sections of the *Morte Darthur* that seem the most creatively independent of earlier tradition, where Malory makes the largest number of idiosyncratic changes. An outline of Malory's view of the Welsh can nevertheless be discerned, although one must begin with that loaded term used earlier: the "Briton."

Michelle Warren uses the phrase "Briton history" to distinguish earlier British history from the later imperial connotations of "British," testifying to the slippery semantics of Briton/Britain/British.[3] This field of reference becomes problematic very early indeed, with the Welsh themselves beginning to abandon "Britannia" as a name for Wales and "Britons" as a name for themselves as early as the twelfth century, shifting to either "Cymry" or "Gualia" for their geographical region, the latter derived ultimately from Anglo-Saxon *Walas* or *Wealas* (but perhaps more directly from French and Latin texts, including Geoffrey of Monmouth), by 1150; following the Norman Conquest, English court documents apply the terms with greater consistency, reserving variations on "Britain" for the whole island and "Wealas" for the inhabitants of modern Wales, probably in an effort to avoid semantic confusion between Britons, Welsh, and Bretons (the very issue that later taxes Warren).[4] The perceived need to change their name as an ethnic group seems to reflect an understanding of their changed circumstances: they had, in R. R. Davies's phrase, "come down in the world" and needed to acknowledge their smaller homeland and more restricted ambitions.[5] However, this did not mean that the Welsh were giving up their identity in favor of one imposed by their English neighbors: "To adopt names such as *Wallia* and *Walenses* did not mean that the Welsh rejected their British inheritance, still less that they ceased to think of themselves and their country as Cymry."[6] There seems to have been a deliberate element of exile in the new vocabulary, as "the use of *Britannia* to signify Wales was predicated on a huge territorial loss": they were no longer Britons, but they might one day reclaim that name in conjunction with a renewed dominion over the whole island of Britain.[7]

The Divided Briton

As many scholars now argue, the Arthurian legend is perhaps the most significant cultural battleground between England and her Celtic neighbors (particularly Wales but also Cornwall and Scotland). "Arthurian literary history," writes Patricia Ingham, "was the object of shared dreamings and political contestations between England and Wales," a conflict that found one outlet in the rebellion of Owain Glyn Dŵr and another very different outlet in the fantastic British history alluded to by Chaucer's Wife of Bath in her Arthurian tale.[8] Ingham notes that criticism of Chaucer's Arthurian story seems "determined to forget Welsh presence on the island at the time Chaucer wrote," defining the Tale's Britons as either inhabitants of Brittany or predecessors of the English, long-vanished inhabitants of "a pastoral, ancient, and united Britain": she argues that "the intimacies of English-Welsh affairs have... meant that Welsh oppositional claims to "British" identity fall victim to a particularly deep invisibility."[9] Davies has argued that, by the time of the annexation of Wales by Edward I in 1282, it seemed to the English that "a new empire had been born, or, rather, an old empire—the monarchy of the whole of Britain—had been reborn."[10] However, the annexation meant to eclipse the Welsh can be seen to have instead inaugurated a "long apprenticeship in English politics" that could often, paradoxically, trouble the peace of the English conquerors.[11] The idea that the Welsh needed to evolve, to become more like the English (socially in the eyes of the English, but politically in the eyes of modern historians) is linked to the long tradition of seeing the Welsh as barbarians. Michael Faletra argues that this tradition is encoded in various versions of Geoffrey of Monmouth's *Historia Regum Britanniae*: following the final defeat of the Britons in Logres, they become the degenerate and fragmented race known as the Welsh.[12]

There is therefore a certain amount of disdain toward the Welsh traceable in Arthurian romance literature, much of it focused on the figure of Perceval. One of Chrétien's knights, upon first encountering the young Perceval, compares the Welsh to ignorant animals, stupid, and less civilized than other peoples (*Perceval*, lines 235–44); both *Perceval* and the *Perlesvaus* insist on the rustic nature of the young man's weapons—javelins and spears associated with the peasantry and hunting (*Perslesvaus*, lines 30–31).[13] This literary dismissal is reflected in contemporary historical accounts, as well. Lodewijk van Veltham describes the Welshmen accompanying Edward I's Flanders expedition of 1297 in similar terms, adding that they were troublemakers as well:

> There you saw the peculiar habits of the Welsh. In the very depth of winter they were running about bare-legged... Their weapons were bows, arrows and swords. They also had javelins. They wore linen clothing. They were great drinkers. They endangered the Flemings very much. Their pay was too small and it came about that they took what did not belong to them.[14]

English chroniclers noted that following the final suppression of rebellion in Gwynedd in 1294–95, the previously poor and uncivilized Welsh were finally learning to behave in a civilized manner (which seems to have meant they were learning to be English, particularly when it came to wealth acquisition and display).[15]

The rebellion of Glyn Dŵr (1400–15), coming at the end of a century of increasing integration, seems to have caught the English by surprise. More alarming, it was not simply a Welsh undertaking: Glyn Dŵr found support and allies along England's borders (the Mortimers in the Welsh Marches and the Percys in Northumberland), as well as in France.[16] The English were often afraid of the possibilities for alliances amongst their neighbors:

> Ideas of a pan-Celtic fraternity, long expressed in poetry and Arthurian prophecies, were read in fifteenth-century gentry households, and were still a curiosity which suspicious English chroniclers felt it wise to mention...[17]

Malory testifies to this continuing English fear of the margins when he notes that Arthur's enemies hail from every possible border region: faced with a Saracen invasion, "they condescended togydir to kepe all the marchis of Cornuwayle, of Walis, and of the Northe" and placing one of their number in "Nauntis in Bretayne" (27: 19–21); they call on "eyght thousand for to fortefye all the fortresse in the marchis of Cornuwayle," and more still on the Welsh and Scottish borders (27: 24–29). The English response to Glyn Dŵr's rebellion was to enact even more repressive laws, including laws governing miscegenation between the Welsh and the English and the inability of the Marcher lords to control their territories.[18] Davies notes that the response of the English was partly rooted in a sense of betrayal:

> The revolt put paid to any move towards dismantling the concepts and machinery of racial distinction in Wales. The Welsh had shown their true colours. They were not submissive and deferential natives. They were not even the merely lightweight people of contemporary reputation. They were a perfidious people, on a par with "the wild Irish, our enemies."[19]

Writing a few decades after Glyn Dŵr's rebellion, Malory might be expected to share a general English disdain for the Welsh, just as he exhibits a fear and loathing of the Scots (admittedly a more consistently threatening enemy within his own lifetime). However, Malory's views on the Welsh are not immediately discernible, at least not to the extent that his distaste for the Scots is readily apparent.

The long border between Wales and England, the Marches, has attracted the attention of postcolonial theorists. Whenever an "English" character, like Gawain in *Sir Gawain and the Green Knight*, crosses that border, it arouses interest: as Patricia Clare Ingham notes, the Marches were "an intimate frontier, a borderland between linked, yet also distinct, cultures."[20] "Lest the English forget" that the Welsh were barbaric, says Lynn Arner, "*Sir Gawain and the Green Knight* was there to remind them."[21] While it may be true that Gawain's journey is through a hostile landscape, one in which the natural world is seen as an Other to the knight, some stretching is required to force the poem into a strictly postcolonial mode. Helen Young notes that Wales has only a few inhabitants whom "God other gome with goud hert loved,"[22] and that this implies that "they are uncivilized and therefore the proper objects of colonization"; this may be true, but to then argue that these same inhabitants "are so unhelpful [to Gawain]" that they create "a sense of alienation and isolation" seems unfair.[23] They are simply telling Gawain the truth when they say that they have not seen any green men around, not an unreasonable assertion under any circumstances (lines 706–8). The Green Knight himself is best seen as a hybrid figure, Welsh/uncivilized and English/urban:

> His size and greenness recall the Otherworld often associated with Wales, while the fashionable clothing and fine materials relate to the conspicuous finery of metropolitan court culture.[24]

If anything, what Ingham elsewhere says about the Wife of Bath's tale also applies to *Sir Gawain and the Green Knight*: the Welsh are nearly invisible in the poem, replaced by a handful of hardy but faceless souls and a castle inhabited by a man who can replace his own head upon decapitation, and whose identity perhaps reveals the extent to which Welsh identity can be subsumed within that of the English. The role of magic in the tale reminds us of Morgan—no more Welsh than Arthur is, as ambiguous as that statement might be—and Morgan is a figure associated with wild places, as Michael Twomey has convincingly argued in the context of "Hautdesert" itself, the high wasteland or desert.[25] An important facet of colonization propaganda is exactly the imperative to depopulate a landscape, and claim that it was always empty. Malory's Welsh have a degree of this hybridity, and it is another border group that attracts his condescension.

The Cornish are Malory's "lightweight people of contemporary reputation." Arthur's knights routinely comment on the inadequacies of their Cornish counterparts, although it is rarely the best of the Round Table who make such comments. Kay, Brandiles, and Tor all agree that good knights never come from Cornwall; Kay remarks that "as yet harde I never that evir good knyght com oute of Cornwayle" (299: 21–22), and he and his comrades spend a pleasant evening rehearsing "all the shame by Cornysh knyghtes that coude be seyde" (299: 35–37). Even the valiant Bors once refuses to joust with a Cornish knight because "...they ar nat called men of worship"—there is little point in matching lances with them (310: 38–39). When Ector de Maris thinks he has been defeated by a Cornish knight he laments his lost reputation:

> "Alas!" seyde sir Ector, "now am I ashamed that ony Cornysshe knyght sholde overcome me!" And than for dispyte sir Ector put of his armoure fro hym and wente on foot wolde nat ryde. (252: 16–18)

Ector's reaction points toward Malory's reasons for this anti-Cornish theme: the insults launched at Cornish chivalry almost all come in the *Tristram* books, and are based directly on similar statements in Malory's immediate source for this section, the Prose *Tristan*. There, the comments serve to heighten the reputation of Tristram, who is always there (as he is in Malory) to overhear the insults and avenge Cornish renown. Muriel Whitaker believes that the anti-Cornish sentiment also serves to bolster a "deliberate contrast" between the courts of King Mark and King Arthur, a contrast illuminated substantially by Edward Donald Kennedy: where Mark is cowardly and treacherous, Arthur is brave and generous.[26] "For the honour of bothe courtes be nat lyke," says Lamorak de Galis (276: 20–22), a sentiment confirmed much later by Bors when he notes that Arthur and Mark "were never lyke of condycions" (681: 29–32). The anti-Cornish sentiment largely does not linger past the end of the *Tristram*, nor is it strongly attested beforehand: Cornish knights serve in the Roman War; Duke Gorlois of Cornwall is clearly a valiant man and his followers the equal of Uther's; and Constantine, son of Cador of Cornwall and "a ful noble knyght" (725: 32–34), becomes Arthur's heir. What interests me is that Malory retains these anti-Cornish sentiments, at least in the context of the *Tristram*, but does not indulge in anti-Welsh sentiment at any stage (even when he introduces Perceval into his narrative, as discussed below).

Malory declares that Arthur's realm was initially England, but that "within fewe years after Arthur wan alle the North, Scotland, and alle that were under their obeissaunce, also Walys" (10: 43–11: 1). He immediately qualifies this statement by stating that a "part of it helde ayenst Arthur, but he overcame hem al, as he did the remenaunt, thurgh the noble prowesse of himself and his knyghtes of the

Round Table" (11: 1–3). Wales, in the first quotation, seems like an afterthought: indeed, much of Malory's early narrative is concerned with enemies in the north, as he himself notes that "the Northe fro Trent forwardes...was that tyme the most party the kynges enemyes" (10: 42–43). Our question revolves around the qualification that a "part of it helde ayenst Arthur": is this a part of the British Isles, or of Wales in particular, or both? Certainly, despite Malory's association of Arthur with England, the young Arthur is closely linked with southern Wales in Malory's own text: "Thenne the kyng removed into Walys and lete crye a grete feste, that it shold be holdyn at Pentecost after the incoronacion of hym at the cyté of Carlyon" (11: 4–6). The subsequent rebellion of his own guests (led by Lot of Lothian and Orkney), who besiege him in Caerleon, is defeated in part when "the comyns of Carlyon aroos with clubbis and stavys and slewe many knyghtes" (13: 1–3). This peasants' uprising, which might normally prompt aristocratic uneasiness, seems justifiable here because it is in the service of the text's central authority figure, Arthur; the "comyns" had earlier insisted that the test of the sword in the stone had revealed God's will, and their single voice helps to prevent an immediate crisis at the moment of Arthur's revelation as king (10: 20–33). The central point for our purposes is that Arthur's earliest support comes from a Welsh city, one firmly in his hands, and even more particularly from those citizens who are armed with nonaristocratic weapons: "clubbis and stavys," weapons sometimes associated with the primitive Welsh. If the "remenaunt" that Arthur must conquer is Welsh, that remnant is not in the region of Caerleon and Cardiff—it is not southern Wales that is Arthur's problem, but North Wales or Norgales. The word "remenaunt" is used in reverse when North Wales faces the "remenaunte of Walys" in a tournament (416: 1), strongly implying that Wales remains strictly divided throughout Arthur's reign.

Malory will sometimes praise knights who are associated with Wales (the Captain of Cardiff, 136: 25; Edward of Caernarfon, 666: 17; Lamyell or Camyell of Cardiff, 667: 8). However, it should be noted that an implicit distinction may already be at work here: Cardiff and southern Wales have a hybrid identity from at least the Norman Conquest onward, an Anglo-Norman identity built on a Welsh foundation (through intermarriage with the daughters of local princes, including Nest, daughter of Rhys ap Tewdwr, prince of Deheubarth in southern Wales). South Wales was said to be entirely under the control of Alfred in Asser's *De rebus gestis Ælfredi*; Cardiff, for example, was in non-Welsh hands since the Norman Robert fitz Hamo (d. 1107) seized it following the death of Rhys ap Tewdwr in 1093.[27] Cardiff is also the port from which the exiled Lancelot and his followers leave England, implying that the city is directly under Arthur's control: "And so they shypped at Cardyff, and sayled unto Benwyke" (699: 19–20). Caernarfon is associated with the 1282 conquest through the castle built there by Edward I, a castle in which his heir Edward II (the first English heir to hold the title "Prince of Wales") was born: it is not too much of a stretch to see Malory, a writer who likes to borrow names from whatever available sources to identify otherwise anonymous characters, including Edward of Caernarfon as a gesture toward the monarch who finally annexed the previously semi-independent North Wales. These Welsh knights, it seems, are actually sometimes English. The Captain of

Cardiff is reminiscent of historical figures such as Sir Richard Gethyn of Builth, captain of Conches and Mantes during the 1430s, described as "the jewel of Wales" and "the lion of England" at separate times, and once explicitly compared to Arthur and Lancelot.[28] The distinction between south Wales, more settled and more English, and the wilder Welsh of Norgales is an important one. Malory makes two divisions within the general category of Britons: the first is between the Welsh and the Cornish, with the latter taking on many of the negative attributes of the Welsh stereotype (albeit as a result of one of his major sources, the Prose *Tristan*); the second is between the Welsh of the settled south and the more dangerous Welsh of "Norgales."

Norgales and the Isles

While Arthur seems to rule in south Wales, the picture in Malory's Norgales is far more complex, in large part because he has inherited a number of figures associated with the rule of this area from a variety of contradictory sources. Malory does not leave a clear sense of his design here, as he does with the Scots in his final books; nevertheless, at the risk of drawing conclusions that are too tenuous from the slight evidence, I would suggest that he does have an opinion about Norgales and its rulers. Malory's opinion is delineated in his depiction of several figures: one is Arthur's early enemy "kynge Riens of North Walis" whom Arthur hates because "allwayes he was ayenst hym" (26: 13–16), while many of the others are members of the family of Pellinore, whose son and heir Lamorak is always said to be "of Walis" (34: 38–40) or "de Galis" (268: 34, also at 276: 6–7, 371: 4–6, 376: 26–30, etc.). Malory's Perceval is a member of this clan.

Ryons is "kynge of all Irelonde and of Iles" in addition to Norgales (36: 26–27), a status he may hold because he has conquered eleven other kingdoms (36: 29–30), eleven being the number of kings who previously kept "the marchis of Cornuwayle, of Walis, and of the Northe" and who had used their power to threaten Arthur (27: 19–20). Ryons is initially seen in some kind of political alliance with them (27: 29–31); previous to the appearance of Ryons and his brother Nero, Norgales was ruled by "kynge Cradilment of North Walis" (19: 23–25). Ryons enters Arthurian narrative in Geoffrey, where a giant named Retho collects the beards of his vassal kings, just as Malory's Ryons does (36: 30–32). Ryons appears as Rion in Chrétien's *Perceval*, where he is called the King of the Isles: a charcoal-burner informs Perceval that Arthur and his men have just defeated Rion, a joyous event for the Arthurian court (*Perceval*, 851). In Malory, as in the *Suite du Merlin*, Ryons is defeated by the doomed knights Balin and Balan (46: 33–38), and survives the battle to complain to Arthur of his "harde adventure" (47: 10). As Malory moves into other sources, the name Ryons disappears and a nameless "kynge of North Walis" begins to make several appearances: at the tournament of Lonazep, conceived as a tournament in which (suggestively) Cornwall and North Wales "shulde juste ayenst all that wolde com of other contereyes" (420: 19–22), the King of North Wales consistently assists Tristram in that knight's latest attempt to test himself against Arthur's court—Tristram unhorses Arthur and gives the king's steed to his North Welsh benefactor (447: 6–29). These tournaments, which seem to reflect shifting alliances and friendships between the monarchs of Britain, often reveal a treacherous Norgales; the North Welsh king is rarely on Arthur's side (276: 36–37, 621: 31, 624: 25, 635: 20–21), with the one exception being a tournament called by Arthur in which he specifies that Logres is to fight alongside Cornwall and North Wales (415: 43–44), perhaps as an attempt to improve relations. The King of Norgales is often seen conspiring against Arthur or Lancelot, sometimes cheating to achieve his ends.[29] The Queen of Norgales is often seen in alliance with Morgan le Fay, once jointly receiving a request for aid from Arthur's rebellious vassal Mark of Cornwall (152: 10) and later accompanying Arthur to his last rest (717: 15–16). The King of North Wales is said to be "passynge hevy" when he hears of another of Arthur's successful wars, the battle against the invading Five Kings (80: 6–8). It is perhaps not coincidental that one of these Five Kings is "the kyng of Irelonde" (77: 20) and that the invaders "passed forth with hir oste thorow North Walys" to reach Arthur's army (78: 14–16). The passage testifies to a lingering confusion concerning the names and kingdoms of Arthur's royal enemies, but it does confirm that for Malory, as for his sources, the idea of danger coming out of North Wales was not beyond the pale.

The importance of the Ryons' other kingdoms of Ireland and the seemingly vague "Iles" cannot be overestimated. Pellinore, too, is called "the kynge of the Iles" (73: 20–21), requiring some discussion of where Malory understood these islands to be. The historical reality that lies behind the title of the "kings of the Isles" has been largely forgotten today; as F. J. Byrne noted, the story of the United Kingdom forces an amnesia concerning alternate paths that history might have taken:

> The writing of national history as a genre has had the unfortunate result of obscuring entities once important in their own right that have not survived as nation states or even as geographical units.[30]

The islands that now form part of Scotland's western seaboard were once the center of a potential political power unit within the British Isles, often dominating surrounding areas: Galloway, the Isle of Man, Anglesey, Cumbria, and Ulster. In the twelfth and thirteenth centuries, Davies has argued, a realm or series of allied realms embracing these islands and coastal kingdoms was entirely possible; indeed, in "terms of power structures, ease of communications, ecclesiastical and economic conditions, ethnic and cultural links, such a unit would have made a great deal of sense."[31] These cultural links were first Celtic and then Scandinavian, and in some areas (notably Galloway) a true hybrid culture was the result of centuries of expansion, conquest, and interbreeding: references to the size and aggression of Viking invaders might help us to understand the nature of the giant Ryons, and might also aid us in seeing that North Wales was a potential path for invasion from the sea during the Arthurian tradition's formative years. In 1098, the Norwegian king Magnus Barelegs invaded Anglesey as a prelude to conquering Britain, only to encounter an Anglo-Irish raiding force also invading Anglesey under Hugh, Earl of Chester, and Hugh, Earl of Shrewsbury. As late as 1164, Somerled of Argyll and the Isles was able to challenge the King of the Scots with a fleet of nearly 160 galleys.[32] Before they adopted the title *dominus Insularum* or "King of the Isles" in 1336, these monarchs were known by the Gaelic title *rí Insse Gall*, a phrase that may hint that the personal name "Rions/Ryons" (*rí Insse*) might have originated as a title. Exactly during the period when the Arthurian legend was being developed and reported by authors such as Geoffrey and William of Malmesbury, the Kings of the Isles were potential powerful threats to mainland England, and their best route for invasion was from the north, through Wales. The military success of Ryons, exemplified by his beard and kingdom collection, may not have seemed as fantastic to a medieval audience as it does to us. The Arthurian tradition, for sound historical reasons, therefore does not draw the same sharp distinction between Wales and the islands and coastal kingdoms with which it shares the Irish Sea. Instead, the tradition seems to insist on a division between north and south Wales, which Malory picks up on: in another of his political summaries, Malory tells us that while there were "many kynges" in the north, and "two or three kynges" in Ireland, Wales had exactly "two kynges" (229: 11–18). One of these kings is the King of North Wales or Norgales, an anonymous figure after the defeat of Ryons; the other is Pellinore, with his heir Lamorak de Galis.

When Chrétien's Perceval asks why King Arthur is both happy and sad at the same time, he is told that victory over Rion has led to the diminishment of Arthur's court:

> King Arthur and his entire army have been fighting against King Rion: the King of the Isles was defeated, which made King Arthur happy; and he's sad on account of his companions, who dispersed to go and stay in the castles they found most attractive, and he doesn't know how they are faring—that's the reason for the king's grief.[33]

As Madeleine Blaess and Brigitte Cazelles have noted, there seem to be strong links between Perceval's parents and the Isles, and this in turn implies a relationship between Perceval and the defeated Rion. Perceval's mother claims that at one time, there was "no knight in all the Isles of the Sea who was of such great merit or so feared and dreaded" as Perceval's father (lines 416–26), but that following the death of Uther Pendragon, he was one of many "noble men who were impoverished, disinherited and wrongly brought to destitution" (lines 432–58). Indeed, criticism has long identified the Hebrides specifically as the homeland of Perceval's family; while Luttrell believes this identification is too specific and does not allow for instances in which the phrase "toutes les illes de mer" seems to function as a formula for the British Isles as a whole, King Rion of the Isles is clearly a specific figure with a specific kingdom.[34] For Cazelles, Perceval is concerned with the "cyclical nature of vendetta," a vendetta she sees as a feud between an Arthurian chivalry, represented primarily by Chrétien's second protagonist Gawain, and a Grail lineage represented by Perceval; both groups, she argues, "promote violence and aggression" as they spiral toward a "denouement [that] could prove lethal for one of the two protagonists, if not both."[35] Cazelles thus disagrees with Donald Maddox, who postulates a difference between the Grail lineage and the secular clans that surround and threaten it.[36] For my purposes, and I suspect for Malory's, the implication that the Grail family, Perceval's family, was the victim of aggressive behavior by Rion/Ryons or Arthur, or both, is the most salient point.

For Malory and his immediate sources, Perceval's father has become Pellinore, already noted above as a King of the Isles. Pellinore fights in the battle against Ryons, facing and killing Gawain's father Lot (48: 32–38) and starting a feud that will end with his death (48: 40–43, 375: 4–13) and the deaths of three of his five sons. While Chrétien left the deaths of Perceval's immediate male kin in a vaguely told past, subsequent versions place the extinction of Pellinore's line closer to the center of their narratives. Pellinore benefits from his alliance with Arthur, and is shown giving advice to the younger king concerning the composition of the Round Table (80: 9–13); he is further the subject of two prophecies by Merlin, one that he will wed Arthur's unnamed sister (36: 2–4) and the other that he will have two sons, Perceval and "sir Lamorake of Walis" (34: 36–41). Malory's interest in this family extends beyond their feud with the Orkney clan under Gawain, despite critical attention focusing almost exclusively on that issue.[37] Perceval's eventual arrival at Camelot is preceded by one of Malory's engaged, chronicle-style commentaries, clearly meant to position the young knight politically:

> Now torne we ageyne to syr Lamorak and speke we of his bretheren: syr Tor, whiche was kynge Pellenors first sone and bygoten of Aryes wyf, the couherd, for he was a bastard; and sire Aglovale was hys fyrste sone begotten in wedlock; syre Lamorak, Dornar, Percyvale, these were his sones to in wedlock. (376: 26–30)

Aglovale is not Pellinore's heir, as Lamorak claims that status a few pages before Aglovale's appearance with Perceval: "Than, sir, ye shall undirstonde my name is sir Lameroke de Galys, sonne and ayre unto the good knyght and kynge, kynge Pellynore" (371: 4–5). Why Agglovale should be overlooked is never explained—the only romance in which he plays a major role is the Dutch *Moriaen*, in which he engages in a love affair with a Moorish princess—but it is probably his very obscurity that is the culprit. Malory wants the valor of his heroes to be matched by their economic or hierarchical circumstances; Lamorak, as the third best knight of Arthur's court, must be the heir.[38] The eventual extinction of the house of Pellinore comes about through a combination of factional dispute (Lamorak and Pellinore die at the hands of the Orkneys, Tor and Agglovale in the confusion surrounding Lancelot's rescue of the queen from the stake) and holy asceticism (Perceval himself, who dies as a hermit after seeing the Grail). The feud between the de Galis clan and the Orkneys is one of Malory's most important subplots, a conflict that bears on the dichotomy between the imagined equality of the Round Table and the family ambitions of Arthur's nephews. For all this thematic importance, however, much of the feud takes place away from the narrative itself: Malory delights in combat, but the fights in which Lamorak and Pellinore die are somehow never shown, only reported.

Dhira Mahoney has recently argued that "Malory's Percivale is drawn from competing literary traditions and, as a result, seems to have something of a split personality" in his initial appearances in the tradition: "he is a type of naïf, brought up in the wilds of Wales by his widowed mother, who wishes to keep him from knowledge of his parentage and therefore of knightly behavior."[39] Malory does not even show Perceval's adolescence; he first appears at court under relatively normal circumstances, introduced to Arthur by his brother Agglovale (376: 35–377: 27). If Malory had wanted to keep the parodic aspects of Perceval's Welsh background, this scene would be the time to do it. Instead, the reader is told that Arthur will knight Perceval for the love of Pellinore and Lamorak (377: 3–5); that his seat at the Round Table should be "to the right side of the Sege Perillous" (377: 21–22); and that Mordred and Kay have some reason to later remark that he was " 'full unlykly to preve a good knyght' " (493: 43–44). Perceval remains a Grail knight in Malory, although second to Galahad, but also becomes a "spokesman of knightly values"; Mahoney believes that the lines between the two Percevals "become blurred," and that Malory is forced into an "attempt to reconcile these two personalities."[40] It does seem as though Malory is moved to modify his sources here, largely by deleting anything that seems extraneous to his purpose; that purpose is twofold, and not contradictory. On the one hand, Perceval was destined to be a Grail knight; on the other, the Prose *Tristan* had specifically stated that the feud that destroyed Perceval's family was with Gawain's kin:

> Now the prose *Tristan*, which combines details from both Chrétien and the *Lancelot*, not only identifies Perceval's father as Pellinor, but adds a new theme, the feud between Gauvain and Pellinor's line, to explain how Perceval's father and brothers were killed.[41]

What is most germane to an understanding of Malory is the link between Perceval's family, associated with either the Isles or North Wales (or both) and with the Grail (through his uncle, the Fisher King), and the destruction of that family in a feud with Gawain's Scottish kin.

The implication that Lamorak and Perceval are Arthur's nephews through a marriage, like Gawain and his brothers, is intriguing; indeed, Perceval is known in at least one Middle English text as Arthur's nephew: in *Percyvell of Gales*, Perceval's father (here also named Percyvell) is rewarded by Arthur with a marriage to his sister, Acheflour.[42] The similarity to Pellinore's story is suggestive, and Malory may well have this particular narrative in mind. At the Assumption Day tournament in the *Tale of Gareth*, Malory shows Lamorak and his brothers accompanying Arthur in a procession; the order of entry is suggestive:

> Than turne we to kynge Arthure that brought wyth hym sir Gawayne, Aggravayne, Gaherys, his brethern; and than his nevewys, as sir Uwayne le Blaunche Maynes, and sir Agglovale, sir Tor, sir Percivale de Galys, sir Lamerok de Galys. (213: 6–9)

Only after Arthur's kin do we see the entry of Lancelot and "his bretherne, nevewys, and cosyns" (213: 9–15); it seems clear that in the *Gareth*, at least, Lamorak and his brothers are King Arthur's nephews. Malory never again explicitly draws out the connection, perhaps because the Lot-Pellinore subplot is so concerned with the problem of royal authority and the troublesome relatives of kings.

The Importance of Wales

Malory's Wales, then, is divided geographically into two halves, north and south; the people of Wales are divided into those who are loyal to Arthur (the people of Caerleon, the house of Pellinore) and a North Welsh royal family that is either overtly hostile or moderately subversive throughout Arthur's reign. Despite Malory's connection of Camelot with Winchester, firmly in England, Arthur's own base of power seems to be southern Wales: his earliest support comes from the citizens of Caerleon, and his earliest wars take place in Welsh territory. Arthur is apparently allied, through marriage, to at least one significant Welsh family, the kin of Pellinore. Norgales is seen as a place of potential danger: the Forest Perilous to which sorceress Annowre lures Arthur is said to be "in North Walis" (300: 33–37), and the country sometimes look like an invasion path from the islands and kingdoms of the Celtic northwest. The de Galis family is associated with feuding, first as allies with Arthur against his enemies, and later between themselves and the Scottish kin of Gawain.

It is this feud that gives us, indirectly, our last real glimpse of Malory's Norgales (and, perhaps not coincidentally, of the equally troublesome Cornwall). As the Round Table begins to break up, Lancelot calls together his followers in the aftermath of Mordred and Aggravayne's ambush:

> So these two-and-twenty knyghtes drew hem togydirs, and by than they were armed and on horsbak they promised sir Launcelot to do what he wolde. Than there felle to them, what of Northe Walys and of Cornwayle, for sir Lamorakes sake and for sir Trystrames sake, to the numbir of a seven score knyghtes. (679: 33–37)

The presence of North Welsh knights in Lancelot's army is reiterated later, when "seven brethirn of Northe Walis whych were seven noble knyghtes, for a man myghte seke seven kyngis londis or he might fynde such seven knyghtes" ask Lancelot for permission to ride out against Arthur's forces, "for we were never wonte to coure in castels nother in noble townys" (701: 4–8). Both moments are Malorian innovations, and it is tempting to see in the boast of the seven brothers from Norgales a rejection of English civilized life: they do not wish to cower in castels or noble towns, and their enemies are Arthur's Englishmen. Less tenuously, these North Welsh knights serve Lancelot for the sake of their dead leader, Lamorak, killed by the Scots who now (led by Gawain) form the bulk of Arthur's remaining men.[43] Malory's distrust of the Scots shows strongly here—the North Welsh arguably have as much reason to hate Lancelot, as he killed the last two sons of Pellinore (Agglovale and Tor) when he rescued the queen from execution (684: 19). With the deaths of Pellinore's last surviving sons, the alliance between the Welsh (north or south) and Arthur seems to be finally, irrevocably, broken. The men of Norgales are never going to join forces with Gawain's Scots—the feud has gone on too long for that—and arguably they were always one step away from rebelling against Arthur anyways.

Notes

1. (Page 11, lines 43–44). All quotations from Malory are by page and line numbers from the one volume *Malory: Works*, ed. Eugène Vinaver, 2nd edn. (Oxford: Oxford University Press, 1971).

2. Cory James Rushton, "'Of an uncouthe stede': The Scottish Knight in Middle English Arthurian Romances," in *The Scots and Medieval Arthurian Tradition*, ed. Rhiannon Purdie and Nicola Royan (Cambridge: D. S. Brewer, 2005), 109–19.

3. Michelle Warren, *History on the Edge: Excalibur and the Borders of Britain, 1100–1300* (Minneapolis: University of Minnesota Press, 2000), 1.

4. Huw Pryce, "British or Welsh? National Identity in Twelfth-Century Wales." *English Historical Review* 116 (September 2001): 775–801.

5. R. R. Davies, *Conquest, Coexistence, and Change: Wales, 1063–1415* (Oxford: Clarendon Press and University of Wales Press, 1987), 19.

6. Pryce, "British or Welsh?" 799.

7. Pryce, "British or Welsh?" 786–87, 800.

8. Patricia Clare Ingham, "Pastoral Histories: Utopia, Conquest, and the Wife of Bath's Tale," *Texas Studies in Literature and Language* 44 (2002): 34–46 [35–38].

9. Ingham, "Pastoral Histories," 38–39.

10. R. R. Davies, *The First English Empire: Power and Identities in the British Isles, 1093–1343* (Oxford: Oxford University Press, 2000), 36–37.

11. James Given, *State and Society in Medieval Europe: Gwynedd and Languedoc under Outside Rule* (Ithaca and London: Cornell University Press, 1990), 208–24.

12. Michael A. Faletra, "Narrating the Matter of Britain: Geoffrey of Monmouth and the Norman Colonization of Wales," *Chaucer Review* 35.1 (2000): 60–85.

13. Chrétien de Troyes, *Arthurian Romances*, trans. and ed. D. D. R. Owen (London: J. M. Dent, 1993); Nigel Bryant, trans., *The High Book of the Grail* (Cambridge: D. S. Brewer, 1978).

14. Lodiwijk, quoted in A. C. Carr, "Welshmen and the Hundred Years' War," *Welsh Historical Review* 4.1 (1968): 21–46, at 22.

15. Davies, *First English Empire*, 113–14.

16. R. R. Davies, *The Revolt of Owain Glyn Dŵr* (Oxford: Oxford University Press, 1997), 125; Margaret Robson, "Local Hero: Gawain and the Politics of Arthurianism," *Arthurian Literature* 23 (2006): 81–94, at 81.

17. Ralph Griffiths, "The Island of England in the Fifteenth Century: Perceptions of the Peoples of the British Isles," *Journal of Medieval History* 29 (2003): 177–200, at 179.

18. Davies, *Conquest*, 457–58.

19. Davies, *Conquest*, 458.

20. Patricia Clare Ingham, *Sovereign Fantasies: Arthurian Romance and the Making of Britain* (Philadelphia: University of Pennsylvania Press, 2001), 108.

21. Lynn Arner, "The Ends of Enchantment: Colonialism and *Sir Gawain and the Green Knight*," *Texas Studies in Literature and Language* 48.2 (Summer 2006): 79–101, at 79.

22. *Sir Gawain and the Green Knight*, line 702.

23. Helen Young, "'Bi contray caryez this knyght': Journeys of Colonisation in Sir Gawain and the Green Knight," *Philament* 1 (September 2003), 14 April 2007. http://www.arts.usyd.edu.au/publications/philament/issue1_HelenYoung.htm.

24. Rhonda Knight, "All Dressed Up with Someplace to Go: Regional Identity in *Sir Gawain and the Green Knight*," *Studies in the Age of Chaucer* 25 (2003): 259–84, at 265.

25. Michael Twomey, "Morgan le Fay at Hautdesert," in *On Arthurian Women*, ed. Bonnie Wheeler and Fiona Tolhurst (Dallas: Scriptorium Press, 2001), 103–19.

26. Muriel Whitaker, *Arthur's Kingdom of Adventure* (Cambridge: D. S. Brewer, 1984), 42–43; E. D. Kennedy, "Malory's King Arthur and King Mark," in *King Arthur: A Casebook*, ed. Edward Donald Kennedy (London: Routledge, 1996), 139–71.

27. David Walker, *The Normans in Britain* (Oxford: Blackwell, 1995), 56–57; Roger Turvey, *The Welsh Princes: 1063–1283* (London and New York: Longman Press, 2002), 44; Pryce, "British or Welsh?" 777.

28. Griffiths, "The Island of England," 194. See J. Ll. Williams and I. Williams, *Gwaith Guto'r Glyn* (Cardiff: University of Wales Press, 1961).

29. Robert R. Hellenga, "The Tournaments in Malory's *Morte Darthur*," *Forum for Modern Language Studies* 10 (1974): 67–78, at 70–73.

30. F. J. Byrne, "The Trembling Sod: Ireland in 1169," in *A New History of Ireland 2: Medieval Ireland, 1169–1534*, ed. A. Cosgrove (Oxford: Oxford University Press, 1987), 1–42, at 18.

31. Davies, *First English Empire*, 62.

32. Davies, *First English Empire*, 66–69. For Guillaume le Clerc's *Fergus of Galloway*, see the edition by D. D. R. Owen (London: Dent, 1991).

33. Chrétien, *Perceval*, lines 834–59.

34. Claude Luttrell, "Arthurian Geography: The Islands of the Sea." *Neophilologus* 83 (1999): 187–96, at 187–89.

35. Brigitte Cazelles, *The Unholy Grail: A Social Reading of Chrétien de Troyes's "Conte du Graal"* (Stanford: Stanford University Press, 1996), 7–8, 40, 302 note 61.

36. Donald Maddox, *The Arthurian Romances of Chrétien de Troyes: Once and Future Fictions* (Cambridge: Cambridge University Press, 1991), 134–39.

37. Charles Moorman believed the feud was one of Malory's three principal themes in *The Book of Kyng Arthur* (Lexington: University of Kentucky Press, 1965), 28; see also Beverley Kennedy, *Knighthood in the* Morte Darthur (Cambridge: D. S. Brewer, 1985), 206.

38. Hyonjin Kim, *The Knight without the Sword* (Cambridge: D. S. Brewer, 2000), 48.

39. Dhira Mahoney, "Malory's Percivale: A Case of Competing Genealogies," in *Perceval/Parzival: A Casebook*, ed. Arthur Groos and Norris J. Lacy (New York: Routledge, 2002): 253–65, at 254.

40. Mahoney, "Malory's Percivale," 254–63.

41. Fanni Bogdanow, *The Romance of the Grail* (Manchester: Manchester University Press, 1966), 20–21. Pellinor is Percivale's father in the *Suite du Merlin*, one of Malory's sources, but the Vulgate *Lancelot-Grail* names this figure Pellehan.

42. Maldwyn Mills, *Ywain and Gawain, Sir Percyvell of Gales, The Anturs of Arther* (London: Dent, 1992).

43. Rushton, "Of an uncouthe stede," 117.

CHAPTER 10

CLASS AND NATION: DEFINING THE ENGLISH IN LATE-MEDIEVAL WELSH POETRY

Helen Fulton

Relations between English and Welsh in medieval Wales are often contextualized by modern historians in terms of twentieth-century imperialism, as a struggle between two nations, at least one of which was "endowed with a sense of racial superiority."[1] When the English king Edward I conquered north Wales, the last remaining princedom in Wales, in 1282, Wales seemed to have lost all hope of retaining its status as an independent nation. Governed as a provincial outpost of the English empire, the royal lands in north Wales were manacled by chains of castles and towns populated largely by English settlers. The borough towns, most of them newly planted, held a monopoly of trade that excluded the local Welsh population on the grounds that they were "foreigners." As R. R. Davies observed, "Nowhere was the spirit of conquest and of racial superiority so vigorously and selfishly kept alive as in the Edwardian boroughs."[2]

Yet, as in other colonial histories, the Welsh did not simply disappear beneath the legal and economic blanket of Englishness. While the most senior posts in the new provincial government inevitably went to members of the Edwardian aristocracy, many of the Welsh gentry were able to keep their lands and to serve in local administration. Almost immediately after 1284, when Edward issued his Statute of Wales at Rhuddlan describing the way in which Wales was to be governed, existing divisions among the Welsh became intensified and refracted through the imposition of English rule. In the very large corpus of Welsh court poetry of the fourteenth and fifteenth centuries, addressed to the native gentry but also to English churchmen and officials, these divisions are made manifest. The poems express some contradictory attitudes toward the English, and in fact problematize the distinction between Welsh and English as singular national identities. For every anti-English remark in the poetry, there are other references that praise the English. For every appeal to remove the English from Wales, there are testimonials to the greatness of English lordship. Such ambiguities and contradictions are symptomatic of a colonial ideology in which the discourses of colonizer and colonized cut across national and cultural boundaries.

The first significant effort by a modern historian to analyze the complex relations between English and Welsh after 1282 came in an article by Glyn Roberts that appeared in the first volume of the *Welsh History Review* in 1963.[3] The article was called "Wales and England: Antipathy and Sympathy 1281–1485," and it remains an essential point of reference for Welsh historical and literary studies. It was the first survey of medieval Wales that challenged the prevailing view of Wales as a plucky little nation crushed by the imperialist boot of England in 1284 and thenceforth at the mercy of a hated enemy. By looking at the administrative structures in Wales that positioned the Welsh gentry within the English ruling system, and at some of the individuals who held official posts in the English administration in Wales, Roberts was able to put forward a convincing case for Welsh cooperation with the English both before and after the conquest by Edward I in 1284. Forming part of a skilled bureaucracy that supplied the needs of Welsh princes and Anglo-Norman lords, these Welsh officials were "sophisticated men of the world":

> Frequently in touch with the king's court, whether as envoys or hostages, they were very much at home in baronial circles. The princes of Gwynedd were not their sole source of royal patronage, and their wide travels enabled them to mix on intimate terms with their traditional enemies. Their horizons, therefore, were not bounded by purely Welsh considerations.[4]

In the context of this pattern of service to the English administration, the anti-English revolts immediately after the Edwardian conquest, led by Rhys ap Maredudd in 1287 and Madog ap Llywelyn in 1294, mark the different factions at work in Wales. These revolts can be interpreted not simply as a nationalistic expression of Welsh hostility toward the new English regime but as the voice of a specific disaffected group: those men described by Roberts as

> . . . minor Welsh lords of the traditional type, men who had consistently opposed the policy of Llywelyn the Last, who had sided with Edward I, but found that they did not like their position under the dispensation which they had done so much to bring about.[5]

Even the great revolt of Owain Glyn Dŵr, which broke out in 1400, cannot be taken as absolute proof that a subjugated Wales was attempting to throw off the shackles of a hated conqueror. The causes of the revolt went beyond local Welsh affairs, and the numbers of Welsh gentry families who supported Owain Glyn Dŵr were relatively small. As Roberts concludes, "there is nothing here to suggest that Glyn Dŵr stood outside the pattern of cooperation already described."[6]

After the revolt ended, more Welshmen than before gravitated toward the royal court of the Lancastrian kings and took up allegiances in the Wars of the Roses.

Roberts' article is also significant in terms of the weight it gives to medieval Welsh poetry as historical evidence for the relations between Welsh and English. It has to be acknowledged that there is very little historical material written in Welsh that survives from medieval Wales, where the dominant languages of record were Latin, French, and finally English.[7] The evidence of the large surviving corpus of Welsh court poetry, along with other literary texts such as prose tales and religious material, is therefore an important witness to the native responses to English occupation. Assumptions about the interdependence of literature and history, from the reflexive model of New Historicism through to the post-structuralist theory of discourse and representation, are now commonplace in critical scholarship but they were virtually unexplored when Roberts was writing in the early 1960s. His interweaving of historical records such as ministers' accounts and legal documents with wide-ranging references to fourteenth- and fifteenth-century Welsh poetry implies a somewhat problematic model of poetry (and indeed historical documents) as virtually unmediated social commentary, but his willingness to include poetry as a significant part of the historical record is dynamic and forward-thinking.

Roberts suggested that the evidence of the poetry reveals most clearly what he calls the "double attitude" toward English rule and its inevitable influences on traditional Welsh life. On the one hand, none of the court poets of the fourteenth century refers back to the fall of Llywelyn ap Gruffudd as a national tragedy; but on the other hand, occasional anti-English comments, and the large body of prophetic poetry, suggest deep wells of nationalistic resentment against the English. Roberts sees a clear distinction between the relatively benign poetry of the fourteenth century, which assimilates the realities of English rule into the native bardic tradition, and the more hostile poetry of the fifteenth century, when court poets drew more extensively on prophecy and voiced hopes that the Wars of the Roses would create a power vacuum into which a Welshman could be inserted. Ultimately, he argues, this disjunction between the "anglophobia" of the poets and the efforts of their patrons—the career administrators and politicians in Wales—to collaborate with English systems of power led to the decline of the bardic order. He states:

> The native culture was to decline because the gentry increasingly listened to the siren songs which they heard coming from England. But it was not Henry VIII who first persuaded them to listen; they had already been doing so, with growing preoccupation, for some two and a half centuries previously.[8]

In this groundbreaking article, then, Glyn Roberts reconfigured the standard view of medieval Wales as an oppressed, resentful, and rebellious nation beneath England's heel, and outlined the complexities of the relations between Welsh and English. He argued that the undeniable sympathy of political and economic interests between Welsh gentry and the English Crown was subverted throughout the period by a strong antipathy articulated through poetry and rebellion. In the end, he concludes, sympathy and pragmatism prevailed. Given the practical necessity of Welsh cooperation in the government of their own country, combined with the opportunities for Welsh advancement under the English Crown, there was little motivation for an institutionalized program of dissent from the status quo. In the euphoria of 1485 and the accession of Henry Tudor, with his links to the Welsh nobility, even the anti-English rhetoric of the court poets began to subside.

There are a number of issues arising from Roberts' article that could be followed up in the context of recent scholarship, but I want to focus particularly on his concepts of "nation" and the "double attitude" toward English influence that is evident in the Welsh written record. Roberts' theory of nation and nationhood is what might be called the commonsense view, established in the Enlightenment and reinforced by centuries of imperialism and warfare. According to this view, a nation is effectively synonymous with the modern nation-state, that is, a politically autonomous unit that has been theorized as a particular assemblage of "territory, authority, and rights."[9] Though nations are constantly in flux—national borders are regularly changing, larger nations can become smaller ones, and so on—such events do not fundamentally alter the commonsense view that nations preexist the people who live in them. It follows from this belief that, if there are nations called "Wales" and "England," these nations must be inhabited by people called "Welsh" and "English" respectively.

Social identity, however, is far more complex than this model allows. The fact that there was a recognized distinction between Welsh and English within the borders of Wales in the Middle Ages means that identity had to be based on something other than nation—in this case language, culture, and legal status. In fact, we have to move closer toward the post-structuralist view that identity, whether national, social, or personal, is a constant process of construction through discursive and cultural practices. R. R. Davies (though no post-structuralist himself) recognized this when he listed some of the ways in which medieval nationalism expressed itself:

> For national identity, like class, is a matter of perception as much as of institutions. The institutions of centralised authority are by no means its only or most powerful focus. In medieval society, it could also manifest itself in an awareness of the common genealogical descent of a people, in a shared belief in a particular version of historical mythology and prophecy, in an emotional attachment to the geographical boundaries of a country, in a heightened awareness of the distinctiveness of a common language and of common customs, in the yearning for the prospect of unitary rule, in the articulation of a "we-they" dichotomy to express the distinction between natives and aliens.[10]

Since identity—national or otherwise—depends on what I will call discursive acculturation, the naturalized use of a range of available discourses, it follows that identity is seldom coherent and stable; since individuals might participate in many different discourses and social practices, their identity will correspondingly cross a number of cultural boundaries. Members of the Welsh gentry, the *uchelwyr*, might be marked as Welsh by their language and cultural traditions, but as English in terms of other kinds of political and class-based practices in which they might engage. The assumption of singular, preexistent, and stable national identity, as evidenced in Glyn Roberts's article, leads to a binary opposition between English and Welsh that can only be explained in terms similar to those used by Roberts, such as "double attitudes," "racial tensions," "antipathy and sympathy." From an Althusserian perspective, the terms "Welsh" and "English" are social and discursive constructs that interpellate individuals, not preexisting categories into which individuals might be fitted.[11] The contemporary poetry of fourteenth- and fifteenth-century Wales therefore performed an ideological agenda of defining and constructing these concepts of "Welsh" and "English," as keeping in place the "we-they" dichotomy. At the same time, the historical and legal records of the English administration construct these concepts in different ways, so that the idea of "Welshness" emanating from these discourses is not the same as the poetic idea. It is the conflict between these differently imagined concepts of social identity that results in the paradoxes at the heart of medieval Welsh poetry.

In the next section, I will survey some of the references to Welsh-English relations in medieval Welsh verse, before going on to activate issues of identity based on the work of Homi Bhabha. Bhabha's postcolonial theory, particularly his concepts of "doubling" and "mimicry," provide a useful way of considering the conflicting attitudes expressed in the poetry as a reflex of colonialism.[12] It will also become clear that class identity, as much as national identity—both unstable and contingent—motivate the attitudes of the Welsh poets toward the English.

Poetic Ambivalence in Fourteenth-Century Wales

The fourteenth-century Welsh poet, Dafydd ap Gwilym, is famously rude about the English. In one of his comic poems, "Trafferth Mewn Tafarn" [Trouble in a Tavern], the narrator is a hotel guest creeping around at night to keep an assignation with the barmaid. He manages to make so much noise that he wakes some of the other guests: "[tri]sais mewn gwely drewsawr, yn trafferth am eu triphac—Hicin a Siencin a Siac" [three Englishmen in a stinking bed, in a bother about their three packs—Hickin and Jenkin and Jack].[13] There is more than a touch of slapstick humor here, with the three men and their three packs, all in the same bed, and their plain Saxon surnames elaborately Cambrianized and turned into metrically perfect *cynghanedd*.

Even in more serious moments, Dafydd takes the occasional side-swipe at the brutish English, who are unable to understand or appreciate the cultural practices of the Welsh nobility. In one of his praise-poems to his patron, Ifor Hael, Dafydd defines the nature of his love for Ifor by distinguishing it from any kind of love that might be felt by an Englishman:

Mawrserch Ifor a'm goryw,
Mwy no serch ar ordderch yw.

Serch Ifor a glodforais,
Nid fal serch anwydful Sais.
  (*Gwaith Dafydd ap Gwilym*,
              8: 13–16)

[Great love of Ifor overcomes me; it's greater than love for a mistress.
I have extolled the love of Ifor; it's not like the love of a simple-minded
Englishman.]

But not all of Dafydd's contemporaries shared his scathing view of the English
as boorish, foolish, and—perhaps their greatest crime—noncourtly. Iolo Goch,
writing toward the end of the fourteenth century, tends to embrace the English,
certainly their ruling classes, as leaders and role models for the Welsh. He composed
praise poems to the English king, Edward III, and to Roger Mortimer, the Earl
of March, who died in 1398. Edward III is saluted as the lion-hearted conqueror
of Scotland, France, and the Holy Land, the king whose military triumphs have
long been prophesied. Yet this is the same king whose grandfather conquered
north Wales in 1284. Roger Mortimer, one of a long line of Marcher lords related
to the royal house of York, was lord of Denbigh and therefore Iolo Goch's feudal
lord.[14] Iolo's praise poem recognizes Mortimer's role as one of the great feudal
lords of England:

Rhyswr, cwncwerwr can caer,
Calon engylion Englont
A'i phen-cynheiliad a'i phont.[15]

[Champion, conqueror of a hundred castles, heart of the angels of England
and her chief supporter and her bridge.]

At the same time, Iolo Goch recuperates Mortimer for Wales, on the basis
of his Welsh blood through his grandmother, Gwladus Du, the daughter of
Llywelyn Fawr (Llywelyn ap Iorwerth). Using this connection, the poet suggests
that Mortimer makes a fitting leader for Wales, that he is in fact the *mab darogan*,
the one prophesied to liberate Wales from its oppression:

Wŷr burffrwyth iôr Aberffraw,
Draig ynysoedd yr eigiawn,
Dragwn aer—darogan iawn
Ydd wyf—madws it ddyfod
Gymru lle rhyglyddy glod.
  (*Gwaith Iolo Goch*, 20: 14–18)

[Descendant of the pure-fruited lord of Aberffraw {i.e., Llywelyn Fawr},
dragon of the islands of the ocean, dragon of battle—I prophesy accurately—it
is time for you to come to Wales where you merit praise.]

Elsewhere in his work, however, Iolo Goch tends to ignore the English as
a nation of people, or to dismiss them as being of little account. In his poem

to Roger Mortimer, he refers to the earls of England with the phrase *gnawd erllugrwydd* [typical {their} insolence] (line 65). In a satire on the Grey Friar, he calls him *y Brawd Sais* [the English Friar] (*Gwaith Iolo Goch*, 25: 6), before launching into a series of gross and slanderous images. We can compare Iolo's ambivalence toward the English with that of Gruffudd Gryg (fl. 1357–70), who is highly complimentary toward the English king, Richard II, calling him *Risiart eryr aesawr* [Richard, eagle and shield], but unequivocal about what he regards as the natural hostility between English and Welsh: seeking reconciliation with the seven sons of Iorwerth ap Gruffudd, he says of them, "saith a'm casaodd fal Sais" [seven who hated me like an Englishman].[16]

These few examples represent the complexity of the political and social relations between England and Wales in the fourteenth and fifteenth centuries. There was indeed no particular reason why the Welsh should like the English, who had conquered the last independent Welsh kingdom in 1284, built a chain of castles to suppress the rebellious natives, imposed English government in most areas of the country, and established a number of English towns populated by imported English settlers in which Welshmen were not allowed to conduct any trade or business. However, as in most cases of political conquest, it was not simply a matter of all the Welsh hating all the English. Normans and Anglo-Normans had been settling in Wales since 1066 and were already assimilated in south Wales as a cultural group before the English conquest. There was a pattern of cooperation, power-sharing, and intermarriage between Welsh and English in south Wales that was spreading to north Wales well before 1284. Llywelyn ap Iorwerth, ruler of Gwynedd in the early thirteenth century, married Joan, daughter of King John, his children, including his daughter, Gwladus Du, married into powerful English families, and his grandson, Llywelyn ap Gruffudd, the last independent prince of Wales, married the daughter of Simon de Montfort, one of Henry III's most powerful barons. The Welsh nobility had always known the value of strategic alliances with the English.

After the conquest of Wales in 1284 by Edward I, the consequence of inter-marriage was to strengthen the position of the English in Wales and, at the same time, to give the new Welsh nobility access to the English hegemony. From the time when the first Anglo-Norman lordships had been established in Wales, there had been a growth of opportunities for Welshmen to hold office under Anglo-Norman and then English rule, and this pattern increased after the loss of Welsh independence. So it would be a mistake to assume that all Welsh people hated the English—on the contrary, many of them resented their own Welsh princes and were more than happy to ally themselves with Anglo-Norman and English lords if this conferred greater power and status on themselves.

In the wake of 1284, the new class of Welsh nobles, the *uchelwyr*, began to consolidate their position as the surviving Welsh nobility whose power depended on serving the English Crown. It was they who, more than anyone in Wales, had a foot in both camps. On the one hand they aspired to the same power and privileges as the English ruling class, and therefore married into their families and imitated their French-based culture and fashions, notably in literature and imported consumer goods. On the other hand they were acutely aware of their role as the inheritors of the native Welsh "high" culture, with its concomitant obligation to support poets and musicians and to conserve the ancient traditions of their aristocratic predecessors. The strategy they adopted, of participating in the dominant English culture while simultaneously supporting the Welsh "high" culture, worked to define the *uchelwyr* as a class of noblemen.

From the central Middle Ages until the beginnings of the modern period, it was the *uchelwyr* who held high office in service to the English Crown, who owned lands and courts, who acted as patrons to native Welsh poets and musicians, who, in short, represented a Welsh nobility in the absence of a hereditary aristocracy. As such, the *uchelwyr* had been mixing, socially and politically, with the ruling English at least since 1284. So, in the poetry specifically addressed to them by the *cywyddwyr*, the native court bards, we might expect quite a large number of references to the English as friends or colleagues, as feudal lords or business partners, as participants in the same social and professional milieux.

Such references are not uncommon, as in Iolo Goch's poems to Edward III and Roger Mortimer, or Dafydd ap Gwilym's friendship with Robin Nordd, or Robert le Northern, one of the English burgesses of Aberystwyth.[17] But neither are they particularly common. Often these references are less than flattering; but occasionally they acknowledge the benign commercial influence of the English in Wales in terms of the expanded market in consumer goods. In a satire on the stock figure of *yr Eiddig* [the Jealous Husband], Dafydd ap Gwilym describes the husband's foul breath spoiling the beauty of his beloved, just as the smoke from a lamp or fire will damage domestic consumables—ornamental carving and a fur coat—that are specifically defined as English:

> Delw o bren gwern dan fernais,
> Dogn benrhaith o saerwaith Sais,
> Drwg gadwad, dygiad agwyr,
> Llugorn llon a'i llwgr yn llwyr.
> Y pân Seisnig da ddigawn
> A fydd drwg ym mwg y mawn.
>   (*Gwaith Dafydd ap Gwilym*,
>   81: 25–30)

[A varnished carving of alder-wood, a lord's piece of English carpentry, badly kept and awkwardly placed, an over-bright lamp will ruin it completely. A perfectly good English fur will go bad in peat smoke.]

References to manufactured goods bought in a marketplace or fair allude to the economy of urban consumption associated with the English towns planted after 1284, and the increased availability of a range of consumer goods to Welsh and English alike. Court records suggest that the towns were significant locations for fraternization and collaborations between Welsh and English, and that Welshmen formed an increasing percentage of the burgesses in a number of towns from the late fourteenth century.[18] The huge number of English loanwords into Welsh, beginning before the Norman Conquest and rapidly accelerating after 1284, also attests to some level of bilingualism among the inhabitants of

Wales.[19] Nevertheless, despite all the evidence for assimilation, actual praise of the English by Welsh poets is quite rare, and is reserved mainly for those members of the English aristocracy, such as Roger Mortimer and William Herbert, whose interests can be aligned with those of Wales, either by blood or politics or both.

It is worth noting—as Simon Meecham-Jones has documented in an earlier chapter in this book—that the Welsh people and language are almost completely ignored in medieval English writing, apart from historical documents, particularly royal proclamations, that denounce the Welsh as rebels, false prophesiers, and general troublemakers. Peter Langtoft's chronicle, written early in the reign of Edward II, lambasts both Wales and Scotland for daring to defy the king:

> Gales soit maldit de Deus e de Saint Symoun!
> Car tuz jours ad esté pleins de tresoun.
> Escoce soit maldit de la Mere Dé!
> E parfount à diable Gales enfoundré![20]

> [May Wales be cursed by God and Saint Simon, for always it has been full of treason. May Scotland be cursed by the mother of God, and Wales sunk deep down to the devil.]

English literary texts, while appropriating Arthur as an English king, exclude the Welsh language completely, unless we can count the odd loanword, such as *wolc*, "hawk," apparently from Welsh *gwalch*, which occurs in the Harley Lyrics.[21]

Colonial Politics, Colonial Ambivalence

What is striking about references to the English in medieval Welsh poetry is the variety of attitudes expressed, from bitterness to admiration, mocking satire to subservient respect. Such ambivalence is characteristic of colonial rule, in which resentment and resistance are balanced by the pragmatics of collaboration. In his influential analysis of colonial representation, Homi Bhabha has theorized the relationship between colonizer and colonized as one of doubling and mimicry.[22] As subjects of colonial discourse, both colonizer and colonized are constructed as doubles of each other, subjects split between self and other. Homi Bhabha says: "To exist is to be called into being in relation to an otherness," and medieval Welsh identity was in large part constructed by the "other" of Englishness, an otherness that was both desired and feared.[23] Yet at the same time, the binary opposition of the two national and cultural labels is undermined by what Bhabha calls "the in-between" or "the margin of hybridity," the space where claims to singular or authentic identity are problematized, "where difference is neither One nor the Other but *something else besides, in-between*."[24] In medieval Welsh poetry, this in-between space is marked by the interchangeability of the discourses and agency of colonizer and colonized. The Welsh voice can speak for both colonized nation and colonial authority.

From the English point of view, Wales as a political entity had been definitively subsumed into England in 1284—in other words, it had been colonized. Contemporary chronicles and historical records kept by the English Crown refer to the castles and districts of Wales not as distinctively Welsh but as provincial extensions of England, whose revenues flowed back, as a matter of course, to the central administration. In matters construed as examples of social deviance, however, including the use of prophecy, the Welsh were singled out as the "other," a group whose cultural practices marked them out as "not English." In the discourse of the historical record, the Welsh are constructed as doubles, as both English (because Wales is part of England) and not English (because of differences in social and linguistic practices).

The literary discourse of medieval Wales articulates the same process of doubling. When Iolo Goch sings the praises of Edward III, he expresses the loyalty of an English subject toward an English king through a distinctively Welsh poetic discourse, doubling himself as both English and Welsh, splitting the subjectivity of the poem between colonizer and colonized, between fear and desire. As Homi Bhabha says, "The fantasy of the native is precisely to occupy the master's place while keeping his place in the slave's *avenging* anger"—that is, the double or split subjectivity of being in two places at once.[25] When Dafydd ap Gwilym sneers at Hickin and Jenkin and Jack, he is occupying "the master's place," constructing the subjectivity of the ruler while at the same time keeping his place in the discourse of resistance.

To explain further the structures of ambivalence in colonial discourse, Bhabha makes use of the term "mimicry" adapted from the psychoanalytical theory of Jacques Lacan. This is the strategy by which the colonizing power imposes its own cultural practices on the colonized; yet it insists on a residue of difference, an inevitable otherness despite the apparent sameness. "Colonial mimicry," says Bhabha, "is the desire for a reformed, recognizable Other, *as a subject of a difference that is almost the same, but not quite.*"[26] Members of the Welsh nobility, the *uchelwyr*, could and did participate in the same economic sphere as the English gentry, send their sons to English universities, accept knighthoods and other honors from the English Crown, even anglicize their names, but a residue of difference remained, manifesting itself through language, discourse, and cultural practice.

These discourses of mimicry produced a profound ambivalence, for both colonizer and colonized. In imposing an English system of government through-out Wales after 1284, with its infrastructure of shires, sheriffs, and constables, the colonizing power mimicked the administration of England while maintaining an observable difference between Wales and England. Wales must be "almost the same, but not quite." One aspect of that "not-quiteness" was the appointment of prominent *uchelwyr*, rather than Englishmen, to positions of administrative power, a strategy that drew attention to the otherness of the Welsh. Because the Welsh population were perceived as "foreign" in terms of their language and social behaviors, local intermediaries, men who could translate the foreign into the normative discourses of power, were required.

This role of the *uchelwyr* as intermediaries, who mimicked English officialdom, produced the ambivalent subjectivity of the poetry addressed to them by the Welsh bards. The eulogized patrons of Welsh poetry, whose power depended on the extent to which they could successfully mimic the cultural practices of the English ruling elite, must also be constantly reminded of their difference, reminded that their authentic identity resided within the traditions and history of Wales as a country and nation other than England. The written evidence from both England and Wales therefore constructs a form of colonial subjectivity based on doubling and mimicry, revealing a complex set of ambivalent negotiations that go beyond a simple "pattern of cooperation" or "racial tensions" between English and Welsh, as Glyn Roberts describes the situation.[27] As the colonizing power, England has little interest in Wales beyond its potential for economic exploitation, which means that any sign of civil unrest or deviance must be violently suppressed and punished, as it was during the rising of Madog in 1294 and again during the Glyn Dŵr rebellion of 1400–1415. The anti-Welsh rhetoric of chroniclers such as Peter Langtoft legitimizes the use of force to maintain hegemonic stability.

On the other hand, the structures of economic feudalism problematize the simple binaries of colonization. The English living within Wales, mainly in the towns, are hardly a dominant class; rather, they often appear in historical documents as equally disempowered as many of the Welsh, overgoverned by royal or Marcher lords and oppressed by demands for taxation and other services to the Crown. Glyn Roberts points out that resident Englishmen as well as the Welsh were punished by the post–Glyn Dŵr punitive legislation that assumed that "Englishmen whose families had long been settled in Wales were no more trustworthy than native Welshmen."[28] At the same time, the resident English asserted their difference by calling for sanctions against the unruly Welsh that would reinvigorate their colonial power and justify their political and economic privileges. The burgesses of the town of Hope, whose charter of 1351 was the first in north Wales explicitly to exclude Welshmen, stipulated in 1401 that "no Welshman can or ought to acquire to himself or his heirs...any English land...for any price, so long as an English burgess is willing to buy and hold it."[29] Here is the mimicry of colonial discourse. The Welsh are almost the same but not quite, clearly differentiated as the "other" despite the similarities of economic oppression and exploitation that afflicted English and Welsh alike.

As the subjects of colonization, the Welsh responded with a keen interest in the English, who govern them, live alongside them, and operate their own linguistic, commercial, and cultural practices that directly impinge, in any number of ways, on traditional Welsh practices. Welsh literary output in the Middle Ages therefore conducts a more or less perpetually ongoing commentary, often oblique and sotto voce, like a sort of subtextual grumbling, on the English presence in Wales, and in so doing, exposes the resentments and disempowerment shared by colonized and colonizers. The processes of collaboration and assimilation identified by Glyn Roberts result in the doubling and split subjectivities that are the inevitable by-products of colonial rule.

Welsh Nationhood and Anti-English Rhetoric in the Fifteenth Century

In considering the relations between English and Welsh, we can follow Glyn Roberts in seeing a clear distinction, even a dramatic break, between the

fourteenth and fifteenth centuries, that is, before and after the rebellion of
Owain Glyn Dŵr, which had profound consequences for Welsh identity politics.
In the fourteenth century, the double subject of Welsh poetry, which collaborated with English rule while also resisting it, was split along class lines. The
native Welsh gentry, the *uchelwyr*, shared a class identity with the ruling English
administration, mimicking its authority but constantly reaffirming their own
residue of Welshness, particularly through their patronage of Welsh poetry.
The kind of anti-English rhetoric expressed in the work of Dafydd ap Gwilym
and his contemporaries was mainly directed at the urban English, those small
farmers and migrant burgesses who populated the new towns planted by Edward
I. Split between the desire to identify with the ruling class and the anger of the
oppressed, Welsh poetic subjectivity appropriates a master discourse of satire and
turns its contempt toward the bourgeois *Saeson* (literally "Saxons"), authentically
English yet distinctively noncourtly.

In the fifteenth century, this class-based rhetoric is overshadowed by the rapid
development of a poetic theme laid down by Iolo Goch in his praise poem to
Roger Mortimer. This theme was nothing less than the reassertion of Welsh
nationhood by means of an imagined collaboration with the English political
aristocracy. This collaboration, already partly realized by the penetration of the
uchelwyr into the English ruling class, had been dramatically enacted in the Glyn
Dŵr rebellion, when Owain's most significant supporters were English noblemen, including the Earl of Northumberland and Edmund Mortimer. After the
rebellion, as Glyn Roberts reminds us, Welshmen rushed to receive a pardon
and serve Henry V in the French wars, including Maredudd ab Owain, the only
surviving son of Owain Glyn Dŵr.[30] The poetic discourse of fifteenth-century
Wales constructs a subjectivity that is even more violently ruptured than that of
the fourteenth century, one that is not merely doubled but almost schizophrenic.
It is a subjectivity determined to reside in two places at once—perhaps the most
meaningful definition of Bhabha's hybridity—just as Owain Glyn Dŵr tried to
run with the hare and hunt with the hounds.

This ruptured subjectivity, brought into being in the aftermath of the Glyn
Dŵr rebellion, is constructed through an anti-English rhetoric that is far more
powerful than the jokes and mockery of the fourteenth century. Yet it is in many
ways less effective, since far from articulating or imitating a master discourse, it
merely rattles the chains of the enslaved. After the rebellion, punitive legislation by the English Crown deprived the Welsh of many of the concessions they
had previously enjoyed, such as access to the economy of the borough towns.
The gloves came off and the Welsh poets lost no opportunities to revile the
English in the most bitter and implacably hostile terms. Rees Davies refers to the
"collective psychological trauma" suffered in Wales as a result of the rebellion
and its aftermath, resulting in a cultural rupture that changed the whole nature
of English-Welsh relations.[31]

The scars left by the rebellion turned the thoughts of many of the Welsh back
to the old idea, dating back at least to the time of the tenth-century prophecy,
Armes Prydein, of a more or less complete break with England.[32] Throughout
most of the fifteenth century, Welsh hopes for a Welsh king on the English

throne grew into an almost frantic desire, encouraged by the factionalism of the Wars of the Roses and fuelled by the revival of an ancient tradition of prophecy with which the poets galvanized the nation. Dafydd Johnston says:

> Y math amlycaf o farddoniaeth wleidyddol yn yr Oesoedd Canol oedd y canu brud, corff mawr o gerddi'n proffwydo dyfodiad y Mab Darogan, gwaredwr a fyddai'n arwain y Cymry i fuddugoliaeth derfynol dros y Saeson ac yn adfer eu hen hawl dros Ynys Prydain.[33]

[The most obvious type of political poetry in the Middle Ages was *canu brud*, the large body of poems that prophesied the coming of the *mab darogan*, "son of prophecy," the savior who would lead the Welsh to a final victory over the Saxons and restore their old rights over the Island of Britain.]

This was the time when Welsh poets urged on their favorite contenders for the English throne, whether it was Jasper Tudor, Edward IV, or William Herbert, favorite of the Earl of Warwick. In a famous praise-song to William Herbert, Guto'r Glyn exhorts him to unite Wales as a single nation, empowered to throw off English rule:

> Dwg Forgannwg a Gwynedd,
> Gwna'n un o Gonwy i Nedd.
> O digia Lloegr a'i dugiaid,
> Cymru a dry yn dy raid.[34]

[Take Morgannwg and Gwynedd, make them into one from Conwy to Nedd. If England and her dukes are angry, Wales will turn to you in your need.]

This was the time when hatred for the English overrode any deep commitment to either York or Lancaster, when the only imperative was to empower the Welsh through access to the English throne.[35] Dafydd Llwyd of Mathafarn (ca. 1395–1486), one of the foremost composers of *cywyddau brud*—the genre of Welsh prophetic poetry that was particularly vigorous in the fifteenth century—envisages an apocalyptic termination of English power in a final bloodbath:

> A'r Saeson ffeilsion eu ffydd,
> A'u gwaed hyd eu hegwydydd.[36]

[And the Saxons, false in their faith, with their blood up to their fetlocks.]

This was the time when intermarriage, the bedrock of assimilation and the building of a new nation in the fourteenth century, was no longer in fashion and was openly discouraged. In the middle decades of the fifteenth century, when the *uchelwyr*, already factionalized by the Glyn Dŵr rebellion, were squaring up to each other in the York corner and the Lancaster corner, disapproval of the

English was not confined to the burgess class. The Welsh gentry were being told to be careful about whom they married. One of Dafydd ab Edmwnd's (fl. ca. 1450–97) major patrons was Rhys Wyn ap Llywelyn ap Tudur of Môn, from an illustrious line of north Welsh lords, and Dafydd commands him not to marry an Englishwoman, Alice, or he will lose the praise of the poets.[37] In the same vein, Hywel Dafi (fl. 1450–80) advises his patron, Harri Mil of Gwent (probably of Norman extraction) to choose a Welsh rather than an English wife:

Cymer ferch Cymro farchawg
Aur i gyd ei war a'i gawg.
Cais ferch addfain ugeinmlwydd
Ac na chais ferch Sais o'r swydd.[38]

[Take the daughter of a Welsh knight, his tableware and basins all of gold. Find a slender girl of twenty years, and don't get an English girl from the county.]

Yet even in the hectic decades of the Wars of the Roses, anti-English sentiment was invoked only for specific purposes and could just as easily be abandoned if the occasion called for a more cooperative attitude. Welsh and English were often aligned against common enemies, as they had been during the Glyn Dŵr rebellion, when Owain's most significant supporters were English noblemen, the Earl of Northumberland and Edmund Mortimer. So Lewis Glyn Cothi (ca. 1420–89) celebrates the lineage of Elspeth, the English wife of Huw Conwy, as signifying the union of two nations, carefully incorporating English names into Welsh orthography and *cynghanedd* in a purposeful way that appropriates English into the dominant discourse of Welsh court poetry:

Aeth cenedl Elsbeth Conwy
o Ferwig wen hyd fôr Gwy.
Hi o Domas Salsbri sydd
i alw'r genedl ar gynnydd.[39]

[Elspeth Conwy's people come from Berwick, fair as far as the water of Wye. It is she, daughter of Thomas Salisbury, who is to call the nation forward.]

Mythic and Contemporary Discourses

In both the fourteenth and fifteenth centuries, then, relations between the Welsh and English, as defined by the Welsh poets, are intricate and complex. Though the political fervor of the postrebellion period and the factionalism of the Wars of the Roses led to a more explicit expression of anti-English rhetoric, we can still discern a continuity of attitudes toward the English across these two centuries.

These attitudes can be categorized as "mythic" and "contemporary," the former expressing the traditional division between British sovereignty and

Saxon invasion, and the latter articulating a more ambivalent set of responses to the presence of the English. "Mythic" references are those that draw on older literary and oral traditions to construct Wales as the rightful ruler of the Island of Britain, shamefully disinherited by the coming of the Saxons. This is the position that emerges in the earliest stratum of Welsh poetry, notably the tenth-century prophecy *Armes Prydein*, and is consistently reiterated throughout the whole period of medieval Welsh court poetry. Explicitly proclaimed by most of the *cywyddau brud* and the political poems of the fifteenth century, it is also alluded to by Iolo Goch and his contemporaries in the fourteenth. It is a self-consciously political and polemical stance that assumes a vision of nationhood, the vision of a unified and distinctive nation, existing since time immemorial, and unproblematically identified by its cultural practices, including language.

What I am calling "contemporary" attitudes, on the other hand, refer to the day-to-day realities of living alongside the English in Wales, with the advantages of a consumer economy offset by the disadvantages of institutional prejudice. This perspective accounts for most of the satires and other kinds of explicit anti-English rhetoric, and is based almost exclusively on social class. It is not members of the ruling English nobility or the English monarchy or the important Anglo-Welsh Marcher families who are contemptuously invoked as *Sais*, "Englishman." It is the burgesses and the small farmers, the minstrels and artisans, who are ridiculed, more because of their class than because of their nationality.

The mythic view of the English as Saxon oppressors is used to praise those patrons, whether Welsh or English, who can resist this oppression, or to prophesy the coming of a *mab darogan* who will liberate Wales. In a praise poem to Rhys Gethin of Nanconwy (attributed to Iolo Goch but not included in the canon edited by Dafydd Johnston), the poet says:

> Lle bu'r Brython Saeson sydd,
> A'r boen ar Gymry beunydd.
> Oes dewrfalch sy falch a saif
> O Lywelyn â'i loywlaif?
> Oes, Rys, â'i ddurgrys ddewrgryf,
> Gethin, i hynt Erbin tyf.[40]

[Where the Briton was, the Saxon now is, and Welshmen suffer pain daily. Is there a proud hero from Llywelyn's line who stands proud with his bright sword? Yes, Rhys Gethin, with his steel shirt, strong and valiant, reared in the manner of Erbin.]

Images of Hengist and Horsa as the baleful progenitors of the reviled race of Saxons permeate the mythic representation of Wales as overrun by the English:

> Cawn o Wynedd Is Conwy
> Eryr gwâr ar oror Gwy,
> A phlant Hors ym mhob gorsedd,
> Gŵr o fôr a'u gyr i fedd.

Gwae'r Saeson gweinion bob gant,
Ac i Wynedd ogoniant.[41]

[From Gwynedd Is Conwy we shall get a gentle eagle on the edge of the
Wye, and with Horsa's children in every seat, a man of the sea will drive
them to a grave. Woe to every hundred feeble Englishmen, and glory to
Gwynedd.]

Such a discourse invokes a mythic and seemingly coherent identity for Wales
as the rightful ruler of the Island of Britain, brutally disinherited by the coming
of the Saxons. Yet the idea of Wales itself is an imaginary concept, an "always
already" compromised "other," unable to remember a time of authentic cultural
autonomy except through reconstituted images of a pre-Saxon Britain. This myth
of nation, of an autochthonous *pura Wallia* so eagerly asserted in Welsh writing,
is itself an expression of a colonized subjectivity. The split subject, doubling up as
both colonizer and colonized, mimicking the master discourse while asserting its
difference, claims an illusory freedom from an illusory enemy.

As in the time of Owain Glyn Dŵr, Welsh politics in the later fifteenth century
are entirely subordinated to the dominant political struggle of the era, the fight for
the English Crown. Contemporary English historical documents construct Wales
as marginal and unimportant to the affairs of the English, or British, state. The
Welsh poetic discourse of a mythic freedom achieved by the *mab darogan* merely
confirms its subaltern position in the insular politics of Britain. At the same time,
Welsh claims to a coherent and freestanding national identity are problematized
by the assimilation of the *uchelwyr* with the English nobility. Magnetized by the
common interests of power and land, they formed an elite class in which cultural
differences were less important than political alliances.

The mythic construction of the English as the ancient Saxon enemy operates
alongside a more contemporary, and pragmatic, view of the English as incoming
settlers, who brought with them all the advantages of a consumer economy and all
the disadvantages of institutional power and prejudice. This contemporary construction of the English in their day-to-day dealings with the Welsh intensifies the
class-based priorities that were first articulated in the work of Dafydd ap Gwilym.

Guto'r Glyn's praise-poem to William Herbert, composed after the fall
of Harlech castle in 1468, combines what I have identified as the mythic and
contemporary views of the English. Despite the almost entirely English sphere
in which Herbert operated during the 1450s and 1460s, the Welsh poets focused
on his Welsh ancestry to construct him as a *mab darogan*, one who would lead the
Welsh nation to victory over the English invaders. Commanding Herbert to unite
the country, Guto'r Glyn abjures him not to allow the English to take over:

Nâd trwy Wynedd blant Ronwen
Na phlant Hors yn y Fflint hen.
Na ad, f'arglwydd, swydd i Sais,
Na'i bardwn i un bwrdais.
    (*Gwaith Guto'r Glyn*, 48: 59–62)

[Do not allow the children of Rowena [daughter of Hengist] throughout Gwynedd, nor the children of Horsa into old Flint. Do not allow any job to an Englishman, my lord, nor a pardon to a single burgess.]

"No jobs for the English" is an uncanny echo of the modern master discourse of anti-immigration, expressing the fears of established settlers in the face of new movements of incomers. These fears were felt particularly by the poets themselves, whose literary and highly skilled discourse represented one of the last remaining residues of an authentic national culture. The satire on the English burgesses of Flint, attributed to Tudur Penllyn, expresses the disgust of the Welsh musician whose services at a local wedding were rejected in favor of an English piper. The poet goes to the borough town of Flint in search of work:

Lle'r oedd, neithiawr, heb fawr fedd,
Sais aneglur, Seisnigwledd.[42]

[Where there was a wedding feast, without much mead, of a devious Englishman, an English feast.]

The poet is hoping to play at the wedding, but instead an Englishman described as "Wiliam Bibydd," "William the Piper," plays the pipes, making an excruciating noise that is described in grotesque detail by the poet. The piper's fee is paid by "Wiliam Cawl Ffa," "William Pea-Soup," another anti-English insult, and the poet leaves the town with a curse on its English inhabitants:

Ei ffwrn faith fal uffern fydd,
A'i phobl Seisnig a'i phibydd.
(61–62)

[May its burning be as long as hell, and its English people and its piper.]

Another aspect of the contemporary relations between Welsh and English that articulates the class-based fears of immigration is the concern that the Welsh uchelwyr would be tempted to adopt the customs and manners of the dominant English. We know that the uchelwyr did participate in the courtly culture of the English and French nobilities as a way of asserting their own high status within Wales. But the poets make it very clear that one of the main roles of the uchelwyr is to support the native Welsh culture, particularly its music and poetry. There is a single poem, an awdl, attributed to a fourteenth-century poet, Iorwerth Beli (ca. 1300–25), that is addressed to an unnamed bishop of Bangor who, despite his Welsh origins, patronized English singers and musicians. These new rivals to Welsh culture were regarded as low grade and untrained compared to the Welsh poets who deeply resented their influence and the threat they posed to the traditional livelihoods of the Welsh bards. Iorwerth Beli expresses an unequivocal rebuke to the bishop on account of his patronage of such low-class players:

Am wybod Saesneg Seisnig dôn—drygwas,
Gwisg a gafas las laes odreon...

Gwehelyth nis câr gwehilion—cerddau
        Tabyrddau, swysau iangwyr Saeson.[43]

[For knowing English, an evil lad with an English tune got a blue garment
with long hems...Good breeding does not like the rubbishy tunes of the
tabors, senses of Saxon yeomen.]

But when it suited them, Welsh poets, and the Welsh population in general,
took advantage of the benefits that came with conquest, particularly in terms of
the new consumerism introduced with the English urban economy. Both Guto'r
Glyn and Tudur Aled sang praise poems to the border town of Oswestry, owned
by an English Marcher lord but having a sizeable proportion of Welsh burgesses.
As far as Guto'r Glyn is concerned, the town can take its place among the great
cities of Europe, while Tudur Aled focuses on the variety of luxury goods that
are now available to the Welsh community because of the growth of the urban
economy, the increased population, and Welsh access to trade:

Cistiau da, 'n costio dierth,
Cwmin, bocs, caem win heb werth;
Siwgr, sarsned, ffelfed a phân,
Siêp-Seid yn siopau sidan...
Cwrw a siwgr caer wresowgwin,
Cwnffets, pomgarnets, a gwin.[44]

[Chests of goods, expensive for outsiders, cummin, box, we get wine
without tax; sugar sarsnet, velvet and fur, silk shops like Cheapside...Beer
and sugar in a mulled-wine castle, comfits, pomegranates, and wine.]

The barrage of English consumer items, barely assimilated into a rudimentary
Welsh phonetics and orthography, mirrors the invasion of English urban
consumerism into traditional Welsh life. Here the split subject is represented
linguistically, doubling itself into a Welsh Englishness or an English Welshness
that articulates the double vision of biculturalism and bilingualism. The references to London and to Cheapside in both poems reveal a subjectivity that is
located in the periphery and yet drawn inexorably, like a moth to a flame, to the
metropolis, the heart and center of economic and colonial power. In its attraction
to the center, the periphery confirms its own marginality.

Class and Nation

Welsh poetry of the fourteenth and fifteenth centuries tells us a good deal about
the fluctuating and complex relations between Welsh and English after 1284.
Unlike many of the colonized lands of eighteenth and nineteenth-century
empire-building in Europe, medieval Wales has left us a rich record of its experiences of colonization, written in the voice of the colonized rather than the
colonizer. History is not always written by the victor.

The Welsh poetic discourse is full of contradictions and tensions that reveal the struggle for identity in a colonized country. The two fundamental issues that inform Welsh perceptions of the English are those of class and nation. In their contemporary dealings with the English settlers in their midst, the *uchelwyr* gravitate toward power, toward the English ruling class, while ignoring or scorning peasants and burgesses, English and Welsh alike. In the mythic representation of Wales as a Saxon-free zone, the nobility of both England and Wales are commandeered into restoring the former nation to its sovereign glory.

In both positions, the contemporary and the mythic, there is not only an anti-English rhetoric but also a rhetoric of appropriation, collaboration, and assimilation. These competing voices can be read as the articulation of the doubled or split subject of colonial discourse that both desires to join the dominant class while maintaining the struggle for freedom. Lewis Glyn Cothi's appropriation of Elspeth Conwy, just as much as Hywel Dafi's rejection of an English wife, express the ambivalence of the split subject, both poems mimicking a dominant discourse of power and prestige that seems to subvert the colonial discourse of England.

The potential for subversion is a constant presence in the *cywyddau*, particularly in those that draw on a class-based rhetoric. The antibourgeois satire of Dafydd ap Gwilym and Tudur Penllyn constructs the subjectivity of the colonizer rather than the colonized, appropriating a master discourse that inverts the relative positions of Welsh and English as self and other. The issue of class itself problematizes relations between the oppressor and the oppressed, since the peasant English might be regarded as more oppressed by feudalism than the *uchelwyr* were by colonialism.

Nevertheless, in political terms, Wales had been colonized by England and this political condition is immanent in the cultural production of medieval Wales. Whenever the Welsh language and meter seem their most authentic and untouched, English loanwords and place names perform the work of linguistic colonization. Whenever the authenticity of the *cywydd* as a prestige native meter seems about to subvert the colonized condition, Guto'r Glyn's appeal for nationhood to an English lord, or Tudur Aled's praise of the shops in Cheapside, return us to the discourse of mimicry, or even ventriloquism. The *uchelwyr* might share the administrative rule of Wales, they might reclaim the self by constructing the bourgeois English as "other," but they are defined by the split subjectivity of their own poetry that constantly reminds them that they almost, but not quite, belong to the culture of the metropolis.

It is tempting to read medieval Welsh poetry as a prestige discourse, utterly authentic, unmarked by doubling or mimicry, whose anti-English rhetoric resists the subjectivity of the colonized and articulates only the certainties of the culturally autonomous. The class-based critique found in many of the *cywyddau* seems to appropriate or reerect the power structures of colonial discourse in which the Welsh are confidently themselves and the English are most definitely the other. But such a reading is undermined by the processes of collaboration between English and Welsh that complicate their relations and force a binary opposition between colonizing English and colonized Welsh to collapse into a space in between. It is the series of collaborations, especially between the elite *uchelwyr* and the ruling English, which splits the subject of Welsh poetic discourse and locates it in two places at once, in the ruling culture of the colonizer and in the appropriated culture of the colonized.

The sociology of class runs like a fault line through colonial discourses and is often inadequately explained in standard accounts of colonial and postcolonial theory. In these accounts, the subject of colonial discourses is inevitably split, doubled, in two places at once, almost but not quite belonging. But if there could be a site of cohesion and singular subjectivity, it might be found in the structures of social class, where the governing nobility, both colonizing and colonized, find common ground in their contempt for the governed.

Notes

1. Gwyn A. Williams, *When Was Wales? A History of the Welsh* (Harmondsworth: Penguin, 1985), 89.
2. R. R. Davies, *Conquest, Co-existence and Change: Wales 1063–1415* (Oxford: Oxford University Press, 1987), 373. See also his article "Colonial Wales," *Past and Present* 65 (1974): 3–23.
3. Glyn Roberts, "Wales and England: Antipathy and Sympathy 1282–1485," *Welsh History Review* 1.4 (1963): 375–96. The article was subsequently reprinted in a collection of Glyn Roberts' papers, *Aspects of Welsh History* (Cardiff: University of Wales Press, 1969), 295–318. All subsequent references are to the original article, abbreviated to "Antipathy and Sympathy."
4. Roberts, "Antipathy and Sympathy," 380–81.
5. Roberts, "Antipathy and Sympathy," 385.
6. Roberts, "Antipathy and Sympathy," 393.
7. For an account of surviving medieval records of Wales, see R. Ian Jack, *Medieval Wales*, Sources of Medieval History (London: Hodder and Stoughton, 1972).
8. Roberts, "Antipathy and Sympathy," 396.
9. This model has been developed by Saskia Sassen, *Territory, Authority, Rights: From Medieval to Global Assemblages* (Princeton and Oxford: Princeton University Press, 2006). Sassen explicitly interrogates the "commonsense" model of "nation," arguing that "it took work to make society national" (18).
10. R. R. Davies, "Law and National Identity in Thirteenth-Century Wales," in *Welsh Society and Nationhood. Historical Essays Presented to Glanmor Williams*, ed. R. R. Davies, Ralph A. Griffiths, Ieuan Gwynedd Jones, and Kenneth O. Morgan (Cardiff: University of Wales Press, 1984), 51–69, at 52.
11. On Althusser's theory of interpellation, the way in which individuals are "hailed" as the subjects of discourse, see his 1969 essay "Ideology and Ideological State Apparatuses," in *Lenin and Philosophy and Other*

Essays, trans. Ben Brewster (London: New Left Books, 1971), 160–65, at 123–73.

12. On Bhabha's theory and its application to medieval Welsh literature, see Dylan Foster Evans, "'Bardd arallwlad': Dafydd ap Gwilym a Theori Ôl-Drefedigaethol," in *Llenyddiaeth mewn Theori*, ed. Owen Thomas (Cardiff: University of Wales Press, 2006), 39–72; Stephen Knight, "Resemblance and Menace: A Post-colonial Reading of *Peredur*," in *Canhwyll Marchogyon: Cyd-destunoli Peredur*, ed. Sioned Davies and Peter Wynn Thomas (Cardiff: University of Wales Press, 2000), 128–47.

13. Thomas Parry, *Gwaith Dafydd ap Gwilym* (Cardiff: University of Wales Press, 1952), 124: lines 48–50. All English translations are my own. For the most recent text and translation of the Dafydd ap Gwilym corpus, see Dafydd Johnston, Huw Meirion Edwards, Dylan Foster Evans, and A. Cynfael Lake, eds., www.dafyddapgwilym.net.

14. Dafydd Johnston, ed., *Iolo Goch: Poems* (Llandysul: Gomer Press, 1993), 173.

15. Dafydd Johnston, ed., *Gwaith Iolo Goch* (Cardiff: University of Wales Press, 1988), 20: lines 6–8.

16. Ifor Williams and Thomas Roberts, eds., *Cywyddau Dafydd ap Gwilym a'i Gyfoeswyr* (Cardiff: University of Wales Press, 1935), 80: lines 32, 79, and 45. The reference to Richard II occurs in a poem addressed to Rhys ap Tudur. According to Glyn Roberts, "the Tudors, so far as the evidence goes, were followers of Richard II; those who survived his death were supporters of Owain Glyn Dŵr." Roberts also suggests that Rhys may have been personally connected to Richard II. See "Wyrion Eden: The Anglesey Descendants of Ednyfed Fychan in the Fourteenth Century," in Roberts, *Aspects of Welsh History*, 179–214, at 198 and 202.

17. *Gwaith Dafydd ap Gwilym*, 98, line 16. On the likely identification of Robin Nordd as Robert le Northern, a burgess of Aberystwyth, see Dafydd Jenkins, "Enwau Personau a Lleoedd yng Nghywyddau Dafydd ap Gwilym," *Bulletin of the Board of Celtic Studies* 8 (1937): 140–45.

18. Davies, *Conquest, Co-existence and Change*, 421–22.

19. T. H. Parry-Williams, *The English Element in Welsh* (London: Honourable Society of Cymmrodorion, 1923); Marie Surridge, "Romance Linguistic Influence on Middle Welsh," *Studia Celtica* 1 (1966): 63–92.

20. Peter Coss, ed., *Thomas Wright's Political Songs of England from the Reign of John to That of Edward II* (Cambridge: Cambridge University Press, 1996), 273.

21. G. L. Brook, ed., *The Harley Lyrics* (Manchester: Manchester University Press, 1956), "Annot and John," line 24. See also A. T. E. Matonis, "An Investigation of Celtic Influences on MS Harley 2253," *Modern Philology* 70 (1972): 91–108; Helen Fulton, "The Theory of Celtic Influence on the Harley Lyrics," *Modern Philology* 82 (1985): 239–54; Dafydd Jenkins, "*Gwalch*: Welsh," *Cambridge Medieval Celtic Studies* 19 (1990): 55–68.

22. Homi Bhabha, *The Location of Culture* (London: Routledge, 1994).

23. Bhabha, *Location of Culture*, 44.

24. Bhabha, *Location of Culture*, 219, original italics.

25. Bhabha, *Location of Culture*, 44, original italics.

26. Bhabha, *Location of Culture*, 86, original italics.

27. Roberts, "Antipathy and Sympathy," 315.

28. Roberts, "Antipathy and Sympathy," 312.

29. R. R. Davies, *The Revolt of Owain Glyn Dŵr* (Oxford and New York: Oxford University Press, 1995), 283.

30. Roberts, "Antipathy and Sympathy," 316–7.

31. Davies, *Revolt of Owain Glyn Dŵr*, 281. Davies describes the anti-Welsh legislation on pages 285–87.

32. The text of *Armes Prydein*, "The Prophecy of Britain," has been edited by Ifor Williams and translated by Rachel Bromwich in *Armes Prydein: The Prophecy of Britain* (Dublin: Dublin Institute for Advanced Studies, 1972). See also Helen Fulton, "Tenth-Century Wales and *Armes Prydein*," *Transactions of the Honourable Society of Cymmrodorion* n.s. 7 (2001): 5–18.

33. Dafydd Johnston, " 'Propaganda'r Prydydd': Gwleidyddiaeth Beirdd yr Uchelwyr," *Cof Cenedl* 14 (1999): 39–67, at 39.

34. Ifor Williams, ed., *Gwaith Guto'r Glyn* (Cardiff: University of Wales Press, 1939), 48: lines 67–70.

35. See Glanmor Williams, *Renewal and Reformation, Wales c. 1415–1642* (Oxford and New York: Oxford University Press, 1993), 6–8.

36. W. Leslie Richards, ed., *Gwaith Dafydd Llwyd o Fathafarn* (Cardiff: University of Wales Press, 1964), 2: lines 7–8.

37. Thomas Roberts, ed., *Gwaith Dafydd ab Edmwnd*, Bangor Welsh Manuscripts Society 47 (Bangor: Printed for Bangor Welsh Manuscripts Society by Jarvis & Foster, 1914). See also Johnston, "Propaganda'r Prydydd," 42–43.

38. Cited by Johnston, "Propaganda'r Prydydd," 43.

39. Dafydd Johnston, ed., *Gwaith Lewys Glyn Cothi* (Cardiff: University of Wales Press, 1995), 222: lines 49–52.

40. Henry Lewis, Thomas Roberts, and Ifor Williams, eds., *Cywyddau Iolo Goch ac Eraill*, 2nd edn. (Cardiff: University of Wales Press, 1937), 37: lines 2–8.

41. Richards, *Gwaith Dafydd Llwyd o Fathafarn*, 43, lines 25–30.

42. D. J. Bowen, ed., *Barddoniaeth yr Uchelwyr* (Cardiff: University of Wales Press, 1959), 23: lines 5–6. For a translation of this poem to Flint, see Joseph P. Clancy, *Medieval Welsh Lyrics* (London: Macmillan, 1965), 166–68.

43. N. G. Costigan, R. Iestyn Daniel, and Dafydd Johnston, eds., *Gwaith Gruffudd ap Dafydd ap Tudur, Gwilym Ddu o Arfon, Trahaearn Brydydd Mawr ac Iorwerth Beli* (Aberystwyth: University of Wales Centre for Advanced Welsh and Celtic Studies, 1995), 15: lines 47–48 and 53–54.

44. T. Gwynn Jones, ed., *Gwaith Tudur Aled* (Cardiff: University of Wales Press, 1926), 65: lines 61–64 and 89–90.

CHAPTER 11

ENGLISH ECONOMIES AND WELSH
REALITIES: DRAMA IN MEDIEVAL
AND EARLY MODERN WALES

David N. Klausner

It has long been a commonplace of Welsh literary history that Wales had nothing to compare to the great proliferation of drama—public and private, amateur and professional, civic and parish—that flourished in England in the fifteenth and sixteenth centuries. In Wales, the subject has for the most part been dealt with by ignoring it. Thomas Parry's *History of Welsh Literature* (1955) devoted three brief pages to drama; the multivolume *Guide to Welsh Literature* (1976–97) ignores the subject altogether, and Cecil Price's *English Theatre in Wales* gives a short summary of the previous three centuries.[1] Gwenan Jones' edition of the two surviving biblical plays was privately printed in Bala in 1939 and has never been reprinted.[2] It is not, on the whole, a subject that has sparked much interest. This is unfortunate since, although there is no question that the situation was very different in Wales from the extensive dramatic traditions east of the border, it suggests that drama was virtually unknown in early Wales. The records suggest otherwise: that while dramatic performance was never as vital and pervasive a part of the Welsh tradition as it was of the English, early Wales did have plays and performances, and that these were often quite different from plays in England. These plays were geographically widespread, from Llanelli to Beaumaris to Chirk, and in both Welsh and English. This chapter will survey the evidence for drama and dramatic performance in Wales up to the earliest *anterliwtau*, the first Welsh popular dramatic tradition. I will examine first the surviving play texts, then the documentary evidence for performance, in both cases comparing the Welsh evidence to the far more extensive English material.

Play texts do not survive in abundance from early Wales, but this fact hardly accounts for the neglect that has been lavished on those plays that have come down to us. Pride of place ought to go to the two biblical plays, a Nativity Play and a Passion Play. Although the earliest manuscript of these plays is dated 1552, the range and variety of surviving texts implies with little question that they represent a much earlier composition. Gwenan Jones, whose pioneering study of these plays was completed in 1918 but not published until 1939, concluded conservatively that, on the evidence of the manuscripts, "the plays had been put into writing before 1552..., and very possibly some considerable time before this date."[3] In fact, the evidence allows this conclusion to be phrased rather more forcefully. The two biblical plays survive either complete or partially in about twelve manuscripts.[4] In date these manuscripts range from 1552 to the middle of the seventeenth century, and although the dialect of the texts strongly suggests an origin in the northeast of Wales, two of the manuscripts were likely written in Glamorgan, and two show dialectal characteristics associated with Gwent. Jones demonstrated that the manuscripts could be grouped into three families, although substantial differences even within these families as well as connections between manuscripts of different families also implies a substantial level of cross-fertilization. The sum of these facts—the number of manuscripts, the range of both date and dialect, and the considerable differences between individual texts, even of the same family—describes a situation in which the playtexts must have existed in written form for a considerable period of time before our earliest manuscript. I see little doubt that the original composition of the plays can be pushed back at least into the fifteenth century. Although the attribution of the Nativity play to Iolo Goch (d. ca. 1397/98) that appears in London, British Library MS Add. 15038 is not supported by other evidence and is unlikely in the extreme, there is no overwhelming reason why the plays could not date from his lifetime. Jones thought that the relatively small number of medieval word forms in the playtexts in comparison with, say, the poetry of Dafydd ap Gwilym, would argue against an early date, but the substantial differences in the surviving texts (again in contrast to the work of a well-known poet like Dafydd) suggests a less careful process of transmission, in which early vocabulary and word forms would be far more likely to be updated.

Given the wealth of local dramatic traditions throughout late medieval England, a pervasiveness that the Records of Early English Drama project is only now bringing fully to light, perhaps the most striking aspect of the two Welsh biblical plays is their virtually complete alienation from the English context. These differences can be seen both in the structure and the content of the Welsh plays. Gwenan Jones examined their sequence of events from the point of view of their possible derivation from English biblical plays (especially those of nearby Chester) on the one hand, or liturgical and biblical sources on the other, concluding that while the playwright showed a clear familiarity with both the liturgy and the New Testament, his work was essentially independent of English dramatic traditions.[5] We might go further; the Chester plays, like those of York and the Towneley compilation, are highly episodic—a necessity given the division of the narrative among craft guilds (at least in the cases of Chester and York). The Welsh plays are essentially through-composed, with only one structural division in the middle of the Passion play. Of the surviving English plays, only the two plays from Coventry show such a structure. The playlist from Hereford, a likely comparator due to its proximity to the Welsh border, implies a sequence of discrete episodes similar to the plays of Chester, though it is not clear from the list whether Hereford's festivities involved full plays or *tableaux vivants*.[6]

The sequence of episodes making up a single play that constitutes Coventry's nativity pageant of the Shearmen and Tailors is similar in style to the Welsh play, though rather longer, including eleven episodes (from an opening prophecy by Isaiah and the Annunciation to the Slaughter of the Innocents) in its 845 lines. In contrast, the Welsh play presents only three of these episodes in 254 lines: the Kings and Herod, the Flight into Egypt, and the Slaughter of the Innocents. It also includes substantial material not found in any of the English plays and likely to derive from native Welsh sources, notably an extended scene with Herod's messenger and, first, the Porter's comic servant who refuses him entry, and then the Porter himself who, afraid of Herod's wrath, buys the messenger's silence before giving him the bad news that the Kings have taken a different route home. The same Porter then assists Mary and Joseph to escape to Egypt. Dialogue scenes with porters restricting entry to a dwelling have long been a commonplace of Welsh literature, and the appearance of the motif here would seem likely to derive from such tales.[7]

A further cognate to the structure of the Welsh biblical plays—though considerably more extensive—is afforded by the Cornish Passion play, whose 3242 lines cover the events from the Temptation to the Deposition from the Cross. In contrast, the Welsh Passion play deals in 1016 lines with the story from the Trial to the Resurrection. However, although it is possible to see a parallel between the Welsh and Cornish Passion plays, the Cornish play is self-consciously theatrical in a way that the Welsh play never is, with extensive stage directions and frequent reference to the action itself. Clear evidence of the Welsh Passion as a performance text is limited for the most part to passages of direct address to the audience.

Gwenan Jones noted that the sequence of events in both the Nativity and Passion plays does not correspond precisely to any obvious source; neither to the English plays, the Gospel texts, nor any liturgical practice. This difference in structure would strongly suggest that the Welsh plays do not derive directly from any of the contemporary English materials. This does not mean, however, that the Welsh playwright had never seen the plays of Chester or (perhaps more likely, given the structural similarities) Coventry or, for that matter, Cornwall. None of the surviving sequences of biblical plays (including such artificial series as that of Towneley[8]) mirrors exactly the sequence of events of any other, so the Welsh plays are not unusual in this respect.

Perhaps the most striking difference between the Welsh plays and their English and Cornish analogues is the complete absence of stage directions. Indeed, it is often difficult in the Welsh plays to understand exactly how the physical action might have worked: the Crucifixion itself, for example, seems to occur in the space of four lines. The Bishop commands Jesus to put down the Cross and shows the three nails to the crowd, and the First Knight orders both the nailing and the lifting of the Cross.

> Trewch vyneidie yr hoelon
> yni draed ai ddwylo
> kodwch yn ychel efo
> mal i gwelo yr iddewon.
> (289–92)

[Friends, drive the nails deep into his feet and hands; lift him up high so that the Jews may see.]

The soldiers then turn to the crucifixion of the two thieves, giving no indication of how (or whether) the Cross is raised, in stark contrast to the Crucifixion play from York in which every technical detail of the Crucifixion is made clear in the soldiers' banter.[9] The Welsh play suggests a dramaturgy radically different to that of all the English and Cornish plays, one in which the physical action is constantly subordinated to the spoken word.

English drama of the fourteenth and fifteenth centuries also includes the morality plays, or moral interludes, in which the life (and sometimes death) of a representative human figure is seen in the allegorical context of a struggle between forces of good and evil for his allegiance. The sole surviving Welsh morality play, *Y Gŵr Kadarn* [The Strong Man], is significantly different from the English exemplars in several ways.[10] The play survives in four manuscripts, the earliest from the late sixteenth century, but it begins in a manner that connects it with the fifteenth-century *Castle of Perseverance*. Like Humanum Genus, the protagonist of *Castle*, the Strong Man begins as a servant of the World, Master Mundus. He describes his relationship to his master in terms that strongly recall the action of *Castle*:

> Deythym atto yn dranoeth
> yn fab bychan tryan llednoeth
> heb un ede amdana.
> (70–72)

[I came to him quite naked, a little boy, a wretch, half-naked, without a stitch of clothes on me.]

Both Humanum Genus and the Strong Man receive their wealth from Mundus:

> Yddo y diolcha fi fy ffortyn
> yn gwissgo melfed a sidan.
> (75–76)

[To him I give thanks for my fortune, wearing velvet and silk.]

The Priest warns the Strong Man that Mundus is untrustworthy and that what he gives, he can also take away, mirroring the theft of Humanum Genus' goods by Mundus' new servant, "the boy," in *Castle*:[11]

> Er maint dy goel di arno
> Fe fydd tebig yth dwyllo
> a rhoir kyfoeth y arall.
> (88–90)

[Despite how much you trust him, chances are he will deceive you, and give your wealth to another.]

The first half of the play consists of an argument between the Strong Man and the Priest, who tries with limited success, like the Good Angel of *Castle*, to convince the Strong Man of the folly of his attachment to the world. The situation changes, however, when the Priest points out that the Strong Man has but one day to live. Terrified by the prospect of imminent death, the Strong Man is guided by the Priest to free himself from the trappings of the World and to repent his sins; he dies with the Priest's absolution and blessing. If the play ended at this point it would conform in a general way to the structure of most of the surviving morality plays, especially *Castle* and *Everyman*. However, it continues for a further two hundred lines as the Strong Man's wife is wooed by his servant Sion, a poor man who pretends to have no interest in the Strong Man's wealth. Once married, he becomes dictatorial and overbearing and the Wife concludes the play,

> pei medraswn gyfarch i ddyw
> Ny ffriodasswn ddim oth gyfryw.
> (806–7)

[If I had known how to beseech God in prayer, I would not have married this man.]

The two halves of the play, then, represent two quite different perspectives: the first, the common material of the morality play familiar from English sources in which the protagonist turns from sinful ways toward repentance and salvation, the second a cautionary tale of marital deception. There are no English analogues for this combination, and the two halves fit together awkwardly.

Dialogue poems are common in medieval Welsh literature (*Ymddiddan Myrddin a Thaliesin* [Dialogue between Myrddin and Taliesin], *Ymddiddan Arthur a'r Eryr* [Dialogue between Arthur and the Eagle], *Ymddiddan Arthur a'i Chwaer* [Dialogue between Arthur and His Sister]) as well as in English (*The Owl and the Nightingale, Winner and Wastour*), but it is quite clear from the use of narrators and speech indicators that, while all of them may have been intended for oral performance, none was intended to be staged by multiple speakers incorporating dramatic action. Surprisingly, then, *Ymddiddan y Corff a'r Enaid* [Dialogue of the Body and Soul] is the most clearly dramatic of the early Welsh plays, beginning with an extensive address to the audience, and including a number of stage directions. These give the distinct impression of an author unused to writing in a dramatic idiom, since they are phrased in the preterit: "A chida hyny iesu a mair a ddoeth yno" [And then Jesus and Mary came there].[12] The play is also considerably more extensive than the dialogue between the body and soul that forms its first section. This is followed by a verbal battle between Michael and the devil for possession of the body and soul, and then by a third section in which a Strong Man (perhaps reflecting the character of the morality play) claims to have no interest in the ten commandments until an Angel describes to him the certainty of death and the fate of the body. Although body/soul dialogues are common in most European languages (the versions of Robert Grosseteste and Andrew Marvell being merely the best known), none gives as clear indication of staging as the Welsh poem.

Finally, in a genre very different from the religious plays previously discussed, the play *Troelus a Chresyd* contained in Aberystwyth, National Library of Wales MS Peniarth 106 comes as close as anything in early Welsh literature to the theater world of London.[13] It also bears a closer relationship to the English literary context than other early Welsh plays, since it is based closely, indeed much of the play is directly translated from, Chaucer's *Troilus and Criseyde* and Henryson's *Testament of Cresseid*. The unique manuscript was copied by John Jones, Gellilyfdy, who completed copying the first part of the text on 14 February 1613, returning to continue his work on 11 September 1622 and completing the copying on 5 October of that year (Jones records these dates in the manuscript). The play itself, however, dates from earlier than the time of its copying, and the principal question is whether it should be seen as part of the vogue for Troy plays in the last few years of Elizabeth's reign. Was the Welsh playwright influenced by such plays as Shakespeare's *Troilus and Cressida* (1601–2) or Thomas Heywood's *The Iron Age* (1612)? The evidence in favor of such influence is weak, although the second scene of the Welsh play includes a council in which the Trojan princes discuss whether or not to return Helen to the Greeks, a scene not derived from Chaucer, but paralleled in both Shakespeare (Act II, scene 2) and Heywood (Act II, scene 1). In neither case is there evidence of direct borrowing, and the three plays hardly show the "remarkable similarities" claimed by Stephens Jones.[14] Jones is closer to the truth when he notes that the Welsh play is "as unlike late Elizabethan drama, and the 'Troy' plays in particular, as is possible."[15] Early editions of Chaucer are not helpful in dating the play, since all editions from William Thynne's of 1532 had included Henryson's poem as a sixth book to *Troilus and Criseyde*. The only really useful evidence, as Stephens Jones points out, is that metrically and stylistically *Troelus a Chresyd* is much closer to the English plays of the 1560s—*Cambyses, Appius and Virginia, Damon and Pythias*—than to the blank verse–dominated plays of the end of the century.[16] A number of suggestions have been made concerning the identity of the playwright, none based on any real evidence, and they remain mere speculation.[17]

The play presents an interesting problem in its inclusion of stage directions and rubrics very much out of line with the norm for Elizabethan plays. Along with quite standard stage directions indicating movement and action like entrances and exits ("Priaf yn troi at ei feibion" [Priam, turning toward his sons]), there are several that speak to states of mind; thus the indication for Troelus when Kressyd is called before the Trojan council: "ac ar hynn mae yn syrthio mewn kariad" [and now he falls in love].[18] Even more distant from the contemporary norms for stage directions are the narrative summaries that appear scattered through the text; these might have been added by John Jones, who seems likely not to have been familiar with the London theatrical world or with the norms of play copying and publishing. That he was copying the stage directions from his exemplar seems certain, however, as one later in the play reads, "Diomedes ar yr ystaeds, a Chressyd yn dyfod yno" [Diomedes on the stage, and Kressyd coming there].[19] More curious are the very elaborate descriptions of the planets that assemble in judgment over Kressyd, following Henryson. Here, for example, is the description of Jupiter:

> Yn nessaf y doeth Iubiter a golwc tec kariadus; duw a llyfodraethwr y sêr yn yr wybren; yn anghyffelib y'w dad Sadwrn, ac wyneb llydan howddgar a golygiad ysgafn; ac ar ei benn yr oedd penddelau o lyssiau gleission megis pette hi galan Mai; ei wallt fal yr aur yn ddisglair, ei lais yn eglur, ei ddillad yn wyrddion ac yn hafaidd, ac yn ei law yr oedd ffon wayw.[20]

> [Next came Jupiter with a beautiful and friendly appearance; god and ruler of the stars in the heavens; unlike his father Saturn, with a broad, pleasant face and jolly expression; and on his head there was a headdress of green leaves as if it were May-day; his hair like gold in brightness, his voice clear, his apparel verdant and summery, and in his hand there was a spear shaft.]

The description, though in prose, is clearly derived from Henryson:

> Than Juppiter richt fair and amiabill,
> God of the starnis in the firmament,
> And nureis to all thing generabill,
> Fra his father Saturne far different,
> With burelie face, and browis bricht and brent,
> Upon his heid ane garland wonder gay
> Of flouris fair, as it had bene in May.

> His voice was cleir, as cristall wer his ene,
> As goldin wyre sa glitterand was his hair,
> His garmound and his gyis full gay of gre[n]e,
> With golden listis gilt on everie gair;
> Ane burelie brand about his middill bair,
> In his right hand he had ane groundin speir,
> Of his father the wraith fra us to weir.[21]

These descriptive passages, despite their clear derivation from Henryson's poem, have taken on a dramatic sense and are clearly intended to indicate the entrances of the planets, since they are followed by the stage direction, "Yno pan gyfarfu y saith dduw yma yn yr un lle..." [Then, when the seven deities are assembled there in one place...].[22] Descriptions carrying this level of detail not intended to be spoken as part of the play are extremely unusual for the period with one important exception: they resemble closely the kind of elaborate description found in the text of court masques, and would suggest a playwright with some experience in this direction. Compare, for example, the opening description of Boreas from Ben Jonson's *Masque of Beauty* (1608):

> In a robe of Russet, and White mixt, full, and bagg'd: his haire, and beard rough: and horrid; his wings gray, and ful of snow, and icycles. His mantle borne from him with wires, & in seueral puffes; his feet a ending in serpents tayles; and in his hand a leaueles Branch, laden with icycles.[23]

Troelus a Chresyd is not modeled directly on the English drama of the later Elizabethan period. The playwright's use of metrics shows no influence of the blank verse of the English plays, but is based on couplets of various lengths and on several different stanza forms. Although the playwright's five-part division of the action would seem to reflect the five act structure that had by the 1590s become common, it seems more likely to mirror the five books of Chaucer's *Troilus and Criseyde* (with the fifth book largely replaced by Henryson's *Testament*); he describes his divisions as "llyfrau" [books] rather than "actau" or "actiau," although the use of the latter in a theatrical sense is only attested from the late eighteenth century. He clearly has some familiarity with the professional theater, and I suspect also with the court masque, though this familiarity may in some cases have been obscured by the copyist, John Jones.

Surviving plays from Wales during the period between *Troelus a Chresyd* and the Civil War are limited to those emanating from the households of Salusbury (Lleweni, Denbighshire) and Myddelton (Chirk, Denbighshire). These are all in English and are wholly within the English tradition; since I have discussed them at length elsewhere I will omit consideration of them here.[24] The importance of the English theatrical tradition in Wales expands in the mid-seventeenth century, especially in the school context, with enterprising schoolmasters like the Rev. William Williams staging such plays at Beaumaris as Thomas Bayly's *Rebellion of Naples, or the Tragedy of Massanello* and Thomas Randolph's *The Muses' Looking Glass* in the 1550s.[25] The Welsh language *anterliwt* tradition, which was to become popular in the eighteenth century, seems to have begun around this time; although the manuscript cannot be dated with precision, the earliest surviving example of the genre, the fragmentary *anterliwt* of Argolws and Simoniax, appears to date from the middle of the seventeenth century.[26]

When we turn to documentary evidence for drama in early Wales we encounter similar limits. A 1320 visitation by Bishop Adam Orleton to the Benedictine Priory of Abergavenny, Monmouthshire, recorded in his register revealed that monks were engaged in miming the Crucifixion in the presence of an audience:

> ...& quosdam ipsorum spectaculum / suorum corporum facientes & aliquociens quod non sine cordis amaritudine referimus nudi extensis brachiis cum baculis & ligatis ad modum crucifixi stramine vel alio aliquo ad modum corone / capitibus eorum superposito de ipsorum dormitorio nocturno tempore descedentes & sic incedentes ac ludentes coram sociis suis / & aliis inibi morantibus & alia enormia facientes que ad presens / propter ipsorum enormitatem nimiam subticemus.[27]

> [...and some of them make a spectacle of their bodies, and sometimes— which we did not learn without bitterness of heart—they come down naked from their dormitory at night, with arms stretched out with rods and tied in the manner of someone crucified, with straw or something else in the manner of a crown put upon their heads, and walk in that way and play before their fellows and others staying there and do other outrageous things, about which we are silent because of their excessive outrageousness.]

Taking Orleton's outrage with a grain of salt, it seems reasonably clear that the brothers were staging a Crucifixion pageant. This pageant may well have been staged without words, since the description concentrates on the action, but the monks were clearly miming the Crucifixion itself [ad modum crucifixi] as well as the crown of thorns [ad modum corone] and acting [ludentes] before an audience from both within and without the Priory [coram sociis suis /& aliis inibi morantibus].

This record is unusual in giving us the content of the performance; for the most part the documentary evidence simply indicates that a play performance took place without indicating whether the play was biblical, moral, secular, in Welsh or in English, much less its title or author. No records survive for the rest of the fourteenth and fifteenth centuries, but from the early sixteenth century a set of depositions (also from Abergavenny) before the Court of Augmentations in 1537 gives some further information. The context of the case has nothing to do with drama: following the dissolution of Abergavenny Priory, the court was attempting to clarify the ownership of the three bells in the priory church, which the citizens claimed belonged to the town and not to the priory since the towns- people had raised the money to pay for them. John ap polle ap John deposed that "he was one of them with one Ienkyn da blether Iohn bengreth Thomas coke Ienkyn ap gwillim llwelyn vynneth and william ap polle ap Ieuan that went aboute into the countrie with games and playse to gather money to pay for the foresaide belles." His evidence is supported by his brother, Maredudd ap polle ap John, who added that "he neuer sawe no man pay any thynge for the same belles but only the towne and the countrie that they gatte apon theym with games and plays..."[28] While the phrase "games and plays" is not entirely unambiguous, it seems likely that the parishioners were raising funds for the bells by one of the most popular English methods, the parish play.[29] Although the purchase of the bells cannot be dated exactly, it is likely that the brothers (eighty and eighty-eight years of age respectively) were remembering events from their youth, and the plays took place sometime in the last quarter of the fifteenth century.

Less clarity is offered by a pair of Chester consistory court depositions from 1570 concerning an altercation in a matrimonial suit that took place following a play at Penley, Flintshire. The play took place on the village green, and while it is marginally possible that the reference is to a sporting event such as football, such occasions are usually identified as such in depositions, and the phrase "after the play was done" suggests a performance. Penley lies in the region of Maelor Saesneg, an area of strong English influence, and the play might well have been a further example of parish-sponsored drama.

The documentation of a play in Llanelli, Carmarthenshire, in 1604 is unambiguous, but is also one of the most puzzling of the surviving records. A group of about a dozen men, led by one Phillip Bowen and his son David Phillip Bowen, are the subject of a bill of complaint brought to the Court of Star Chamber. Described as "Men of contentious spirittes, lewde liues and evell conversacons," the Bowens and their cohorts are accused of a series of assaults and disturbances, capped by the attempted murder of a customs official. Following this sequence of bloodthirsty attacks,

> ...the said Phillippe Bowen beinge Cheiftaine and Ringleader vnto all the reste coulde not be satisfied onelye with Causing a moste profaine and scurrulous stage playe to be acted and played vpon or aboute the twentith daye of Maye laste within the perishe Churche of Llanelly aforesaid to the great dishonor of god the prophayninge of his Temple the breache of your Maiesties lawes and the greevous offence of manye trewe Christian protestantes and loyall Subiectes...[30]

The sectarian note with which this account ends suggests that the offending play may well have been perceived as Catholic in its subject matter.[31] The court records do not provide answers to most of our questions, however: what was a band of ruffians doing putting on a play in a church? If the play was, as the bill of complaint suggests, Catholic or anti-Protestant, by whose authority was it staged in the parish church? All that can be gleaned from the document is that a play was performed, and even that may be suspect, since the Court of Star Chamber was frequently used as a method of tying one's enemies up in litigation, and the factual content of bills of complaint is often impossible to substantiate. Even so, the fact that the plaintiff (one John Vaughan of Westminster) would make such an accusation indicates that at least one person saw such an event as a possibility.

A case brought before the Flintshire Great Sessions in 1608 concerns an assault that took place in "an Arbor or play place" on Tallarn Green, not far from Penley.[32] The phrase "play place" is ambiguous, and could indicate either a site used for local (parish?) performances, or a playing field for games such as football. The alternative description of the site as an arbor, however, would seem to eliminate the "playing field" reading. As with the Penley record, the proximity of Tallarn Green to the English border would suggest plays in English, perhaps under parish auspices. The green at Burgedin, Montgomeryshire, is similarly called a "pleing place" in a 1591 Great Sessions deposition.[33]

All the records cited so far involve performers and performances that we would define as "nonprofessional"; the first evidence for professional performers lies in the municipal accounts of Swansea's common attorneys during the period from 1617 to 1634, in which almost every year there is a receipt from "stage players" for repairing the windows of the Town Hall.[34] Sadly, the accounts give no indication of the nature of the players' performances, nor why they so consistently resulted in broken windows. Performances do not seem to have been associated with a particular time of year; the only two dates noted in the entries (for the payments, not for the performances) are October 24 and January 8. The Town Hall as venue for stage performances is consistent with the use of municipal buildings in English towns, and the lack of further evidence for civic sponsorship of drama in Wales is likely a factor both of the very limited survival of municipal records and the relative poverty of most Welsh towns.[35] Swansea would also be a more likely town than most in Wales for visits by professional players. Travel in Wales was exceptionally difficult, with roads of generally poor quality traversing mountainous terrain; like Cardiff and Haverfordwest (where the Earl of Essex's musicians appeared in 1596–97), Swansea could be approached by water with relative ease, and the surviving port books give ample evidence of regular communication with a variety of English ports such as Bristol and Barnstaple.[36]

The diary that Robert Bulkeley of Dronwy, Anglesey, kept through much of the 1630s contains four references to his attendance at plays. In three of the cases, the phrasing is ambiguous ("rid to a play at llanddaysant") and could possibly refer to gaming; the fourth record, however, is clear: "post prandium I rid to the schoole to heare a play."[37] The plays of Maelor Saesneg (Penley, Tallarn Green) and Swansea could well have been in English, but although Bulkeley kept his diary in English, the plays that he saw in rural Anglesey must have been in Welsh. Bulkeley himself was well educated. He had been a student at Christ Church, Oxford, and went into the service of Theophilus Field, bishop of Llandaff, in the early 1620s. By September 1621 he had returned to Oxford, likely to pursue an MA, but by 16 June 1622 he had returned to his family home at Dronwy to assist his widowed mother in running the estate. He stayed there for the rest of his life and—while his university training and service in the bishop's household meant that he kept his journal in English, the language of administration—the language of his daily life must have been Welsh, and the plays he saw in small towns like Llanddeusant and Bodedern would only have found an audience in Welsh.

The only place on Anglesey where an English-language play would have been viable was in the highly anglicized borough of Beaumaris. The enterprising headmaster of the Free School of Beaumaris, the Rev. William Williams, mounted productions of several English plays, among them Thomas Bayly's *Rebellion of Naples, or The Tragedy of Massenello* (Wing B199), performed in 1652, and Thomas Randolph's *The Muses' Looking Glass* (STC 20694), performed in 1655. For both of these plays Williams composed prologues for school performances.[38] Randolph's pastoral comedy seems unexceptionable school fare, but *The Rebellion of Naples* is a very curious choice for a school. This story of the 1647 Neapolitan rebellion against the Spanish centers on its leader, the fisherman Massenello, who is driven mad by the acquisition of political power. Although the story was often used as antimonarchist propaganda, Bayly reads it in precisely the opposite way, as an example of power corrupting the mind not trained to wield it. How the Beaumaris schoolboys dealt with the two onstage beheadings (including Massenello's head being ripped off by the citizens of Naples) is anybody's guess.

Several references appear in the records using the word "interlude." These seem in most cases to be references to plays in a more or less English tradition, not to the Welsh *anterliwtau* of the later seventeenth century. So in a Hereford consistory court prosecution in 1589, the schoolmaster of Churchstoke, Montgomeryshire, a stone's throw from the English border, is cited "for makinge and setting forthe of enterludes on the sabothe daye." The performers appear to have been local, for one Lewis Powell, who was both a player and a churchwarden, was cited to appear at the next sitting of the court.[39] In April of 1621 Mr. Justice James Whitelock recorded in his journal that the Chester circuit was entertained in Ruthin "withe the waites of the towne & a banquet a latin oration & an enterlude."[40] One document, however, is very likely to refer to the early stages of the *anterliwt* tradition. Though neither localized nor dated, a poignant letter to a father concerning his wayward son was sent by a schoolmaster named Robert Lloyd in the mid-seventeenth century, complaining that the boy had "misimploy'd his time in composeing something, which they call an interlude...." Lloyd notes that instead of translating Martial's epigrams into Welsh, as he had been set to do, the unnamed boy preferred to "trifle away his usefull houres in welch rimeing."[41]

Finally, we have the record of a performance of a play that was certainly in Welsh, and very likely given by professional players. It is an extraordinary record, since it attests both to the existence of such drama in early Wales, but also to its relative infrequency. The documents survive in the Caernarfonshire Quarter Sessions records, and the case concerns an affray that broke out in a private house called Derwyn Bach in the village of Dolbenmaen, south of Caernarfon at the foot of the Llŷn peninsula on 29 May 1654.[42] The disagreement behind the affray involved stock access to a meadow by means of a bridge over the river Llecheiddior; the immediate occasion for the fight was the gathering together of the participants to see a play performed in the house. The nature of the play itself is unknown, since it was peripheral to the case, but the various depositions include the following information: the play was performed by two men and a boy, who were paid 1s 6d by the assembled company. The play was announced on the previous Sunday by the minister after morning service. The performance involved a substantial amount of doubling, with the three participants playing multiple characters, and several of the deponents express their satisfaction at having observed this:

> ...all three beinge disguised & some tymes one of them in womans apparell all three at seuerall tymes apperinge in seuerall changes of apparell after divers sorts & in ye shape of others some tymes in blacke some tyme<.> in redd & some tymes in all other Collurs yet this deponent knoweth

the acters were the three straungers whoe Continued thus actinge; and diliueringe seuerall parts by heart for an houre or two...[43]

Contemporary audience reactions to plays are very unusual; the reaction of a naive audience member to a specific theatrical practice, such as doubling, is rare in the extreme. The payment to the players indicates their professional status; the location of the performance strongly indicates that it must have been in Welsh. Banns from the pulpit would suggest that the play might have been religious in its content.

The only other hints concerning the nature of the play appear in the Articles of Misdemeanor presented to the justices of the peace in connection with the case. Since these were drawn up (as their heading makes clear) with the assistance of the plaintiff in the case (the owner of the bridge whose refusal to allow access provoked the affray) they must be taken with a measure of salt. The intention of the articles seems to be to place the blame for the disturbance on the players:

> ...there were three persons vnknowen disguised in chaunge of apparell that acted sometymes in one habyt & sometymes in an other habitt behaveing themselues very diso<..>erly and vncivill to the Manifest breach of ther good behauior...

It is not entirely clear whether the basis of the accusation is the disturbance of the peace or the disguising, but this point is incidental to the description of the play.[44]

We have, then, limited evidence—both textual and documentary—for dramatic performance in early Wales. Given what information we can assemble on the destruction of manuscript and documentary material from the dissolution of the monasteries to the middle of the nineteenth century, it is very likely that we are only able to see a small part of the picture.[45] In England, outside of the professional theater and the London court theater, the predominate backing for performances came from parishes and municipalities. Given the economics of early Welsh society (easily seen in the surviving civic account books, few though they may be), most Welsh towns were not in a financial position to support any kind of civic drama or to hire professional players.[46]

Even on the basis of this limited evidence, however, several points can be made. There is no doubt that drama existed in early Wales, though the description of the Derwyn Bach interlude implies that it was far less common than in England. This drama was widespread geographically, from Maelor Saesneg in the northeast to Anglesey and Caernarfonshire in the northwest, to Swansea in the south; this geographical distribution, as well as the surviving playtexts, indicates that performances took place in both Welsh and English. From the documentary evidence it may also be concluded that drama existed on both local nonprofessional and traveling professional levels. Although the stage players who regularly broke the windows in the Swansea town hall might well have traveled from England, there is no evidence that players crossed the border into Wales. There would have been little reason for them to do so, for the most part the pickings would have been slim. In 1535/36 Rowland Lee, bishop of Coventry

and Lichfield, fought the plan to place control over law and order in the hands
of local justices on the basis that few Welshmen could meet the £20.00 property requirement for a justice of the peace: "there be ffew welshemen in wales
above Breknock that maye dispende ten pounds lande..."[47] The few municipal
accounts that survive show that civic entertainment was not high on the list
of priorities, though the highly anglicized borough of Beaumaris, Anglesey, in
1585 appointed a lord of misrule, as Richard Price was excused his burgage dues
"in consideration that he is lord of the mery pastimes..."[48] This is an exception,
and although the evidence is scanty, it is very unlikely that English performance
traditions were common in the Welsh towns or countryside.

In the houses of the gentry, especially those who spent a substantial amount
of time in London, dramatic entertainment occasionally flourished, as in the
Salusbury and Myddelton households. These instances remained entirely within
the English tradition, emulating the entertainments of the distant capital, in
English, for an English-speaking audience. Welsh drama, though not common,
was to be found elsewhere.

Notes

1. Thomas Parry, *A History of Welsh Literature* (Oxford: Clarendon Press,
   1955); A. O .H. Jarman and Gwilym R. Hughes, *A Guide to Welsh
   Literature*, 2 vols. (Swansea: Christopher Davies, 1979, 1984); R. Geraint
   Gruffydd, *A Guide to Welsh Literature, c. 1530–1700* (Cardiff: University
   of Wales Press, 1997); Cecil Price, *English Theatre in Wales in the
   Eighteenth and Early Nineteenth Century* (Cardiff: University of Wales
   Press, 1948), 6.
2. Gwenan Jones, *A Study of Three Welsh Religious Plays* (Bala: Bala Press,
   1939).
3. Jones, *Three Welsh Religious Plays*, 30.
4. The complete texts of the Nativity are in BL MSS Add. 14986 and 14882;
   NLW MSS Cwrtmawr 530A, Peniarth 65, and Peniarth 73; the fragmentary texts are in BL MS Add. 15038, 14973, and 14975, Cardiff Central
   Library MSS 2.4, 2.5 (olim 11i.,ii.) and 2.632 (olim Hafod 22); NLW MSS
   874 (olim MS Wrexham 3), and Llanstephan 135. The full texts of the
   Passion are in BL MSS Add. 14986, Add. 14812, and Add. 14973; NLW
   MS Cwrtmawr 530A; the fragmentary texts are in BL MS Add. 14975 and
   15038, Cardiff Central Library MSS 2.4, 2.5 (olim 11.i., ii) and 2.632 (olim
   Hafod 22); NLW MSS 874 (olim MS Wrexham 3 [two copies]), Peniarth
   65, Peniarth 73, Llanstephan 135. NLW MS Peniarth 73 and BL MS Add.
   14975 were originally a single manuscript, and the text of the Passion play
   is divided between them.
5. Jones, *Three Welsh Religious Plays*, 49–99.
6. David Klausner, ed., *Herefordshire and Worcestershire*, Records of Early
   English Drama (Toronto: University of Toronto Press, 1990), 115–16.
7. Probably the best known example is the poem "Pa gur yv y porthaur"
   in the Black Book of Carmarthen (NLW Peniarth 1, fols. 47v–49r), in

which Arthur is challenged by the gatekeeper, Glewlwyd Gafaelfawr, and responds by listing his accomplishments and those of his companions, Cei and Bedwyr. Glewlwyd appears in other texts in a similar context, notably in *Culhwch ac Olwen* and the romances *Owein* and *Gereint uab Erbin*.

8. On the artificial origin and redating of the Towneley plays, see Barbara D. Palmer, "Recycling 'The Wakefield Cycle': The Records," *Research Opportunities in Renaissance Drama* 41 (2002): 88–130 and Garrett P. J. Epp, "The Towneley Plays and the Hazards of Cycling," *Research Opportunities in Renaissance Drama* 32 (1993): 121–50.

9. See my forthcoming article "Staging the Unstageable: Performing the Crucifixion in Medieval England and Wales," in *Aspects of Medieval Civic Drama: Essays in Honour of David Mills, Medieval English Theatre*, (2008).

10. Sarah Campbell, ed., *"The Strong Man* and Its Contexts: An Edition, Translation, and Study of a Medieval Welsh Morality Play" (Ph.D. diss., Catholic University of America, 2005). Quotations and translations are from Campell's edition.

11. *Castle of Perseverance*, lines 2896–94.

12. Jones, *Three Welsh Religious Plays*, 248.

13. W. Beynon Davies, ed., *Troelus a Chresyd* (Cardiff: University of Wales Press, 1976); the text is also available online at the Historical Corpus of the Welsh Language site, http://people.pwf.cam.ac.uk/dwew2/hcwl/tch/tch_frames.htm.

14. R. I. Stephens Jones, "The Date of *Troelus a Chresyd* (Peniarth 106)," *Bulletin of the Board of Celtic Studies* 26.4 (1976): 430.

15. Jones, "Date of *Troelus a Chresyd*," 432.

16. Jones, "Date of *Troelus a Chresyd*," 435.

17. J. S. P. Tatlock, "The Welsh *Troilus and Cressida* and Its Relation to the Elizabethan Drama," *Modern Language Review* 10.3 (1915): 277, note 1; R. I. Stephens Jones, "The Authorship of *Troelus a Chresyd*," *Bulletin of the Board of Celtic Studies* 28.2 (1979): 223–28; Gwyn Williams, " 'Troelus a Chresyd': A Welsh Tragedy," in *Person and Persona: Studies in Shakespeare* (Cardiff: University of Wales Press, 1981), 109–10 (reprinted from *Transactions of the Honourable Society of Cymmrodorion*, 1954).

18. Davies, *Troelus a Chresyd*, 54, 58.

19. Davies, *Troelus a Chresyd*, 127.

20. Davies, *Troelus a Chresyd*, 129.

21. Robert Henryson, *The Testament of Cresseid*, ed. Denton Fox (London: Nelson, 1968), lines 169–82.

22. Davies, *Troelus a Chresyd*, 131.

23. *The Characters of Two Royall Masques: The One of Blacknesse, the Other of Beautie, etc.* (London: Thomas Thorp, 1608 [STC 14761]), sig C2v.

24. David Klausner, "Family Entertainments among the Salusburys of Lleweni, Denbighshire and Their Circle, 1595–1641," *Welsh Music History/Hanes Cerddoriaeth Cymru* 6 (2004): 129–54.

25. The prologues that Williams wrote for his productions are printed in David Klausner, ed., *Records of Early Drama: Wales* (Toronto: University of Toronto Press, 2005), 43–45. Alfred Harbage lists *The Rebellion of Naples* as "closet drama," but it is clear from Williams' prologue that it received at least one performance, even though that was very distant from London (*Annals of English Drama: 975–1700*, rev. edn. S. Schoenbaum [London: Methuen, 1964], 146–47).

26. NLW MS 5269B, fols. 531r–34v.

27. Klausner, ed., *Records: Wales*, 216 (text), 378 (trans.).

28. Klausner, ed., *Records: Wales*, 218–19.

29. On parish drama, especially as a fund-raising tool, see the essays in *English Parish Drama* ed. A. F. Johnston and Wim Hüsken, *Ludus I* (Amsterdam: Rodopi, 1996).

30. Klausner, ed., *Records: Wales*, 99.

31. The 1572 letter-book of the Chester Puritan preacher Christopher Goodwin gives some indication of the aspects of the city's biblical plays that he found particularly objectionable, especially in his list of the plays' "absurdities"; see Elizabeth Baldwin, Lawrence M. Clopper, and David Mills, eds., *Records of Early English Drama: Cheshire (including Chester)*, 2 vols. (Toronto: University of Toronto Press, 2007), 1: 143–48, esp. 147–48.

32. Klausner, ed., *Records: Wales*, 199.

33. Klausner, ed., *Records: Wales*, 225.

34. Klausner, ed., *Records: Wales*, 206–9. An engraving of Swansea's early town hall is reproduced at lxxv.

35. See the discussion of the use of Exeter's Guildhall in Sally-Beth Maclean, "The Southwest Entertains: Exeter and Local Performance Patronage," in *Bring Furth the Pagants: Essays in Early English Drama presented to Alexandra F. Johnston,* ed. David Klausner and Karen S. Marsalek (Toronto: University of Toronto Press, 2007), 58–71.

36. Klausner, ed., *Records: Wales*, 251; E. A. Lewis *Welsh Port Books, 1550–1603* Cymmrodorion Record Series 12 (London: Cymmrodorion Society, 1927), 350.

37. Klausner, ed., *Records: Wales*, 48–52.

38. Klausner, ed., *Records: Wales*, 42–45, 403–4. The 1649 print of the play gives the author as "T. B." and Williams' identification of him as Thomas Bayly is by no means a certainty. Bayly, a staunch royalist, was the youngest son of Lewis Bayly, bishop of Bangor (d. 1631).

39. Klausner, ed., *Records: Wales*, 235.

40. Klausner, ed., *Records: Wales*, 130.

41. Klausner, ed., *Records: Wales*, 271–72.

42. The house still exists, and a photograph of it appears in Klausner, ed., *Records: Wales*, lxxiii.

43. Klausner, ed., *Records: Wales*, 65.

44. In 1597 Elizabeth's statute on Rogues, Vagabonds, and Sturdy Beggars was extended to prohibit disguising, including in its purview "all such persons not being Felons wandering and pretending to be Egyptians,

or wandering in the Habit, Form or Attire of counterfeit Egyptians," *Statutes of the Realm*, ed. A. Luders et al. (London: Records Commission, 1810–18), 39, vol. 4, part. 2, p. 899 (39 Elizabeth c. 4/2).

45. Records of the Court of Great Sessions, for example, do not survive from all jurisdictions. When the court was abolished in 1830, control of the records was left in the hands of the county administrator who had previously kept them, but no further funds were provided for their storage. In many jurisdictions this meant that the records were junked. Parchment documents from Caernarfonshire were sold to tailors to line cuffs and collars; paper documents were tossed unceremoniously in the Menai Straits. In the light of such treatment, we are lucky that anything at all has survived. See Kenneth O. Fox, "The Records of the Court of Great Sessions," *Journal of the Society of Archivists* 3 (1966): 177–82.

46. See, for example, the accounts of the borough of Haverfordwest, B. G. Charles, ed., *Calendar of the Records of the Borough of Haverfordwest 1539–1660*, Board of Celtic Studies, History and Law Series 24 (Cardiff: University of Wales Press, 1967). The one payment of five shillings to the Earl of Essex's musicians in 1596–97 is a striking exception to the rule. Devereux had close connections with Haverfordwest, having been brought up at the family seat of Lamphey Hall in the southern part of the county.

47. The National Archives, SP 1/102/453.

48. Klausner, ed., *Records: Wales*, 42.

CHAPTER 12

"SONGES OF THE DOEINGES OF THEIR AUNCESTORS": ASPECTS OF WELSH AND ENGLISH MUSICAL TRADITIONS

Sally Harper

An imaginary juxtaposition of the contrasting soundscapes that might have characterized Wales and England during the 1430s is found in an anonymous dialogue ballad of the early seventeenth century.[1] Purportedly a translation from a Welsh original, this fanciful recreation of the courtship of the future grandparents of Henry VII—Owain Tudor of Anglesey (ca. 1400–1461) and the widow of Henry V, Catherine de Valois (1401–37)—has Owain attempting to woo the aristocratic Catherine by laying before her the charms of his homeland. Wales is defined by a series of pastoral delights; among them the "murmuring musick" of its clear fountains, the "musicall moanes" of its harps, tabors and "sweet humming drones," its Whitsuntide maypoles and dancing on the village green, and the serenading of a bride with bagpipes as she makes her way to church. Catherine, accustomed to tilting and tournaments, masques and revels, inevitably has very different expectations. For her the music of courtship requires a soothing "silver-like melody" that "rocks up" the senses; Welsh music, to her refined ear, is "clownish," for it "soundeth not sweet."

Frivolous though it is, this ballad raises some interesting questions. To what extent was there a genuine dichotomy between Welsh and English secular repertories, instruments, and practices during the medieval period, and how far was the role of the professional musician distinct in these two countries? How, indeed, did Welsh and English perceive the musical traditions of the other, and to what extent did musicians and musical styles "cross the border?" Surprisingly such questions have received little attention to date. Analogues for Welsh instrumental music of the Middle Ages, so intimately bound up with "bardism" and strict-meter poetry, are more commonly sought in medieval Ireland—a country with a similarly elevated bardic tradition and a comparable dependence on oral transmission.[2] This chapter thus makes a preliminary attempt to evaluate the possibility of a Welsh-English musical interchange, with particular reference to bardic and minstrel practice. It explores the function and status of harpers (or poet-harpers) in both countries, and attempts to quantify their associated musical and poetic repertories. It also examines that profound Welsh emphasis on panegyric, where bardic musicians were often defined as champions of their native culture—not least in singing "the doeings of their auncestors."[3] Sharp contrasts inevitably emerge between the two traditions, but there is also a degree of common ground.

The Welsh Tradition of Harp and Crwth

The dominant genre of secular music in medieval Wales up to the late sixteenth century was *cerdd dant* [string craft], a highly distinctive repertory played on the harp or sometimes the crwth (a form of bowed lyre that bears a close relationship to the English crowd).[4] The term has an obvious parallel with *cerdd dafod* [tongue craft], a sophisticated vernacular strict-meter poetry that was composed orally and declaimed publicly. Both crafts were an intrinsic part of Welsh medieval "high culture" and were patronized by the nobility; both were highly distinctive forms without direct parallel beyond Wales; both were propagated by skilled professional bards who had undergone intensive training and belonged to an exclusive bardic order. But whereas Welsh strict-meter poetry survives in relative quantity, we know less about medieval *cerdd dant*. Just thirty or so pieces, the majority almost certainly conceived during the second half of the fifteenth century, are found in an obscure tablature copied out by Robert ap Huw of Anglesey in ca. 1613.[5] All are intended for solo harp, and most are based on one of the twenty-four *mesurau*—simple "measures" or chordal patterns that echo the twenty-four strict meters of *cerdd dafod*. Many of the *mesurau* have Irish-sounding titles, which has fuelled speculation that aspects of the repertory were born in Ireland (though the absence of musical material from that country leaves this inconclusive). The Welsh pieces themselves mostly feature a variation structure based on related *mesur*-based sections known as *ceinciau* (from *cainc*, here meaning "branch"), and they employ complex patterns of decorative figuration that can only be executed effectively on the medieval harp. The overall effect of the music is not unattractive, though it features a great deal of repetition and a relatively high level of dissonance. A seventeenth-century Englishman, raised on the instrumental fantasia and various types of native song, might perhaps have been forgiven for finding Welsh music of this type "not sweet."

This extant repertory is also supplemented by lengthy inventories of "lost" pieces whose titles were recorded by bardic or antiquarian scribes from at least 1500.[6] Some of these items were named after particular harp techniques; some incorporate the name of an associated master harper; others honor saints or Welsh heroes (see below). Taken as a whole, they suggest that the great flowering of *cerdd dant* came during the later fifteenth century: the style of the extant music is highly consistent, and none of the titles suggests an association after 1500. (No known bardic musician of the sixteenth century seems to have given his name to a composition, even though harp and crwth players certainly continued to play such pieces until at least 1600.) Rather there is a focus on an earlier, often mythological Wales. One of the surviving pieces, "Gosteg yr Halen" [Prelude of the Salt], is followed by a gloss indicating that it used to be played before King Arthur's knights as the salt cellar was placed on the table [yr hwn a feddid yn i ganu o flaen marchogion Arthur pan roid y salter ar halen ar y bwrdd]; another, "Caniad Ystafell" [caniad of the chamber] recalls those occasions when the poet-harpers of the Welsh princes played privately for the queen in her chamber (see below). All four of the gostegion or "preludes" found in Robert ap Huw's book perhaps functioned as prebanqueting pieces in the hall of king or nobleman, while items in other named genres (such as the caniad and cwlwm) may have served as a general accompaniment to dining, as solo interludes between poetic recitations, or simply as more intimate chamber pieces. The range of implied functions was probably typical of the duties required of the medieval harper Europe-wide. Feasts were occasions when harpers came into their own, but many also fulfilled a more intimate role in the chamber: the Franciscan bishop Robert Grosseteste (ca. 1175–1253), for instance, who allegedly "loued moche to here the harpe," accommodated his harper in a chamber next to his study so that "he had solace of notes and layys" both day and night.[7]

Aside from these various solo functions, harp and crwth in medieval Wales also fulfilled another significant role—provision of a simultaneous accompaniment for the poetry itself. Perhaps surprisingly, there is far more evidence for oral performance of "lyric verse" in Wales (if we may indeed apply the term "lyric" to such distinct strict-meter poetry) than there is in England.[8] Whereas a good deal of English medieval verse was surely designed for private reading, Welsh bardic verse was a much more public affair, and there is plentiful evidence that declamation with some form of accompaniment was the norm. The exact nature of this accompaniment remains ambiguous and it may well have changed over time, though it is clear that the harp was the favored instrument. The poet-harpers of the Welsh princes accompanied their own verse, as did the great Dafydd ap Gwilym (fl. 1330–50), whose cywydd "Y Gainc" (in this context "the melody") talks of the simultaneous construction of poem and accompaniment at his harp. Dafydd's poetic successor Gruffudd Fychan ap Gruffudd ab Ednyfed, active in the second half of the fourteenth century, also declared that a poem was as nothing without a harp, and that he himself had earned disgrace by daring to declaim a "cywydd sengl"—a poem without accompaniment [Cenais, pan rygryddais glod, Cywydd sengl, cuddiais anglod].[9] At some point, however, professional reciters [datgeiniaid] seem to have displaced self-accompanying poets, and although they were sometimes viewed with suspicion and castigated for their unreliability, they gradually became an accepted part of the bardic hierarchy. The duties and status of such reciters are discussed at some length in the lengthy bardic tract known as the "Statute of Gruffudd ap Cynan," compiled in ca. 1523.[10]

Provision of a suitable accompaniment, whether it fell to the poet himself or to a professional declaimer, was a delicate matter. Welsh medieval poetry—unlike its English and European counterparts—does not use lyrical song meters; it is counted in syllables rather than feet, lacks a predictable pattern of stresses, and employs a unique ornamental sound system known as *cynghanedd*, a "harmony" that arises from internal correspondences of rhyme, alliteration, and assonance. Any form of accompaniment thus needs to support and enhance the intricate 'verbal music' that results, so that simplicity is a prerequisite. The imagery used in some poems (including that by Dafydd ap Gwilym himself) suggests that one form of accompaniment may have involved constant repetition of a short "tune" (or perhaps simply a metrical pattern) known as a *cainc*. This was apparently a unit of unvarying length based on a very simple *mesur* with a fixed number of "beats," which could then be matched to a regular textual unit (such as the couplet). The beats provided by the instrument (or a stick in more primitive cases) thus formed a stable framework for the poem itself, and an experienced reciter—who probably used heightened speech rather than melody—could use this simple framework to enhance both the natural speech rhythms of the verse and the music intrinsic to it. Several experiments based on this principle have been undertaken recently, using *ceinciau* from Robert ap Huw's book, although the results remain inconclusive.[11]

That self-accompaniment on the harp was the norm in the princely courts of Wales prior to the invasion of Edward I in 1282 is known from the earliest redactions (ca. 1250) of *Cyfraith Hywel*, the Law of Hywel Dda (Hywel ap Cadell, d. 949/950). This makes reference to two distinct types of professional poet-harper, each with a distinct function and repertory.[12] The first was the *pencerdd* or "chief poet" whose harp was equivalent in value to that of the king, and who operated within his own domain outside the confines of the court. The second was the *bardd teulu* or "bard of the retinue" (called *poeta familie* in some of the Latin redactions), one of the twenty-four officials who served within the royal household itself: his lifelong badge of office was a harp given by the king.[13] The *pencerdd* was responsible for overseeing and instructing the lesser *cerddorion* (*joculatores*) within his domain, though he was a regular visitor to the court hall, where he was expected to sing twice, first of God and then of kingship. These items were then followed by "songs of another sort" [*tria carmina de kerd amgan*][14] performed by the resident *bardd teulu*, who was also to sing sotto voce for the queen in a quiet area of the hall if requested to do so. Some redactions of the Law make further reference to a "bard stauell" who performed privately in the queen's chamber,[15] perhaps suggesting that the function of the *bardd teulu* evolved over time. These various performance contexts are probably reflected in the surviving verse itself: R. Geraint Gruffudd has calculated that the extant poetry of the princes divides roughly into 75 percent secular panegyric (including elegy), 20 percent in praise of God and his saints, and just 5 percent in praise of women.[16]

The *bardd teulu* also had one other distinct function (at least up to the twelfth century): he was required to sing for the king's bodyguard both as it went into battle and as the spoils were divided after a raid (when the songs likely recorded individual feats of military prowess). The title of the prebattle song is recorded unvaryingly in the various redactions of the Law as "Unbeiniaeth Prydain" [The Sovereignty of Britain], perhaps synonymous with the great vaticinatory poem of ca. 930 found in the Book of Taliesin, "Armes Prydain" [The Great Prophecy of Britain].[17] This text yearns for a lost Welsh sovereignty, foretelling the reconquest of Britain and the overthrow of the Saxon invaders by a Celtic alliance under the patronage of Saint David. The apparent place of the court harper among (or alongside) the war band is also confirmed in a near-contemporary biography of the prince Gruffudd ap Cynan (d. 1137), which records the loss of Gruffudd's own master harper, Gellan *telynor pencerdd*, at the Battle of Aberlleiniog, Anglesey, who fought against the Normans in 1094.[18] However, battle-harpers were by no means unique to Wales. *Le Roman de Rou* [Rollo], the Anglo-French text of Wace (ca. 1110–71+), includes a vivid account of Taillefer, household minstrel of William, Duke of Normandy, emerging from the ranks on the approach to Hastings to hearten the men by singing of the military heritage of Charlemagne and Roland ("chantant / de Karlemaigne e de Rollant, / e d'Oliver e des vassals / qui morurent de Rencevals") before riding forward to his death.[19] Harpers of a later period seem also to have rallied the troops: all of the lords at the battle of Falkirk in 1298 allegedly had attendant harpers,[20] and some relic of the custom even survived in mid-Tudor Wales. A carved bedstead frieze from Dinefwr, Carmarthenshire—probably commissioned in or soon after 1507, by Henry VII's greatest Welsh ally, Sir Rhys ap Thomas—depicts a harper processing into battle alongside crossbowmen and lancers.[21] It may well have been a commemoration of the great 1507 tournament held at Carew Castle to celebrate the first anniversary of Rhys's admission into the Order of the Garter (an occasion for which "manie new hymnes and anthemes" in honor of King Henry and Saint George were allegedly composed).[22]

The disappearance of Welsh court patronage after the defeat of the Last Prince, Llywelyn ap Gruffudd, in 1282 inevitably caused Anglophobic sentiment to run high in some quarters, not least for its impact on the bards. Sir John Wynn of Gwydir, near Conwy (1553–1627) was even to claim that Edward I had ordered blanket extermination of all Welsh poets and musicians, who were to "be hanged by martial law as stirrers of the people to sedition."[23] (This entirely unproven legend subsequently inspired Thomas Gray's celebrated "Pindaric Ode" of 1754 and a series of related paintings, where Gray's solitary bard, harp in hand, escapes the massacre by hurling himself from a precipice into the River Conwy.) But in reality the situation for professional bards under English occupation was probably much less clear-cut. Though they were indeed forced to forego the security of royal patronage, the land-owning *uchelwyr* that they came to serve were often supporters of the new order imposed by the English themselves. Many of these "high men" were in the service of the English Crown, spoke English, and married English wives, and by the fifteenth century a fair proportion of the families who patronized the bards were of English descent themselves.[24] The sons of Tudur Fychan of Penmynydd in Anglesey, for example, had significant English associations: Gronwy (d. 1382) fought in France, probably for the Black Prince, while both Rhys and Gwilym are thought to have enjoyed a close relationship with Richard II. But at the same time their generosity to the bards was exceptional. The poet Iolo Goch (ca. 1325–98) reports that travelling musicians and minstrels [*cerddorion* and *clerwyr*] who visited the family household were rewarded with "liveries / And splendid chequered cloth / And the best green available" [lifreioedd / A brethynnau brith honnaid / Ac o'r gwyrdd gorau a gaid].[25]

Celebration of the Ancestors in Song

The chief function of Iolo Goch and the other "bards of the nobility" [beirdd yr uchelwyr], like their courtly predecessors, was to provide a steady stream of panegyric, feting the patron's deeds, his generosity, the splendor of his house, his possessions, and above all his ancestry. The bards had long been the recognized keepers of genealogy. Giraldus Cambrensis observed in his *Descriptio Kambriae* (1193) that Welsh poets recited pedigrees from memory and recorded the gene-alogies of the princes in their ancient books,[26] and almost four centuries later the Denbighshire historian David Powel (1552?–98) confirmed that the bards were still greatly esteemed for their keeping of "records of Gentlemens armes and petegrees."[27] Harp (or crwth) remained an essential adjunct to such eulo-gizing, whether at feasts, weddings, or on occasions when elegies [*marwnadau*] were pronounced. The account of the 1507 Carew tournament makes specific reference to harp-song of this kind: the welcoming feast was graced by "bards and *prydydds* accompanied by the harp" who sang "manie a song in commemora-tion of the virtues and famous achievements of those gentleman's ancestors there present."[28]

Public celebration of ancestry was, however, not confined to the nobility. A report entitled "The State of North Wales Touching Religion," apparently compiled somewhere between ca. 1572 and ca. 1598, possibly at the request of William Cecil, Lord Burghley, attacks various Welsh superstitions—among them the large assemblies that would gather outdoors on Sundays and feasts to celebrate the "songes of the doeinges of their Auncestors" and other aspects of their native mythology. Such gatherings may have carried more than a hint of sedition, not least in their celebration of "warrs againste the kinges of this realme and the English nacion":

> Vpon the sondaies and hollidaies the multitude of all sortes of men woomen and Childerne of everie parish doe vse to meete in sondrie places either one some hill or one the side of some mountaine where theire harp-ers and Crowthers singe them songes of the doeinges of theire Auncestors namelie of theire warrs against the kinges of this realme and the English nacion, and then doe they ripp vpp [recite] theire petigres at lenght howe eche of them is discended from those theire ould princes. Here alsoe doe they spend theire time in hearinge some parte of the lives of Thalaassyn Marlin Beno Kybbye Iernin, and suche other the intended Prophettes and Sainctes of that cuntrie.[29]

Some features of this account also have interesting resonance with the *cerdd dant* repertory itself. Recitation of the *vitae* of Saints Beuno, Cybi, and Ernin (all of them local to north Wales)[30] may well have been interwoven with comple-mentary musical items on harp and crwth: the repertory lists contain a number of *caniadau* for saints, including Beuno, Dewi, Gwenfrewi (Winefride), and Padarn.[31] Equally, the two "prophettes," Taliesin and Merlin, belong to an earlier, independent Wales that also finds expression in lost musical *caniadau* addressed to figures such as Llywarch Hwlbwrch, chamberlain to Gruffudd ap Llewelyn (d. 1063), and Rhys ap Tewder, the last ruler of the ancient southern kingdom of Deheubarth (d. 1093). Other pieces even have seditious overtones. Just as Merlin is viewed as a great vaticinatory figure in the political prophecy *Armes Prydein*, the harp repertory sometimes feted Welsh patriots in resolute opposition to English authority. A lost "Caniad y Brenin Lawgoch" is evidently associated with Owain Lawgoch or Owain ap Thomas ap Rhodri (d. 1378). Owain was a figure of continued Welsh resistance to English rule in later vaticinatory poetry: he became the stuff of legend, a sleeper king resting in a cave until the call came to rise and redeem the Welsh people.[32] Association with prophetic recitation seems even to have conditioned the stereotypical English view of the Welsh harper in the mid-sixteenth century. The caricature of the Welshman drawn by the English physician Andrew Borde in *The First Book of the Introduction of Knowledge* (1542) is defined not merely by his intimate attachment to the horsehair-strung harp with which he accompanies himself, but also for his "good pastime / In tellyng of prophyces, whyche be not in ryme."[33]

Border Crossings

What, then, of those Welsh musicians and poets who crossed the border into England? Some evidently found favor. Welsh trumpeters were popular at the court of Edward I, for two such instrumentalists (along with two crwth players and their grooms) received handsome payments to travel from Wales to Westminster for the wedding of Edward's daughters in 1290.[34] Edward II also rewarded six named Welsh trumpeters in 1307/8—Ieuan and Ithel, who apparently operated as a duo, and a "quartet" comprising David ap Rees, Lewelin, Tuder ap Caudel, and Maddok Arlgouth.[35] Several Welsh crwth players are also listed among those who attended the great Pentecost feast held at Westminster to celebrate the knighting of Edward as Prince of Wales in 1306: one of them, "Teguareth le Crouther," was even a part of a favored "inner circle" of minstrels known as "La Comune."[36] Surprisingly, however, there seem to be no Welsh names among the large numbers of harpers who served these two monarchs.

Named Welsh musicians appear but rarely in the later court records, although some Welshmen may be hidden within groups of anonymous household minstrels, and others were surely occasional court visitors. Henry Tudor himself was apparently served by an English harper (James Hides),[37] though two unnamed harpers were brought to court in January 1497 by one of the Welsh gentlemen ushers in the Privy Chamber, Hugh Vaughan, and the 1502 accounts of Margaret Beaufort (mother of the king) record a payment to "a walshe man oon of the kynges mystrels."[38] This individual was perhaps one of three unnamed "stringmynstrelx" cited in the king's accounts, who received regular payments of 100 shillings.[39] Henry VIII also appointed two long-serving "Welsh minstrels" in 1537, Robert Reynoldes and Thomas Glyn:[40] Reynolds was a crwth player, synonymous with the "Robin ap Rheinallt" celebrated in several Welsh poems; his father Rheinallt was also an esteemed crythor, and is mentioned in Dafydd ab Edmwnd's famous lament for the harper Siôn Eos (see below).

One other fascinating court partnership—if such it was—is suggested by a set of Shrewsbury Bailiffs' Accounts from the later 1470s. On two occasions, Guto'r Glyn (fl. ca. 1435–93), the faithful Yorkist poet who served in Edward IV's guard (and according to Gutun Owain wore the king's collar and badge), received a joint payment for working with one "Walter [?Gwallter] harper" in Shrewsbury.[41] Both are described as "minstralles principis." Guto's exact movements at this period are unknown, although his companion is almost certainly the "Walter harper" listed within the accounts of the household of Edward, Prince of Wales (son of Edward IV) in 1479, and the minstrel Walter who subsequently received livery for the coronation of Richard III in 1483.[42] The three-year-old prince had been sent to Ludlow in 1473 to serve as nominal president of his father's newly appointed Council of Wales and the Marches, and a separate household was established for him later that year; its resident harper may well have been recruited from Wales. The visits of Guto and Walter to Shrewsbury were likely occasioned by the presence in that town of the Council, which indeed met there in 1478 to promote "the wele rest [and] tranquillity of the same Towne and for good Rule to be kepte [among] thofficers."[43] Although joint payments to minstrels do not automatically signal concurrent performance,[44] it seems a fair assumption that Walter (or Gwallter) provided some form of musical accompaniment for Guto's poetry that year.

Welsh and English cultures probably coexisted with relative ease in some towns—Guto'r Glyn himself was not only familiar with Shrewsbury, but also its near neighbor Oswestry, which he praised in glowing terms, comparing it with Rome, London, and Canterbury.[45] English- and Welsh-speaking communities seem also to have enjoyed reasonable integration in places like St. Davids, Carmarthen, and Brecon (which for Huw Cae Llwyd was "the Constantinople of Wales"),[46] while at an earlier period, the Marcher courts were probably productive centers for the cross-fertilization of music and poetry. Constance Bullock-Davies has argued for bilingualism and literary exchange in these centers on several counts, envisioning a situation where "French, Welsh and English minstrels lived together in the same castles from the time of the Conquest." She also speculates that Welsh melodies and songs must have been known in the English court as early as the twelfth century, for "common sense and ordinary experience teach us that it is in this way that popular music and song travel."[47]

But cross-border relations were not always warm. Those English musicians who ventured into Wales (or even Welsh musicians with English pretensions) were often treated by the Welsh poets with suspicion, if not downright hostility. An *awdl* (a poem in the traditional meters) by the early fourteenth-century poet Iorwerth Beli provides a scathing description of the English-style musicians and poets who served the Anglophile bishop of Bangor, "Anian Sais" (1309–28): Iorwerth remarks a general tendency for "excellent servants of true poetry" (by implication those of the era of the princes) to go unrewarded, whereas nasty churls like Tudur Wion, who "knows English and has the English accent of a rogue" [Am wybod Saesneg Seisnig dôn—drygwas], are paid handsomely for producing new-fangled poetry and ugly music on objectionable English-style instruments.[48] The instruments cited still include harp and crwth, but in this case it is an uneven willow crwth with broken insides that squeals like piglets, and a harp covered in false wolf skin, with tight strings fashioned from gut.[49] The gut-strung harp receives much fuller condemnation in a *cywydd* by Iolo Goch for its inferiority to the *telyn rawn* [horsehair-strung harp]—the true instrument of bardic tradition.[50] In contrast, the new "leather harp" that now invades Wales— one made for an old Englishman [*Sais hen*]—has disturbingly alien characteristics. Iolo despises it not only for its ugly jaundiced yellow color and bowed front, but also for its hoarse sound, which recalls the sound of geese squabbling over territory [Gwyddau yn dadlau am dir] or young crows wallowing [Cywion brain yn ymgreiniaw].

The undermining of superior indigenous culture and authority by English imposters is also condemned in a famous late fifteenth-century *marwnad* for the master harper Siôn Eos [John Nightingale], hanged by a Chirkland jury for killing a man in a chance mêlée.[51] Its author, Dafydd ab Edmwnd (fl. 1450–97), denounces bitterly "the law of London" [cyfraith Lundain] that has taken away this "nightingale of song," for, under native law, "cyfraith Hywel," Siôn would have been pardoned on payment of compensation. In a series of images drawn from the musical repertory itself, Dafydd grieves for "the man who was father of *cerdd dant*" [Y gŵr oedd dad y gerdd dant], one whose rendition of *gosteg, profiad,* and *caniad* (all genres represented in Robert ap Huw's book) was matched by no other. Siôn's death also occasioned at least one (lost) musical tribute: a "Caniad Marwnad Siôn Eos," whose existence raises interesting questions about the context for musical *marwnadau* and their possible partnership with poetic elegy.

Those who most incurred the wrath of the Welsh bards, however, were the English pipers. In their own right, pipes could be perfectly acceptable: Gerald of Wales cites them as one of the three traditional instruments of Wales (together with harp and crwth) in his *Descriptio Kambriae*,[52] and both pipes and bagpipes are acknowledged (together with organ) as the three instruments of "wind craft" [*cerdd fegin*] in a set of bardic triads attached to an early redaction of the bardic grammar (Aberystwyth, National Library of Wales MS Peniarth 20, copied ca. 1330). Iolo Goch also celebrated the sound of the pipes (or bagpipes) and their potential for accompanying dancing in two eulogies: a *cywydd* addressed to Syr Hywel y Fwyall [Hywel of the Axe], constable of Cricieth, delights in the "lively music of pipes / and bag, and fine-looking men / enjoying dance and carol" [A cherdd chwibenygl a chod / Gorhoenus, a gwŷr hynod / Yn chwarae dawns a charawl], while a second poem feting the court of Ieuan, bishop of St. Asaph, notes that guests were fortunate to "have pipes and dance every day" [Pibau, dawns, a gawn pob dydd].[53] A very different stance is nevertheless taken in a fifteenth-century satire on the bagpiper who plays at an English wedding in Flint (the first of Edward I's plantation towns and still regarded as English at this period).[54] The poet is humiliated by having his own *awdl* cut short: the English audience laughs at him and chatters of other things—peas and manure—while clamoring for "Wiliam Bibydd." Wiliam duly appears with his "sad bag, gut-stuffed belly, / A stick betwixt arm and breast" [Â chod leddf, fol berfeddfaich, / Wrth ffon rhwng ei fron a'i fraich] and the pipes respond with "a wasp's buzzing" [llais cacynen], like "an old goose butchered...a thousand cat's tendons / Unwanted goat with one note..." [Gwaedd hunlle'n lladd gŵydd henllom /...Mal gwythi mil o gathod / Gafr un llais, heb gyfran llog].[55] A century later the poet Lewis Dwnn (fl. 1568–1616) similarly mocked the "foul-voiced Englishman who rolls around Britain" [Sais dryglais a dreiglo Prydain] for turning away highly honored poets from his cold table while insisting on "his beloved piper," while for Lewis ap Siôn ap Sienkyn the piper was the "bogeyman of little boys / With filthy cheeks and jowls" [bibydd di-bibydd bwbach y bechgin / a bochgern / gern afiach].[56] Castigation of English musicians became even more generalized for the itinerant Merioneth poet Siôn Mawddwy (fl. 1575–1613), who visited a fair in an unnamed shire town while the Court of the Great Sessions [Sesiwn Mawr] was in residence.[57] He satirizes not only the ugly sounds of the English language, with its "this that which what when," but also a whole parade of musical instruments and their players—lute, tabor, "dungpipe" [bawbib], bagpipes, bandor[a], and viol, which growls out a persistent "bwm, bwm, bwm."

The Welsh insistence on revering and preserving their own "superior" culture finds interesting expression in a list of "pedair kamp ar hugain," the "twenty-four feats" required of the late medieval Welsh gentleman. First mentioned in a poem by Lewys Glyn Cothi (ca. 1420–89),[58] the feats all embody traditional values: it is no accident that they were copied into various manuscript collections from ca. 1500 onward that collate specialized bardic lore (including cerdd dant repertory lists and extracts from poetic and musical grammars). Five main groups of skills are defined, beginning with the six feats of physical strength (weights, running, leaping, swimming, wrestling, riding), the four strengths with weapons (archery, fencing with sword and buckler, fencing with two-handed sword, using the quarter-staff), the three feats of hunting (hunting with greyhounds, fishing, hawking), and the seven "household" feats or camp deuluaidd. The last group draws directly on bardic practice, comprising composition of poetry [barddoniaeth], play-ing the harp [canu telyn], reading Welsh [darllain cymraeg], singing a cywydd to a string instrument [canu cywydd gan dant], the more recent practice of singing a cywydd pedwar to a tune [canu cywydd pedwar, ac accenu],[59] and two related genea-logical feats—drawing coats of arms [tynnu arfau] and general heraldic knowledge [herodraeth]. The four "lesser feats" or gogampau that complete the list also have bardic overtones. They comprise three types of game—gwyddbwyll ("wood-sense," mentioned three times in the cycle of tales known as the Mabinogi), tawlbwrdd (a board game cited in Cyfraith Hywel) and dicing—together with tuning the harp [cyweirio telyn]. This last feat also resonates with native Law: the three "legal" harps of king, pencerdd and nobleman all came with their own cyweirgorn or "tun-ing horn," in itself an emblem of status and skill. Seen as a whole, this entire portfolio of feats seems to encapsulate the bardic view of the ideal patron: one who displays heroism and physical prowess, but who also has an enthusiasm for his native culture and is a distinguished amateur poet and musician.

The catalogue of Welsh feats serves as an interesting foil to another gentle-manly "syllabus" of similar date—one devised for the henchmen of Edward IV, which survives among the general household reforms of ca. 1471–72 in the Liber Niger. Although the gentle "curtsey" embodied here still has an old-fashioned quality, some of the required accomplishments are worlds away from their Welsh counterpart. The master of the henchmen is charged "to shew the schooles of urbanitie and nourture of Englond, to lerne them to ryde clenely and surely [jousting, harness, "curtesy, "rules of goynges and sittinges"]. Moreover to teche them sundry languages, and otyr lerninges virtuous, to harping, to pype, sing, daunce...with remembraunce dayly of Goddes service accustumed."[60] A Welsh gentleman of the late fifteenth century would surely have recognized "nurture of [one's country]," jousting, harping and "Goddes service," but mastery of foreign languages and courtly dancing were emphasized only from the later sixteenth century, when it became the norm for the sons of the Welsh nobility to cross the border to acquire their education.

The Status and Function of the Welsh and English Musician Compared

Leaving aside these fundamental distinctions of ethos and repertory for a moment, are there any indications of common ground between the status and function of harpers and poet-harpers in Wales and England? The harp evidently reigned supreme in Wales throughout the medieval period—the crwth never achieving quite the same emphasis—but what of its status in England? Its versatility certainly offered many advantages—it is the instrument most commonly associated with the musically literate, and its potential for both melody and harmony must have rendered it invaluable to the medieval composer. Richard Rastall has also speculated that its popularity at the English court may have arisen from its suitability for accompanying *gestes*, those lengthy narrative romances sung in either English or French that generally record heroic deeds.[61] But there are also some fundamental distinctions of usage to be noted. First, the harp was beginning to decline in England (at least in court circles) by 1480, at the very period when composition of Welsh *cerdd dant* was apparently at its height; second, the Welsh favored a rather different sort of harp from the English, with horsehair strings remaining the norm; third, it is impossible to identify any form of repertory specific to the harp in England before the seventeenth century; and fourth, harpers in England were often classified in very general terms as "minstrels," irrespective of their status. There was no real English counterpart to the elevated bardic harper of medieval Wales, where the term "minstrel" was generally used in a very different way. Welsh minstrels (often termed *y glêr*) certainly existed, but they were mostly common entertainers who pedaled a lesser repertory and moved within a different social order from the bards themselves.[62]

But there were also some striking parallels. A number of English harpers—at least those fortunate enough to find employment at court or in the houses of magnates and prelates—must have enjoyed comparable status to the best of the Welsh bardic musicians, and Richard Rastall has shown that harpers were more highly favored than other liveried musicians (with the possible exception of trumpeters).[63] From the reign of Edward III, when the administration of court minstrels became more specialized and a single harper became the norm within the king's household, the appointment often carried special responsibility: harpers appear making payments, exchanging horses, or delivering letters. Equally, any single minstrel accompanying a man of rank was generally a harper.[64]

English and Welsh harpers must also have shared more general musical functions. We have already noted their presence on the battle field, at feasts and in the chamber, and in the English pay rolls they are also found in the sickroom and at the shrine: one harper received 20 shillings for playing as Edward I had his blood let, while another was paid for playing before the tomb of Saint Richard in Chichester, and another played as the king made his offering at St. Augustine's, Canterbury.[65] Like their Welsh counterparts, many of these individuals surely sang or recited, as well as playing. Explicit evidence is limited, but John, Lord Howard (Duke of Norfolk from 1483), arranged in October 1481 that the London harper William Wastell should take the son of John Colet, harper of Colchester, "to teach him to harp and to sing,"[66] and in 1304/5, Edward, Prince of Wales, son of Edward I, made special arrangements with the abbot of Shrewsbury for his "rymour" Richard to learn "la menestralcie de Crouther," presumably with a view to accompanying himself. The prince had heard that the abbot had "vn bon Croutheour" (perhaps a Welshman?), and asked that Richard be permitted to stay at the abbey until he was proficient on that instrument.[67]

Just *what* was played by such instrumentalists in England, as emphasized above, nevertheless remains ambiguous. For all the complexity of interpreting the exact nature of the musico-poetic partnership in medieval Wales, we can at least be certain that harpers did indeed accompany early strict-meter poetry in some manner, just as we know that some part of an idiomatic Welsh harp repertory for solo harp survives in Robert ap Huw's problematic tablature. But in England the boundaries are much more difficult to draw. Such instrumental music as survives in written form is often highly mobile: some pieces occur in several different adaptations for different instruments, while others are intabulations of vocal items. The English harper likely had a wide instrumental repertory, but there is no evidence that any of it was conceived specifically for harp in the manner of Welsh *cerdd dant*. At a more general level, there was also less sense of instrumental integrity—a much wider range of instruments was used to accompany verse in England, with Chaucer himself mentioning singers who accompany themselves on rebec, gittern, and psaltery.[68] In Wales, however, that standard "trio" of harp, crwth, and pipes remained dominant throughout the Middle Ages, with harp and crwth as the only acknowledged instruments of bardic accompaniment.

The nature of minstrel-song itself also raises questions beyond the Welsh border. Andrew Taylor speculates that it was probably diverse, embracing songs of praise and blame, satire and victory, elegies, short *lais*—and up to at least the fourteenth century, extended narrative *gestes*. The repertory must also have called for fluency in both English and French, for the latter was the first language of all of England's rulers from the conquest to Henry IV (1366–1413).[69] The Middle English romances (such as *King Horn* or *Sir Orfeo*) now survive mostly as literary texts, but at least some of them probably originated as oral compositions performed by self-accompanying minstrels. Though explicit terms such as "rhymer" or *gestour* are very rare in the pay records, a *joculator* called Herebert is known to have performed two narratives in the prior's hall at St. Swithun's, Winchester in 1338—the first a song [*canticum*] of Colbrond (apparently the legend of Guy, earl of Warwick, who defeated a Danish giant); the second a *geste* of Queen Emma (mother of Edward the Confessor), who was "freed from the ordeal by fire."[70] This in itself suggests another important cross-border distinction: the Middle English romance was a highly significant genre in England, but there is no comparable tradition of narrative verse in Middle Welsh. Storytelling was important in Wales and fragments of oral stories survive, but they were generally associated with a lower grade of poet than the professional bard.[71] The magician-poet Gwydion, one of the main characters in the last of the Four Branches of the *Mabinogi*, is shown entertaining the court of another king with after-dinner stories, but the context makes clear that tale-telling was not the usual function of a master-poet.

Poet-harpers on both sides of the border nevertheless seem to have been united in delivering another type of song on occasion—that of abuse. Thomas Malory's minstrel Elyas, for instance, is sent by Sir Dynadan to sing a lay "whyche spake the most vylany by Kinge Marke and of his treson that ever man herde," and Taylor speculates that extant fragments of this type probably reflect what was once "a stream of discourse."[72] Wales itself, of course, had a strong tradition of bardic "flyting," although vicious satire and vituperation were primarily the specialty of those lesser poet-minstrels, *y glêr*. Most of their material remained unwritten, although the rhymesters themselves are occasionally derided in the great poetic compendium known as the Red Book of Hergest (copied 1382 x 1410). The satirical harpist Darre, whose "dinner would fill Carmarthen Castle" [lloneit kaer vyrdin oed yginyaw] is censured by Y Prydydd Breuan for both his gluttony and general moral depravity,[73] while Hywel Ystorm ridicules a base poet-crythor as "athro cler" [teacher of the clêr], whose mouth is "a pit of mocking verse" [ryw bydew kerd wattwar].[74] Such lesser poetasters—who wandered the country competing for the same rewards as the professional bards themselves—became the subject of stringent legislation in Wales, just as comparable statutes were passed to regulate minstrel traffic in England and protect the livelihood of the liveried musician.[75]

The real mainstay of Welsh tradition, however, was that elevated panegyric that sustained the bardic livelihood; that celebration of ancestry that enabled nobleman and commoner alike to retain a superior sense of heritage and native mythology, and in some cases an optimism that the Welsh might yet be delivered from English oppression. Long after English music became fashionable among late sixteenth-century Welsh gentlemen (confirmed in part by their purchase of lutes and viols and hire of English music tutors), the bards remained welcome at the noble houses. John Salusbury (ca. 1566–1612) of Lleweni in Denbughshire, the Welsh-speaking poet-courtier who penned English sonnets, consistently patronized native poets and musicians, while as late as 1654, two Welsh poets and a harper were paid for performing *cywyddau* for the Middleton family of Chirk Castle near Wrexham.[76]

Direct association between the native Welsh secular tradition and its English counterpart was surely limited by the end of the sixteenth century, yet harp and crwth were still to be found accompanying certain types of English verse. The writer and critic George Puttenham (1529–90/91) claimed in *The Arte of English Poesie* (1589) to have "written for pleasure a litle brief Romance or historicall

ditty in the English tong of the Isle of great Britaine in short and long meetres,"
which, he remarked, was to be

> ...commodiously song to the harpe in places of assembly, where the company
> shalbe desirous to heare of old aduentures & valiaunces of noble knights in
> times past, as are those of king Arthur and his knights of the round table,
> Sir Beuys of Southampton, Guy of Warwicke and others like.[77]

Strange, indeed, to find here faint English echoes of those "meatinges" held on
the Welsh hillsides in Puttenham's own lifetime. But we should also not assume
that all Welshmen would necessarily have favored such activities. The antiquary
and map maker Humphrey Llwyd (1527–68) was far keener to vaunt the cultural and professional advances made in his country since the coming of the
Tudors than to dwell on certain aspects of an earlier culture—and in his view
the dependence of the Welsh harper on oral tradition was by now tantamount to
illiteracy. His short historical and geographical description of Britain, written in
1568 (and subsequently translated by Thomas Twyne as *The Breviary of Britayne*
in 1573) expresses relief that the new Tudor Wales nowadays contains "but few
of the ruder sorte, which cannot reade, and write their own name, and play on
the Harpe after their own maner."[78]

But perhaps the last word may go to the poet-courtier Sir Philip Sidney
(1554–86), who famously admitted in his "Defence of Poetry" (1582–83?) to being
moved by the crwth—an instrument that might well have epitomized musical
"clownishness" for that anonymous seventeenth-century English balladeer: "I
never heard the old Song of Percy and Duglas, that I founde not my heart moved
more than with a Trumpet; and yet it is sung but by some blinde Crowder, with
no rougher voice, then rude stile."[79] Sidney also proclaimed in this same work a
heartfelt admiration for the longevity of Welsh bardic practice (an admiration that
surely embraced the role of the harper as well as the poet). "In Wales, the true remnant of the ancient Britons...they had poets which they called bards, so through
all the conquests of Romans, Saxons, Danes, and Normans, some of whom did
seek to ruin all memory of learning from among them, yet do their poets even
to this day last; so as it is not more notable in soon beginning, than in long
continuing." How fitting that this archetypal Elizabethan courtier should have
expressed genuine respect for that "long continuing" bardic tradition: a tradition
that had survived against the odds, and was still defined and sustained not only by
its reverence for a glorious Welsh past, but also by the poets and musicians who
joined forces "to singe [the] songes of the doeinges of their Auncestors."

Notes

I am very grateful to Professor Richard Rastall for commenting most helpfully
on a draft version of this chapter.

1. "A New Song of the Wooing of Queene Katherine, by a Gallant Yong
   Gentleman of Wales Named Owen Tudor: Lately Translated Out of

Welch into Our English Phrase. To the Tune of Light in Love Ladies," in *The Golden Garland of Princely Pleasures and Delicate Delights*, ed. Richard Johnson, 3rd edn. (London: By A. M[athewes] for Thomas Langley, and are to be sold at his shop ouer against the Sarazens Head without Newgate, 1620 [STC 14674]), A6. The ballad was probably inspired by Shakespeare's courtship scene between Catherine and Henry at the end of *Henry V.* See also Michael Drayton, "Owen Tudor to Queen Katherine," *Englands Heroicall Epistles* (London: printed by I[ames] R[oberts] for N. Ling, and are to be sold at his shop at the vvest doore of Poules, 1597 [STC 7193]), and Hugh Holland, *Pancharis the First Booke. Containing the Preparation of the Loue betweene Ovven Tudyr, and the Queene, Long since Intended to Her Maiden Maiestie* (London: By V. S[immes] for Clement Knight, M D CIII, 1603 [STC 13592]).

2. See, for instance, Sally Harper, "So How Many Irishmen Went to Glyn Achlach? Early Accounts of the Formation of *cerdd dant*," *Cambrian Medieval Celtic Studies* 42 (2001): 1–25.

3. Fuller discussion of Welsh music in its cultural context appears in Sally Harper, *Music in Welsh Culture before 1650: A Study of the Principal Sources* (Aldershot: Ashgate, 2007). This also explores the much closer relationship between England and Wales where music for the liturgy is concerned—see especially Chap. 11, "Shaping a New Liturgy: The Adoption of Sarum Use in Wales."

4. Mary Remnant, *English Bowed Instruments from Anglo-Saxon to Tudor Times* (Oxford: Clarendon Press, 1986), Chap. 4, "The Crowd."

5. Robert ap Huw's manuscript survives as London, British Library MS Add. 14905. Two facsimiles are available: Henry Lewis, ed., *Musica: British Museum Additional Manuscript 14905* (Cardiff: University of Wales Press, 1936), and Wyn Thomas, ed., *Musica: Llawysgrif Robert ap Huw* (Godstone: Scolar Press, 1982).

6. Key sources are collated in Bethan Miles, "Swyddogaeth a Chelfyddyd y Crythor," 2 vols. (M.A. diss., University of Wales, 1983), vol. 2; see also David Klausner, ed., *Records of Early Drama: Wales*, Records of Early English Drama 18 (Toronto: University of Toronto Press, 2005), 159–81 (trans. 349–68); 273–86 (trans. 390–95).

7. *Robert Mannyng of Brunne, Handlynge Synne* (1303), ed. F. J. Furnivall, EETS os 119 (London: Trübner, 1901), 158.

8. One of the most enlightening discussions of early English song remains John Stevens, *Music and Poetry in the Early Tudor Court* (Cambridge: Cambridge University Press, 1961).

9. *Gwaith Sefnyn, Rhisierdyn, Gruffudd Fychan ap Gruffudd ab Ednyfed a Llywarch Bentwrch*, ed. N. A. Jones and E. H. Rheinallt (Aberystwyth: University of Wales Centre for Advanced Welsh and Celtic Studies, 1995); 11, cited Patrick K. Ford, "Performance and Literacy in Medieval Welsh Poetry," *The Modern Language Review* 100 (2005): xxxvii.

10. Two versions of the Statute, together with various other associated documents, are given in Klausner, ed., *Records: Wales*, 159–83 (trans. 349–70)

11. For fuller exploration of this question, see Sally Harper, "Dafydd ap Gwilym, poet and musician," in *Gwaith Dafydd ap Gwilym*, ed. Dafydd Johnston (Published Online, University of Wales, Swansea, http://www.dafyddapgwilym.net). The site also features video recordings of experimental declamations.

12. Relevant extracts from several different redactions of the law are given in Klausner, ed., *Records: Wales*, 4–7 and 11–28 (trans. 310–11 and 314–26); see also Dafydd Jenkins, ed. and trans., *The Law of Hywel Dda: Law Texts from Medieval Wales*, The Welsh Classics 2 (Llandysul: Gomer Press, 1986).

13. For fuller reference, see Dafydd Jenkins, "*Bardd Teulu* and *Pencerdd*," in *The Welsh King and His Court*, ed. Thomas Charles-Edwards, Morfydd E. Owen, and Paul Russell (Cardiff, University of Wales Press, 2000), 142–66.

14. Klausner, ed., *Records: Wales*, 12, 316.

15. Klausner, ed., *Records: Wales*, 13–14, 317–18.

16. See R. Geraint Gruffydd, "Gogynfeirdd," *Oxford Dictionary of National Biography*.

17. Rachel Bromwich, "Review of *A Guide to Welsh Literature Volume 1*," *Llên Cymru* 13: 4 (1981): 298–301, at 300. See also Gruffydd Aled Williams, "The Bardic Road to Bosworth: A Welsh View of Henry Tudor," *Transactions of the Honourable Society of Cymmrodorion* (1986): 7–31.

18. "Ac ena y diguydus Gellan telynyaur penkerd o barthret Gruffud en e llynges" [then fell Gellan harpist and chief poet on the side of Gruffudd in the fleet], in *A Medieval Prince of Wales: The Life of Gruffudd ap Cynan*, ed. D. Simon Evans (Felinfach: Llanerch Press, 1990), 42 (trans. 73).

19. See Andrew Taylor, "Fragmentation, Corruption, and Minstrel Narration: The Question of the Middle English Romances," *The Yearbook of English Studies* 22 (1992): 38–62, at 34.

20. Cited John Southworth, *The English Medieval Minstrel* (Woodbridge, Suffolk: Boydell and Brewer, 1989), 88.

21. See Peter Lord, *The Visual Culture of Wales: Medieval Wales* (Cardiff: University of Wales Press, 2003), 268 for reproduction.

22. See Harper, *Music in Welsh Culture*, 281–82. The account of the tournament is part of the Life of Sir Rhys ap Thomas (ca. 1449–1525), written by his direct descendant Henry Rice (ca. 1590–1651). See Klausner, ed., *Records: Wales*, 256–67; also Ralph A. Griffiths, *Sir Rhys ap Thomas and His Family: A Study in the Wars of the Roses and Early Tudor Politics* (Cardiff: University of Wales Press, 1993), 245–58.

23. Sir John Wynn, *The History of the Gwydir Family and Memoirs*, ed. J. Gwynfor Jones (Llandysul: Gomer Press, 1990), 24.

24. Dafydd Johnston, "Cywyddwyr," *Oxford Dictionary of National Biography*.

25. "Marwnad Meibion Tudur Fychan," poem 6 in Dafydd Johnston, ed., *Iolo Goch: Poems* (Llandysul: Gomer Press, 1993). Robes of the king's livery were also given to the "minstrels of Wales de Radyngges" serving within the French household of the Black Prince at Eastertide (10–12 Edward III): see Richard Rastall, "Secular Musicians in Late Medieval England," 2 vols. (Ph.D. diss., Manchester, 1968), 1: 26.

26. "You have to bear in mind that the Welsh bards, singers and jongleurs kept accurate copies of the genealogies of these princes in their old manuscripts, which were, of course, written in Welsh. They would also recite them from memory, going back from Rhodri Mawr to the time of the Blessed Virgin Mary...," *Descriptio Kambriae*, in *Giraldi Cambrensis Opera*, ed. J. F. Dimock. 8 vols. (London: Rolls Series, 1861–91), 7: 167, L. Thorpe, trans., *The Description of Wales* (London: Penguin, 1978), 223.

27. David Powel, *The Historie of Cambria, Now Called Wales, etc.* (London: Rafe Newberie and Henrie Denham, 1584 [STC 4606]); facsimile edn. in *The English Experience, its record in early printed books published in facsimile* 163 (Amsterdam: Theatrum Orbis Terrarum; New York: Da Capo Press, 1969), 191–92.

28. Klausner, ed., *Records: Wales*, 256–67. It should be acknowledged, however, that eulogizing of ancestry seems even to have occurred in England: Andrew Taylor notes that two mid-sixteenth-century ballads, "The Hunting of the Cheviot" and "The Lords of the North Country"—associated with the Tamworth harper Richard Sheale—celebrate those who fought against the Scots in the border territories; the second text flatters two contemporary northern magnates by juxtaposing their names with those of champions from an earlier era. See Andrew Taylor, "Songs of Praise and Blame and the Repertoire of the *Gestour*," in *The Entertainer in Medieval and Traditional Culture*, ed. Flemming Andersen, Thomas Pettitt, and Rheinhold Schröder (Odense: Odense University Press, 1997), 47–72, at 69–72.

29. London, British Library MS Lansdowne 111, fols. 10r, 10v, transcribed in Klausner, ed., *Records: Wales*, 29.

30. Ernin was allegedly a sixth-century monk of Bardsey who went to Brittany: see Terry D. Breverton, *The Book of Welsh Saints* (St. Tathan: Glyndŵr Publishing, 2000), 241, who cites an extinct chapel of Llanhernin near Llanegwad in Caernarfonshire.

31. For further comment on the repertory lists, see Sally Harper, "Issues in Dating the Repertory of *Cerdd Dant*," *Studia Celtica* 35 (2001): 325–40.

32. Anthony Carr, "Owen of Wales," *Oxford Dictionary of National Biography*.

33. *Andrew Borde's Introduction of Knowledge and Dyetary of Health*, ed. F. J. Furnivall, EETS ES 10 (London: Trübner, 1906), 126.

34. Constance Bullock-Davies, *Register of Royal and Baronial Domestic Minstrels 1272–1327* (Woodbridge, Suffolk: Boydell and Brewer, 1986), 217.

35. Bullock-Davies, *Register of Minstrels*, 39, 98, 107, 211, 226.

36. Constance Bullock-Davies, *Menestrellorum Multitudo: Minstrels at a Royal Feast* (Cardiff: University of Wales Press, 1978), 50.

37. A payment for a case for James Hides' harp was made on 8 May 1492: see *Records of English Court Music*, calendared and edited by Andrew Ashbee (9 vols.), vol. 7 (Aldershot: Scolar Press; Brookfield, Vt.: Ashgate, 1993), 151; also Fiona Kisby, "Royal Minstrels in the City

and Suburbs of Early Tudor London: Professional Activities and Private Interests," *Early Music* 25 (1997): 199–219, at 205.

38. Ashbee, *Records of English Court Music*, 8: 1

39. Ashbee, *Records of English Court Music*, 7: 153–70; also Rastall, "Secular Musicians," 2: 133.

40. Ashbee, *Records of English Court Music*, 7: 269; also *A Biographical Dictionary of English Court Musicians 1485–1714*, 2 vols., ed. Andrew Ashbee and David Lasocki (Aldershot: Ashgate, 1998), 1: 486 (Glynn); 2: 954 (Reynolds).

41. Shrewsbury Bailiffs' Accounts, 1474–75 (6s. 8d.) and 1477–78 (3s. 4d.). Alan Somerset, ed., *Records of Early English Drama: Shropshire* (Toronto: Toronto University Press, 1994), 1: 150, 152–53; 2: 580–82. Gutun Owain's elegy for Guto recalls "Dwyn coler gwychder y gard / A nod y brenin Edward," poem 124 in *Gwaith Guto'r Glyn*, ed. Ifor Williams (Cardiff: University of Wales Press, 1939). Guto is also the author of a *cywydd* to "Wiliam Talbot ap John Talbot ap Richard Talbot" of Shrewsbury (poem 28).

42. Richard Rastall, "The Minstrels of the Royal Households, 25 Edward I: 1 Henry VIII: An Inventory," *Royal Music Association Research Chronicle* 4 (1964): 1–41, at 33–34; H. C. de Lafontaine, *The King's Musick: A Transcript of Records Relating to Music and Musicians (1460–1700)* (London: Novello, 1909), 1.

43. Penry Williams, *The Council in the Marches of Wales under Elizabeth I* (Cardiff: University of Wales Press, 1958), 7–9.

44. Richard Rastall, "Some English Consort-Groupings of the Late Middle Ages," *Music and Letters* 55 (1974): 179–202, at 180.

45. "Canmol Croesoswallt," in Williams, ed., *Gwaith Guto'r Glyn*, poem 69.

46. Ralph A. Griffiths, "Wales and the Marches," in *The Cambridge Urban History of Britain, I: 600–1540*, ed. D. M. Palliser (Cambridge: Cambridge University Press, 2000), 681–714.

47. Bullock-Davies, "Welsh Minstrels," 121.

48. Iorwerth Beli, "Cwyn yn erbyn esgob Bangor," in *Gwaith Gruffudd ap Dafydd ap Tudur, Gwilym Ddu o Arfon, Trahaearn Brydydd Mawr ac Iorwerth Beli*, ed. N. G. Costigan (Bosco), R. Iestyn Daniel, and Dafydd Johnston (Aberystwyth: University of Wales Centre for Advanced Welsh and Celtic Studies, 1995), 149–69, at 151.

49. Nid ef a berchid berchyllson—debig / Grwth helig terrrig, tor goluddion. /...Agarw oedd glybod eigion—telynau / O gau wisg fleiddiau, tannau tynion [There was no respect for the uneven willow crwth / Like the sound of piglets, with its insides broken /...It was horrible to hear the entrails of harps / Of false wolf skin, tight strings].

50. Johnston, ed., *Iolo Goch: Poems*, 130–32.

51. "Marwnad Siôn Eos, Poem 75," *The Oxford Book of Welsh Verse*, ed. Thomas Parry (Oxford: Clarendon Press, 1962); loose translation in Joseph P. Clancy, *Medieval Welsh Lyrics* (London, New York: St. Martin's Press, 1965), 229–31.

52. *Descriptio Kambriae*, in *Giraldus Cambrensis Opera*, ed. J. S. Brewer, James F. Dimock, and G. F. Warner, 8 vols., RS 21 (1861–91), 6: 183; L. Thorpe, trans. *The Description of Wales* (London: Penguin, 1978), 223.

53. Johnston, ed., *Iolo Goch: Poems*, poems 2, 70.

54. Helen Fulton, "Trading Places: Representations of Urban Culture in Medieval Welsh Poetry," *Studia Celtica* 31 (1997): 219–30 [225–26]; D. J. Bowen, *Barddoniaeth yr Uchelwyr* (Cardiff: University of Wales Press, 1959), poem 23.

55. Bowen, *Barddoniaeth yr Uchelwyr*, 57; free translation in Clancy, *Medieval Welsh Lyrics*, 166–68.

56. Three poems, including the two cited here, were copied by John Jones of Gellilyfdy into NLW MS Peniarth 313 under the heading "Yr Ofergerddorion" [The Wastrel Musicians]. See D. J. Bowen, "Detholiad o Englynion," *Bulletin of the Board of Celtic Studies* 15 (1954): 186–87; also Richard Suggett, "Vagabonds and Minstrels in Sixteenth-Century Wales," in *The Spoken Word: Oral Culture in Britain, 1500–1850*, ed. Adam Fox and Daniel Woolf (Manchester: Manchester University Press; New York: Palgrave, 2002), 138–72, at 161.

57. A version of the text appears in T. Gwynn Jones, *Llên Cymru: Detholiad o Ryddiaith a Phrydyddiaeth* (Aberystwyth: Cambrian News, 1926), 3: 67–68.

58. "Dug bedair camp ar hugain / hyddgarw hir a ddygai'r rhain": "Moliant Wiliam ap Tomas Fychan," in Dafydd Johnston, ed., *Gwaith Lewys Glyn Cothi* (Cardiff: University of Wales Press, 1995), 119–20. See also Thomas ap Ieuan Madog, "Marwnad Siôn Stradling," in *Hen Gwndidau, Carolau a Chywyddau being Sermons in Song*, ed. Hopcyn and Cadrawd (Lemuel J. Hopkin James and T. C. Evans of Llangynwyd) (Bangor: Jarvis and Foster, 1910), 53–55. Brief comment is also given by Glanmor Williams, "Glamorgan Society 1536–1642," *Glamorgan County History* 4: 136–37. The earliest list appears in NLW MS Peniarth 56 (ca. 1500), 28: "Pedair kamp arugain y sydd ardeniodd dyfnwal moel mud yn yvort gron i pwy bynag a vyno goruhaviayth." These were reproduced in facsimile in *Dr John Davies Mallwyd, Antiquae linguae britannicae et linguae latinae, dictionarium duplex, 1632,* English Linguistics 1500–1800, 99 (Menston: Scolar Press, 1968) and (with loose translation) in Edward Jones, *Musical and Poetical Relicks of the Welsh Bards* (London: Printed for the Author, 1784; repr. London: Morley, 1985), 18.

59. For discussion of this particular feat, see Daniel Huws, "Dressing Women in Tunes," in *Bearers of Song: Essays in Honour of Phyllis Kinney and Meredydd Evans*, ed. Sally Harper and Wyn Thomas (Cardiff: University of Wales Press, 2007), 180–88, at 184–85.

60. A. R. Myers, *The Household of Edward IV: The Black Book and the Ordinances of 1478* (Manchester: Manchester University Press, 1959), 126–27; see also Stevens, *Music and Poetry*, 273.

61. Rastall, "Secular Musicians," 1: 167; Richard Rastall, "Some English Consort-Groupings of the Late Middle Ages," *Music and Letters* 55 (1974): 179–202 at 184–85; also Taylor, "Fragmentation, Corruption, and Minstrel Narration," 49.

62. For a valuable exploration of *y glêr*, see Huw M. Edwards, *Dafydd ap Gwilym: Influences and Analogues*, Oxford Modern Languages and Literature Monographs (Oxford: Clarendon Press, 1996), 1–37.

63. Rastall, "Secular Musicians," 1: 145.

64. Rastall, "Secular Musicians," 1: 145, 164.

65. Rastall, "Secular Musicians," 2: 17, 114.

66. Rastall, "Secular Musicians," 2: 159. Wastell was to receive 13s. 4d. as a payment of good faith, followed by a gown and an additional 6s. 8d. at the end of the year.

67. Letter from Edward, Prince of Wales, to the Abbot of Shrewsbury: PRO E 163/5/2 mb 14, transcr. *Records of Early English Drama: Shropshire*, 2 vols., ed. J. Alan B. Somerset (Toronto: University of Toronto Press, 1994), 126, 562.

68. Rastall, "Secular Musicians," 1: 166.

69. For fuller discussion, see Andrew Taylor, "Songs of Praise and Blame," 47–72, at 61–62.

70. Cited Taylor, "Songs of Praise and Blame," 49.

71. See Brynley F. Roberts, "Oral Tradition and Welsh Literature: A Description and Survey," *Oral Tradition* 3 (1988): 61–87, at 63.

72. *Malory Works*, ed. Eugene Vinaver, 2nd edn. (Oxford: Clarendon Press, 1971), 626; cited Taylor, "Songs of Praise and Blame," 67.

73. Cited Edwards, *ap Gwilym: Influences and Analogues*, 44, 56.

74. Edwards, *ap Gwilym: Influences and Analogues*, 44–45.

75. For a valuable study of the later legislation and its impact, see Suggett, "Vagabonds and Minstrels" (n. 56).

76. Klauser, ed., *Records: Wales*, 151.

77. See George Puttenham, *The Arte of English Poesie*, ed. G. Gregory Smith, Elizabethan Critical Essays 2 (London: Oxford University Press, 1959), 43–44.

78. See *The History of Great Britain, from the First Inhabitants Thereof, Till the Death of Cadwalader, Last King of the Britains, etc. . . . To Which Is Added, the Breviary of Britayne, Written in Latin by H. Lhuyd, . . . Englished by T. Twine. L. P.* (London: F. Giles, 1729).

79. Philip Sidney, "A Defence of Poetry," in *Miscellaneous Prose of Sir Philip Sidney*, ed. Katherine Duncan-Jones and Jan van Dorsten (Oxford: Clarendon Press, 1973).

CHAPTER 13

WILLIAM SALESBURY AND WELSH
PRINTING IN LONDON BEFORE 1557

Geraint Evans

William Salesbury is one of the most celebrated figures in Welsh history. He was, as R. Brinley Jones has said, "the outstanding example of the Welsh Renaissance scholar" whose "genius for matching the new with the old" allowed him to straddle the eras of manuscript and print and help to create a modern, standard, national language for Wales, as Luther had done for Germany.[1] Yet Salesbury's most significant connection as a scholarly pioneer in the new world of print lies not with early modern Wales, but with London.

Printing in Britain and Ireland was more closely regulated and controlled than in any of the centers of printing in continental Europe. A series of Acts between 1512 and 1534 had outlawed the importation of bound, printed books from the continent, all domestic printing was controlled through the stationers' guild (the Stationers' Company after 1557) and many categories of text, religious and otherwise, could only be produced by royal licence.[2] Although there were some retailers and retailer-binders working outside London, by the mid-sixteenth century there were no provincial printers apart from those authorized to work in university towns.[3] The greater part of all printing in Britain and Ireland before 1695 took place in and around the cities of Westminster and London and there was no authorized printing in Wales before the eighteenth century.[4] So it is in Salesbury's relationship with the London printing establishment of the mid-sixteenth century that the early story of Welsh printing must be contextualized.

This context also helps to underline the extent to which the Welsh urban experience in pre-industrial times must include the experience of London. In the Welsh social and textual experience of town life after 1485 London is a constant presence, and it could hardly be otherwise. London was the metropolis of Britain. It was the center of government and trade and the only major center of printing. With a growing population in 1547 of between 55,000 and 70,000 it

was perhaps the twelfth largest town in Europe. For size and wealth it already had
no British competitors, yet by 1600 it would have a population of some 200,000.[5]
Its greatest significance for Wales, however, was not just its size but the fact that
there were probably more Welsh people living and working there than in any
one of the Welsh towns before the nineteenth century.[6] London continued to
be remembered in Welsh literature as the capital of the Island of Britain in pre-
Saxon times but it is also the main point of reference for town life with a number
of references to London and to "Siep" or "Siep-Seid" in Welsh poems, mainly
cywyddau of the fourteenth and fifteenth centuries. Iolo Goch's praise-poem to
Owain Glyn Dŵr's court at Sycharth describes it as containing:

> Naw neuadd gyfladd gyflun,
> A naw gwardrob ar bob un,
> Siopau glân glwys cynnwys cain,
> Siop lawndeg fal Siêp Lundain.[7]

[Nine symmetrical identical halls, / And nine wardrobes by each one,
Bright fair shops with fine contents, / A lovely full shop like London's
Cheapside.]

Even when a town in Wales or the March is being praised, London is the
paradigm, as in the famous description of Oswestry by Tudur Aled (ca. 1465–ca.
1525), which Helen Fulton discusses on page 208. Oswestry is said to have silk
shops like Cheapside, "Siep-Seid yn siopau sidan" and exotic consumer goods
such as "cwmin" and "bocs" and "pomgarnets," and the Cambrianized borrowings of these items emphasizes both the essential Englishness of the commodity
and its assimilation into Welsh life.[8]

Salesbury's early career as a writer is bounded by two events: the publication in 1546 of Sir John Price's *Yny lhyvyr hwnn* [In This Book], the first Welsh
printed book,[9] and the accession, in 1553, of Queen Mary, which brought an
end to state support for vernacular worship and related publication.[10] The early
years of Edward's reign saw the largest amount of printing and publishing in
England since printing was established there in the 1470s as "Protestant propaganda flooded London bookstalls and provincial markets" following the renun-
ciation of earlier censorship and licensing regulations.[11] This was the period
during which Salesbury was first active in London, when the first Welsh books
were printed and when the foundations were laid for the later translation into
Welsh of the Bible and the Book of Common Prayer, a process that was interrupted by the accession of Mary in 1553. No Welsh books were printed in
London during Mary's reign, which also saw a decline in the total amount of
printing and a complete halt to the printing of vernacular Bibles.[12] In the five
nontransitional years of Edward's reign (1548–52) there were over a hundred
editions of the Bible printed in England, half of which were in English. In
the four nontransitional years of Mary's reign (1554–57) there were only ten
editions printed, none of which were in English.[13] Salesbury seems to have

been in Wales throughout Mary's reign and there is a tradition that it was during these years that he systematically engaged with the task of translating the whole of the New Testament into Welsh. He had already begun this work in translating the excerpts from the gospels and letters that comprised *Kynniver Llith a Ban* (1551), his early Welsh equivalent of the English Prayer Book of 1549. The story persists that it was in the discomfort of a secret chamber in Cae Du, a family house near Llansannan in North Wales, that Salesbury laid the foundations for his Welsh edition of the New Testament, an edition that was eventually published in London in 1567. The real importance of this tradition, its function in the emerging cultural nationalism that helped to form modern Wales, is that it supports the romantic notion of Salesbury enduring any hardship in order to achieve this nation-building act of religious devotion. There is no doubt that Salesbury's books were enormously important and influential, and that printing in Welsh, of which he was the chief pioneer, played a pivotal role in the survival of the language, but the reason the image of Salesbury translating the New Testament while in hiding in fear of his life was so appealing is because it is such a wonderful metaphor not just for the sacrifice of the religious life, but for the Welsh language itself, struggling to take possession of this new, life-giving technology in opposition to a tyrannical state for whom enforced conformity was the basis of power.

From the first appearance of Welsh printing in 1546 until the death of Edward VI in 1553 William Salesbury wrote or published at least eight works in Welsh and English, one of which, *Kynniver Llith a Ban*, also includes a substantial "Dedication to the Bishops" in Latin.[14] Of these eight works, seven were published and one remained in manuscript. The one that remained in manuscript was Salesbury's translation into Welsh of *Tabulae de schematibus et tropis* [Tables of Schemes and Tropes], a work on rhetoric by Petrus Schade which was first published in Antwerp in 1533.[15] Salesbury's eight early works are:

1. *A Dictionary in Englyshe and Welshe* (1547) [N. Hill for] "J[ohn] Waley." STC 21616.
2. *Oll synnwyr pen Kembero ygyd* [The Sum of Welsh Wisdom] (1547?) "Nycholas Hyll." STC 12403.9.
3. *The Description of the Sphere or the Frame of the Worlde* (1550) "R[obert]. Wyer." STC 20398.7 and 20399. Thavies Inn.
4. *A Brief and a Playne Introduction . . . [to] . . . the Brytysh Tongue* (1550) [R. Grafton for] "Roberte Crowley." STC 21614. Thavies Inn.
5. *Ban wedi i dynny . . . o gyfreith Howel dda* [An Excerpt Taken from the Law of Hywel] (1550) [R. Grafton for] "Roberte Crowley." STC 21612. Ely Rentes.
6. *The Baterie of the Popes Botereulx, Commonly Called the High Altare* (1550) [R. Grafton for] "Roberte Crowley." STC 21613. Ely Rentes.
7. *Kynniver Llith a Ban* [As Many Readings and Excerpts] (1551) [?R. Grafton for] "Roberte Crowley for William Salesbury." STC 2983 [=21617]. Ely Rentes.

8. *Llyfr rhetoreg Petrus Mosellanus* [The Book of Rhetoric by Petrus Mosellanus] (1552) Aberystwyth, National Library of Wales Cardiff MS 2.39 (formerly Cardiff MS 21).

At least three of these works were to play a significant role in the establishment of Welsh as an institutional language in the middle decades of the sixteenth century. *A Dictionary in Englyshe and Welshe* and *A Brief and a Playne Introduction* are important linguistic works that provided practical assistance to non-Welsh-speaking clergy in Wales in the early years of vernacular worship, while *Kynniver Llith a Ban* provided a Welsh translation of the "epistles and gospels" of the 1549 English Prayer Book.[16] The compulsory use of the English Prayer Book and its revised successor of 1552 marked the beginning of a crucial period of linguistic history in which vernacular worship in Wales (and probably, there-fore, vernacular literacy) would have been in English had there not been Welsh translations available and sufficient official support to allow their use. While it is difficult to know how extensively *Kynniver Llith a Ban* was used in Welsh churches, its importance was that it provided the only alternative to English worship in Welsh parishes prior to the publication of the Welsh New Testament and Book of Common Prayer in 1567, both of which were also translated by William Salesbury and printed in London.[17]

Welsh people had been attracted to London in increasing numbers since Henry Tudor became king in 1485. There are numerous Welshmen recorded as serving in the royal household, some 169 in the period 1500–1549 and in Edward's reign Welshmen became much more influential at the center of power with William Thomas, for example, becoming clerk to the Privy Council and fulfilling ambas-sadorial roles, and (Sir) Thomas Parry becoming a privy counselor. The diocese of London also continued to attract Welsh clerics throughout the sixteenth century.[18] We also have a valuable account of Welsh life in London in the early sixteenth century in the work of Elis Gruffydd, whose chronicle is full of references to Welsh life in early Tudor London.[19] This was a period of rapid population growth. Between 1541 and 1582 the population of London grew from less than 50,000 to about 112,000, and 20 years later it would reach 200,000. Outside London, though, town life was not a universal experience. In 1547 only some 10 percent of the population of Britain lived in towns with 2,000 inhabitants or more and Carmarthen was the only town in Wales with a population of 2,000 by the later sixteenth century. Other significant Welsh towns included Brecon that was some-what smaller than Carmarthen and Caernarfon and Denbigh that had barely a thousand inhabitants apiece.[20] Estimates of the Welsh population in London in the mid-sixteenth century vary from one to three percent of the total, although Emrys Jones points out that one reading of the figures for 1582 suggests that the Welsh element of the population was by then 6,336 people, that is, some 5.6 percent of the total population. Even the more conservative of the estimates makes it clear that there would have been significant numbers of Welsh people in London around 1550, when Welsh printing began. This is not to say, of course, that even several thousand Welsh speakers scattered throughout a large, cosmopolitan city could in any sense replicate the linguistic dynamics of a small, Welsh-speaking town in

Wales, but the figures are nevertheless significant. It seems that the Welsh were not particularly identified with any one part of the city and in attempts to identify the Welsh in London by location in the sixteenth century, Holborn, where Salesbury lived, is not mentioned. But one piece of topographical evidence is interesting: an attempt to estimate the origins by county of the Welsh in London for the mid-sixteenth century puts Denbighshire first with Flintshire a close second.[21]

William Salesbury, that "most exact critic of British antiquities,"[22] was born in Denbighshire sometime around 1520, perhaps at a house called Cae Du in the village of Llansannan, and spent much of his early years, in the 1520s and 1530s, at the family home in Llanrwst.[23] The details are unclear but he may have received his early education in Wales, and in his youth he spent some time in Lancashire.[24] He also appears to have studied at Oxford. According to one history of Oxford University's most famous graduates, Salesbury "Spent several years in academic learning either in St. Albans, or Broadgate-hall, or both. Thence, he went to an inn of chancery in Holbourn near London, called Thavies inn…and thence, as 'tis probable, to Lincolns Inn."[25] However, although there are a number of secondary references indicating that Salesbury studied at Oxford his name is not recorded in Joseph Foster's transcript of the members of the university in the sixteenth century.[26]

From Oxford, as *Athenae Oxonienses* tells us, Salesbury moved to Thavies Inn at "Holbourn near London" to study the law. "Holbourn near London" refers to the fact that while Holborn was within the liberty of the city for the purposes of trade, it was outside the city walls. Thavies Inn was one of a number of extra-parochial precincts or liberties of London, and was located west of the city of London in the parish of St. Andrew, Holborn. The professors and students of law had established themselves in buildings outside the Roman wall in the thirteenth century after the law schools in London had been closed by a writ of Henry III in 1234.[27]

In his *Survey of London*, first published in 1598, John Stow says that "Thauies Inne in Oldborne" is one of the nine Inns of Court that lie "within the liberties of this Citie" that houses "students of the common lawes."[28] Thavies Inn was an Inn of Chancery by ca. 1400 and in the fifteenth century was known as Davys Inn.[29] By the late sixteenth century there were a total of fourteen Inns of Court and they had complete control of legal education in England until the end of the Tudor period. It is not known how long Salesbury studied law, although in the years that followed the accession of Edward VI his other interests seem to have taken greater priority. One reason, perhaps, why he later moved from Thavies Inn to Ely House.[30] Although Salesbury's career, seems to us now to be entirely defined by writing and printing, and hardly at all by the law, it has been suggested that during this time he may have made use of his legal training while serving Sir Richard Rich, to whom Salesbury was to dedicate his anti-Catholic pamphlet, *The Baterie of the Popes Botereulx*.[31] However, an equally significant role for the Inns of Court, in terms of Salesbury's career was that they were "hotbeds of the ideological struggle almost as much as the universities, in some ways more so because of the lack of institutional control over the membership before the 1580s."[32] Moreover, it was a recognized career path. As Emrys Jones has argued, the law was the professional and intellectual area that was most associated with the Welsh at that time offering as it did "real possibilities of advancement for the sons of the middling orders as well as sons of gentry."[33]

Salesbury's first book to be published was *A Dictionary in Englyshe and Welshe*, printed in 1547 for "J[ohn] Waley" of Hart's Horn in Foster Lane.[34] The relationship with John Waley was to last for twenty years, for this is the same John Waley who is named with William Salesbury in Elizabeth's patent of 1563, granting them an exclusive seven-year licence for the printing of the scriptures in Welsh, following the authorizing act of 1563.[35] The original patent survives in the British Library, and is reproduced in facsimile in John Ballinger's survey of the Bible in Wales.[36] The *Dictionary* was probably printed between January and Easter of 1547[37] and may have appeared very shortly, perhaps only a few weeks, after John Price's *Yny Lhyvyr Hwnn*. Salesbury's second book, which also appeared in 1547, was *Oll synnwyr pen Kembero ygyd*, printed by the Dutchman "Nycholas Hyll in Saynte Iohns Strete, Clerkenwell, London," another printer who worked outside the western edge of the city of walls. Nicholas Hill is also the same printer who is now credited by STC with printing *A Dictionary in Englyshe and Welshe* for John Waley.[38] *Oll synnwyr pen Kembero ygyd* was a collection of over nine hundred proverbs, a genre much in vogue in humanist Europe, taken mainly from a manuscript by Gruffydd Hiraethog, but with a few additional proverbs that Salesbury "thought necessarie to be had in remembraunce." These were translated by him from works by Erasmus, whom Salesbury calls "yr athro dyscediaf, huotlaf, ac awdurusaf yn cred oll or a vu in oes ni ac ys llawer oes or blaen" [The most learned, eloquent, and authoritative teacher in this age and many previous ages].[39]

Whether or not Salesbury was at Thavies Inn in 1547 when he published *A Dictionary in Englyshe and Welshe* and *Oll synnwyr pen Kembero ygyd*, he was certainly there by 1550. During that year he published four books, the first two of which include references to Thavies Inn. The first was a perfect example of humanist scholarship, an English translation of a well-known classical work on the theory of the spheres. *The Descripcion of the Sphere or the Frame of the Worlde* was "Englysshed by...W. Salysburye" from Thomas Linacre's Latin version of Diadochus Proclus's Greek work on the spheres or planets, and was printed by "R[obert] Wyer."[40] The letter of dedication to John Edwards, which precedes *The Descripcion of the Sphere* concludes: "Thus fare ye well. At Thauies Inne, in Houlborne. Anno domine. 1.5.5.0."[41] The second book published that year was one of Salesbury's best known works. On the face of it this looks like a companion volume to the *Dictionary*, but its function was more likely to have been conceived as a guide to pronunciation for non-Welsh clerics, and others, who would be reading from *Kynniver Llith a Ban*, which had been planned for some time and was to be published in the following year. *A Brief and a Playne Introduction* was published by Robert Crowley, the first of four works that he would produce for Salesbury, and its probable function as a linguistic guide for non-Welsh speaking clerics is made clear by the fact that a revised version was republished in 1567, as *A Playne and a Familiar Introduction*, to accompany the publication of the Welsh New Testament and Prayer Book. Salesbury was still at Thavies Inn when this book was written, as the dedication makes clear: "To hys louynge frende, maistre Rychard Colyngborne...Thus fare ye hartelye / well. At Thauies Inn in Holburne / more hastely, than spedelye. / M.D.L."

Sometime during 1550 Salesbury moved from Thavies Inn to Ely House. Although the move did not take him very far, he may have thereby achieved a closer working arrangement with a man whom he already knew from his time at Oxford. STC includes an index that lists all London addresses associated with the printing trade in London prior to 1640 with a map of:

> ...all stationers and other publishers appearing in STC imprints and with known addresses, whether they had signs or not, in a context showing who were their colleagues nearby. The addresses have been grouped geographically in twenty-four small areas labelled A-X, organised in five major districts.[42]

Section twenty two, labelled "V," is in the fifth of these districts, which is described as "west of the Fleet Ditch" in Holborn. Ely House is located as no. 158f. on the STC map, on the north side of High Holborn, nearer to Hatton Garden than Saffron Hill. There are just four entries for Ely House for the whole period covered by STC. They are as follows:

W. Seres (in rentes) 1548
R. Crowley (author; in rents) 1549–51
W. Salisbury (author; in rents) 1551
R. Ward (ov[er]/ag[ainst the] House) 1593.[43]

Leaving aside the entry for 1593, this index of addresses brings together three people who worked closely together in the years 1548–1551.

Robert Crowley was born in Gloucestershire, in the second decade of the sixteenth century, and, like Salesbury, was educated at Oxford.[44] According to *Athenae Oxonienses*, Crowley became a student in the university about 1534, and was soon after "made demy of Magd[alen] coll[ege]." By 1542 he was a bachelor of arts and was made "probationer-fellow of the said house by the name of Rob. Crole."[45] Without making it clear whether he took an MA, or when exactly he left Oxford, the same source tells us it is likely "that he left the university when K. Hen. 8 began to settle a mongrel religion in the nation."[46] It seems likely that he gave up his fellowship in 1544 and was established in London by 1546.[47] The question of whether Salesbury and Crowley were at Oxford at the same time is difficult to answer in the absence of clear records. Crowley's movements are also open to speculation: it has been suggested that he may have left Oxford, or at least left Magdalen, as early as 1538, when John Foxe "was accused by other fellows of belonging to 'a new religion,' and abandoned the university [with his] colleagues Robert Crowley...[and] Thomas Cooper."[48] It is possible, however, that Salesbury and Crowley were contemporaries at Oxford who both moved to Holborn at about the same time and shared a growing enthusiasm for proto-Protestant reforms and the potential of the printing press as an agent of change. Whatever the circumstances of their first meeting, Salesbury was certainly in London by early 1547, and Crowley was certainly involved in printing by 1548, when he published three controversial works that were printed by John Day and William Seres, who was based at Ely Rents. It seems likely that it was through William Seres that Crowley learned the business of printing, and he is soon publishing his own works, also from premises at "Elye rentes in Holbourne,"[49] perhaps the same premises that Seres vacated in 1548 when he moved from Ely Rents to Peter College in Paul's churchyard.[50] Robert Crowley published four of Salesbury's books in 1550 and 1551, and in total he is associated with nineteen publications between 1549 and 1551. He was also a prolific author, writing some twenty books himself, most of which postdate his career as a printer.[51] He abandoned book production before the death of Edward VI and never practiced it again. Crowley's career is a remarkable example of the versatility and technological utilitarianism of writers and printers whose work was informed by the proselytizing ideals of the Reformation. Apart from printing some of the earliest Welsh books, he made two other significant contributions to literary and publishing history. In 1549 he wrote and published the first complete English metrical version of the psalms, *The Psalter of David Newly Translated into Englysh Metre*, and the following year published the first ever printed version of *The Vision of Pierce Plowman*, the first of three editions that he produced that year.[52] He published all these works under his own name only from 1549 to 1551, having probably learned the craft while seeing three of his pamphlets through the press, at the office of Day and Seres during 1548.[53]

Crowley's abandonment of printing seems to have coincided with his ordination by Bishop Ridley in September 1551, and with the accession of Queen Mary, Crowley was one of many English protestants who sought refuge in Germany, returning to England in 1559. Although he did not publish any books after 1551, he did maintain a lifelong interest in book production and bookselling. He is recorded as taking apprentices and was made a freeman of the Stationers' Company by redemption in 1578.[54] Throughout his career, Crowley remained loyal to the ideals of the Reformation. He was at times ejected from livings and, in 1566, briefly imprisoned, for continuing to oppose the preservation or use of religious vestments and other traditions that he saw as too reminiscent of the Church of Rome. In 1564, for example, there had been an attempt to enforce the clergy to use the square cap, tippet, and surplice, but Crowley was a leading opponent of this, saying that he would not minister in what he called the "conjuring garments of popery."[55] This particular piece of sartorial conservatism, as Crowley saw it, had been promoted by Matthew Parker, the Pierpont Morgan of sixteenth-century book collectors, who was to become Archbishop of Canterbury in late 1559 and correspond with William Salesbury in the 1560s. As H. S. Bennett has suggested, we should not think of Crowley as "a professional printer," but as someone who "acquired a press to further his antipapal activities" and used other printers to produce the books that he sold.[56] A more recent summary of Crowley's career puts it succinctly, while locating his role firmly in the area of bookselling rather than book production:

> After Crowley established a book shop specialising in the sale of popular octavo chap-books, he published 19 texts under his own imprint between 1549 and 1551.[57]

The printer most likely to have been working with Crowley, apart from Jugge and Day, was Richard Grafton, who was the King's Printer from 1547 to 1553, and whose printing house "in the parish of Christ Church within Newgate," was one of the closest to Crowley's bookshop near Ely House.[58] Grafton printed books for Crowley without identifying himself in the imprint and Crowley also enjoyed the patronage of Elizabeth, Lady Fane, the wife of Sir Ralph Fane, a close associate of Protector Somerset. This suggests, as John King has argued, "that Crowley's shop served as a conduit for controversial works favouring the Protestant regime."[59] It also means that during these years Salesbury had allied himself, or could be seen to have allied himself, with one of the most radical elements in London printing circles, in a way that others, such as Sir John Price, did not. It also meant that Salesbury became a potential target after 1553.

Later in 1550, after he had moved from Thavies Inn to Ely House, Salesbury published two books, which carry Robert Crowley's imprint, relating to two important contemporary questions: the Catholic altar and the marrying of priests. Geoffrey Elton has called these issues the two major doctrinal issues of the day in Reformation England, and in both issues, Salesbury allies himself strongly with the radical reforms of the Edwardian regime.[60] Salesbury's *The Baterie of the Popes Botereulx* was part of a concerted protestant campaign to gain popular support for the removal of "ye popish altars out of Christes Churches."[61] He also published a short excerpt, with an English translation, of part of the Welsh Laws, which purportedly supported the argument for the marriage of priests. The bilingual title page describes it as

A CERTAINE CASE EXTRACTE / out of the auncient Law of Hoel da, kyng of Wales / in the yere of oure Lorde, nyne hundred and fourtene / passed: whereby it maye gathered that prie- / stes had lawfully maried wyves / at that tyme.[62]

Ban wedy i dynny . . . o hen gyfreith Howel dda was "Imprinted at London by Roberte Crowley, dwellyng in Elye rentes in Holbourne" in 1550, the year in which he published four separate works and was working on what was arguably the most important Welsh book to be published before 1567. That book was the most substantial Welsh printed book of these early years and it appeared in the following year, when, in the absence of any initiative from the Welsh bishops, Salesbury attempted to supply a Welsh equivalent to the 1549 English Prayer Book for the people of Wales.[63] The title page describes the contents as

Kynniver / llith a ban or yscry / thur lan ac a ddarlleir yr Eccleis pryd / Commun / y Sulieu a'r Gwilieu / trwy'r vlwyddyn : o Cam- / bereiciat / W.S.

[As many readings and excerpts from holy scripture as are needed to be read in Church at Communion, Sundays and Feast Days throughout the year: translated into Welsh by W.S.][64]

Once more, Salesbury's publisher was Robert Crowley, despite the fact that the King's *Patent*, which was reproduced by way of authority opposite Crowley's colophon, had been awarded in 1546 to Salesbury and John Waley.[65] *Kynniver Llith a Ban* was a Welsh version of the Epistles and Gospels for every Sunday and holy day throughout the year, and was the only Welsh text that could have been used in Wales, alongside the 1549 English Prayer Book, until the publication of Salesbury's complete Welsh Prayer Book, *Lliver gweddi gyffredin*, in 1567.[66] It was Salesbury's first published attempt at scriptural translation and while his etymologically informed orthography was not universally popular, it clearly established the approach he would take in the 1567 New Testament. Crowley's imprint appears on four of Salesbury's books in 1550 and 1551 and their names are most famously linked together in the colophon *of Kynniver Llith a Ban*:

> Imprinted at / London by Roberte Crow- / ley for William Sales- / bury dwellynge in / Elye rentes in / Holbourne. / Anno Domini. / M.D.L.I.[67]

This may seem to be at least potentially ambiguous in terms of which of the two might be dwelling in "Elye rentes" but a number of other sources are available that make it clear that, for a least some of the time, both were resident there. The buildings of Ely House covered all of the land that is now called Ely Place, together with substantial gardens to the north and west and was the London residence of the bishop of Ely, consisting of the bishop's palace and chapel, a large and famous garden and a number of other buildings including those that were called Ely Rents. The precise location of Ely Rents is referred to in a court case about the boundary of the liberties of the city, in which judgment was given in 1570, that the bishop's house, garden, and other property are outside the liberty except for the "tenements" fronting Holborn called "Elye Rentes."[68] So we can be fairly sure that in 1550, just twenty years earlier, William Salesbury was living and Robert Crowley was trading in one of the properties fronting High Holborn, on the northern side of present-day Holborn Circus, directly opposite Thavies Inn. That these buildings were adjacent in the sixteenth century is suggested by a description in John Stow's *Survey of London*:

> From this church of S. Andrew vp Oldborne hill bee diuers fayre builded houses, amongst the which on the left hand there standeth three Innes of Chauncery, whereof the first adioyning vnto Crookham Alley is called Thaueis Inn, and standeth opposite or ouer against the said Elie house.[69]

The most remarkable architectural survival from this period, which Salesbury would have known, is the bishop's chapel and crypt in Ely Place, which is the only complete building in London to survive from the reign of Edward I.[70] It is interesting to note, given the nature of the enterprise to which Salesbury and

Crowley were so committed, that this chapel was also the first "Anglican" church in England to be returned to the Roman Catholic Church, and is now once again a Catholic place of worship.[71] A further coincidence is that immediately prior to its being purchased by the Catholic church in the 1870s it had been leased for forty years to a congregation of Welsh Presbyterians in London.[72]

At the time when Salesbury moved from Thavies Inn, across the street into Ely Rents, the bishop's palace was playing a major role in the power struggle to control English affairs. In the early years of the reign of Edward VI Ely House was in the possession of the John Dudley, Duke of Northumberland, and according to Elijah Williams, the historian of Holborn, "Dudley was still living in Ely Palace in January, 1552, but his efforts to acquire ownership had not been successful."[73] The bishop of Ely did eventually lose the property when Ely House was given to Elizabeth's lord chancellor, Sir Christopher Hatton, whose family name survives in the development that became Hatton Garden.[74]

The parish church of St. Andrew Holborn, which formed a triangle with Thavies Inn and Ely Rents, was also changing rapidly as the Reformation gathered momentum. The church had undergone substantial rebuilding over the previous two centuries and by the final years of Henry's reign contained several chantry chapels as well as the private chapel of the future Earl of Southampton, Thomas Wriothesley. On 24 April 1545, the future second Earl, Henry, was baptised at St. Andrew, with Henry VIII among the godparents. His son, the future third Earl of Southampton, would become famous as the patron of William Shakespeare.[75] It is interesting, if perhaps just a little fanciful, to speculate that of all Shakespeare's connections with Wales and the Welsh the earliest may have been William Salesbury witnessing the ceremonial trappings of the christening of the father of Shakespeare's future patron, while living next to the bishop of Ely's palace, whose splendid garden would be immortalized, for its strawberries, in Shakespeare's *Richard III*.[76]

In a period of some five years covering most of Edward's reign, William Salesbury wrote at least eight works covering many of the interests of European humanism, including classical learning, philology and rhetoric, and the theology of reformation. He was the central figure in the transition of the Welsh language from manuscript to print, whose example laid the foundations for the survival of the language through his enthusiastic adoption of the new technology and his promotion of the relevance and necessity of printing in Welsh. He achieved most of this in London, the metropolis of Britain and the center of the Welsh book trade until the eighteenth century. While the significance of London to the history of Wales in the early modern period has perhaps been understated in a Welsh historical tradition that was part of what Kenneth O. Morgan has called the rebirth of a nation,[77] the early career of William Salesbury is a reminder of the importance of that link. During these years in London Salesbury was at the center of a rapidly changing world, a world in which humanist ideas were the currency of change and printing was its instrument.

Notes

1. R. Brinley Jones, *William Salesbury*, Writers of Wales (Cardiff: University of Wales Press, 1994), 64–65.

2. See C. Paul Christianson, "The Rise of the London Booktrade," Chap. 6 in *The Cambridge History of the Book in Britain, Volume III: 1400–1557*, ed. Lotte Hellinga and J. B. Trapp (Cambridge: Cambridge University Press, 1999), 145–47; the Act of 1534 is reproduced as an Appendix at 608–10.

3. Philip Gaskell, *A New Introduction to Bibliography* (Oxford: Clarendon Press, 1985), 171–85.

4. For an account of printing in Wales before 1820, see Eiluned Rees, *Libri Walliae: A Catalogue of Welsh Books and Books Printed in Wales, 1546–1820* (Aberystwyth: National Library of Wales, 1987).

5. See Penry Williams, *The Later Tudors: England, 1547–1603* (Oxford: Clarendon Press, 1995), 10–11 and A. L. Beier and R. Finlay, eds., *London 1500–1800: The Making of a Metropolis* (London: Longman, 1986), 2–10.

6. Emrys Jones, ed., *The Welsh in London, 1500–2000* (Cardiff: University of Wales Press for the Honourable Society of Cymmrodorion, 2001), 9–11, 36.

7. See Dafydd Johnston, ed., *Iolo Goch: Poems* (Landysul: Gomer Press, 1993), poem 10, lines 49–52.

8. On towns and commodity culture in medieval Welsh poetry, see Helen Fulton, "Trading Places: Representations of Urban Culture in Medieval Welsh Poetry," *Studia Celtica* 31 (1997): 219–30 and "The *Encomium Urbis* in Medieval Welsh Poetry," in *Proceedings of the Harvard Celtic Colloquium* 22 (Cambridge, Mass.: Harvard University Press, 2008).

9. See Rees, *Libri Walliae*; A. W. Pollard and G. R. Redgrave, *A Short-Title Catalogue of Books Printed in England, Scotland and Ireland and of English Books Printed Abroad 1475–1640* (London: Bibliographical Society, 1991), hereafter STC; John Ballinger, *The Bible in Wales* (London: Sotheran, 1906). The catalogue numbers for *Yny lhyvyr hwnn* are Rees, *Libri Walliae* 4079, STC 20310, and Ballinger, *Bible in Wales*, 1. The most important articles about Yny lhyvyr hwnn and about early Welsh printing in general are R. Geraint Gruffydd, "Yny lhyvyr hwnn (1546): The Earliest Welsh Printed Book," *Bulletin of the Board of Celtic Studies* 22 (1969): 105–16; R. Geraint Gruffydd, "Y print yn dwyn ffrwyth i'r Cymro: Yny lhyvyr hwnn, 1546," *Welsh Book Studies* 1 (1998): 1–20.

10. See G. R. Elton, *England under the Tudors*, 3rd edn. (London: Routledge, 1991), 193–223.

11. See John N. King, "The Book Trade under Edward VI and Mary I," Chap. 8 in Hellinga and Trapp, eds., *Cambridge History of the Book, III*, 164–178. The peak years of London book production prior to 1597 were 1548 and 1550.

12. B. J. McMullin, "The Bible Trade," Chap. 22 in *The Cambridge History of the Book in Britain, IV: 1557–1695*, ed. John Barnard and D. F. McKenzie, assist. Maureen Bell (Cambridge: Cambridge University Press, 2002), 455.

13. The one exception is the so-called Queen Mary Bible (STC 2091) that was largely printed before the accession of Mary. This was the ninth folio edition of the Great Bible and only a handful of copies survive. According to a manuscript note in the British Library copy, most of the edition was destroyed in 1553 at her command. See the statistical breakdown of book production between 1547 and 1557 in King, "Book Trade under Edward VI and Mary I," 175–78.

14. See also the section in the Introduction regarding the "Dedication to the Bishops," in *Kynniver Llith a Ban*, ed. John Fisher (Cardiff: University of Wales Press, 1931), xxiii–xxvi.

15. Schade was commonly known as Petrus Mosellanus. Salesbury's work was not published but survives in Cardiff MS 2.39 (formerly Cardiff MS 21), and in later copies; see Jones, *William Salesbury*, 33.

16. The Act of Uniformity was passed on 21 January 1549 for use of the Book of Common Prayer from Whitsuntide 1549. The Second Act of Uniformity was passed in April 1552 for the use of the 1552 Prayer Book from November 1552. Both Acts also made church attendance compulsory. See Glanmor Williams, *Wales and the Reformation* (Cardiff: University of Wales Press, 1997), 163–66.

17. See Isaac Thomas, "Translating the Bible," in *A Guide to Welsh Literature c. 1530–1700*, ed. R. Geraint Gruffydd (Cardiff: University of Wales Press, 1997), 154–75.

18. Jones, ed., *The Welsh in London*, 19–24.

19. See Jerry Hunter, "Taliesin at the Court of Henry VIII: Aspects of the Writing of Elis Gruffydd," *Transactions of the Honourable Society of Cymmrodorion* 10 (2004): 41–56; see also Thomas Jones, "A Welsh Chronicler in Tudor England," *The Welsh History Review* 1 (1960): 1–17.

20. Jones, ed., *The Welsh in London*, 36.

21. Jones, ed., *The Welsh in London*, 10–12.

22. Anthony à Wood, *Athenae Oxonienses, An Exact History of All the Writers and Bishops Who Have Had Their Education in the Most Ancient and Famous University of Oxford from the Fifteenth Year of King Henry, etc.*: new edn. ed. Philip Bliss 4 vols. (London: Rivington et al. Oxford: Parker, 1813–20), 1: col. 358.

23. For details of Salesbury's life see Jones, *William Salesbury* and D. R. Thomas, *The Life and Work of Bishop Davies and William Salesbury, etc.* (Oswestry: Caxton, 1902).

24. See Isaac Thomas, "William Salesbury—ei gyfnod cynnar," *Y Testament Newydd Cymraeg, 1551–1620* (Cardiff: University of Wales Press, 1976), 60–69.

25. à Wood, *Athenae Oxonienses*, 1: col. 358.

26. Joseph Foster, ed., *Alumni Oxonienses: The Members of the University of Oxford, 1500–1714* (Oxford: Parker, 1891).

27. Robert Blackham, *Wig and Gown: The Story of the Temple, Gray's and Lincoln's Inn* (London: Sampson Low, 1932), 25–26.

28. John Stow, *A Survey of London: Reproduced from the Text of 1603*, ed. C. L. Kingsford, 2 vols. (Oxford: Clarendon Press, 1971), 1: 77.

29. E. Williams, *Early Holborn and the Legal Quarter of London*, 2 vols. (London: Sweet and Maxwell, 1927), 833–67.

30. None of the sixteenth-century buildings that comprised Thavies Inn in Salesbury's time have survived, although the name Thavies Inn is still used for the location. See Simon Bradley and Nikolaus Pevsner, *The Buildings of England, London 1: The City of London* (Harmondsworth: Penguin, 1997), 56.

31. See Peter Roberts, "The Welsh Language, English Law and Tudor legislation," *Transaction of the Honourable Society of Cymmrodorion* (1989): 38.

32. Jones, ed., *The Welsh in London*, 29.

33. Jones, ed., *The Welsh in London*, 18–29.

34. William Salesbury, *A Dictionary in Englyshe and Welshe*, English Linguistics, 1500–1800: A Collection of Facsimile Reprints 180 (Menston: Scolar Press, 1969); STC 21616. See the entry for John Walley [*sic*] in E. Gordon Duff, *A Century of the English Book Trade, 1457 to 1557* (1905; repr. London: Bibliographical Society, 1948); STC now attributes the printing to Nicholas Hill for John Waley.

35. Act V. Elizabeth, Chap. 28 (1563). The measure had been supported through Parliament by Richard Davies and Humphrey Llwyd; see Glanmor Williams, *Welsh Reformation Essays* (Cardiff: University of Wales Press, 1967), 166, 183; Jones, *William Salesbury*, 51.

36. See Ballinger, *Bible in Wales*, 14.

37. The arguments about priority, and therefore about dating, are summarised in Gruffydd, "Yny lhyvyr hwnn."

38. See STC 21616 and 12403.9; see also Gruffydd Hiraethog, *Oll synnwyr pen Kembero ygyd*, ed. J. Gwenogvryn Evans, Reprints of Welsh Prose Works 3 (Bangor: Jarvis and Foster; London: Dent, 1902). On Salesbury's use of a Dutch printer see Stan Wicklen, "William Salesbury and the Dutch Connection," *Denbighshire Historical Society Transactions* 46 (1997): 52–58.

39. The proverbs from Erasmus are taken from *Adagia* (1500) and *Apophthegmata* (1531).

40. William Salesbury, *The description of the sphere or the frame of the worlde: right worthy to be red and studyed on of all noble wyttes. Spetyally of all those that be desyrous to attayne any perfect knowledge in cosmographie /...Englysshed by me Wyllyam Salysbury* (London: Robert Wyer, 1550); STC 20398.7, 20399. There were two editions in the same year, see W. A. Mathias, "Gweithiau William Salesbury," *Journal of the Welsh Bibliographical Society* (1952): 137. Salesbury probably used Thomas Linacre, *Procli Diadochi Sphaera...T. L....Interprete...* (London: Richard Pynson, 1522). Between the 1522 edition and Salesbury's 1550 translation there were a number of editions printed in London and else-where, often under the title De Sphaera. The London editions of 1536, 1539, 1547, and 1549 contained both the Greek text and Linacre's Latin version.

41. See Mathias, "Gweithiau William Salesbury," that quotes the dedication from the second edition, STC 20399, at 137.

42. "London Addresses," STC, Index 3E, 241.

43. STC, 3: 256.

44. For details of Crowley's life and career see the *Dictionary of National Biography* and J. W. Martin, "The Publishing Career of Robert Crowley: A Sidelight on the Tudor Book Trade," *Publishing History* 14 (1983): 85–98, to which I am particularly indebted.

45. à Wood, *Athenae Oxonienses*, 1: cols. 542–46. The term "demy" is unique to Magdalen College, Oxford, and denotes, following the College Statutes of 1486, "a foundation scholar...so called because their allowance or "commons" was originally half that of a Fellow..."; see OED 2 demy 4.

46. à Wood, *Athenae Oxonienses*, 1: col. 542.

47. See Martin, "Publishing Career of Robert Crowley," 85–86.

48. James McConica, ed., *The History of the University of Oxford*, vol. 3, *The Collegiate University* (Oxford: Clarendon Press, 1986), 367–68.

49. Colophon to William Salesbury, *A brief and a playne introduction, teachyng how to pronounce the letters in the British tong, now commenly called Walsh* [1550], English Linguistics, 1500–1800: A Collection of Facsimile Reprints, 179 (Menston: Scolar Press, 1969); Rees, *Libri Walliae* 4559, STC 21614.

50. See STC 3: 152.

51. See Robert Crowley, *Selected Works*, EETS es 15 (London: Trübner, 1872).

52. STC 2725; STC 19906, 19907, 19907a.

53. The origin of this idea seems to be the account in Thomas Frognall Dibdin, *Typographical Antiquities or the History of Printing in England, Scotland, and Ireland: Containing Memoirs of Our Ancient Printers, and a Register of the Books Printed by Them, etc.,* 4 vols. (London: William Miller, 1810–19), 2: 758.

54. See DNB and Duff, Century of the English Book Trade.

55. Quoted in John Strype, *The Life and Acts of Matthew Parker, the First Archbishop of Canterbury in the Reign of Queen Elizabeth, etc.,* 2 vols. (London: John Wyat, 1711), 1: 301.

56. H. S. Bennett, *English Books and Readers, 1475–1557* (Cambridge: Cambridge University Press, 1969), 194–95.

57. Hellinga and Trapp, eds., *Cambridge History of the Book*, 3: 167.

58. See STC entry for Richard Grafton.

59. Hellinga and Trapp, eds., *Cambridge History of the Book,* 3: 167–68; see also Martin, "Publishing Career of Robert Crowley," 87; Gruffydd, "Y print yn dwyn ffrwyth," 3.

60. See Elton, "Introduction," in *The Reformation, 1520–1559*. For a general account of the dispute see Eamon Duffy, *The Stripping of the Altars: Traditional Religion in England, c. 1400 to c. 1580* (New Haven and London: Yale University Press, 1992).

61. William Salesbury, *The baterie of the Popes boterculx, commonly called the High Altare* (London: R. Grafton for Robert Crowley, 1550); STC 21613. See also Glanmor Williams, "William Salesbury's *Baterie of the Popes Boterculx*," *Bulletin of the Board of Celtic Studies* 13.3 (1949): 146–50.

62. STC 21612. See John H. Davies, *Yny lhyvyr hwnn a Ban o gyfreith Howel*, Reprints of Welsh Prose Works, 4 (Bangor: Jarvis and Foster, 1902).

63. See Thomas, *Y Testament Newydd Cymraeg*, 71–74.

64. See John Fisher, ed., *Kynniver Llith a Ban* (Cardiff: University of Wales Press, 1931); my translation.

65. Fisher, *Kynniver Llith a Ban*, 170–71.

66. See Melville Richards and Glanmor Williams, eds., *Llyfr Gweddi Gyffredin, 1567* (Cardiff: University of Wales Press, 1953).

67. John Fisher, *Kynniver Llith a Ban*, 171; STC attributes the printing to "?R. Grafton" for R. Crowley for W. Salesbury.

68. Williams, *Early Holborn*, 360.

69. Stow, *A Survey of London*, 2: 39.

70. Parts of Westminster Abbey also survive from this period. For Ely Place and St. Ethelreda's see Bridget Cherry and Nikolaus Pevsner, *The Buildings of England, London 4: North* (Harmondsworth: Penguin, 1998), 260–61, 300.

71. The sign outside the chapel in Ely Place today reads: "St. Ethelreda's / Ancient chapel of / the bishops of Ely / Built 1250–1290 / Restored to the Old Faith 1874 / In the care of the Rosminian Fathers (Institute of Charity)."

72. See Jones, ed., *The Welsh in London*.

73. Williams, *Early Holborn*, 359–60.

74. See Douglas Newton, *Catholic London* (London: Robert Bale, 1950), 221–23.

75. See Margaret Troke, *A Medieval Legacy: John Thavie's Bequest to St. Andrew Holborn* (London: St. Andrew Holborn Church Foundation, 1998), 22; the event is also commemorated by a plaque in the church.

76. "My lord of Ely, when I was last in Holborn / I saw good strawberries in your garden there / I do beseech you send for some of them" (William Shakespeare, *Richard III*, III, iv, 31–33); see also Williams, *Early Holborn*, 356.

77. Kenneth O. Morgan, *Rebirth of a Nation: Wales, 1880–1980* (Oxford: Oxford University Press, 1982).

INDEX

INDEX OF MANUSCRIPTS